D1570580

The Road to Respectability

The Road to Respectability

James A. Garfield and His World, 1844–1852

Hendrik Booraem V

A Western Reserve Historical Society Publication

LEWISBURG: Bucknell University Press
LONDON: Associated University Presses

Associated University Presses
440 Forsgate Drive
Cranbury, NJ 08512

Associated University Presses
25 Sicilian Avenue
London WC1A 2QH, England

Associated University Presses
P.O. Box 488, Port Credit
Mississauga, Ontario
Canada L5G4M2

The paper used in this publication meets the requirements of the American National Standard for Permanence of Paper for Printed Library Materials Z39.48-1984.

Library of Congress Cataloging-in-Publication Data

Booraem, Hendrik, 1939–
The road to respectability.

Bibliography: p.
Includes index.
1. Garfield, James A. (James Abram), 1831–1881—Childhood and youth. 2. Presidents—United States—Biography. I. Title.
E687.B72 1988 973.8′4′0924 86-50895
ISBN 0-8387-5135-0 (alk. paper)

Printed in the United States of America

Contents

Preface

THIS book is not quite a standard biography. Its focus is a person, true; but it uses only part of its subject's life, and uses it as a lens through which to view a portion of the American past. James A. Garfield, twentieth president of the United States, is the central figure—not during his political career, but during eight years of his adolescence, from the ages of thirteen to twenty-one.

Adolescence, in America, is a time of peculiar significance. The classic American novel, whether by Twain, Fitzgerald, Farrell, Kerouac, or Albert G. Riddle, Garfield's friend and neighbor in the Western Reserve, is about a young person, often a young man, as he matures, becomes aware of his environment, and takes a few fateful steps of interaction with it. Something about a young person's first independent contact with society seems to possess special meaning and validity for our culture. The young person who tests his illusions and school knowledge against the reality of society sees that reality with a sharpness and detail he will probably lose in later years; at the same time, his first attempts at joining society are apt to have immense influence on the way his own life develops. Thus a study of one famous American's adolescence, though not the pinnacle of his career, illuminates two areas of genuine importance—a man and his surroundings—in such a way that each sheds light on the other.

Though a very important time of life, adolescence is a difficult one to delimit. There is certainly nothing magic in the concept of the teens or in the number twenty-one. But the possible yardsticks for determining the bounds of adolescence are so numerous, and often give such conflicting results, that one cannot apply them consistently to a given individual. Garfield, for instance, at age twenty-one was clearly an adult by a number of criteria; he was living away from home, and he had been supporting himself for several years. On the other hand, his emotional bond with his family was still very strong, and in some areas of his life, notably his romance with Mary Hubbell, there was still the same tentativeness and emotional turmoil one associates with adolescence. His own later judgment leaned to the adolescent side: "I was a very pulpy boy until I was at least twenty-two years old." The lack of definition is even more true of the beginning of adolescence. Here puberty is clearly the physical trigger for the psychosocial phenomenon known as adolescence; but puberty itself is a collection of physical changes that occur at varying times and have varying social meanings. Few of us could look back over our own lives and say with confidence, "My adolescence began (or ended) here."

In view of these difficulties, there is a strong case to be made for falling back on the conventional limits of adolescence: beginning with the teens and ending at age twenty-one. That is what I have done here. I make no claim that Garfield left childhood on 19 November 1844, on that he became an adult precisely on that same date in 1852; but I do suppose that the center of his journey from childhood to adulthood is somewhere between these dates, and that the reader will see how, in this period, he developed the basis of a clear adult identity.

But why James A. Garfield at all? First, because he was president, although only briefly. Holders of the nation's highest office have tended to generate material about their early lives from a variety of sources—not only their own personal papers, but recollections of friends and neighbors, anecdotes, campaign biographies, documents—which offer a usefully broad perspective on what is usually a rather obscure part of a person's life. Not all presidents' early lives are well documented, but most are. Moreover, the presidents are an interestingly varied group, with talents far less specialized than a comparable group of American artists, say, or jurists, or athletes. Some were verbally skilled; others were almost inarticulate. A few were highly intelligent, whereas others approached the average. Some were bookish, and others were basically outdoorsmen. All were politicians, of course; but some were reluctant ones, dragged into politics by circumstance, while others had begun campaigning for office before they were old enough to vote.

Why Garfield in particular? He had an interesting adolescence, as this book attempts to show; more importantly, there is an abundance of source material about it. An intensely self-conscious man, and something of a romantic who saw his own life as a great adventure, Garfield from an early age got into the habit of saving his papers and writing down reminiscences of his youth. His papers contain dozens of letters to him and from him during the years before he was twenty-one. There are reminiscences written at various times. Finally, there is a diary that covers almost every day of his life from age sixteen through his early twenties. Few other presidential collections can match this volume of documentary material.

Another reason for the abundance of sources about Garfield's youth is that he died so young—at forty-nine, younger than any other president except John F. Kennedy. Many people who had grown up with Garfield, family members, friends, and fellow students, were still alive at his death and willing to share their recollections. Quite a few had already done so during the presidential campaign of 1880, but now that their friend was gone, they could speak with the frankness that death permitted and reveal memories that might have gone unmentioned while he was still alive. Most, of course, were anxious to keep his name unsullied and to avoid mention of anything discreditable, but the posthumous memories had a sweep and inclusiveness not often found in those published during his lifetime. Garfield's friend Corydon E. Fuller wrote an entire book of his recollections entitled *Reminiscences of James A. Garfield*. When it was published in 1887, his widow wrote Garfield's widow to assure her that everything which could possibly cause offense had been edited out; nevertheless, the book is copious and often revealing. As time went on, other early acquaintances of the president shared their memories, and even into the early twentieth century some were still giving interviews to reporters.

In addition to these sources on Garfield himself, there is a surprising amount of peripheral source material generated by the lively, literate culture of the rural Western Reserve: the papers of Lucretia Rudolph, who became Garfield's wife, and of his first cousin Henry Boynton; the papers of his friend and biographer Albert Gallatin Riddle; the papers of Orlando J. Hodge, his friend at Geauga Seminary; the recollections of the Henry family who lived only a few miles across the river in Bainbridge; the recollections of Perry Mapes, who grew up down the road from Garfield; the proceedings of the literary society Garfield and his friends founded; the elaborate digests of Cleveland newspapers and court records for this period, done under Work Projects Administration (WPA) auspices in the 1930s. Finally, there are the campaign biographies of Garfield produced in 1880 for the presidential canvass. Previous biographers have generally ignored these as political shoddy unworthy of serious attention, but in fact most of them rested on original interviews and, in some cases, considerable research. I contend (and argue the case more fully in the appendix) that these biographies, critically examined, are useful and sometimes valuable source documents. All these sources have contributed to this study; most have not been utilized by any previous biographer.

This wealth of material also provides a detailed, informative picture of the world in which Garfield grew up, the rural Western Reserve—specifically, Cuyahoga, Geauga, Lake, and Portage counties. One cannot understand Garfield without understanding this world, and in these pages I attempt to give a thorough picture of what life was like in the Reserve in the 1840s and 1850s—what people ate, what they read, how they amused themselves, what they wore. The reader will find extended discussions of courtship and dating customs, of life on a canal boat, of phrenology and its significance, of carpenter's tools and house building. Most of this material is directly from primary sources; there are few good secondary works on the Reserve during this period. Perhaps the material presented here will stimulate some reader to undertake a general social history of the Reserve in the 1800s; the sources for it are ample, and it would be a fascinating book.

A word of caution needs to be added about the sources for Garfield's early adolescence. Before 1848, when his diary begins, they are comparatively skimpy and rest mainly on oral reminiscences; these, it turns out, are far from reliable. The Garfield scholar Allan Peskin discovered some years ago that Garfield's mother had married a second time in 1842, that the marriage had ended in divorce, and that Garfield had assiduously concealed this episode all his life, editing it out of his reminiscences and diary. In fact, if it had not been for an unguarded reference in the diary during the last year of his life, it might have remained a secret. Thus a biographer of Garfield begins with the knowledge that the apparent candor and fullness of his own testimony about his life may be deceptive at points. There were things Garfield wanted concealed, and he did not hesitate to conceal them. In reading over the sparse evidence about his early adolescence, I have found evidence that suggests other important omissions—for instance, another unsuccessful marriage by Garfield's mother during his early childhood, and a brief residence in another region or state when he was eleven. These questions are discussed more fully in the notes to chapter 3.

This book makes no pretense to finality; it presents the evidence I have been able to accumulate in several years of searching. There remain unsolved questions, big and small, about Garfield's early life. Additional evidence may exist to answer many of them and, consequently, I will greatly appreciate anyone's calling attention to source material I may have overlooked, or to errors of fact, or of interpretation in the book as it stands.

An author's most pleasant obligation is to mention the people who have helped him. By far my most important debt is to the Western Reserve Historical Society and its staff, who were instrumental in introducing an outsider to the riches of the society's holdings on the history and culture of the Reserve. Without its collections, this book would have been impossible. Lawnfield, the Garfield home at Mentor, Ohio, now a property of the Western Reserve Historical Society, was still operated by the Lake County Historical Society at the time of my researches, and the people there were unfailingly helpful. Other institutions where I consulted books or manuscripts included the Library of Congress, the New York Public Library, the Ohio Historical Society, Hiram College, and the Johns Hopkins University. Thanks to those twin twentieth-century marvels, microfilm and inter-library loan, I was able to consult many important sources fairly close to home at the University of South Carolina's Thomas Cooper Library. The Grand Rapids (Michigan) Public Library and the Bentley Historical Library of the University of Michigan responded promptly to my appeals for information.

To an uncommon degree, this book leans on the assistance of individuals who made themselves available to help an author with limited resources of time, mobility, and money. Professor James Banks of Cuyahoga Courty Community College gave me the benefit of his discussion and research skills; Nelson P. Bard, of his knowledge of Solon history; Miriam Goldbach showed me around the Chagrin Falls Historical Society; Dwight Hendricks of the Booth Library at Hiram College went out of his way to hunt up relevant source material. Phyllis McLaughlin of Des Moines, Iowa, aided me in investigating the important papers of Corydon E. Fuller in the Iowa Historical Society. Dr. Robert A. Wheeler of Cleveland steered me to a useful source, the George Starr diary; and Patricia Woodward of Berea, Ohio, has been of immense assistance in trying to unravel the Garfield family's tangled history.

Thanks are due also to the people who assisted in publication of the book, especially Ted Sande, director of the Western Reserve Historical Society, and Keimit Pike, director of the Society's Library; also to Beth Gianfagna of Associated University Presses and to Ann Harvey, a splendid copyeditor. I am grateful to Margie Whitehurst for typing a portion of the manuscript at a time when accuracy and speed were vital.

Finally, I should mention Dolores Lashley, of Greenville, South Carolina, whose generosity made the beginning of this research possible; and my wife, Lynn Allen Booraem, whose forbearance allowed it to continue.

The Road to Respectability

1

The Black-Salter

Fall 1847

If you had been picking your way along a mud road in the northern part of Solon Township, Cuyahoga County, Ohio, in the fall of 1847 . . .

Not that there was much reason why you should have been. The neighborhood was not on the direct route to such places of importance as there were in northeastern Ohio in 1847; it was poor, thinly settled country, with nothing to offer except some steep hills to pull and some boggy spots where the land sloped down toward the center of town . . .

You would have traversed a landscape characteristic of Ohio at the passing of the frontier. Stands of immense trees, survivors of the primeval forest, still dominated the land; sometimes they occupied large areas. But they alternated with cleared lands where frame farm houses and barns overlooked acres of pasture or recently harvested wheat fields. The struggle between Americans and the forest was over here, and humans had obviously won. The woodland was retreating; the wolf and bear were gone, the deer disappearing, only the smaller denizens, squirrels, woodchucks, foxes, remaining.[1]

There was a splendor about the landscape, for this part of Ohio, the old Connecticut Western Reserve, rivaled New England in spectacular autumn foliage. The giant hickories with their sulfur-yellow leaves, and the tulip poplar, called whitewood by the settlers, with its broad canary-yellow leaves, mixed with the blazing yellow, orange, and fiery pink of the rock maple, and the yellow and brown tones of oak, ash, and beech. In spots, deep in the woods, groves of hemlock provided a thick, blackish-green backdrop. Fallen leaves, red, brown, and yellow, drifted across the hard light brown soil of the roads.[2]

But though there was a splendor, there was also a rawness. The fields where cattle grazed and wheat grew were thickly dotted with enormous, jagged stumps, a foot or two high, blackened by fire—the remains of the recently cleared forest. Charles Dickens, traveling through central Ohio a few years before, had commented on the odd shapes these stumps could assume in the glimmering of dusk, ". . . a Grecian urn in the center of a lonely field; . . . now a student poring on a book; now a crouching Negro; now a horse, a dog, a cannon, an armed man; a hunchback throwing off his cloak and stepping into the light."[3]

And still the assault on the forest went on. This time of year particularly, the air over Solon was pungent with wood smoke, not only from farm stoves and fireplaces, but from mass burnings of timber and brush. The land had been cut over, typically, in late spring or early summer by gangs of wood-choppers, and the felled trees left to dry several months under the summer sun. Now it was time to burn them, first the brush, then the logs not needed for building or fencing.

Burning over fifteen or twenty acres was, as a young man from the general area later recalled, "a grand and sometimes almost a fearsome spectacle." The brush particularly went up in a crackling, thunderous conflagration, with white smoke twisting and billowing into a high column visible for miles, leaving the foliage on the standing leaves of the surrounding forest limp and withered from the great heat. Then it took men and oxen a week or ten days to haul the blackened logs into piles for the final burning, which might last as long as a week, with fires slowly licking at the enormous trunks and the loggers, black from head to foot, working to keep them from rolling out of place.

Even when the last spark flickered out, work was not quite over. Teams and wagonloads of men arrived with baskets and long-handled scrapers; working carefully but quickly, before any rain could fall, they scooped up the soft gray ashes and loaded them into the wagons, to be carted off for black salts.[4]

Black-salting, the final stage in the clearing process, was a business that existed only within a very specialized economic niche. It flourished thanks to three conditions: the surplus of wood and scarcity of cash on the American and Canadian frontiers, and the need of English wool manufacturers for potash to clean raw fleeces before they could be spun. American pioneers had found that by leaching wood ashes with water and boiling the resultant lye into a black, hard, gritty cake called black salts, and then cooking it in a kiln until it turned into light gray pearlash, a form of potash, they had a commodity easily transportable and capable of bringing a good price in England or, what was more important, cash at the nearest large town.

In the economic history of any Ohio community, black-salting was a phase that lasted as long as wood was abundant. In the early days of settlement, asheries—the places where wood ashes were boiled into black salts and sometimes baked into pearlash—sprang up all over a township, usually wherever there was a country store, since local merchants found it convenient to take ashes in exchange for their merchandise. Knowledge of the craft spread among the people: which kinds of trees, for example, produced the richest ashes (water elm, beech, basswood, maple, and hickory were among the best; evergreen ashes, poor in potash, were worthless). Later, as the forest became depleted, the asheries closed. This was happening all over the Reserve in

1847; not far away, in Randolph, the last ashery closed that year for a shortage of material.[5] But Solon and the area around it had been settled late, because of the poverty of the soil, and for that reason ashes were still plentiful there.[6]

There were at least three asheries operating in Solon in the 1840s. A man named Alvin Harris had one in the southern part of the town. At the center, from 1840 on, there was a store run by an ex-seaman from Connecticut, Archibald Robbins, who took ashes in trade and manufactured black salts and pearlash. And in the northwest corner of the township, in an area called Hampshire Road, recently settled by families of some social pretensions from New Hampshire and Maine, there was another, run by Daniel Morse.[7]

If you had been walking down the right road on a certain fall morning in 1847, you would have encountered a young man who had just quit work at Morse's ashery.[8] He was fifteen going on sixteen, but tall for his age, and he walked with determination. He was a farm boy, and dressed like one—heavy cowhide boots covering woolen stockings, baggy woolen trousers held up by a sturdy suspender or two, a rumpled flannel shirt, perhaps a wamus, a loose jacket dyed madder red—all in the awkward cut and dull colors, butternut drab or sheep's gray, that marked homemade men's clothing. But his appearance was striking. He looked big and truculent. His burly, strong-shouldered body was surmounted by a big head, almost overgrown; his legs seemed a size too short, his hands oddly small. He had a round, thick-lipped face, with a set expression that struck different people as grim, or preoccupied, or surly. His hair, stiff, wiry, light brown, discolored red in front by the fumes from the black salts, stood up like a tangled mane. His name was James Garfield, and he was going back to his home in the neighboring township of Orange.[9]

Unlike Archibald Robbins, who had several sons to help him with the work of the ashery, Daniel Morse had only daughters at home; he had made it a practice, therefore, to hire a boy in his early teens to help with the work, collecting ashes, shoveling them into the leaching vats, keeping the fires going, and stirring the lye as it boiled in the tall black kettles shaped like half-eggshells, with extra thick bottoms to resist being eaten away by the chemicals in the salts. Although not arduous, it was a smelly and unpleasant job—the young black-salters often looked their name, grimy all over like charcoal-burners. Morse paid nine dollars a month, with room and board, and had no difficulty finding help.[10]

The Garfield boy ("Gaffield" to the people of the vicinity, most of them New Englanders like the Morses)[11] lived four or five miles away, with his brother and widowed mother, and was always looking for odd jobs to bring the family extra cash; he had worked in an ashery before and knew something of the business, a fact which may have commended him to Morse. But Morse may have hesitated, too, before hiring him, for the boy had the reputation of being difficult—not mean and not dishonest, but sensitive, short-tempered, and, alas, not terribly hard-working. If he did hesitate, then perhaps the way the boy left his employ confirmed his doubts.[12]

The stories do not agree in every detail, but the general outline is the same; for several weeks the boy and the Morse family got on well. Young Garfield was fond of books, and Mrs. Morse permitted him to stay in the sitting room reading some of their books after he finished his work in the evening and before he retired to his room. The Morse home no longer stands, but the scores of Reserve houses from that era which have survived make it easy to envision the house, and the sitting room within it. Like any Reserve home beyond the log-cabin stage, it was frame, and built on the New England–farmhouse pattern. The sitting room was at what was called the front, although in practice the house was almost always entered from the kitchen. It was a small room, plastered and painted some dark color, perhaps blue, with a low ceiling. There were neat curtains at the windows, a rag carpet on the floor, and a warm fire on the brick hearth. Perhaps, if the Morses were affluent enough, there was a wooden mantelpiece painted to resemble the marble counterpart in an elegant city home. But one must not exaggerate the comfort. The furniture, in all likelihood, was both simple and sparse—a chest or two, a couple of tables, a couple of chairs, perhaps a settee. Apart from the firelight, a few candles on the tables provided all the light there was—and the boy probably sat at a small table near the bookcase, poring over his evening's reading by the flickering light from a single tallow taper.[13]

One evening the Morses' daughter Zeruiah was entertaining a young man named Bigelow, a teacher at an academy some miles away. He seemed a good catch for a young lady, being smart, self-assured, a Vermont Yankee by birth, and Mrs. Morse wanted to see that the couple had a chance to chat without being disturbed. The small front room seemed the best place; so she tactlessly announced to young Garfield that it was time for the "servants" to go to bed.

It was always a mistake to use the word "servant" in a frontier area, even where the frontier atmosphere had worn as thin as it had in northeastern Ohio. Frontier people jealously guarded the idea that they were all equal in social status, and strongly resisted anyone's claim to superiority. Mrs. Morse's use of the word suggests, at the least, a certain insensitivity, not to say pretension. But young Garfield was infuriated to an unusual degree. He stalked off to bed; next morning, he announced flatly that he was quitting. He may not have made a scene of it—despite his reputation as a fighter among other boys, he had a fairly consistent respect for his elders. But he was definitely, irrevocably through at the Morses'.[14]

He stumped off toward home, his social status vindicated, seething inside; for years afterward he could not mention the incident without anger. The loss of income for himself and his family probably did not bother him; or if it did, it was counterbalanced by the certainty that his mother would be glad to see him after an absence of over a month. She always preferred to have all her children near her. All in all, his heart was reasonably light as he prepared for the long climb up Orange Hill.

2

James and His Reveries

Fall 1847

In half an hour's walk, young Garfield was at the hilltop, where, in the manner of climbers, he could turn around to view the prospect behind him.

He could see far to the west, over fields and multicolored woods, visible through the autumn haze. The land in that direction flattened out as it approached the Cuyahoga River, seven or eight miles distant. But what he saw was more than the Cuyahoga valley—it was really the beginning of the great interior plain of North America. Except for occasional bluffs bordering large rivers, there were no hills of any size west of him until the Rocky Mountains, one thousand miles away.

Eastward the land had a different look—hilly, irregular, with "ledges," rock outcroppings, on some of the heights. A couple of miles further it plunged into the deep, narrow cutting of the Chagrin River, a medium-sized, shallow stream which flowed northward into Lake Erie. The Chagrin descended from the hills in a series of falls, all more or less spectacular, where the water dropped in a silver sheet from one rock shelf to another. The energetic Yankees who had settled the area had built dams and millraces all along it to power a series of tiny industries—chair factories (water power supplied the force for turning the legs), grist mills, axe factories, paper mills. The area reminded well-traveled visitors of the hill country in western Massachusetts or northern Connecticut. On across the Chagrin valley, one could see a country of gentle hills rolling away to the east.[1]

He stood, really, at the boundary of two distinct geographical provinces. East of him the winter snows were deeper and lasted longer. In the country west of him, where the lake moderated the climate, the last frost was in mid-April; in Orange, Solon, and the country eastward, in mid-May. Pine and hemlock, familiar trees to New Englanders, grew well in Orange, Solon, and the country east—but hardly at all to the west. People in the eastern townships felt a little detached from the rest of the county; they did their ordinary trading not at Cleveland, the county seat, but at the small manufacturing village of Chagrin Falls, across the valley.[2]

It was eastward that he went now, perhaps down the narrow dirt road that ran, straight as a shot, along the Orange–Solon town line. More likely, though, he took a path through the woods. The old settlers, families like the Garfields, had known the area before the roads were put through, and knew all the old shortcuts through the forest.

The boy knew the Orange woods like an extension of his own body. He had walked in them, hunted in them, run wild in them, searched in them for strayed cattle, almost since he could walk. As a child, perhaps, he had been afraid of the forest and the wild things in it; but now that he was half a man, he had made the woods his own. Not just in the color of fall; he knew the summer woods, the tangles of wild berries that grew rank in abandoned clearings, the honey-dark shade under the poplars and maples, the sudden chill east winds foretokening rain, the calls of the loon and whippoorwill at night; or early spring, when all sorts of unexpected flowers appeared like a miniature collection of precious china from under the dead leaves—bloodroot, ladyslipper, wake robin, spring beauties; June, with bees humming in the fragrant basswood flowers, or midwinter's snow-covered ground, the keen winds, the harsh creaking of branches against each other, and the cry of the white owl.[3]

The most exciting thing about the woods, to him, were the rock out-crops, which lent them a touch of fantasy, of wild romance. Some were large. Up west from the Garfield farm ("up west" because all this part of Orange sloped downward toward the east), at the head of the brook that ran through their pasture, was a big collection of rocks he called the "Stone Bridge." Not far away was another high rock, almost a cliff, from which, as a boy, he had played at preaching. All these places, to him, had names, drawn mainly from his reading.[4] He read constantly and never ceased to amaze his friends with the wealth of facts he knew and the names he applied to the things around him. According to one boyhood friend, he had named all the trees in his apple orchard, each with the name of a famous Indian. His favorite was "Tecumseh."[5]

Indians, it seems, were one thing he associated with the woods he was walking through. Not the real Indians; they had been killed or driven out of the area long before he was born. He had probably never seen an Indian, unless it was one of the sad, drunken ones who hung around the Cleveland docks.[6] In that respect, the area of his boyhood was not at all like a frontier. Only in boyish fantasy did he need to worry about the unknown shadow behind the gleaming bole of a beech. The Indians in his mind were the symbolic ones that have haunted the consciousness of generations of American boys—the crafty, disciplined, merciless hunters who stalked the woods and seemed to be one with wild nature. One feared them, but wanted to be like them—at least, in 1847 one was beginning to want to be like them, as American attitudes toward Indians changed. An admiring biography of Tecumseh had been printed at Cincinnati in 1841; perhaps young Garfield had read it.

From other books he had read, he knew, or felt he knew, the character of the Indians, traced in words both forbidding and alluring: "quick of apprehension, and not wanting in genius"; at times "friendly, and even courteous"; in war, distinguished "for bravery and address"; seeking no pleasures beyond "the strong impulses of public festivity, or burning captives, or seeking murderous revenge, or the chase, or war, or glory."[7]

All this was from the Reverend Charles A. Goodrich's *History of the United States*, which the boy had read repeatedly. Much of what he read was about history. It was a subject generally approved, and easy to find books on. Moreover, it was entertaining. Goodrich's history told not only about the Indians but also about such exciting matters as the English captain John Smith's adventures among the Turks, how he had beheaded two in single combat and received "his picture set in gold" and "a coat of arms, bearing three Turk's heads in a shield," or the destruction of a Massachusetts Indian village, where "five or six hundred Indians lay bleeding on the ground, or smoldering in the ashes."[8]

Equally entertaining was a locally printed history of the Revolution he had run across somewhere, a strange mixture of prose and heroic couplets. Unaware how odd a production it was, he had memorized long stretches, in which the author, Benjamin Eggleston, denounced war and slavery, invoked Mars, Neptune, and other classic gods, and flayed the British ("Old Tryon, that infamous demagogue, / More fit to serve the Devil than his God, / Lands with his army, bred in murder's school— / Fit body to fit head—an arrant fool.")[9]

A third book he read with a thrill on winter nights told the story of Israel Putnam, who had tracked and fought a she-wolf in her rocky den near the Connecticut River.[10] This was almost tribal history, for "Old Put," resourceful, determined, unflinching, belonged to the New England epic that cropped up repeatedly in the history books and had such meaning for the people of the Reserve, New Englanders themselves at one or two removes. (Garfield's mother had been born in New Hampshire, his father in New York, both to Massachusetts people.) Practically all of the history they read was written by, for, and mostly about New Englanders, and was full of encomiums to Yankee virtue. New Englanders possessed not only seriousness and pluck but also "shrewd inquisitiveness" and "keen relish of a jest," according to the Reverend Mr. Goodrich, a Connecticut man himself.[11]

(Fallen twigs crackled under his heavy boots on the forest path. Squirrels chattered overhead high in the yellow hickories.)[12]

The same sort of history was in the songs his mother sang, some of which re-echoed in his head and combined with what he had read in Goodrich's history. Though a small woman, short in stature, with a birdlike alertness, Mrs. Garfield was energetic, tough as a hickory knot, and gifted with a rich true voice of the sort that was the delight of country choirs. She loved to sing, and knew all the kinds of songs then common in the country, hymns ad ballads; years later, as an adult, Garfield guessed she could have sung forty-eight hours straight without exhausting her repertory, if her voice could have held out.[13] He remembered best the songs she sang from her own youth, folk songs of New England, hymns and religious songs like "Safe in the Promised Land," war songs of 1812 about the fight of the *Guerriere*, the *Wasp* and *Hornet*, ballads like "James Bird," whose twenty-eight stanzas ended:

Farewell, Bird! Farewell forever,
Friends and home you'll see no more.
But his mangled corpse lies buried
On Lake Erie's distant shore.

("E-rye," they generally pronounced it.)[14]

James Bird and John Smith, Israel Putnam and Tecumseh, the Indians and their foes seemed to people the woods where he walked, thanks to his powerful, accurate, and extraordinarily vivid memory. These figures—pasteboard and tinsel, some of them, though he could not be expected to know that—were as real to him as the people in his neighborhood, and better company, because they never rebuked or mocked him. Part of a sentence he wrote in a letter a few years later suggests how much comfort he drew from nature and memory, the inanimate and the imaginary: ". . . when the day is down and the moon shines calmly, and old Orion girds on his shining armor to walk forth in the blue fields of heaven I keep him company. . . ."[15]

Orion and the constellations, and other facts like the capital of Ohio or simple interest or the five Great Lakes, were the province of the district school, which young Garfield had attended regularly at least through his early teens. The boy's memory had made him an astonishingly apt student, and in the neighborhood he was thought of as a prodigy, with all the good and bad that that implied. Other children, to his embarrassment, teased him because of his overgrown head, shouting the rhyme:

Little head, little wit;
Big head, not a bit.[16]

But on the whole he liked school. It was a scene of triumph for him, where he did well in reciting and particularly in debating. Some later neighborhood stories affirmed that he had debated against adult men while in his early teens, and that he and some friends had a debating club that met regularly in the schoolhouse, and were not averse to breaking the lock of the schoolhouse door if they had to get in.[17]

(The forest floor felt spongy under his feet, especially heading downhill where the heavy October rains had washed drifts of sodden leaves or humus across the path. The morning air was chilly on his face.)

There was another source of facts, church and the Bible. He, his mother, and his brother attended a church called the Disciples of Christ, which also met in the schoolhouse. The Disciples laid special stress on the duty of reading and knowing the Scripture, and this emphasis, together with the constant hymns, proverbs, and religious discussion that were an invariable feature of life on an American frontier, had made Solomon and Elijah, Barnabas and Apollos and the Syrophenician woman, thoroughly familiar figures to him. As a small boy he had envied the preacher who stood up in meeting and shared the Word of God with the people; he had come home and gone into the woods and preached to the trees and rocks. Now he had outgrown that wish to preach, but the people and concepts of the Bible, the angels, the miracles, the terrible wrath of God, were no less real to him; nor were promises like the one in the familiar hymn, paraphrased from Psalm 103:

Our days are as the grass,
Or like the morning flower;
If one sharp blast sweep o'er the field,
It withers in an hour.

But thy compassions, Lord,
To countless years endure;
And children's children ever find
The words of promise sure.[18]

Like any reading boy in the Reserve, too, he knew the pair of religious classics that were in most farm households—*The Pilgrim's Progress* and Whiston's translation of the *Histories* of Josephus. These were books there was no objection to his reading, if he liked, late at night by the light of a tallow candle, while the rest of the family slept.[19]

Another class of books, much more questionable, he had been reading since he was thirteen. Novels—not the elaborate European novels of men like Dickens and Bulwer-Lytton, with which he was totally unacquainted, but silly, simple American productions, mostly about adventure and thwarted love. Harmless as they were, however, they were still novels, and many devout Christians in the 1840s felt all novels were "demoralizing," in that they tended to arouse emotions which, in the interests of morality and harmony, were better left alone. "The 'common sewers of society,'" one clergyman called them. Apparently the Garfields did not entirely share this view. James and his cousin Harriet Boynton, who lived across the road, read them together avidly, and evidently someone in the Garfield or Boynton families took the trouble to buy them in Cleveland, or possibly, if they were available, in Chagrin Falls.[20]

Alonze and Melissa, by Daniel Jackson, Junior, was among their favorites. Like Goodrich's history, it had a heavily New England flavor, being set in western Connecticut on the eve of the Revolutionary War. It contained romance enough to satisfy cousin Harriet, plus exciting scenes like a series of apparitions that frightened the heroine, confined in a gloomy, castle-like mansion near Long Island Sound. There were, first, a "sulphureous [*sic*] stench," then a "loud hoarse peal of ghostly laughter," followed two pages later by the ghost itself, "tall and robust, wrapped in a tattered white robe, spotted with blood." There were also exciting seafights in the life of the hero, who had become a sailor upon hearing false reports of his beloved's death; changes of scene to exotic locales like Paris and Charleston, South Carolina; and a finale in which the protagonists were rich, honored, and reunited at last, and the "ghosts" revealed as a band of smugglers.

Moreover, since the book was a novel and not a history, it contained extended, elaborate descriptions that may have appealed to a poetic streak in young Garfield. "On high hills beyond, the tops of lofty forests, majestically moved by the billowy gales, caught the sun's last ray. Fleecy summer clouds hovered around the verge of the western horizon, spangled with silver tints or fringed with the gold of evening." This could have been Orange itself in summer, seen from somewhere on the other side of the Chagrin valley.[21]

Always looking for new books, he had moved on from *Alonzo and Melissa* to the kind that now, at age fifteen, bulked largest in his reading—tales of pirates and the sea. There were several varieties of these. Some were innocuous, or even morally uplifting, like John Sherburne Sleeper's *Tales of the Ocean* (which Garfield probably read), from which all profanity had been edited to avoid offending the reader and designed, its author said, to "inculcate principles of sound morality." It consisted of sugar-coated stories of seafaring life, with jolly, witty sailors and romantic plots, interspersed with ringing generalities like "A sailor is habitually brave—he is accustomed to danger in every shape, and is unappalled at the prospect of death. In the hour of difficulty, in shipwreck or in battle, his courage and presence of mind seldom forsake him. . . ."[22]

But Garfield's favorite was a very different sort of work, *The Pirate's Own Book*, a detailed compilation of pirate tales from all ages and all lands, much less sanitized than *Tales of the Ocean*. It held ample bloodshed, treachery enough for a dozen Elizabethan plays, passages where the decks were "ankle deep in blood and gore," adventures in shark-infested waters, grisly public hangings, and slightly racy parts like the one where some Englishmen, captives of Persian Gulf pirates, were examined by Arab women to determine "in what respect an uncircumcised infidel differs from a true believer."[23] To James Garfield, at fifteen, this book was "a kind of bible"; he pored over it constantly. It had everything to fascinate a certain sort of boy just entering adolescence: rebellion, violence, destruction, retribution, with the prospect of freedom and wide-ranging adventure on the immense ocean.[24]

Steeped in pirate lore, young Garfield had developed an obsession with the sea, and with the idea of becoming a sailor. It was a somewhat juvenile passion, appropriate to a naive, spoiled youngest child, who had always been indulged in his reading and imagination, and who even at fifteen was not being pushed at all hard toward adulthood. He spent hours imagining himself a sailor, deep in his dream world, "visiting with himself," as one of his cousins put it. One wonders where he saw himself in *The Pirate's Own Book*—maybe in the career of Charles Gibbs, the Rhode Island boy from a good family, with "a great antipathy to work" and "a great inclination to roam." Gibbs had run away from home at fifteen to become a sailor and subsequently a pirate responsible for the death of over one hundred and fifty persons in the West Indies.[25]

These powerful visions, though wholly unconnected with his daily reality, lost none of their power on that account. He had never even seen the sea; but the calm blue expanse of Lake Erie, which he saw when he went to Cleveland, and could glimpse from some points in Orange, could without difficulty be transformed into the turbulent, blue-green, foaming main. Using the images derived from his reading, he found delight in dreaming of the whistle of wind in the rigging, the tilt of the vessel, the salt smell of the water. . . .

The familiar smell of farm animals, horse- and cow-dirt, the hen park, the pigpen, mingled with woodsmoke in the air.[26] He was coming down, out of the woods, past the orchard of a hundred apple trees his father had planted. Down in the pasture, the little brook in its ravine rippled over flat, brown, squarish stones. There was the well he had helped his brother dig, and beyond, the red house. He was home.[27]

3

The Garfields
1831–1847

THE early settlers of the Western Reserve had their own rule of thumb for determining when the frontier period ended in a given locality: When frame houses replaced log houses, the frontier was a thing of the past. As architectural historians of Ohio have shown, replacement usually took place in three steps. The settler built a log cabin to meet his family's immediate need for shelter. Once established on his land, he replaced it with a more pretentious log house, built of squared logs and sometimes covered with clapboards, which usually contained several rooms and might have such amenities as windows that opened and shut. This, however, was not the change early settlers saw as important. That came some years later, when the settler, if he was doing well, began putting up frame buildings—first a large, impressive barn, then a frame house. The richer settlers began the process; the moderately prosperous followed them; meanwhile, the poorer ones moved away and their cabins collapsed and disappeared. Then the frontier was over. A modern student could perhaps devise additional measures, but hardly a better one.[1]

Judged by this standard, the Garfields' neighborhood in south Orange and the adjacent part of Solon was, in 1847, just at the end of the frontier era. On main roads like the one where the Garfields lived, almost all the houses were frame—simple Greek Revival, on the Yankee pattern, painted red or white. Some log houses lingered on side roads; and, to be sure, every so often a new settler just beginning to develop his land put up a log cabin, as a Manx immigrant to northern Orange named Corlett did in 1844, or a farmer named Burgess did across the river in Russell in 1846.[2] Some land remained completely undeveloped, like the hundred-acre tract just south of the Garfield farm, a chunk of primeval forest that had been sold but, for some reason, never settled.[3] So traces of the frontier still existed, but were fading fast.

The widow Garfield and her sons had barely been able to keep abreast of the tide. Their little red house, with its inevitable complement, a dooryard garden colorful in summer with larkspur, marigolds, hollyhock, sunflowers, and yellow dahlias, and fragrant with traditional herbs like sage, pennyroyal, and "meetin' seed" (fennel),[4] was only a year old in the fall of 1847. The house had been built the summer of the preceding year to replace the ramshackle log cabin where the family had lived for years.[5]

The house was a definite improvement on its predecessor; it looked neat and stood straight. It was, however, undeniably small—four rooms, according to the best source. There was a kitchen, with a bare wood floor religiously scrubbed by Eliza Garfield, a shelf for washing and stacking dishes, a pantry, and with farm products hanging from the walls and ceiling. Possibly a cookstove—large iron cookstoves had been in use in the area for about ten years. They were costly, however, and the Garfields may have had the traditional cooking fireplace, with its large pots, iron cranes, and brick oven. There was a small bedroom for Eliza, and another which James shared with his tall, rawboned, slow-spoken brother Thomas, the nominal head of the family. And there was probably a sitting room more or less like the Morses', with curtains, rag carpet, and whatever nice furniture the family had. (They may not have had much; the only household items still preserved from this period are a clay inkwell, a cast-iron kettle and frying pan, and a wooden scoop.) Eliza's spinning wheels and loom would have been in this room too.[6]

There was no bathroom, of course; the small, malodorous privy out behind

The Chagrin Valley. James Hope's painting of Garfield's birthplace, done in 1882, is not an accurate source for the cabin itself, but does depict the isolation of a newly settled family.

the house took care of elimination. As for bathing itself, this was a matter of bringing in pails of water from the well, heating the water over the fire, pouring it into the washtub, washing rapidly before it cooled, and then emptying the water, pail by pail, outside. The process was long and laborious, and they bathed no oftener than necessary.[7]

The Garfield boys still remembered their previous home, the old cabin, with a kind of affection. James could recall having lain on the floor watching the play of the firelight on the stone-and-clay backwall of the fireplace, the dance of the flames around the big backlog, the warmth emanating from the firestick in front. They had slept in the loft, warmed by the rising heat from the fire. Probably there had been the usual ladder stairs in the corner of the cabin, and probably there had been mornings, common in frontier experience, when the boys had awakened to find their bedclothes finely covered with snow that had sifted down overnight through chinks in the roof. Their mother, and probably their sisters when they were still at home, had slept in the single room downstairs.[8]

During most of their residence in the cabin, that had been all their living space—the twenty-by-thirty-foot single room and the loft. Shortly before they built the new house, Thomas had purchased the old log schoolhouse that the district had just abandoned, and had moved it back of the cabin as an addition. But this makeshift had not helped the rickety cabin itself, whose frame was sagging farther every year, jamming the doors against the ground; every year they had to saw a little bit more off the bottom to be able to close them. It had been a good enough structure in its day, but Abram Garfield had never intended it to last fifteen years.[9]

Abram Garfield, James's father, had built the cabin in 1830, a year before the birth of his youngest son. He had just moved to the area, with his wife and the three children they had then—nine-year-old Mehitable, eight-year-old Thomas, and six-year-old Mary[10]—to take up the fifty acres of land he had bought from the speculator Simon Perkins. There were few neighbors yet in the thick, sloping forests except for his half-brother Amos Boynton, who had bought the rest of the one-hundred-twenty-acre lot and had already begun a similar cabin on his land.[11] John Mapes and his family lived one mile south, and the Smith family a mile or so to the north.[12] The area was still practically wilderness, although an island of wilderness among lands already settled and partially cleared. The soil did not seem fertile, and the land was rocky and irregular; settlers had avoided it as long as more choice land was available.[13] But to Abram Garfield it was full of promise. The strong, burly man had put his best into building the cabin. Its sides were unhewn logs chinked with clay, its floor a slightly irregular surface of logs hewn with the adze. The chimney continued upward from the stone fireplace in the "cat-and-clay" construction (twigs or reeds held together by clay) typical of frontier cabins. Two small windows, one at each end, let daylight in; a plank door

Garfields and Boyntons. These pictures, all dating from the 1850s, convey not only how the Garfields and Boyntons looked but also how respectable farmers of the Reserve dressed for important occasions like being photographed.

Amos Boynton

Eliza Garfield

William Boynton (*left*) and James Garfield (*right*)

Silas Boynton

in the middle of the front permitted entrance. It was a standard pioneer cabin, fully as good as any of the neighbors'; anything Abram Garfield did was bound to be workmanlike.[14]

Abram died three years after building the cabin; James, his youngest son, had never known him. But since his father's loss was such a strong influence on his early life, and since he alone of all the children bore his father's first name—James Abram Garfield—he had always been hungry for information about him. His mother had been more than ready to supply his needs. In repeated conversations she had created in James a clear, vivid image of the man who had fathered him and built the cabin. He had been a tall, large man, of prodigious physical strength, light complexioned, with small feet and hands and ruddy lips, like James. He was originally from Otsego County, New York. His stepfather, a man named Boynton, had moved west to Ohio in the 1810s with a sizable family, four Garfield children and nine Boyntons, and had settled in Independence on the Cuyahoga River. In 1819, Abram, then twenty, had gone south to Muskingum County to visit some old neighbors from New York. There he had met Eliza Ballou, whom he married next year. Abram had no trade; he was a farmer and laborer like the rest of his family. For a while in the 1820s he made money as a contractor on a section of the great Ohio and Erie Canal, then under construction across eastern Ohio. Men respected him. He was hearty and commanding, if somewhat quick-tempered at times. He had lost heavily on his second venture in contracting, however, and in 1830 the family moved to Orange to farm. Then, in 1833, he died.[15]

Naturally, the details of Abram's death were a central part of family tradition. It was due to a forest fire, in the dry, dangerous spring months. The woods around their cabin had been blazing all day, and Abram had been out fighting the fire, as Eliza remembered it. In the afternoon he came home exhausted, sat in the shade of the cabin doorway, and fanned himself with his hat. That evening he developed a sore throat; two days later, despite the family's best efforts, he was dead. In the pattern of the hardworking New England farmer, shortly before he died he looked out the window and called his oxen by name. Then he leaned on his wife's shoulder, murmured something like "I have to leave you" and died.[16]

His death put Eliza in a difficult, though hardly uncommon, situation. She had herself and four children, all of them under thirteen, to feed. She owned fifty acres of land only partly paid for, most of it uncleared and useless for cultivation. In the short run, her predicament was not desperate, for her brother-in-law and other neighbors could help get in the crop Abram had planted, and she was entitled by law to a year's support of $120. But in the long run, with no man in the house able to handle an axe to clear land, or even a maul and wedge to split rails for fencing, her prospects of holding on to the land were bleak indeed.[17]

There were three options commonly available to a woman in Eliza's situation. She could throw herself and children on the bounty of some richer relative until they got reestablished; in Eliza's case, unfortunately, there was none. She could parcel out the children among various kinfolk and stay on at the cabin herself, eking out a living at some craft like weaving or spinning. Or she could remarry after the shortest decent interval possible.

There is fragmentary evidence to suggest that Eliza tried the last of these alternatives. Years later a niece recalled her marrying a man who "left her, taking with him horse and wagon and any other valuables he saw fit." A cryptic note in the family papers suggests that a marriage took place in 1835, two years after Abram's death, to a man whose last name began with C. It lasted only seven months. No reason whatever is given why he abandoned her, and one has to suppose that Eliza, desperate for a way out, simply made a bad choice and ended by inadvertently compounding her misery. At least the episode, short lived as it was, was easy to suppress from the record and from memory; it is no surprise that printed lives of Garfield failed to mention it, or that the traces of it are so very tenuous.[18] But the neighbors in Orange were aware and pitied the family; and Eliza, angry and shaken, was more determined than ever to keep her family together somehow. She adored her four children, and they her. There was an unusual warmth in her household, and she wanted to preserve it.[19]

In 1836, the year after the failed marriage, the children were almost old enough to be of some help, Mehitable, whom the family called Hitty, fifteen that year, was a cheerful, hardworking girl who was ready to tackle any job, even splitting firewood, to help the household. Thomas, who would turn fourteen in October, was probably beginning to develop some height and strength. The younger children, eleven-year-old Mary and five-year-old James ("Jimmy" to the family), were still too young for heavy work but could help with lesser jobs. "We all had to work," Hitty recalled later, "every one who could lift a pound." With all their labor combined, it was just possible for them to survive together.[20]

That they managed to do so was, nevertheless, a tribute to Eliza's stubbornness and her capacity for sacrifice. Day by day, they had to wring a living from the farm. Eliza, Hitty, and Thomas together were not strong enough to clear land, plant and harvest grain, the mainstay of most Reserve farms, so they channeled their efforts into easier crops—corn, vegetables, potatoes. A couple of cows provided milk and butter. There were nuts and berries in the woods. Altogether, they subsisted on a very plain diet, and sometimes went hungry. Getting firewood was a problem too, until Thomas acquired strength and skill with an axe. Before that time, Eliza either leased some of her land to a neighbor to clear and cultivate, taking the cleared wood as payment, or, with the younger children, gathered sticks and branches at the edge of the woods. As for light, store-bought candles were out of the question, as were any bought goods, sugar, coffee, or cloth; probably the fire was all the light they had. Their garments were scratchy homespun; Eliza kept a few sheep, whose wool she, Hitty, and Mary carded, spun, dyed, and wove.[21]

One of Eliza's first decisions was to sell Amos Boynton twenty acres from Abram's fifty, and use the proceeds to pay off the debt on the remaining thirty acres.[22] By so doing she got rid of a heavy cash obligation. But for a few purposes, like property taxes, cash remained necessary. Eliza used her spinning wheel and loom to make money, taking in work as new settlers moved into the area, sewing a man's pants and vest from heavy fulled cloth, her daughter remembered, for seventy-five cents. Sometimes she could work out an arrangement with a craftsman to avoid the need for cash, like sewing clothes for the itinerant shoemaker and his family while he cobbled for hers. Despite these makeshifts, however, there was never much money in the Garfield home. Their existence, as a rule, was very poor, their food meager, their clothing coarse.[23]

And yet, without wishing to seem saccharine, one must note that, as they grew up, all the Garfield children looked back on these childhood days with nostalgia, as happy times. What they recalled was certainly not material comforts. It must have been the quality of life around the stone fireplace. Eliza Garfield read to her children; she sang to them and told them stories; she was a cheerful, hearty, bustling woman, indeed something of a busybody in the neighborhood, but one of those indispensable people who could always find time to be at a sick neighbor's bedside. From her New England background she had derived a great respect for learning, and was always glad to board the district school teacher and ply him with questions. Her devotion made it possible for the children, as long as they were very young, to avoid feeling the pain of poverty.[24]

Ill luck continued to haunt the family. In the late 1830s, Hitty, then in her middle teens, decided to get married. Perhaps her aim was to relieve the family of an extra mouth or to ally them with another local family that could help in case of financial crisis. If so, she was disappointed. Her marriage turned out to be as much a mistake as her mother's second attempt, though longer lasting. The groom, Stephen Trowbridge, was the son of a fairly prosperous Solon farmer who had settled about the same time as the Garfields. Superficially, he was attractive—bright, ready of speech, with a sort of transparent honesty. A few years, though, were to show him to be shiftless, a dreamer, uninterested in supporting his own family, let alone his in-laws. Hitty had their first child when she was eighteen.[25]

Then, Thomas. He had not been able to take time to attend school since his father died, and for that reason perhaps seemed slow. But in his teens he also began to be bothered by seizures of some sort, perhaps epileptic. They did not threaten his health, but what they did, apparently, was to rob him of sustained energy and drive. By his late teens (around 1840), it must have been obvious that Thomas, though strong, loyal, and devoted, strictly and deeply pious, capable of earning money from odd jobs and doing all necessary work around the farm, was not the man to restore prosperity to the Garfield family.[26]

The one bright spot in this dark picture, the brighter because of the general bleakness of its surroundings, was the development of little Jimmy. From the time he was three or four, it was clear that his intelligence was out of the ordinary. He learned to read early; he said surprising, clever things; he began school early and almost at once became the star pupil. Eliza and the rest of the family doted on him. He should go to college, they agreed, though in their situation the dream seemed absurd. They showed him off to visitors; very often they let him out of his household duties. This suited Jimmy, who hated work. He was a restless, inquisitive child, incapable of staying still long enough to do anything well (except, of course, read—he was a voracious reader).[27]

As time went on, however, Jimmy became a problem to the family, too. The problem was that no one had any control over him. Half the time he was shut up in his books or in some dream world, and the other half wilfully determined to have his own way, whether that meant cutting church on Sundays or walking ahead of Thomas, instead of behind, during spring plowing. Neither Eliza nor Thomas was able to make him obey. Uncle Amos Boynton once tried to straighten him out, but Jimmy simply sulked and felt that his uncle disliked him. Bright as he was—and he was very bright—his talents seemed doomed to waste unless the family could get some money and Jimmy could acquire some self-control.[28]

Worries about Jimmy may well have prompted Eliza's decision, in 1842, to marry again.[29] It is hard to see what other reason she could have had. Financially, her worst years were behind; Thomas was now old enough to run the farm, Mary would soon be old enough to marry, and there was only Jimmy to provide for. Granted, the cabin was in scandalous shape, but in time they would be able to replace it too. It seems unlikely, in other words, that she needed the financial support of a husband in order to get by.

Nor was the marriage a matter of love, to judge by the apparent ease with which it broke off only a year later. The man, Alfred Belding, was ten years younger than she, a decent man, of good family—he lived on his father's place between Independence and Bedford, in the flatlands ten miles west of the Garfields—responsible, hard-working, perhaps a little fussy. He may have been a widower. What Eliza may have wanted from such a man was financial security in her later years, a strong hand to bring Jimmy into line, and perhaps eventually money to send the boy to an academy, where he could get a proper education, and on to college.[30]

In any event, she and Belding were married in April 1842, when Jimmy was ten and a half. At once Eliza and the younger children said farewell to the old cabin and the old neighborhood. Thomas probably stayed to work for Amos Boynton, who was buying the farm from them. At first, it appears, they lived at the Belding place in Independence, but shortly they moved elsewhere, so that Belding and his new wife could begin a home of their own. It is not clear from the evidence where they settled, but it was probably some distance from Cleveland. Perhaps they went to Michigan, a favorite destination for migrants from the Reserve. On the journey, Jimmy saw things he had never seen before in his life—brick houses, for instance.[31]

Wherever it was, they did not remain there long as a family. Sometime in 1843, Belding and Eliza had a disagreement, and Eliza, with Jimmy and Mary, walked out. It is tempting to speculate that it had something to do with disciplining Jimmy, who hated Belding ever after. Whatever the cause, shortly afterward Eliza and the children turned up again in Orange at the farm. Belding sent several appeals for her to return. They were unheeded. A year later, he gave up, moved back to Bedford, filed for divorce, and began trying to rebuild his life.[32]

Rebuilding, of course, was also in order for the Garfields. (Eliza kept her first husband's name, and apparently was never referred to as Mrs. Belding.) Amos Boynton let his sister-in-law have the farm back without too much fuss. In 1844 or 1845 Eliza sent Thomas to Michigan to spend the summer on a land-clearing job that would raise money for a new house; in the meantime, they bought the old schoolhouse as an annex to the cabin. In 1845 Mary married a man named Marenus Larabee, and the couple moved immediately to Michigan.[33] Eliza and Jimmy were left to tend the farm.

It was not a good time for trying to get back on one's feet. The winter of 1844–1845, in which Jimmy turned thirteen, was an unusually warm one—"a New Orleans winter," the Cleveland paper called it, that tempted the buds in the Garfields' apple orchard to swell, the grass to sprout in the pastures. Then a killing frost, in early May, so cold that even oak trees reportedly perished, cut down all the corn and potatoes and everything in the orchard. At the same time a serious drought hit the region, and by mid-July, in blistering heat, the pastures were so dry that the cattle raised clouds of dust crossing them in search of something to graze on. Formerly dependable streams and springs dried up. No one in that part of the Reserve made much of a crop that year, least of all, one imagines, the Garfields. Hard pressed as ever, they looked out on a neighborhood that was sharing, to a degree, the sufferings that had become second nature to them.[34]

The neighborhood was changing. At the beginning, it had been a fairly homogeneous bunch of settlers, Yankees from New England or upstate New York with big families. They had shared the transplanted-Yankee values of thrift, industry, and piety. Most of them were Methodists or, like the Garfield family, Disciples of Christ; indeed the neighborhood struck one observer as "rather remarkably religious."[35] Their manners, too, were Yan-

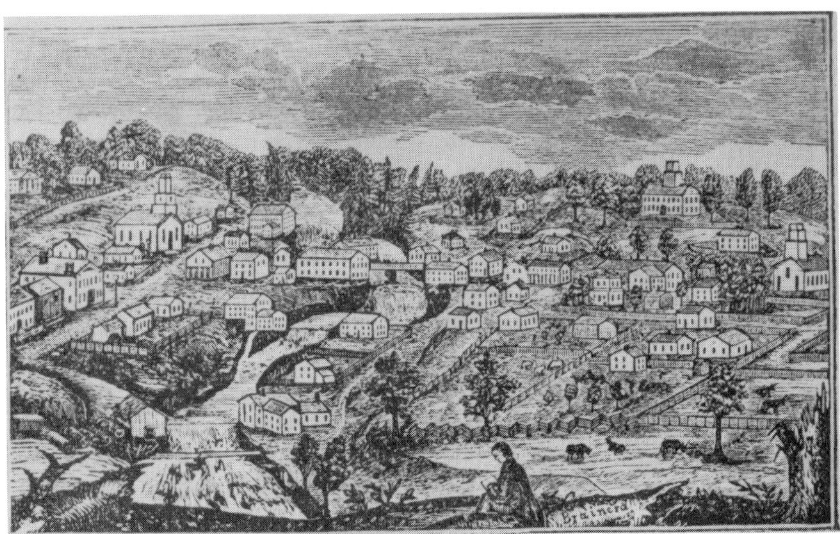

The woodcut of Chagrin Falls, made by a contemporary in 1844, suggests how rapidly the area had developed in fifteen years.

One end of the Chagrin Falls business district in the 1850s. The road in the center led toward Orange and Solon.

kee: caution, blunt speech, and keen interest in other people's business. Orange had been unusual only in the absence of frontier rowdiness. It had few taverns and relatively little drinking, though there must have been some; there always was in rural townships. And there was the usual quota of neighborhood characters, the human flotsam of the frontier.[36] But by and large, Orange had been, and still was to some extent, a sedate, serious-minded, isolated forest neighborhood.[37]

Some of the changes in the dozen years since Abram's death were physical: there were more fields and fewer woods, fewer forest paths and more country roads. Many of the early settlers Abram and Eliza had known had left the area, some for opportunities farther west in Illinois or Michigan, a few for the thriving village of Chagrin Falls across the valley. A new wave of settlers had taken their place, including immigrants from England, the Isle of Man, and Europe.[38] Across the road from the Garfields a German family named Rundt had built and was farming.[39] As the neighborhood developed, its original character was vanishing, but no new direction was visible. Its future seemed uncertain, especially in comparison with Chagrin Falls.

"The Falls," as they called it in Orange, had grown spectacularly. All the Garfields, even Jimmy, could remember when it was a tiny settlement of two or three houses. Now it had a main street with brick buildings, a bridge over the splashing falls, lawyers' offices, an academy, a comfortable two-story inn, Bayard's Hotel. There the Cleveland-to-Pittsburgh stage stopped daily, its driver sounding a blast on his horn before he brought his four horses to a stop with a flourish beside the hotel, handing his sack of mail to the waiting postmaster, and shortly starting off again with another blast on his horn, his progress followed by the envious eyes of the village boys. There was talk of a plank road to Cleveland. The little place struck a visitor a few years later as a "cheery, sociable and charming village."[40]

Thus in 1847, the Falls was flourishing; Orange and Solon were emerging from the frontier stage; but the Garfield family remained where it had been the past fourteen years, at a standstill, poor, rural, matriarchal, and immobile.[41]

4
A Questionable Future
Fall 1847

For young Garfield, life had started turning sour when they moved back to the tumbledown cabin in Orange in 1844. He probably felt, in some obscure way, it was a disgrace to be back among the friends he had so lightheartedly said goodbye to the year before. Worse, the move back meant that he was not to have a kind protector, someone who could help him realize his talents. And the family was back on the same miserable level, two steps from the poorhouse. With Mary gone, there was more work to be done, and Eliza was getting older and less able to bear her share of the burdens. Jim was getting older too, and it was probably evident already that he was not going to be only tall like Thomas, but big like his father. He was the proper age, the proper size. Jimmy, the pet of the family, twelve going on thirteen, was going to have to get out and work as he had never worked before; it could not be put off longer.

Of course, he already knew a lot about farm work—boys' work: bringing in wood for the fire, hauling water from the spring, going to get the four cows down in the meadow on foggy or frosty mornings, calling each by name—they all probably had names like "Star" or "Beauty" like other Reserve cows—and driving them up to the barn, getting out the old three-legged stool morning and evening to milk (this was a job for men and boys on the farms of the Reserve). There was the arm-wracking work of churning, nice, though, because it allowed time for daydreaming while the dasher thumped in the churn; in spring, riding a horse to plow the fields for corn as the leaves began to open on the huge forest trees; dropping the seed into hills in the cool, dark-smelling, gravelly earth; planting potatoes, beans, turnips with their tiny seeds; building fires, weeding the kitchen garden. But now he had to take on man's work, heavy work, the guts of farming.[1]

One pressing need of the family was for firewood, but here the Garfields encountered a serious problem with Jimmy: he was fearfully clumsy. Left-handed, to begin with, he also had the awkwardness of early adolescence. Most of his problem, though, was due to the protective cocoon of daydreams he had been spinning around himself since boyhood, to keep out the un-

GARFIELD'S WORLD

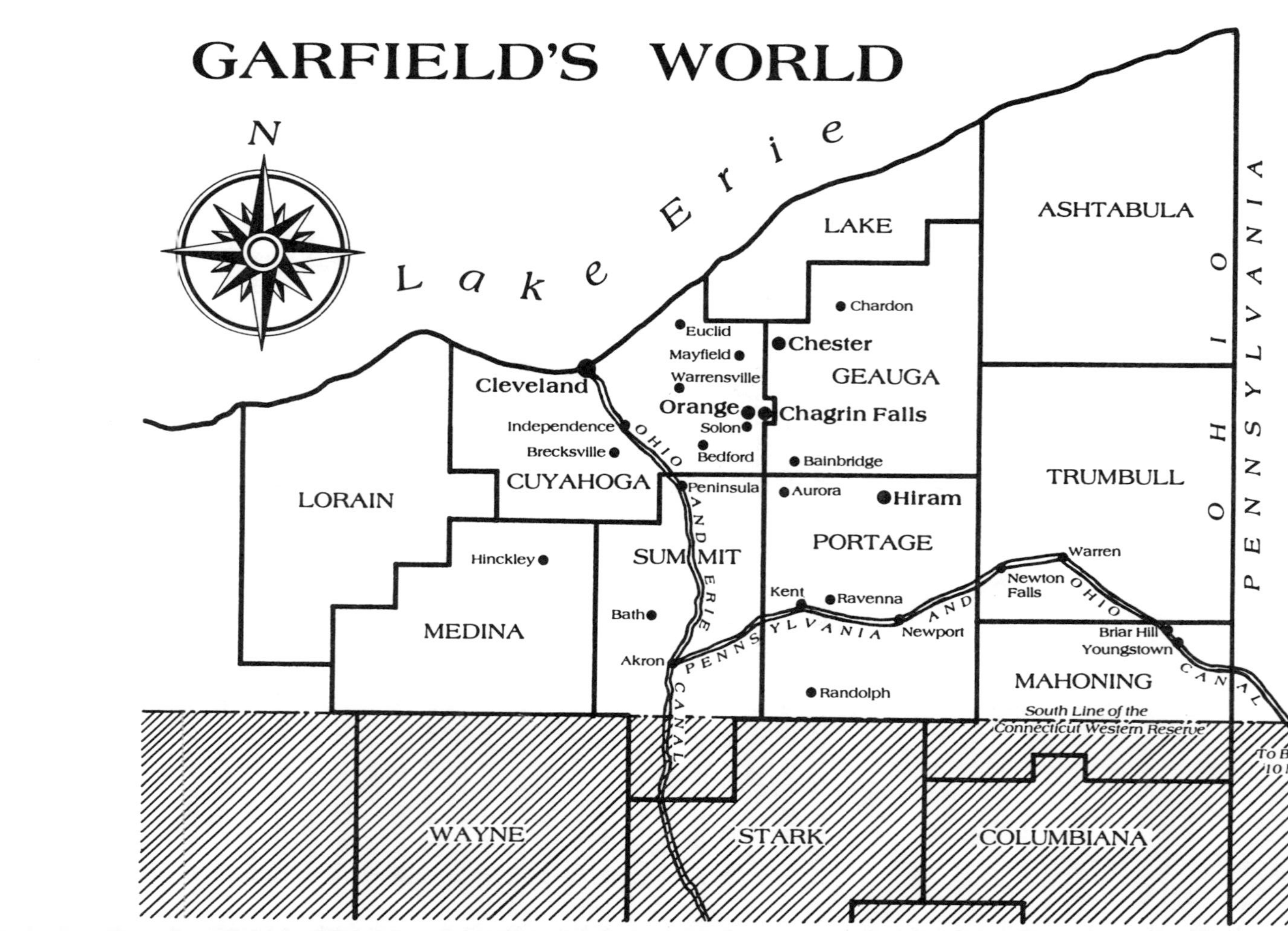

pleasant realities of being poor, feeling different, having no father, having a mother whose marriages were dogged by misfortune. It took him a terribly long time to master the use of any tool, because he could not keep his mind on the task. "He could do anything but hoe corn," Thomas recalled much later. "He would let his mind wander off on something else and cut off the corn every time." The memories of his mother and aunt were a litany of accidents caused by inattention: "He cut his feet with his axe or scythe. He wrenched his back by the fall of a fence rail upon him. He fell from the barn upon a pile of wood." A cut from the gleaming scythe, the sharpest of all farm tools, could be deep and excruciating; and as for axes, he spent weeks convalescing in the house after gashing his feet with an axe the winter he was fourteen and again when he was fifteen. These were only two of many similar incidents. He nearly killed his young cousin Silas Boynton through carelessness with an axe. All the Boyntons could tell tale after tale about his mishaps: how he bruised himself when he fell while wandering in the woods lost in thought; how he barely escaped falling headlong through the works of a mill.[2]

These years, his early teens, were painful in another way. As a child, he had been largely unaware of what other people thought of him and his family; now, back in Orange, he began to understand the looks of pity or scorn he got. The Garfields alone seemed to be falling in the eyes of the community, getting nowhere. Everyone else was advancing. The realization hurt.[3] It was around this time that he began reading novels—as a refuge, perhaps. He seems to have changed his friendships too, taking up with a boy a couple of years older, the son of a farm family from Massachusetts who had just moved into the neighborhood.[4] With other boys his age he became touchy, quick to imagine that he was being ridiculed or sneered at. He began acquiring the reputation of a fighter, responding to taunts with his fists, fighting "instantly," viciously, and "to hurt." Some of his adversaries were bigger than he, and he was not always victorious; but he fought hard, with a touch of desperation, defending his honor and the family's.[5]

By the time he turned sixteen he had learned skill with an axe. He chopped in the small wood lot and regularly supplied the fuel needed in the fireplaces and cookstove; more than that, he hired out to neighbors for similar work. He helped Henry Dunwell clear a big lot in the beech and maple woods across the town line in Solon. The spring he was fifteen and had a passion to own a rifle (which, it is hardly necessary to say, neither Thomas nor Eliza could afford), he got a land-clearing job and chopped until he had the money he needed.[6]

He took on other jobs, too. One winter he spent taking care of his Uncle Amos's cattle. In the summer of 1847, for the first time in his life, he spent a month away from home at work during haying season. This was grueling work, even if he did not use a scythe, but merely raked and pitched the hay under the broiling June sun. Haying, in the light of memory, was apt to seem idyllic, evoking as it did recollections of "the wagon, with its wide ladders; the bright forks, with their long handles; the fragrant odor of the grass, as it was pitched on the wagon," the sweat and banter and camaraderie of the workers, and the blue-steel scythe blades ringing against the grindstone; but people who were closer to the job saw the labor rather than the picturesqueness.[7] "I did the easiest work: raking hay," a German laborer in the Midwest recalled. "Easy as the work was, the burning sun was intolerable. The thermometer rose to 100 and over. After an hour's work I was completely soaked with perspiration . . . Stacking hay with an iron fork is very tiring, and even if one works without a shirt and drinks water constantly, it is almost unbearable." The grain harvest, which followed haying in July, was still more taxing, because of the time pressure to get the grain into the barn before rains could spoil it. It was the real test, the real man's work. Jim, at fifteen, had not hired out at harvest season yet; perhaps next summer. . . .[8]

But in a funny way his mastery of farm tasks was an illusion, a broad highway leading nowhere. Nothing was more certain than that Jim Garfield was not going to be a farmer.[9] His mother's land was coming to Thomas, not to him, and thirty acres was far too small a farm to subdivide, particularly in the scanty soil of Orange; Thomas would need every acre he could get just to make a living. Moreover, Jim disliked farm work. One can interpret the few accidents and self-inflicted wounds that lasted into his later teens as mute protests against the drudgery of what he was doing. Twice in these years, for instance, he managed to sprain his ankle while working on someone's farm; once he had to be carried home. Farm labor, for him, was a handy way of picking up money for his and the family's needs, but as a lifetime occupation it was out of the question.[10]

His mother, too, consciously or not, helped to turn him against farming. She had typed him early as an unusually restless child—"never still a moment at a time" was the way she put it—and in the tightly knit Garfield household Eliza's perceptions generally became family dogma. This is not to suggest that Eliza was wrong; on the contrary, she was probably essentially right. Jim did have a hard time keeping still in his seat; he was apt to toss and turn and fling off all his cover in his sleep; he did get bored easily. But the point here is that he absorbed her perception and made it his own—so that later, for instance, in his early thirties, he would write Eliza that he was "still the same restless being that I ever was." A restless man, by definition, is not cut out for farming. As he explored possible adult identities, he could have felt that it was part of his nature to travel and be free; that farming, or any other trade that would confine him to the forests and plunging hills of the Chagrin Valley, was not for him.[11]

But if he was not to farm, what was he to do? Abandoning farming was almost equivalent to abandoning his home; in the woods of Orange, eighty percent of the men over twenty-one made their living, or tried to, working the land, either theirs or someone else's.[12] Other options were pitifully few; a contemporary who grew up in the Reserve summarized them succinctly: "to chop and clear land, and make black salts, or tend a saw-mill, or drive oxen, or sell tape and calico. . . ."[13] At the Falls, three miles distant, there were a couple of factories, a printing office, several doctors, a few lawyers, and an academy. But the significant opportunities seemed to lie in the other direction, in Cleveland.[14]

Jim had probably been to Cleveland about a dozen time in his life, certainly not more. It was not the distance that discouraged visits; seventeen miles to the county seat was not too far for a young man in good health to walk with ease, if his family, like the Garfields, did not have a horse.[15] But ordinarily Orange people visited the city either to sell or to buy, and needed a wagon to carry their goods. (This was not quite universal. It was later told in Orange that Mrs. John Durant, during the 1840s, had regularly carried butter, eggs, and chickens, up to forty pounds in all, to market in Cleveland, walking the entire distance to the Public Square and back. The Durants, though, were English immigrants, inured to the heavy demands of a semi-feudal system; it is hard to imagine an American settler doing the same thing.)[16] So Jim rode with his uncle Amos Boynton, or occasionally perhaps in the Mapeses' wagon or buggy, in late spring or summer when the roads were good.[17] For him, and no doubt for many boys in the neighborhood, the trip was rare enough to be a thrill.

They would leave early in the morning, and ride north on the Center Road until they came to the Chagrin Falls road, at Phares Thorp's store and the wagon shop; there they would turn left, northwest. As they crossed into the next township, Warrensville, they looked down into the Cuyahoga valley. To the northwest, twelve miles away, they could pick out the cluster of buildings, trees, and masts, that was Cleveland. With the early morning sun behind them, they descended into the flatlands, passed through the little crossroads settlement of Warrensville Center, and drove on west. Around here, usually, they began to run into other farm wagons bound the same way, with produce to sell in town. As they approached Cleveland, they would begin to see big, rather fancy two-story inns here and there by the roadside, then a big apple orchard, then the first scattering of small houses that marked the outskirts.[18]

Cleveland's location on the lowlands at the mouth of the Cuyahoga, where it entered Lake Erie, had been its fortune. When the Ohio Canal, parallel to the river, was put through in the 1830s, a brisk trade had begun, transferring the produce of Ohio farms and forests—lumber, wheat, potash—from the canal onto lake craft, and Eastern goods to the canal. New merchant firms had sprung up, then other businesses serving travelers and merchants. The town's population had jumped from 7,000 in 1840 to 10,000 in 1845, and would reach nearly 18,000 by 1850. Already the business district, Superior Street down from the Public Square, had the air of a city, with its profusion of new brick three- and four-story stores, its elaborate new hotels, its rough wooden planking over which freight wagons rattled down to the river front, its crowds of wagons and carriages, with men in frock coats and women in elegant dresses. There were also, not far away, such signs of city refinement as the "liberally devised and chastely arranged" Erie Street Cemetery, which impressed a New England visitor, and the dim grandeur of the Catholic cathedral. Out Euclid Avenue, richer citizens were starting to build pretentious houses modeled on Italian villas. The city fathers were beginning to talk of major improvements: gas lighting, a railroad connection with the rest of Ohio, even paved streets.[19]

As the country people from Orange drove in, however, down Kinsman Road and Ontario Street, they saw first the older, simpler Cleveland—a quiet, neat small town with a distinct New England stamp in the decorous fence and white churches around the Public Square, the small cottages with

Superior Street, Cleveland, looking toward the Public Square, in 1858.

their shrubbery and hospitable front porches, the broad, tree-lined streets, with here and there a wandering pig; only at the end of their journey, the public market on Michigan Street, did they encounter the urban complexity of the business district.[20]

To a young man in search of opportunity, Superior Street radiated promise, with its specialty stores and commercial and medical colleges; but even more than that, at least to Jim Garfield, the waterfront, the interface between Cleveland and the rest of the world. Cleveland up to 1847 had no pier on the lake front, so that all its water traffic had to crowd into the narrow, winding Cuyahoga. One went down the Superior Street hill toward the forest of masts and columnar stacks of steamboats vomiting black smoke, amid the shouts of teamsters and laborers. Everything was new and exciting—the clumsy canal scows out in the river loading and unloading, the solemn German immigrants pulling on their pipes and regarding the new world around them, the exhilaration of walking among men who had been in Buffalo two days ago and would be in Sault Ste. Marie next week, and of course the sudden views of the lake flecked with sails. Here, if anywhere, a romantic imagination felt all the possibilities, all the openings life had to offer.[21]

Of course, young Garfield was not the only boy in Orange looking for opportunity. There were dozens of boys for whom there was not enough room on the farm, or who had simply decided to get away from the land. There were, to take only the nearest example, the sons of his uncle Amos Boynton.

The Boyntons lived in a white frame house visible from the Garfields', across the road to the north. It was a bigger house than the Garfields', which was no surprise, as Amos Boynton was one of a very few men in the township who actually made money from farming. He was a walking example of the kind of successful farmer James Garfield could never be—"industrious almost to a fault," as an admirer called him, always ready to take a hand with the haying or do all the milking. Moreover, he had a taste for the kind of minutiae necessary to the running of a really well-managed farm—what crops were to be planted in which lot, exactly when logs were to be hauled to the sawmill, how much it cost to fatten a calf in a given period of time. His farm, according to a later sketch, "was the best kept in the neighborhood, his products went to market in the best order and commanded the best prices." Tall, spare, dark, and balding, oddly like the portraits of Sherlock Holmes familiar to a later generation, he was a man of simple, firm religion; later tradition in the neighborhood had it that he used to carry his Bible with him as he plowed and pause periodically to read it while his team rested. The sonorous phrases of the King James Version came as easily to him as those of everyday speech. "Go on then my son always abounding in the work of the Lord," he wrote his son William, "for as much as you know that your labor is not in vain in the Lord." He was the chief man of the South Orange Disciple congregation, and more than once had to take his young nephew in hand. Jim's feeling toward him was a compound of respect, fear, and dislike.[22]

Unlike the Garfields, who farmed mainly for subsistence, Boynton specialized to some extent. Like many another observant Yankee in the Reserve, he had realized that his soil, although third-rate for corn or wheat production, was ideal for grazing, and had moved little by little into dairy farming. He owned around twenty cows, more than four times as many as the Garfields and more than any other farmer in the neighborhood except John Mapes, also a dairyman. They were the small red cows of native stock then common in the region, far from purebred by modern standards but good enough to have earned the Reserve the sobriquet of "Cheesedom," which it had already borne for some twenty years. In addition to his wife and five children old enough to work, he seems to have hired help fairly regularly, for he had a lot to do. The sour smell of cheese hung over the back of the Boynton house. Hoops of pressed curd, turned daily and rubbed with melted butter, cured on racks; tin pans of milk sat on the shelves, lacking only the rennet to be added to begin the cheese-making process. Aunt Alpha, Phebe, and Harriet kept the churns busy. Exactly where Uncle Amos marketed his products is not clear. Some he definitely took to Bedford village, about five miles southwest; some, doubtless, to the Falls. Like John Mapes, he probably had regular customers in Cleveland, merchants whom he supplied with butter and cheese. He and Mapes, in any event, were the two prosperous men of the neighborhood, settlers who had capitalized on their early start to make their farms paying enterprises. Abram Garfield could have been a farmer of the same kind, had he lived.[23]

Thriving as the Boynton farm was, it was only eighty-nine acres, not really big enough to be divided economically among Uncle Amos's three sons; at least one of the boys would have to go west to Michigan or Iowa in search of affordable land if he wanted to stay in farming, or remain in Ohio and go into some other line of work. William, the oldest, three years older than Jim, who was not robust, despite his broad features and stocky build, probably wanted to do something besides farm. He was thus in Jim's situation. Henry, two years younger, though quite bright (as they all were), seemed fairly content with rural life, and more likely to take over from his father. Droll, good-looking Silas, just twelve in 1847, was not yet at a point where he had to choose, but it seemed plausible that he, too, might seek his fortune away from Orange.[24]

One did not have to look far to find other neighborhood boys similarly situated. Amos, Byron, and Oscar, the sons of Zenas Smith, whose farm was just up the Center Road from the Boyntons, were in their late teens and early twenties and looking for trades. One seems to have gone to Cleveland around this time to enroll in a medical college. Orrin Judd, young Garfield's best friend, was in the same position—a younger son of a small farmer, searching for something else to do. Edwin, the oldest Mapes boy, liked farming and seemed likely to follow his father, but he was an exception.[25]

In one respect, Jim was in a better position than most of his contemporaries. The understanding among Reserve farmers was that a boy owed his father "time"—that is, farm labor on demand—until he reached twenty-one. Up to that age, therefore, it was difficult to work seriously at another occupation. The obligation could be liquidated in various ways. Frequently a boy would hire out to neighbors, save his wages, and eventually buy the balance of his time from his father at a rate agreed upon by both. Sometimes a generous father would simply remit the rest of the time owed by his seventeen- or eighteen-year-old son. But the obligation was generally recognized in the region, and most of Jim's friends were among the boys who, to quote a verse of that time, "mowed and hoed and pushed the plow and longed for one-and-twenty."[26] Jim, on the other hand, had nothing tying him to home except the bonds of filial affection. Thomas had no legal claim on his labor, and it had been understood at home for some time that he had a right to hire out to whomever he chose, and to do with his wages whatever he saw fit.[27]

Forehanded as usual, Eliza had already begun trying to steer her youngest toward a trade that she hoped he might like better than farming, one that would let him stay near home; in fact, she had begun almost as soon as her hopes of educating him were dashed. In the summer of 1846, when they were putting up the new house, she had persuaded Thomas and Jimmy, who was then fourteen, to hire on as helpers to the master carpenter, Jedidiah Hubbell of Chagrin Falls. Cutting the cost of the house was the main idea, of course, but there was a definite hope that her younger son would take to the business and decide to follow it.[28] To say nothing of burgeoning Cleveland and smaller towns like Chagrin Falls, carpentry was a good business in the rural Reserve at that time, as the log houses of the settlement days gave way to the understated geometric beauty of Greek Revival in which Reserve farmhouses were commonly built. Besides houses, there were always barns going up, and churches, taverns, and schools.

Certainly there was money to be made in the business. The number of carpenters and joiners in Orange and adjoining towns attested to that. The federal census of 1850 found six in Orange alone. Solon had seven, Chagrin Falls nineteen, Bedford twenty-six. Some of them did very well. Jedidiah Hubbell was among the fifteen or twenty most prosperous men in Chagrin Falls, and another carpenter there was richer than he. His brother Solyman, a carpenter in Warrensville, was also a substantial man. The ordinary carpenter might not do as well as these, but could at least expect to own a house and lot.[29]

Carpentry was not light work. In the Reserve the traditional mortise-and-tenon style of framing a building with interlocked, heavy beams eight or ten inches square still prevailed, despite the lighter balloon-frame style that was beginning to take hold in Cleveland. Framing timbers, along with the siding, shingles, and decorative molding—everything but the flooring, in short—were usually fashioned on the spot from the seemingly inexhaustible forest. (Flooring was usually made at a local sawmill.) A good carpenter, therefore, was concerned not only with things like nailing on siding, making door frames, and laying floor and roofing, but also with selecting and making the basic material. He had to know the use of the felling axe, the broadax (for hewing timbers), molding planes, the zigzag pieces of metal for shaping the varied designs of interior and exterior trim, the froe (for splitting shingles), and similar tools, as well as the properties of the native woods, oak or walnut for flooring, chestnut or oak for shingles, and softer woods like whitewood for interior molding—though, as an early carpenter's helper remarked, the soft wood in the country seemed "a good deal harder than most hard wood."[30]

But Jim was a disappointment in carpentry as he had been in farming, and in much the same way. He learned just enough of the business to get by and pick up a little money, no more. He was accurate with hammer and nails; he could use the large froe to get out clapboard siding, splitting carefully down a quarter section of a log, or the smaller froe to make shingles. Using an auger and chisel, he could make a mortise, the square hole in a framing timber which received the tenon. He did not mind high work on large buildings like barns. But he had absolutely no interest in figuring the pitch of a roof, or the dimensions of a staircase, or getting the proper proportion on a cornice; these problems, which were the work of a master carpenter, held no appeal for his imagination. As a result, he worked sporadically, when the opportunity came up, mostly on barns, doing work many other men and boys could do, no better, no worse. Five years after he had begun "learning" carpentry, he still did not know how to lay flooring.[31]

If Jim had little taste for the life of a carpenter, he seems to have had even less for that of a clerk, the other obvious non-farm job in his area. To a boy so earnest and self-occupied, the casual socializing of the country store, selling tape and calico, exchanging banter with the ladies and dirty jokes with the male customers, was uncongenial. He also lacked the rudimentary polish in dress and manners that the job demanded. Moreover, it may be that, with a head full of ideas from his reading, he found clerking or any other job within the circumscribed world of Orange dull and unpalatable.

With his quick intelligence and the wealth of ideas gathered from his reading, it seems natural that he should have felt attracted to one of the professions. But all of them seemed, for one reason or another, uninviting or unattainable. Medicine, the easiest to enter for a young man of modest background, which had attracted one of the Smith boys and was later to interest his cousin Silas Boynton, did not interest him at all. Then it was hardly a profession, really; more an arcane craft like that of the daguerreotype men who occasionally visited Bedford or the Falls, a matter of mixing mysterious compounds and using a few tricks of the trade to win public confidence. His clumsiness and diffidence made medicine off limits for him.[32]

The ministry as a career was out, because the Disciples of Christ did not believe in a professional ministry. Their preachers were men fully conversant, like all Disciples, with the Word of God, who felt in addition, a call from God to preach, Unsalaried, they supported themselves, for the most part, by their own trades of carpentry, medicine, farming, or whatever. Jim could become a preacher whenever he wanted to—and in early boyhood he had wanted to very much—but he recognized that he would have to earn his living some other way.[33]

Then there was law. The profession called for exactly the talents he had displayed so strikingly since boyhood—reading, debating, verbal ability in general, and Jim probably realized the fact. But the law also called up the most unpleasant memories of his early life: divorce, his mother's bitterness and frustration, lawyer's fees, technicalities. For obvious reasons, he had a "strong prejudice" against the profession. Whatever he became, he was not going to be a lawyer.[34]

Through the boy probably never ran through his future prospects in just this way, all these points must have occurred to him at one time or another, and their cumulative effect must have been deadening; he was trapped in a life he disliked and was not good at, and there was no clear way out. The obvious alternatives were as bad or worse. He had no chance to use the talents he clearly possessed. Life seemed a maze where all the turns led to dead ends.

In a larger sense, young Garfield probably had no clear idea of the alternatives there were. That is, he knew there was such a thing as Latin, but whether he had seen any is questionable. He had never seen a book in Greek. He knew there was a bar examination, but had no notion what it was about. He was, it cannot be emphasized too strongly, a common country boy from a very limited background, dependent almost wholly on his reading for information about the world. His conceptions of the outside world were often romanticized or distorted. All he knew was that he was missing something—he had no real idea what.[35]

Not too surprisingly, at fifteen, Jim to some extent turned against respectability and learning and a lot of things that embodied them. He did not take part in debating as he had at one time. He went to meeting no oftener than he had to. For a time he gave up school, but eventually went back, for social reasons—there was not much else for young people to do in the winter. Basically his life consisted of work for Thomas, odd jobs, and small neighborhood diversions. He still had his thin-skinned pride, his insistence that he was as good as (read "better than") any other boy in the area; but he was beginning to have uneasy premonitions that he, like the others, was headed only for a life of obscurity and hard labor.[36]

At times that fall he must have stood, heavy-limbed and idle, at the back of the red house, gazing with his characteristic abstraction across the muddy yard, the barn, the meadow and its shallow brook, the apple trees heavy with fruit, seeking a solution in the dry cornstalks, the blowing leaves, the fields thick with stubble and stumps, or the shaggy forest looming beyond. In none of them could he see an answer.

5

The Social Season

Winter 1847–1848

In October 1847, Jim could look ahead, utterly without enthusiasm, to what was coming up on the farm, what he and Thomas would have to do. There was the corn to be harvested. He would pick, probably; Thomas would drive the wagon and collect the ears. Then the corn had to be husked. In the early days of Orange, as in most townships, there had been husking bees in plenty; probably there were still some in the late 1840s—as there were still barn raisings. Husking bees benefited short-handed families like the Garfields. All the neighborhood people gathered at someone's barn with their corn; the young ones sat in two long lines, facing one another, and stripped the husks from the ears, with plenty of banter and calling back and forth. The women served cider and refreshments; fundamentally, it was a social occasion, although a lot of work was done. The Garfields would not have included corn husking among the farm work they had to do.[1]

But there were numerous other jobs; late fall, in fact, was the second busiest season of the year. The apples had to be harvested and made into apple butter or cider (for this purpose, there were sometimes apple parings, community affairs like husking bees, where the neighborhood apples were pared, cored, and boiled down); the potatoes had to be dug, a tedious job; next season's wheat had to be sown, with due care to keep the great flocks of wild pigeons that passed through the valley in the fall off the newly sown fields. These birds were beautifully colored, slate blue with buff breasts and feet red as coral, and they flew in incredibly dense flocks, sometimes just above one's head. Shooting them was hardly sport; it was easy to bring down enough for a meal. ("We got enough for pigeon pie and fried pigeon," a neighborhood boy remembered, "till we longed for salt pork.")[2] And in the intervals between other tasks, Jim and his neighbors could range the woods gathering chestnuts to be sold at the Cleveland market.

In November, however, with the last of the harvest in, the rush of farm duties abruptly slackened. Not stopped—there were still important things to be done during the winter months. Farmers who raised wheat generally threshed their grain in winter, especially if they threshed by hand, in the

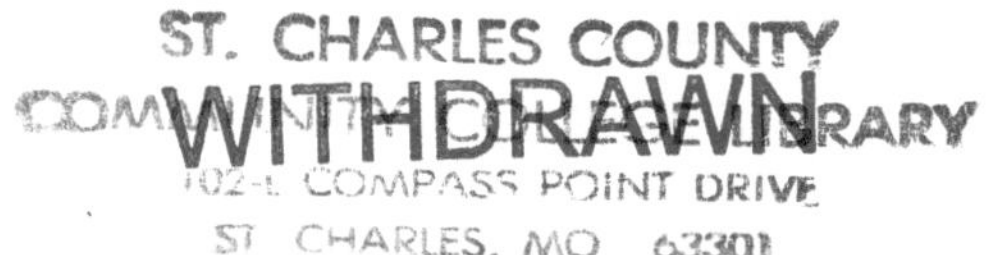

old-fashioned way.[3] Meat animals, cattle and swine, were butchered in cold weather. Cows continued to give milk, and dairy farmers to make cheese; those who were willing to brave the rutted, muddy roads to Cleveland, Bedford, or Chagrin Falls in winter weather could get good prices for their products. Most preferred to stay home. For a majority of farm families, winter was a relatively slack season, a time to relax and enjoy life, to the extent that the strict Yankee culture of the Reserve permitted.[4]

Relaxation did not mean organized, professionally produced entertainment. Winter or summer, that was scarce in the woods of Orange. Once in a long while, posters on roadside trees or barns would announce the coming of a circus or traveling menagerie to Bedford, Cleveland, or the Falls. Occasionally a traveling group of singers or musicians would give a concert even in a country schoolhouse. For the rest, the inhabitants had to rely on each other for amusement.[5]

By far the easiest, cheapest, and most common form of entertainment was simply talking. Conversation, in households like the Garfields' or Boyntons', could be richly diverting, with its tangy, picturesque phrases derived from New England speech. A Reserve boy of a later generation remembered his aunts' expressions like "woes which would make a bird shed tears," or "Now do be a man or a mouse or a long-tailed rat, with your pockets full of gold and silver." Eliza described her shiftless son-in-law Stephen Trowbridge as "so slack he can hardly draw his breath." Aunt Alpha and Eliza, apparently, did most of the talking in their family gatherings, punctuating each other's accounts with "Well, really," and "Great sack," but the younger Boyntons and Garfields were no less observant and critical. Even the men, despite the laconic speech they cultivated in public, enjoyed roasting their neighbors and relatives in private. Deadpan irony was a popular style. Here, for instance, is Uncle Amos on Stephen Trowbridge:

> Stephen D. has bought some cows to drive west and the prospect is quite flattering for he has given 13. here and he will have to pay from fore [*sic*] to five dollars a head to get them half way and by the time he gets them through they will cost him more than he can sell for so he will make his jack out of pocket. . . .[6]

Neighbors, their foibles and their doings, provided an unfailing source of amusement. Joe Cleveland, a half-educated young farmer who lived down the road, who could talk and never bring a story to its conclusion, was always good for a laugh. So was the neighbor named Grant, who was apt to take a drop too much and drive wildly around in his buggy.[7]

Outside the family, too, there were many opportunities for amusing talk. Women at their sewing and quilting bees, men at barn raisings, could relate and savor the latest funny thing said by someone in the vicinity, compare accounts of a recent exciting event, or reach into memory, if necessary, to bring up some tried-and-true bit of local lore. In most Reserve communities, a corps of male idlers, old and young, hung around the store and commented on whoever and whatever passed by; but in this respect the Boynton neighborhood was lacking. Thorp's store was a mile or more to the north, at what would later be called Orange Center; Robbins's two miles south in Solon; the stores at Bentleyville and the Falls, two and three miles, respectively, to the east. It is not clear that any of these served as a focus for the gossip of the neighborhood—but there was gossip, doubtless.[8]

One topic so permeated conversation in Orange, as in most Reserve communities, that it deserves special mention—argument over religious doctrine. Farm hands in the haying field argued predestination and free will during their breaks. A neighborly call could easily turn into a long, involved discussion of justification by faith. Members of the Disciples of Christ, the Garfields' church, frequently went around with Bibles in their pockets, fully armed for controversy with the followers of other doctrines. "Every man was gifted upon that subject," recalled an early Portage County resident. "They would quote the text of Scripture, fire and fire back, and it was entertaining and instructive. . . ."[9]

Entertaining and instructive it certainly was, and also the most democratic variety of debate conceivable; in the intensely Christian Reserve, almost any man, woman, or adolescent knew enough Scripture to hold up one end of a religious argument. Perhaps surprisingly, in view of the strong religious feelings of many residents, it created little ill feeling. People seem to have understood it as basically a game, nicely suited to the Yankee habit of contention, a battle of wits; and a showdown debate like the one of November 1843, in Chagrin Falls, at which two Methodist and two Disciple champions battled it out on three questions: "1. Do the Scriptures teach that to a believing penitent, baptism is a condition of the remission of sins? 2. Do the Scriptures teach that immersion is the mode of baptism? 3. Do the Scriptures teach that infants are subjects of baptism?"[10] took place in an atmosphere more like the World Series than the Diet of Worms.

One did not even have to be a practicing Christian in order to participate. A local character in Bainbridge, Daddy Russ,

> never attended church, but he was voluble in quotations from the Bible, especially the Old Testament. A sort of walking commentary in discussing religious dogmas, he bothered the Calvinists, Methodists, and Baptists with quotations against their respective tenets. He was always ready to argue doctrinal points, and always good-natured, honest, witty, and shiftless. Never known to do a day's work, he was never idle; but always poking about, going to mill with a bushel of corn on his shoulder, or visiting the neighbors to "talk Scriptur."[11]

Jim Garfield, who went to church no oftener than he had to, nonetheless enjoyed this kind of biblical discussion, especially because it demanded faculties he had in abundance: memory and a way with words. A story told of him around this time may or may not be true, but in any event illustrates the kind of debate that absorbed the attention of people in the rural Reserve. He is supposed to have been digging potatoes for Joseph Patrick, one of the more prosperous farmers in the Hampshire Road neighborhood (this much sounds thoroughly plausible) and carrying them in baskets to the cellar, past Patrick's daughter and a neighbor, who were having a lively talk on modes of baptism, mainly the hoary sprinkling-versus-immersion controversy. The neighbor, a defender of the sprinkling side, maintained that "a drop was as good as a fountain," and Jim, on his way back to the field, stopped—one can see him, with tangled hair and dirty trousers, breathing a little hard—and rattled off Hebrews 10:22: "'Let us draw near with a true heart in full assurance of faith, having our hearts sprinkled from an evil conscience.'" "Ah, you see," said the neighbor, "it says 'sprinkled.'" "Wait for the rest of the text," replied Jim, "'and our bodies washed with pure water.' Now, how can you wash your body in a drop of water?" And he headed back to his potatoes.[12]

Any kind of talk was held to be allowable entertainment if combined somehow with instruction. On that principle, Orange, Chagrin Falls, and the surrounding communities gave a warm reception to the lecturers who continually toured the Reserve, holding forth in country schoolhouses on temperance, phrenology, recent scientific discoveries, geography, or the evils of slavery, and often peddling books they had written or were writing.[13] The preaching in local churches was a diversion of a similar kind; even among the lay preachers of the Disciples, verbal skill was as much appreciated as spiritual wisdom.[14] In many parts of the Reserve, political rallies furnished entertainment of the same order, though in the immediate neighborhood of the Garfields they seem not to have been very important.[15]

One widely popular way, at least for men, of combining the entertainment and instructional value of talk was the debating society or "lyceum." Most communities in the Reserve seem to have had one. It would meet in the schoolhouse, usually on winter nights when there was not much else to do. A few candles would be affixed to benches and windows with pocket knives ("toad-stabbers," they were jocularly called), a committee would get the fire going, some local worthy, still in his work clothes, would take the teacher's chair, another the minute book, and debate would begin, with equal time for both sides and each speaker limited to fifteen minutes.[16] In a region where men were apt to take pride in reading a newspaper regularly, debates of this sort tested a man's ability to recall and use the facts he had picked up.[17] There were plenty of chances for sharp exchanges and, for those who wished to attempt it, flowery oratory; and debate often generated, as one secretary noted, considerable "wit & levity." Questions concerned current events like the Mexican War, then in full swing and generally unpopular in the Reserve, or the justice of American policy toward the Indians. Or, when these failed, there were perennials like the relative influence of women and men on society, whether slavery or liquor was more harmful, and the poser propounded in 1845 to the Mayfield Lyceum: "Has civilization enhanced the happiness of mankind?" (The Lyceum decided it had not.)[18] Men and boys who were verbally skilled, like young Garfield, enjoyed taking part; others who were not, like his brother Thomas, came to relax, listen to the proceedings, and serve as judges.[19]

For adults in Orange, it seems fair to say, entertainment meant either talking or listening to someone else talk. There were no organized sports and no holiday celebrations to speak of. Christmas was not observed in any special way (indeed, the phrase "to wish someone a Merry Christmas" was a recent and somewhat exotic innovation) nor were Thanksgiving Day, New Year's, or Easter. There was only the Fourth of July.[20]

For the young, of course, there were more active diversions. Children had all the traditional amusements of childhood (Garfield remembered, as a boy, wading in a brook, marching in a mock parade of children, playing on a cornstalk fiddle, making a cap of burdock burs) as well as some peculiar to a semi-frontier area (a family friend recalled to Garfield the time when "Mary throwed the Wild Cat at you").[21]

As boys entered puberty, around twelve or thirteen, they tended to spend a lot of time roaming the woods together in bands, fishing and hunting, swimming in the occasional deep swimming holes along the shallow, rocky, noisy Chagrin, doing forbidden things like masturbating and telling dirty stories. Strict fathers discouraged or forbade their sons' running around with other boys in this fashion; Amos Boynton, for instance, probably kept his boys under rather tight control.[22] But Jim, accustomed to having his own way, ran wild freely with several boys near his age, George Warren, the Boyntons when they could get out, and his best friend Orrin Judd, a beanpole of a boy, two years older than himself, whose father had recently cleared a small farm on the Orange–Solon town line. Jim and Orrin were both youngest sons, fairly bright and fairly rebellious. To say they got along well would be an understatement; for a couple of years they were all but inseparable. They spent nights at each other's houses, played pranks together, shared private jokes, rambled for hours hunting in the woods. Jim had his treasured rifle, and Orrin most likely had one too. (Probably, like most Reserve boys of their generation, they held shotguns beneath contempt.) They shot mainly squirrels, which abounded in the forest. Sometimes Orrin's older brother Newel came along. It may have been in these days, too, that Jim had the little black dog his mother later remembered as going everywhere with him.[23]

Now, however, he was approaching sixteen (his birthday was 19 November), an age at which many Reserve boys got over what one called, with affectionate disparagement, "the gun and watch fevers," and began to show an interest in the opposite sex. The exact age at which this transformation took place varied, of course, from one youth to another, and for some it never really was complete. Orange, like most communities in the Reserve, had a group of men who lived to hunt, who enjoyed hunting clothes and guns and the whole atavistic style of life, and got tremendously excited when any uncommon animal was reported in the woods. But for most boys, girls eventually superseded hunting as a preoccupation. And winter, with its sleigh rides, its singing schools and revivals, was an ideal time for the change to manifest itself.[24]

Winter was the season when society blossomed in the rural areas of the Reserve. The reasons were fairly obvious. There was not a great deal of work on hand, and the days were shorter. Moreover, after a good snowfall, travel was incomparably easier than at any other time of year. A bunch of young men and women could pile into a sleigh and zip twenty miles over snow-covered roads in an evening to a tavern or a schoolhouse, for country dances and jigs. There were few taverns in the Garfields' township, and no dances; Jim, and probably his contemporaries, grew up thinking of dancing as a waste of time.[25]

There were plenty of other ways, however, for young people in Orange to get together during winter. Most of them revolved around the district school. Every township in Ohio was divided by law into school districts, usually eight or ten (Orange had nine), each with its board of directors who were responsible for providing a building and seeing that classes were held in it. These districts seem to have been quite as important as country stores in defining rural neighborhoods—at least to the young people. Officially, the districts had numbers, but they were commonly known by their names—in Orange, the Abell district, the Marble district, the Center district; in Solon, the Ledge district. The Garfields lived in the Boynton district.[26]

Since state law laid down no specifications for school buildings, each district was free to tackle the problem in its own way. As a result, the appearance of the schoolhouse varied markedly from one district to the next. Some were simple log cabins, like the old one Jim had studied in as a boy and which his family later bought. Schoolhouses of this kind persisted at least to the 1850s; a boy in Garrettsville, Portage County, ten years Garfield's junior, recalled watching a neighbor's cabin catch fire through the chinks in the side of his log schoolhouse. Some schools were small hovels made of slabs nailed together, some little stone houses. The one in Solon District Number 8, for some time, was a rented building that doubled as a blacksmith shop. The pupils ("scholars," in the language of the time) were given a recess when oxen had to be shod. The new Boynton district schoolhouse was perhaps a cut above average. It was a neat, small frame building, painted red, across the brook from the Garfields' farm and visible from their house.[27]

Inside, it looked much like any other Reserve schoolhouse. A cast-iron wood-burning stove with its front legs missing, propped up by bricks, was centrally located near the teacher's desk. In the center were rows of benches for the small children, while the older ones sat at desks in the back and around the sides—perhaps on a U-shaped raised platform that ran around the walls, an arrangement followed in many schools. A pail and dipper, broom and wood box completed the furnishings. Three or four high windows admitted light.[28]

Garfield had many memories of this school, most of them happy ones: the red, beaming faces of wintertime, the dark, coarse paper of the textbooks, the perplexing problems in compound proportion and the Rule of Three, the goose quill pens and ink made at home from oak gall and copperas, the benches and walls, whittled on and sometimes covered with mischievous and obscene drawings.[29] The subjects he and his friends had studied were the same every year—reading from McGuffey's Readers, spelling from Webster's *Speller*, Ray's *Arithmetic*, Morse's *Geography*, and grammar. Once in a while a district had a teacher capable of teaching subjects beyond the standard five—history, "natural philosophy" (as science was then called), botany, even Latin or French, just like the high schools that were beginning to be set up in the larger cities; but the Boynton district appears to have had few such teachers in Garfield's time.[30]

Twice a year, usually, the directors opened the school for classes. "Summer school," generally taught by a young woman, was for the smaller scholars only; it opened during June or July, a time of year when those over eleven or twelve had to be busy in the fields. But "winter school" was held at a time when older boys were finished with seasonal work and the days hung heavy on most girls' hands. Young men in their late teens or early twenties whose schooling had been interrupted earlier by the need to go to work (almost any need took precedence over school) came then to catch up on the fundamentals of arithmetic and grammar; others the same age came just to have something to do. Classes were larger—in some districts, extremely large—and the age range wider than in summer school. A teacher in Geauga County, for example, had forty-one students on his roll (though daily attendance was no doubt less); they included nine pupils between four and seven years of age, one nineteen years old, one twenty-two, and, of course, a wide scattering of ages in between. It was usual to hire for winter school a male teacher who could deal with this motley assortment.[31]

The atmosphere of winter school was perceptibly different from that of summer school, even for the smaller children. It was not just the stuffy heat of the wood stove, nor the heavy smell of wet woolens and unwashed human bodies, nor even the "bustle & confusion" of which one Hudson youth complained, the younger children singing out their letters, or states and capitals in geography, or multiplication tables, while the older ones tried to study more advanced subjects. In many districts, there was a latent tension between a man teacher and the "big boys" in the rear, until it was established who was to be dominant, or the possibility of an attempt by local bullies to show their mettle by "breaking up" the school, or the excitement of a knock-down brawl which would set the school in an uproar. Besides that, from a quite different angle, there was the chance of a young male teacher's becoming romantically interested in one of his female pupils, or, if the teacher was a young woman, as sometimes happened in other districts, vice versa. Many a marriage in the Reserve had begun as a teacher-pupil relationship in a district school.[32]

For young people in the Boynton district, as in any other, the all-important question about winter school each year was the identity of the teacher. This generally became known only a week or two before classes began, in mid-November or early December. (There was no fixed opening date; parents learned the school was open by word of mouth, or by seeing the teacher in the schoolhouse door.)[33] Sometimes the directors succeeded in getting a popular, experienced teacher who lived in the area, like one of the Niece family from Bainbridge, several brothers and a sister who were all highly thought of. If not, they took what they could get; sometimes a local youth who had been off to an academy, sometimes a young man from outside the area who was attending a local academy and needed money to continue his studies. Teachers in Boynton in the recent past had been a fair sample: there had been Lafayette Niece and perhaps his brother Chauncey, as well; another capable local men named Harvey Rutherford; and a young man from New England, a student somewhere nearby, who had boarded at the Garfields' and had fascinated Jim with his tales of the world beyond Orange, particularly its culture and literature.[34]

Some of Jim's happiest and most vivid memories of district school clustered around the single afternoon in the school week—it was usually on Friday, sometimes Saturday—when the teacher held "declamations," or what the pupils called "speaking pieces." Each of the older girls and boys was given a piece to memorize; the girls, in the words of one ex-scholar, "would recite some real nice poetry about Flowers and Love and Heaven and Mother, and the boys would say 'Give me Liberty or Give me Death,' 'Midnight in his guarded tent the Turk lay dreaming of the hour,' and other inspiring poems." All the older scholars were expected to take part, and many dreaded the occasion—but not young Garfield. He had the two main requisites for a successful speaker, a retentive memory and a deep need to win his audience's approval. In declamation he shone. Over the years he had memorized dozens of school pieces to recite and could declaim them, with feeling, at a moment's notice. They formed a great part of the murmurous mental baggage he carried into any situation. One of his favorites, "A Ride to the Moon," a flight of fancy singularly apt for a dreamer like Jim, began "I packed my traveling trunks away in the boot of an air balloon. . . ."[35]

The run of luck which the Boynton district directors had enjoyed for several winters in choosing teachers came to an end in the winter of 1847–48. Their choice was a man named Morrison. Whether he was a local man or not is not clear. His knowledge of his subjects was somewhat spotty—not an entirely unknown phenomenon in the Reserve. (In 1851, Andrew Freese of Cleveland said that one-third of the teachers he examined in Cuyahoga County "knew nothing about fractions, and several could not bound a State.")[36] Under the inquisitive, probing gaze of the Boynton cousins and Garfield in the early weeks of winter school, Morrison's areas of ignorance became apparent. William, Henry, Harriet, and James had been brought up to respect their teachers, but they could not resist commenting on Morrison's mistakes and pointing them out to him. For one thing, the Yankee culture of the Reserve encouraged contentiousness, in education as in religion; for another, it was a great triumph for a Reserve schoolboy to prove his teacher wrong. (Burke Hinsdale, in Medina County, remembered as a high point of his school days the time he showed up his teacher, who had given the class the sentence "Caesar was killed by Antony" as a writing assignment.)[37] Morrison reacted badly to such hectoring; he grew angry and defensive, the classroom situation deteriorated, and the cousins, led apparently by William Boynton, began pressing him harder, pouncing on his errors, and then enjoying his outbursts of temper. By the New Year they had, by one account, "convicted [him] . . . of incapacity to parse a sentence of ordinary English," and took their case that Morrison was, in Garfield's later words, "unfit to teach a school" and ought to be dismissed to the parents. The contest had turned into the best kind of winter entertainment, a neighborhood controversy.

On 3 January, no doubt at Uncle Amos's request, the directors visited the school and observed; next evening they held a heavily attended school meeting, at which the Boyntons and Garfield presented their case and succeeded in securing Morrison's dismissal. Two days later, however, either because of the difficulty of finding a substistute in midwinter or, as Garfield believed, because of some kind of political pressure, the directors reinstated him. Thereupon Garfield, the Boyntons, Orrin Judd, and several others announced, with parental permission, that they were pulling out to attend school in a neighboring district.[38] Doing so was simple, since the Ohio school laws said nothing whatever about attendance, or which school a student ought to attend. Attending a local district school was merely a convenience, not a requirement.[39] So beginning on the seventh, Garfield, Judd, and presumably the Boyntons began attending a nearby school taught by Jim's likeable, feckless brother-in-law, Stephen Trowbridge.[40]

In this winter young Garfield began keeping a diary, "to exercise the hand a little evry [*sic*] day in writing," as he noted on the flyleaf. (Apparently his schoolwork did not involve much writing.) Where he got the idea is uncertain; perhaps one of the Boyntons had started keeping a journal. Actually, though, it was a fairly conventional thing for a serious and introspective young man in his time and place to do, even a young farmhand. In any case, the diary was a cheap little book of lined paper bound with cord, purchased probably at Solon Center or Bentleyville. Though he began it on New Year's Day, at the height of the Morrison controversy, he set down no details of the matter. His diary was not a vehicle for expressing his feelings, at that time; the entries were simple, one-line statements of weather and daily routine, so one can learn a good deal from it about what Jim Garfield, and the adolescents of Orange, in general, did that winter.[41]

Stephen's school, Monday through Saturday, lasted until 26 February, and Jim attended regularly, enjoying it as he had always enjoyed school. Now and then he took a day off for some good reason: one Monday morning he stayed at Stephen's house and helped him butcher; then they washed the blood off and went to school in the afternoon. Another day, after a deep snow, he was out with the sled, hauling hay to the barn and wood to the house from remote areas on their farm ("logging it," was the expression often used in the Reserve). One Thursday morning he had the temerity to drop in on Morrison's school, but he wrote nothing about his reception there.[42]

Two or three times that winter he attended a spelling school in the evening. This was another local kind of amusement, one of Jim's favorites, in which his remarkable memory gave him an edge. Despite the slip on the flyleaf of his diary, in the heat of a spelling match he was almost always right. The big, clumsy boy was known as a crack speller for miles around.[43]

Spelling school was always held at night in a district schoolhouse. Customs varied from one locality to another, but the common format pitted the scholars of the home district against those of another, or against all outsiders, so that the occasion usually drew people from a wide radius; spelling school was one of several institutions that bound the neighborhoods of Orange, Solon, Chagrin Falls, and surrounding townships together. Not only scholars attended; usually there were a large number of adults, spelling buffs and people who enjoyed a social evening. In some districts there was a social hour before the match began. As with the lyceum, candles would be stuck in place on windows, on desks, and in sconces if any existed, and people talked until the teacher called them to order.

Spelling school was as much the teacher's show as the scholars'. Webster's *Speller* was invariably used, and a good teacher with some experience usually got to the point where he or she could impress the assembled farmers by calling the list without looking at the book. One exceptional teacher in Geauga County could go for two hours in this fashion. The procedure was that of the familiar spelling bee, with the bashful scholars, lined up on opposite walls, gradually eliminated as they missed words. The contest often went on for hours, to the rapt attention and applause of the audience.

It was a social occasion for the young too. After an hour or so, the teacher generally called a recess. The girls, by unspoken custom, stayed in the building and socialized, while the boys went outside to roughhouse—"wrestle, collar and elbow, side hold, or back hold, or rough and tumble," a Bainbridge resident recalled; "or else stand and jump; hop, skip, and jump; or play 'crack the whip,' or 'fox and geese' when there was snow. Fist fights were stopped at once, but sometimes occurred on the way home." Big boys as well as small ones took part in the play. Jim enjoyed it, although he had to try hard to be gentle; he was so heavy set that it was easy to hurt a younger boy unintentionally.[44] The socializing after the match was over, when each boy had a chance to ask the girl of his choice to let him walk her home, probably appealed less to him. To judge from his diary, he was either indifferent to or scared of girls. Burke Hinsdale's experience seems to apply almost exactly here, especially the correlation between appearance and awkwardness: "I was a big, stout boy three or four years younger than I seemed, awkward and bashful. My age, size, and appearance exposed me more or less to banter and ridicule. I took small pleasure in company, and in large companies, especially if ladies were present, I was miserable. . . ."[45]

Singing school, an institution which, like spelling school, tried to combine instruction and entertainment, held most of Jim's attention that winter. A Mr. Little held classes on Thursday and Friday nights, probably at the usual fee of one or two dollars for the course, and young Garfield attended almost every one. Where the school met is not clear; singing schools met sometimes in schoolhouses, sometimes in private homes, sometimes in churches. They were exceedingly popular in the Reserve. Originally a late eighteenth-century attempt in New England to reform congregational singing that had become overloaded with ornamentation and had lost any sense of a regular beat, the singing schools had been carried into the Reserve with the rest of Yankee culture and had flourished, even where there was no special emphasis on congregational singing, simply because they provided a very agreeable way of passing a winter night. Around January of each year, regular as a Connecticut clock, either a church would get up a singing school for its members or a singing master from New England would appear in the community and offer to conduct an independent one.[46]

What Webster's *Speller* was to the spelling school, Hastings and Warriner's *Musica Sacra* was to a singing school. First published in Utica, New York, in 1817, it began with a four-page explanation of musical terminology totally confusing to anyone who was not an accomplished musician. One learned, among other things, that the scale consisted of four notes—faw, sol, la, faw, sol, la again, and mi, what modern musicians call the seventh. (The Continental do-re-mi scale had not yet reached America.) Terms like crotchet, quaver, slur, and bar were defined, and there was a little mnemonic for finding the place of mi from the key signature. Most singing masters devoted a session or two to this material, but the bulk of the school consisted of singing the tunes that comprised the rest of the book—some of them still familiar to twentieth-century churchgoers, such as "Easter Hymn," "Old Hundred," and "Coronation," but most of them completely vanished into the limbo of forgotten hymns. Armed with a pitch pipe and a winning manner, the master would test the voices of his students—there were usually twenty or thirty—and assign each to soprano, tenor, or bass (most *Musica Sacra* tunes were in three parts, the tenor being for both men and women), or, if they completely failed to sing on pitch, to the listeners' section.[47]

Singing school was predominantly a "young ladies'" affair. The boys who attended usually did so in hopes of escorting some particular young woman home. Jim Garfield was unusual, however; he came because he liked to sing. Not really a musical connoisseur, he found singing, to use twentieth-century jargon, a liberating experience. Friends of his youth have left amusing records of his appearance in church, head thrown back and belting out with all his might "How Firm A Foundation," his congregation's favorite hymn. How musical his rendition was is not clear; but it was probably no less so that those of most of the others. He apparently enjoyed Little's school greatly in this winter, and was sorry when it was over.[48]

These were his main diversions during the winter. There were other, lesser ones—a week or so of fine sleighing after the heavy snowfall in February, a concert of some sort at Solon Center, a lecture on phrenology at Abell's schoolhouse, occasional visits to the Falls with Orrin. Indeed, most of these activities he and Orrin probably shared. Whether he attended Disciple meeting with his family in these months is not clear from the diary. If he did, he did not trouble to mention it. With this possible exception, his winter seems to have been a fairly typical one for a sixteen-year-old in the Reserve.[49]

The proper finish for a Reserve winter—or the first delight of a Reserve spring—came in March when the sap began rising in the rock maple trees and men and boys headed for the "sugar camps" strategically located around their acres or in unclaimed woods.[50] Tapping the trees and "sugaring off" was a long-awaited event, but it may have been one young Garfield missed in the spring of 1848. By March, circumstances had worked out to gratify Jim's restlessness just a little, so that for the first time in his life, he was to spend more than a month away from home.

6

Independence

Spring–Summer 1848

It was mostly happenstance that James spent the spring of 1848 in Independence rather than Orange, but the consequences were far-reaching.

Ten miles west of Orange, in the flatlands along the Cuyahoga River, Independence was familiar country to the Garfields. Abram Garfield's stepfather and his family had settled there in the 1810s when they first came west from New York; Abram and Eliza had lived there fore several years after their marriage, and Jim's brother Thomas had been born there. None of the original Garfields or Boyntons were left now. In the way of the west, they had all grown up, married, and moved on, although Thomas Garfield, Jim's uncle, a fairly prosperous farmer and builder, still lived in the next township to the north, Newburgh. But Jim's married sister Mary did live in Independence. She and her husband Marenus Larabee had settled there when they moved back from Michigan, sometime after 1845, and they visited Orange fairly regularly.[1]

Early in February, Marenus brought his wife over to visit her mother and brothers for a week or two. Jim enjoyed the visit—he and his dreamy, pretty older sister had always been close—and when the time came for her to leave, he was the one who drove her back home. They used Uncle Amos's buggy; Cousin Harriet came along. It was 19 February, during a thaw, and the roads were so deep in mud, particularly after they came down from the hills, that the journey was slow. By the time they reached the Larabee farm, it was near evening, and they spent the night.[2] While there, Jim learned of a chance for work through his Uncle Thomas, who stopped over to see him. Uncle Thomas was getting set to clear some land right on the Independence-Newburgh town line, and needed hands. His terms, whatever they were exactly, seemed adequate to Jim, who may also have welcomed the prospect of spending a month or two away from Orange. This was a slack time of year on the farm, muddy and idle; if necessary, Thomas could handle the spring plowing easily by himself. So on 7 March, a biting cold day with snow on the ground, Jim showed up at Newburgh, ready to pick up his axe.[3]

In the event, his job for his uncle lasted less time than he expected, only about a month; but when it was over he managed to pick up other land-clearing jobs nearby, one with a farmer in Independence, Edward Barns. After that he planted crops for another local farmer and got other old jobs. One way and another, he stayed around Independence until the end of May, boarding first with a farmer named Watts, then with his sister and brother-in-law, to keep the money in the family. (There is little question he paid the Larabees for his board; Marenus, his brother-in-law, was a sharp man with a dollar. But he did get to enjoy Mary's "good dinners"—she was the best cook in the family.)[4]

He came to feel at home in the area. He went home to Orange, brought back his rifle, and used it for hunting in the woods along the Cuyahoga. During April he went to a couple of house or barn raisings. These affairs, at which the heavy timbered frame of a large structure was lifted into place by the combined strength of the men of the neighborhood, were hard work and often dangerous; every so often someone would get killed at a raising. In Independence, unlike Jim's south Orange neighborhood, a main attraction was the free whiskey and nutcakes furnished to the participants. Jim, no whiskey drinker, probably went mainly for the nutcakes and the socializing.[5]

In one respect, his jobs for his uncle and Barns were different from the land clearing he had previously done. Here, instead of piling the felled wood for burning, the men were expected to chop it into standard lengths and stack it up for cordwood. Some days Jim did nothing but split and pile the freshly chopped, fragrant wood. Much of it was to be boated to Cleveland later in the spring, to be sold to Lake Erie steamboats.[6]

One of these jobs had a glorious fringe benefit. The land where he was working commanded a view straight down the winding Cuyahoga valley and out onto the lake itself—Lake Erie, with its "bright, lively, blue color, so beautiful and rare" that impressed the young Walt Whitman the spring of 1848 as he returned from New Orleans to New York. The lake was alive with ships; at almost any moment he could see half a dozen steamers puffing across it, either the older sidewheelers or the newer, longer "propellers." But what most caught his eye were the sailing ships. Each one seemed a majestic vision straight out of *The Pirate's Own Book*, floating noiselessly across the water. The sight of a sailing vessel, he remembered later, would make him "almost insane with delight"; he would set down his axe and gaze, transfixed, out onto the lake, as his dream world materialized. The next and natural step was to imagine himself aboard, tossed by the cold waves, under the swelling canvas, and then to think of how much money he could be making as a sailor, until the whole vision began to wear an air of solid reality. Then he would have to pick up his axe and attack another tree.[7]

But though the lake was just beyond reach, the canal was not. It paralleled the east side of the river, a broad, empty ditch lined with gray clay, only four feet deep but forty feet wide at the top, tapering to twenty-six at the bottom—this was the way it looked in March, anyway, when Jim first came to Independence. But on the first of April they let water into the canal, and boats began moving on it, big, clumsy, white barges, piled high with freight. He found no difficulty in getting down to it—it was only a short distance from the places where he was working and staying—and from mid-April on he went down there frequently to see what was going on.[8] In May he attended a boat launch in Independence. It was not so impressive as the launching of a ship, just as a canal boat was less complex in construction than a ship—any master carpenter who could build a barn, in fact, could turn out one of the long, box-like craft, with their high, rounded bow and stern, their two or three simple cabins on deck, and the distinctive "wales" or wooden ribs running around the sides, to cushion the boat's bruising contacts with the lock walls.[9] But it was interesting. The canal, he found, was fairly big business in Independence. Many men who worked on it lived there, and some local farmers, like Ben Fisher, a justice of the peace for whom he did several odd jobs, owned all or part of a canal boat.[10]

In a peculiar way, too, the canal was the center of its own little social world. The locks between one level and another necessitated at least a ten-minute delay for every boat, more if there were other boats waiting ahead. They provided time for going ashore to buy necessaries or to toss off a dram or two of whiskey, and consequently each lock—there was one every mile or two—had its own grocery, which usually did a brisk trade in liquors. In Independence, the Gleason brothers kept the grocery at the Twelve-Mile Lock (twelve miles, that is, from Cleveland, the northern end of the canal); there were others at the Eleven-Mile Lock, near the Larabee farm, and the Eight-Mile Lock. Inevitably, these "doggeries" also attracted a clientele from the surrounding country. In Brecksville, south of Independence, the Seventeen-Mile Lock was known as the place where heavy drinkers hung out. In Brecksville, too, and probably in most other places along its length, the canal was the place where men and boys went on Sundays during warm weather to swim and loaf. Criminals from Cleveland, too, seem to have frequented taverns along the canal. To some degree, then, the canal was a focus for several kinds of rough behavior—which possibly added to its allure for a boy from a quiet rural neighborhood.[11]

As spring wore on, Jim began seeing more of his family on the Garfield side. There was his Uncle Thomas, a big, hearty, domineering man like most of the male Garfields, a gambler and plunger in real estate, very different from his upright half-brother Amos Boynton. There were Thomas's two swaggering sons, George and Charles. Ben Fisher, the farmer for whom Jim worked, was also a connection. His wife was a Letcher, a daughter of Jim's Aunt Polly Garfield. Most of the Letchers now lived in northwestern Ohio, but two of Jim's cousins, Thomas and Amos Letcher, men several years older than he, had only recently come back to Independence; Amos, in fact, was co-owner of a canal boat with Fisher.[12] Also, surprisingly, Jim saw a lot of his mother; either because she felt low, as she often did in the spring, and wanted a daughter's care or because she missed her Jimmy, she came over to spend a week or two at the Larabees', fell sick, and ended up not going home until the end of May.[13]

But the most abiding impress on his mind that spring came from the two things mentioned earlier, the visions of sailing on the lake and the business of canaling. Around the middle of May, he got a taste of the latter. A Mr. Doolittle was boating cordwood from Independence to Cleveland and hired Jim to load the boat; Jim ended by riding the boat to Cleveland and unloading the wood there too.[14]

In all probability, this was his first trip on the canal, and his first chance to see in detail how the business operated. The boat, some fourteen feet wide and sixty or seventy feet long, piled high with wood wherever there was room, was drawn by a pair of horses at the other end of a long line. They plodded along the slippery, ten-foot-wide towpath, urged on, and sometimes ridden, by a young boy with a whip, the "driver." Water weeds, cattails, and spring wildflowers glided by, as the boat lumbered quietly on at a speed of two or three miles an hour.[15] A steersman sat at the large wooden tiller in the stern, guiding the boat when there was a curve in the canal; the rest of the crew, the captain, the bowsman, maybe another driver, were idle.[16]

Every so often, as they approached a lock, the tempo changed. Up ahead, the surface of the canal narrowed to a span barely wider than the boat, between low stone walls. At either end of the lock, two gates of heavy timbers, painted Indian red, the common red of barns and schoolhouses, blocked the way, and some distance ahead of the lock there was a wooden distance-post to announce its approach. The men got out their setting-poles as the driver unhitched his team, to guide the craft slowly into its slot. (Unless, of course, there was a boat bound in the opposite direction already coming up through the lock—in which case Jim's boat pulled over to the bank, in the widewater next to the inevitable doggery, and waited for the other to lock through.) Then they were in the lock, the boat tied to the four mooring posts to prevent its banging around, the upstream gates shut tight behind them. The wickets in the downstream gates, butterfly valve-like openings controlled by long brass rods, were opened, and the water beneath the boat began to swirl as it emptied slowly through them. The boat descended with the level of the water. Mossy stone walls loomed up on either side of it. The drop in the average lock of the Ohio Canal was eight to ten feet, so that by the time they were on the lower level they seemed to be in a little, dark, cool-smelling cell with two walls of damp stone and two of timbers, once red, but worn to an old rose with time and use, down which runnels of water trickled. Then the downstream gates opened and they were ready to pole out, hitch up the team, and go on to the next lock.[17]

The only other operation of consequence occurred when the blare of a canal horn announced an oncoming boat headed in the opposite direction. In such a case, the upstream boat always had the right of way. Jim's boat, headed toward Cleveland, pulled over to the far bank, its team to the outside of the towpath, with the line slack between them, while they let the other boat and team pass over. Most of the boats that passed were freight boats like their own, with a cabin fore and one aft, and perhaps a small stable in the middle for the spare horses. In most boats, the center was piled high with cargo, typically cases of merchandise from the East—everything from shoes and hardware to pianos and the latest fashions—bound for the towns of interior Ohio. Once in a while, but far less often than would have been the case five years before, they encountered a gleaming white passenger packet, with wider decks and longer, more pretentious cabins. In the 1830s and early 1840s passenger boats had been numerous on Ohio's canals, but now lake steamers, river steamers, and the railroads inching slowly west, were putting them out of business. American travelers liked to go fast; to most, the smoothness of a ride on the canal was insufficient compensation for the leisurely, almost comically slow pace of a canal packet.[18]

Young Garfield probably saw nothing funny about canaling. To him it was, if not high adventure, at least fascinating and different from anything he knew at home. And the crowning joy of it was that every trip brought him to that jungle of warehouses and drays, that forest of masts and smokestacks, that was the Cleveland waterfront, where he could toy with the idea of signing on a Lake Erie vessel and becoming a "genuine 'old salt'" like the ones he had read of. In May, he got to Cleveland four times, each time with a load of wood. He would help unload it at the steamboat docks, probably amble around the waterfront a little, and then head back up the canal.

At the beginning of June, however, he went back to Orange. Possibly he was needed on the farm; the heaviest time of the year, the beginning of haying, was coming up. An unpleasant incident that took place at this time may also have had something to do with his return. It was night, and he was coming back from Cleveland on a canal boat belonging to a William Weed. It sprang a leak, as canal boats were apt to do, and they had to stop and bail for an hour or two. When they finally had the situation in hand, it was past midnight. Young Garfield, thoroughly tired out, took the lamp, went to a bunk in the cabin, and dropped off instantly to sleep. When he woke the next day, he found his pocket book gone. He suspected Weed had taken it, but said nothing to anyone except his journal, where he wrote the longest entry he had yet put down—not mentioning, however, how much money he had lost. It may have been a fair amount, five or ten dollars; he had worked on several jobs in the past few days. In any event, he helped Weed boat one more load of wood to Cleveland, returned to the Larabees', and went home to Orange.[19]

Before going back, though, he had to go down to the Fourteen-Mile Lock in south Independence to pick up his rifle, which he had apparently left with someone there, and where he had one of those adventures that make good stories afterward but are no fun when they happen. Even in settled Independence there was still enough forest to get lost in, and that was what he did. Coming back with his gun in the afternoon, he decided to do some shooting in a part of the woods he was unfamiliar with; in the wilderness of tree trunks, moss, and vines, the lush foliage of early June, he ranged too far. Evening came, and a thunderstorm blew up. In the rain and the dark Jim lost his way, and took shelter under a fallen tree. It kept raining hard, and he realized he was going to have to spend the night where he was; he buttoned his rifle inside his shirt, covered himself with bark, and slept. In the morning he awoke drenched to find that his hollow was full of water—and also that he had spent the night almost in sight of Marenus and Mary's house.[20]

On 3 June he was back in Orange, nursing a cold from his night in the woods; 5 June, Monday, he was down at the Judds' helping Orrin paint chairs; Wednesday he and Orrin went hunting. After that, the regular routine of summer's work began. He plowed and hoed corn, clad in butternut jeans, tow shirt, and straw hat, the farmer's summer uniform. Thomas was building something, probably a new barn; Jim worked with him as mason's helper.[21] On rainy days, he took a tub or two of butter to trade at one of the stores in the Falls—walking down the hill to the ford at Bentleyville, up the hill, up the muddy streets of the little manufacturing town, past all the familiar landmarks—the carriage works, the paper mill, Church's blacksmith shop, Bayard's tavern where the stagecoach stopped, Champion Hall, the elegant little lyceum built and owned by a wealthy absentee landowner from Rochester, New York, who opened it occasionally to the public, and, up the hill, the cupola of the Methodist seminary. Sundays he went to meeting with his mother and Thomas, if he felt like it; at the beginning of July he went with them to a Disciple meeting in Bedford. It was, in short, the same old life in Orange.[22]

There is evidence that it irked him terribly. As often as he could, he found work elsewhere—off the farm and, if possible, outside the neighborhood; from about the middle of July, he was hardly home at all. Perhaps he quarreled with Thomas, but it is hard to imagine a quarrel with the serious, quiet, simple older brother; more likely it was just the old restlessness, more acute than ever this time, aggravated by a sense of his own strength, of physical maturity, and the remorseless passage of time that was making him, every year, more and more just another Reserve farmhand toiling under the summer sun. For a week in late June he worked down in Solon, hoeing corn for a farmer named Norton, a fellow Disciple. In mid-July, he and John Rundt from across the road teamed up to look for farm work seven or eight miles away in Aurora, where a lot of wheat was grown.[23]

The fact that they teamed up at all was a measure of Jim's desire to get away. They made an odd pair indeed—young Garfield, big, self-occupied, touchy, and his coarse, hard-working, hard-drinking companion, three or four years older, whose phlegmatic German calm struck Jim as perverse ignorance.[24] All they had in common was a need for pocket money and a desire to get away from Orange. Still, they looked like a promising couple of hands and had no difficulty finding a job with a farmer who paid them full men's wages, a dollar a day. It was the first time Jim had ever earned that much. When that job was over, they found another with a neighboring farmer that kept them in Aurora another week, haying. This time they had "some difficulty" with him over wages—he refused to pay Jim a full dollar a day, claiming that he was still too young. Jim took offense, turned on his heel, and walked home through the rain.[25]

Twice during the summer he found a way to get back over to Independence.[26] Once he took a day from his job in Solon and walked over, to collect some back wages from Edward Barns and his Uncle Thomas; once he drove over with Edwin Mapes in his buggy. What drew him, of course, were the memories of the canal, the waterfront, and especially the ships out on the lake, memories that danced continually in the back of his mind like the sparkle of far-off ocean waves seen from an inland spot. The life of a sailor had never seemed so rewarding, so within reach. That his mother, who knew his feelings, or the rest of the family, or for that matter most neighbors in Orange, thought of seafaring life as disreputable and degrading seems not to have bothered him. He understood that the neighbors' opinion of him was equally low: they thought him a difficult boy and a judgment on his mother for having spoiled him.[27] (One of the neighbors much later, when Garfield had become famous, rephrased her censure in words that were meant to be milder, but still carried some of their original sting: ". . . he was determined and was not a Christian in his early life.")[28] If he thought about the question at all, he may well have concluded that since he was not going to amount to anything anyway, he might as well waste his life in the most exciting way possible.

When he finally decided to make a break, it was mid-August. He had been working at various places in his neighborhood for two weeks. On the fourteenth he had joined an itinerant group of farm workers who were headed for the townships to the south, seeking work in harvesting. He tramped ten or fifteen miles with them across the warm, sunny fields, spent the night in Twinsburg, and then suddenly changed his mind. No reason is given in the diary—but he left the group, walked back to Orange, picked up a few belongings, and without a word about his plans, walked the ten miles to Independence. That night he spent with Marenus and Mary; the next day he was off to Cleveland to find a sailor's job on the lake.[29]

7

Making a Break

August 1848

As Garfield recalled much later, when he got to the River Street waterfront on the morning of 16 August, there was only one ship in port of the kind he was interested in.[1] On an average day, there were a dozen or more sailing ships docked at the Cleveland wharves—but the burly young novel-reader, bent on fulfilling his dream, was choosy in assessing prospective vessels. It was still early, presumably on another of the warm, clear mornings northern Ohio had been having, when he strode up the gangplank of his choice and announced to one of the sailors that he was looking for a berth.[2]

Garfield remembered all his life what happened next. The captain, drunk or hung over, staggered onto the deck from below, took one look at the lubberly, thick-lipped, tousle-headed youth in front of him, and told him in scorching language to get off his ship at once. The language was not new to Jim, but he could not cope with the anger. He stumbled ashore in such confusion that he was barely aware that he was being laughed at. He had known rejection before, but always in circumstances that made it possible for him to blame people who thought themselves richer or better. This was different—a mine exploded in the center of his dream world. Possibly for the first time in his life, he felt crushing failure.[3]

He was still wandering the docks in an emotional daze when he caught sight of Ben Fisher's canal boat, the *Evening Star*. She was probably out in the river beside a ship, loading copper ore (although Jim may not have recognized the cargo at once) from Lake Superior. Canal boats often came into the river through the guardlock, a few hundred feet from the foot of Superior Lane, to load. He recognized her at once, and saw his cousin Amos Letcher supervising operations. Presently Letcher, as he remembered (and his memories were usually accurate) felt himself tapped on the shoulder and turned around to see his younger cousin, who said, as nonchalantly as possible, "Hello, Ame, what are you doing here?"

"You see what I'm doing," Letcher said. "What are you doing here?"

Jim explained that he had been hunting work in Cleveland, that he had been "bluffed off" a Lake Erie vessel, where they had called him a "country greenhorn," and that he was still looking. The implication was obvious: he would like to try working on the canal and getting some experience before he sought a job on the lake again. Letcher understood that. He had only one post, however, to offer on the *Evening Star*, that of driver, the least prestigious and lowest paying job. He offered it with some apologies, but Jim, still shaken from his recent experience, accepted without question. The wages were a bit less than he had been making at odd jobs—twelve dollars a month—but they were above average for a driver, and Letcher promised to promote him when a chance came. He went to see about his team.[4]

The *Evening Star* seems to have been fairly typical of the four hundred or so boats that plied the Ohio Canal and its connections in the late forties. Her crew numbered five or six—one captain, one steersman, two drivers, and one or two bowsmen, the hands who went ahead to prepare a lock for the boat, kept the headlamps trimmed, and handled the ropes and poles as the craft went through a lock. Accord to a description which may be apocryphal but is plausible, her layout was also typical, with a fore cabin where the crew slept, a cabin aft with the stove and food, a stable amidships for the second team of horses, and the rest of the boat a cargo hold. She was seventy-five feet long, the standard dimension for the Ohio Canal, where all the locks were that length. The decks were exceedingly narrow and often cluttered with ropes and other gear; often the men had to clamber over cabin roofs to get quickly from bow to stern.[5]

Jim's job of driving was a simple one, which he had often seen done before. It was essentially the management of horses; the only tool was a big blacksnake whip. Each of the drivers had a team for whose care and feeding he was responsible, and they took turns drawing the boat—probably, as the custom was on the canal, in six-hour shifts called "tricks." Each one, when his trick began, walked his team carefully across the planks from boat to shore, trying to keep them from seeing the water and balking. Then he harnessed them to the seventy-foot towline, with the stronger horse, or "leaner," directly connected to the boat and the other in front of him, whipped them up, and set off down the towpath. He could walk alongside, or ride the rear horse, as he preferred.[6]

To a farm boy like Jim, who was familiar with the care and handling of horses even though his own family did not own one, driving seemed easy—but the first day taught him he still had some things to learn. He and his team had the first trick out of Cleveland. When the boat was loaded, the crew poled her back through the guardlock, and Jim hitched up his horses and headed down the towpath, a high earthen bank that ran in long curves between the canal and the winding Cuyahoga. When they met their first boat coming in the other direction, the two drivers got their lines tangled. The fault was probably due to Jim's inexperience, but in any event, by the time they got the lines straight, the *Evening Star*'s momentum had carried her up

These photographs, taken two generations after Garfield's time, when railroads had largely superseded canal traffic, show a quiet, semi-abandoned waterway; but basic features like the lock gates, the "doggeries" at each lock, and the design of the boat itself, remain unchanged.

Near the Eight Mile Lock of the Ohio Canal

The Eleven Mile Lock of the Ohio Canal

level with the horses. A few rods ahead was a wasteway, a sort of sluice for emptying excess water from the canal into the river, over which the towpath passed on a bridge. As the boat passed Jim, the steersman shouted to him, "Hurrah, Jim, whip up that team, or your line will ketch on the bridge." Obediently, Jim cracked the whip and got his team on the trot, but it was too late; just as they reached the center of the bridge, the line, which had indeed snagged somewhere under the murky water, tightened and yanked Jim and the horses backward into the canal. The water, though dirty, was only four feet deep—fortunately for Jim, who could not swim a stroke. He spluttered to the surface, his sun-bleached hair plastered to his head, dripping but unhurt. The horses were all right, too. It was a typical Garfield mishap, clumsy and conspicuous, but with no great harm done, and Jim could laugh it off as he got back to dry land. "I was just taking my morning bath," he told Letcher.[7]

Early in the afternoon, they reached Eleven-Mile Lock, at Fisher's farm in Independence. Here Jim would have gotten off if it had been that spring; instead, he swapped places with the other driver, drove his team on board, rubbed them down, and went on deck to sit with Letcher as the boat glided slowly on down the canal. From other Garfield relatives, the captain had heard a good deal about his brilliant cousin, and had been trying to sort out his impressions since Jim had come on board. He decided to ask him a few questions to test his knowledge. (Letcher felt pretty confident of his own capacity; he had taught school in Indiana for three winters.) The subjects he selected were the Yankee's basic trinity—the areas where a young man prided himself on having accurate knowledge: grammar, mathematics, and geography. In Letcher's words, "I asked him several, and he answered them all, and then turned on me, and asked me several that I could not answer." The captain gave it up, and told Jim he was too smart to be working on the canal. That fact Jim knew only too well; it would be interesting to know what he replied.[8]

They passed Fourteen-Mile Lock, and headed south into parts of Ohio Jim had never seen before. He began to make the acquaintance of his fellow crewmen; if his memory and Letcher's, thirty years later, are to be trusted, some of their names were still known. There was a bowsman named Dave, a hulking man in his middle thirties. The steersman, George Lee, was twenty-eight and lived in Independence. The other driver was called Ikey. He may have been white or black; many blacks worked on the canals. Maybe there was a cook, too—many boats seem to have had a woman who presided over the kitchen; or maybe the crew took turns cooking.[9]

The *Evening Star* continued inching south, parallel to the river. The valley gradually narrowed; as the land rose, locks grew more frequent. Within two or three hours, they came to the village of Boston, the first of several little settlements that catered especially to canal traffic. It had stables to house the relief horses that drew passenger packets, several bars, a grocery or two, and a couple of hotels. Not too surprisingly, it was popular with gamblers, and had a rather rough reputation. Peninsula and Johnny Cake Lock, a few miles farther on, were similar places.[10]

At Peninsula, where they arrived about sunset, the canal crossed the Cuyahoga on a stone aqueduct wide enough for only one boat and turned down the river's west bank. The *Evening Star* crossed and went on; like most canal boats, she ran day and night. The bowsman lit the bull's-eye lantern that served as a headlamp. Those of the crew who were not working turned in, while the driver and his team plodded down the towpath in the growing dark. The beam from the headlamp illuminated just enough for the driver to see where he was going. Jim was probably asleep in his bunk as darkness fell, but later in the night he was awakened to begin his next shift. They were approaching the twenty-one locks of Akron.[11]

Akron was the highest point on the entire length of the canal from Lake Erie to the Ohio River—the "summit," as it was called, where a reservoir called Summit Lake fed water both northward and southward into the canal. It was in origin simply a canal settlement—the name Akron was Greek for "summit"—but had grown into a fair-sized village, and the approach to it from the north was one of the more spectacular sights the canal offered. Turning away from the Cuyahoga, the waterway followed the Little Cuyahoga River until, about two miles north of Akron, it began ascending a hill with a direct succession of locks called the "lock stairs"—twenty-one in all—to Summit Lake. It took several hours to get through them all (an average passage through a single lock was ten or twenty minutes), so that it was perfectly possible, in the daytime, to let passengers off at Lock 10, say, for one or two hours' shopping, and have them rejoin the boat at the Exchange Street lock, Lock 1.

Young Garfield did not see the lock stairs, this first time; he experienced them as a series of operations in the lantern's glare: hitching the team, driving the horses, unhitching, drowsily waiting in the chill of midnight for a downbound boat to lock through, leaning against the horses. He was by no means alone; there were taverns and groceries at every lock, many of them open all night, with candles burning brightly behind the bar and boatmen talking. He may have finished his shift by the time they reached the top and slipped into the lower canal basin, in the first light of dawn.[12]

The copper ore they were carrying was destined for a foundry in Pittsburgh, so at Akron they paid their toll and left the Ohio Canal, heading north out of the basin in a direction almost parallel to the way they had come on another canal—the Pennsylvania and Ohio, nicknamed the "Crosscut." This canal ran right past the brick stores on Akron's main street. Completed in 1840, it was the newest link in the Ohio Canal network—some seventy-five miles, from Akron to New Castle, Pennsylvania—and perhaps the busiest.

Completion of the Crosscut supplied a crucial missing link in the canal network. Heavy goods could now go directly from the Great Lakes to Pittsburgh, and the products of Pittsburgh could find markets in the interior of Ohio. More than that, a large section of the Reserve hitherto isolated was opened to trade and busy experimenting with new crops and new industries. Warehouses and wharves had sprung up all along the canal to handle wool (there was a boom in sheep raising just then), flax, Reserve dairy products like cheese, and coal. Boats to carry his merchandise crowded into the Crosscut. Old documents list the *Sea Bird, Ravenna, Bennington, Algomah, Old Zach, Independence, Spy, Planet, Oaxaca, Blue Bell, American Eagle, Pocahontas, Norway, Golden Rule, Hurricane*, and hosts of others.[13]

Young Garfield saw the Crosscut at the very zenith of its history. In 1848, it had existed only eight years, and flourished only two or three years more. The railroads that would put it out of business were already stretching west from the Atlantic; by the early fifties, they would be rattling all over northern Ohio, drawing away the trade of the area with their superior speed.[14]

There was nothing very remarkable about the Crosscut as a canal. It had no spectacular feature like the lock stairs. It contained fifty-four locks, with an average rise of 7.85 feet; fifty-seven bridges, and two aqueducts. From Akron it descended northeast to rejoin the Cuyahoga; then north of Franklin Mills it began its ascent eastward, up Breakneck Creek, and reached its summit south of Ravenna, where the feeder from Crystal Lake came in. From there it descended slowly, crossed the Mahoning River at Newton Falls on an aqueduct, and followed the north shore of that river on into Pennsylvania. All along it there were little mills—flax, grist, or woolen—using its water power, warehouses, and the customary doggeries. Along the Crosscut's sides, tiny settlements called themselves "ports," so exhilarating was the potential of the canal as a link with the rest of the world.[15]

This stretch of canal—the Crosscut, and the part of the Ohio Canal from Cleveland to Akron—was to be the scene of almost all Jim's experience. One wonders what he noticed, seeing the Crosscut for the first time. Probably it struck him that here, unlike the Ohio and Erie, there were places where canal boats used the river itself; in Franklin Mills, and again below Youngstown, the canal simply exited into the river for some distance.[16] Of course, he was still learning the driver's trade, and doing so in typically awkward fashion; he later remembered falling into the canal fourteen times on this first trip. Possibly the *Evening Star*, too, was having her troubles; although no mishap is mentioned in Garfield's journal, her pace from Akron to Pennsylvania was so slow as to arouse the suspicion that something in addition to this driving went wrong.[17]

However that may be, they slowly advanced east along the Crosscut. Small, neat Reserve communities slid by—Campbellsport, Newport, Newton Falls, Warren. As they approached Pennsylvania, the landscape gradually changed; identical round-topped hills, like something from a primitive painting, dominated the landscape. A few of those close to the canal had mine shafts sunk in their sides and huge piles of coal next to them. There were two or three iron foundries, belching thick coal smoke, next to the canal near Youngstown. This industry was three or four years old at most; it was the beginning of a process that with the coming of the railroads, would transform (some would say ruin) the Mahoning valley.[18]

Just beyond Lowell the canal entered Pennsylvania; probably there was a boundary marker of some kind. Eight miles farther on, the canal ended, its last lock opening into Beaver Creek—or, as it was also called, the Erie Extension. This was a canal of a different sort. The state of Pennsylvania had converted a medium-sized stream to a canal, with a towpath and a series of dams to raise the water level. There was a channel that canal boats were supposed to stay in; if they strayed out of it, they ran the risk of hitting an obstruction, as the canal boat *Pelican* had done in 1846 when she struck a snag near Chewtown and sank with forty hogsheads of sugar and twenty-five barrels aboard. The steersman had more to do in this stretch, the driver less; for some short sections, in fact, they may have taken both teams of horses on board and poled along like a keelboat. Beaver Creek was only twenty-four miles long; its mouth opened into the broad and busy Ohio River, from which it was separated by a long stone dam and an immense guardlock.[19]

From Beaver Point on, there was of course no possibility of horse-drawn travel against the Ohio's strong current. For many canal boats, the journey ended there; they discharged their cargo at the Beaver Point warehouses and took on goods left by steamboats for dispatch to some point in interior Ohio.[20] But the *Evening Star* went on to Pittsburgh, towed by a river steamboat, a fantastic craft—a Reserve traveler had described one as "a two-story farmhouse with a narrow piazza on the side and a sawmill wheel behind."[21] After thirty churning miles they came in sight of the city, a vast jumble of mines, houses, foundries, and shops, bigger than any place young Garfield had seen in his life, and overhung by an ever-present cloud of coal smoke. Their docking area in the Monongahela River was crowded and labyrinthine, an "ugly confusion of backs of buildings, and crazy galleries and stairs," as an English visitor had described it a few years earlier.[22]

The *Evening Star* and her crew spent three days in the grimy coal-and-iron city before they were towed back to Beaver Point to begin their return trip. No doubt Jim and his comrades got out into the crowded maze of streets and tried to see the sights as best they could. Perhaps they were in the city around nightfall, at that magical moment when the day's smoke had thinned and the gas lamps on either side of the streets were turned on. (Cleveland did not yet have gaslight.) In the soft glow, the soot-blackened buildings were not discernible—only the line of lamps, "extending," a country visitor noted with wonder, "until they are lost in themselves as it were." Jim did not mention anything like this in his diary; he recorded only that he had listened to two street preachers the Sunday they spent there.[23]

On 29 August they left Beaver Point. Next day they stopped at the Brier Hill mine, just above Youngstown, to take on coal for Cleveland. The mine, with the gaping mouths of its lateral tunnels, came right up to the canal. They could see the cars full of gleaming chunks emerging from the earth and the black-faced workers adding to the heaps that loomed up against the blue sky of late summer, while lines of canal boats stood by to load. For canal transport, the coal was put into flour barrels or bushel baskets and brought aboard. The *Evening Star* took on sixty tons.[24]

(Coal from the Summit mines near Akron had long been a minor commodity on the canal, but only in the past two or three years, with the opening of the Mahoning valley operations, had it become a major one. Now it was one of the two or three biggest cargoes in the Cleveland trade, as more and more lake steamboats turned from wood to coal. One could already foresee the day when no more cordwood would be boated to the Cleveland wharves.)[25]

From Youngstown to Cleveland, the landscapes of the Crosscut and Ohio Canal unrolled in reverse before Garfield—the brick and stone mills, the brick storefronts of Akron, the tall, boxlike frame warehouses and hotels of the canal villages, clean geometrical shapes painted red, yellow, or white. He became used to the rhythms and sounds of the canal—the card-playing between locks, the dash of cold canal water on one's face at the beginning of a shift, the songs canalmen sang, with gusto if not melodiously, like "Old Dan Tucker" and "Cindy." When they returned to Cleveland, he was ready to continue. Letcher, too, was satisfied with his cousin's work; he promoted him to bowsman, at fourteen dollars a month, not a bad wage, with the prospect of further raises as he gained experience. The only people still skeptical about Jim's future on the canal were the other crewmen, to whom the captain's brainy young relative was an alien, suspect figure.[26]

Their attitude changed, however, on the second trip, after Jim got into his first serious fight on the canal, at Beaver Point. It was with the bowsman Dave. Jim was on board, working with a setting-pole, one of the long iron-tipped poles used to push off from docks or wharves, when the boat gave a sudden lurch.[27] The pole flew out of his hands and struck Dave, who was standing several feet away, in the midriff. Ignoring Jim's apology, the big bowsman started toward him cursing and muttering something about thrashing the careless rascal ("rascal" in the 1840s was a swearword as strong as, say, "son-of-a-bitch" in the twentieth century).[28] Jim, in turn, took offense and decided he was going to fight and, if possible, whip the older man, but he stayed where he was and let Dave come at him. "Remaining perfectly still until he was almost upon me," Garfield remembered later, "I suddenly jumped aside and as he passed I dealt him a terrible blow just back of and under his left ear. With great force he fell with his head between two beams in the bottom of the boat." Jim leaped on him, prepared to follow up, as Letcher shouted, "Pound the damn-fool to death, Jim! Damn me if I'll interfere." But there was no fight left in Dave; he was helpless, and Jim saw no point in beating him to a pulp. He let him up, and a few minutes later the two shook hands.[29]

This short bout had unexpected consequences. It gave Jim prestige, not only on his own boat, but also, as the story spread, on others. He had settled the doubts of the crew, in what would later become standard Western-movie fashion, by speaking to them in their own language, in the neat, quick way he had handled his opponent. Maybe Garfield exaggerated later when he recalled that the fight gave him the rank of "a hero" among "the rough men along the canal," but it certainly did win him full acceptance.[30] If there was anything like an initiation ceremony for canalers, this was it. He had definitely broken with Orange.

8

The Wild Life

September 1848

THE new hand soon learned the routine of the *Evening Star*. His job, bowing, was unchallenging; he had only "to make the locks ready, get the boat through, trim the lamps, etc." Their route was regular; but Pittsburgh, their destination on his first trip, was not part of it. Generally they just worked the Ohio and Erie Canal and the Crosscut from Cleveland to Beaver Point and back.[1] Going down from Cleveland the cargo was usually goods destined for the small interior towns, barrels of Syracuse salt, lath, or lumber. Coming back, they normally stopped at the Brier Hill mine to load up with coal or occasionally at one of the forges near Youngstown to take on a load of iron. There were several factories there turning out iron in one form or another; in fact, the canal passed right through the yard of a rolling mill, and workers had to cross on bridges to get from one building to another. Every so often one of the younger workers would get a laugh by leaping off the bridge onto a slow-moving canal boat underneath, and riding it down to the next bridge.[2]

On the second trip a minor incident occurred that Jim was to remember for a long time. Probably he polished or embellished it a little in the retelling; even so, it tells something about the canal, and more about him. At Newport, a canal village southeast of Ravenna, the *Evening Star* was in the lock, shifting and bumping aimlessly as the water rose beneath its keel; Garfield, standing on the bow, could see on shore "a group of men seated on a bench in front of a liquor doggery, and prominent among them . . . a dashing young man with dark eyes and raven locks," who "seemed to be enjoying the rowdyism of the bacchanal group"—an image like a painting by William Sidney Mount or Richard Caton Woodville—the row of round, convivial faces, a little crafty, a little bloated, far inferior, Garfield thought, to the dashing young man "in intelligence, and respectability of dress." Garfield was "struck with the thought that one of so superior intellect should be pleased with such comrades," and he looked "intently" at the dark young man as his boat rose to the top of the lock. For a long moment their eyes met. Then the *Evening Star* had to go on, which it did, with its young bowsman "musing on my own headlong course of life. . . ."[3]

The urge to compare was ever-present in young Garfield. Unsure of his own worth, his masculinity, his place in society, he measured himself against every male his own age that he encountered. One can be confident that, as the boat drew slowly away from Newport, he was thinking over the contrast between himself and the dark-haired stranger.

One thing on his mind, clearly, was "respectability of dress." He was wearing, as he recalled, a "coarse, heavy oilcloth coat and pants," necessary for a man on the bow, where water leaking through crevices in the upper lock gates was apt to fall in a fine, continuous spray as a boat locked through.[4] The dark young man had "respectable" clothes on: black shoes or boots, and woolen trousers, probably of the light cloth called casimere; a pressed white shirt, with stiff stand-up collar, and a vest; a neck handkerchief, of solid color or spotted, tied at a jaunty angle beneath his chin; a dark broadcloth coat, either a frock coat reaching to the knees or the increasingly popular sack coat without a waist seam, which stopped a little below the hips; and probably a "plug hat," one of the silk top hats that had recently supplanted the traditional beaver. Between the two styles of dress yawned a social gap.[5]

It may, at first, seem odd that in the supposedly egalitarian Midwest of the 1840s it should have mattered how men were dressed. But it did. "How many judge," a Cleveland newspaper editorialized, "of a person's character by the cut of his coat, his manners, and conversation! A person well dressed is supposed to possess a good mind and a virtuous heart, while a ragged man with a patch on his knee, passes for a villain or simpleton." Even if this was a conventional sentiment borrowed from elsewhere and applied more or less offhand to the dress of the Reserve, it still matched a reality. Garfield, who was very much aware of the social meaning of what he wore, mentioned several times being slighted because of his dress in his youth. A Reserve novelist of the period could portray it as an event of symbolic importance when a respectable character took off his coat and neckcloth and went into the field, with open collar, to work with the hands—adding, to reassure his readers that the change was purely sartorial and not moral, that he still "looked like a gentleman."[6]

Essentially, there were two uniforms for males in the Reserve—the respectable one, already described, and the working garb of Jim and his friends on the farms or the canal—light cotton shirts, in solid colors or stripes, with puffed, blousy sleeves and loose cuffs; light pants of some cotton material like satinet, held up by a pair of suspenders; sometimes a vest; heavy, clodhopper-type shoes, and a broad-brimmed hat of felt or straw. No underwear; underwear for men was a fashion just beginning to take hold among the respectable. One could see it advertised in city papers, but country people and workingmen had not yet adopted it. Rich men, professionals, and other men with some status to assert wore the respectable uniform. Artisans and farmers wore it on Sundays when they were in company with God and the womenfolk—otherwise, they wore work clothes.[7] Uncle Amos and the Boynton boys, and Jim, for that matter, when he was in Orange, had coats of store-bought broadcloth, pressed shirts, and cravats for Sunday meeting and daguerreotypes. On the canal, Sunday was not generally observed, and men wore the worker's uniform exclusively—except the captains of some boats, who proclaimed their station with a broadcloth coat and neck handkerchief.[8]

In some ways, the dress of the respectable and the workingmen differed little. Neither class changed clothes often. A jocular newspaperman who wrote of packing clothes for a fortnight's trip—"six collars and a shirt"—strengthened the impression given by Charles Dickens, who wrote in *Martin Chuzzlewit* how the respectable men of America kept up appearances by changing their detachable shirtfronts (like the detachable collar, an American invention) while continuing to wear the same shirt. And the two classes bathed with equal frequency—that is, rarely, beyond washing face and hands daily. Nonetheless, there were two uniforms, and Jim could not help feeling, as he gazed at the young man, that he was equally entitled to be wearing the superior one, both intellectually and morally.[9]

Morality: that was the real reason for his fascination with the dark-haired young man. Respectability in dress, social respectability in general, was only a token of moral respectability. The young man had seemed to be seeking out the degradation of a life below his station, just as Jim, in his "headlong course of life," was allowing himself to be drawn into a life rougher and more corrupt than any he had known; and despite occasional qualms, he was going knowingly and willingly.[10]

Canal life was rougher in many ways than life in Orange. Take language, for instance—profanity was common, almost universal, on the canal. Swearing, like many other features of American life, was in a state of transition at this period. The four-letter words for bodily functions, which were to become the ultimate in profanity by the late nineteenth century, were still considered merely gross indelicacies and used only in their literal meanings. The staple of swearing was still, as it had been for centuries, oaths concerning God and religion, although these were beginning to fade as the other group advanced. Jim found "hell" and "Goddamn," and words like "bastard," coming more readily to his lips than they had ever done.[11]

Then there was fighting. Jim had been known in Orange as a fighter, although there he had fought more out of desperation than from any love of combat. On the canal, fighting was different; it was a regular part of life, almost a recreation, a welcome break from the work routine, invariably good for plenty of conversation, stories, and wagers among the work-weary, uneducated hands. Canal boat crews fought with other crews over whose boat had the right to go through a lock first; if the same two crews met later anywhere along the canal, they often set to in a rematch. On the Cleveland waterfront, canalmen and lake sailors were apt to plunge into bloody brawls in which knives and clubs were used; at small interior places like Youngstown, local bucks would come down to the basin to try picking a fight with the boatmen.[12]

Jim had no zest for fist fights when he came on to the canal. If Letcher's memory is correct, on the first trip his cousin talked him out of fighting with the crew of another boat at a lock north of Akron.[13] But a few weeks worked changes. Somewhere on the Crosscut in September, when Jim was bowsman, he ran ahead and started opening the gates of a lock before another boat, which was approaching from the opposite direction and was actually closer, could get to it. The bowsman from the other boat, a burly Irishman, stormed up to the lock, indulging, Garfield recalled, "in all the versatility of cursing peculiar to his nationality." But Jim faced him down; the big sixteen-year-old, standing immobile, told him in a few words to give up the lock or get whipped, and the Irishman backed down. Apparently Garfield had some other fights, too; he later told a friend he had learned to box while on the canal. A not terribly well-authenticated story from another canalman has him knocking down an opponent by hurling a driver's heavy blacksnake whip at him.[14] There is Garfield's own recollection of having "to whip a man or two" while on the canal,[15] and he also remembered that he swore until his conversion in 1850.

As to his drinking, the evidence is much more equivocal. Alcohol permeated canal life to an even greater extent than it did the rest of American life. True, there were few spirits carried or drunk on board, but that was because there was no need for them, with a doggery every mile or so. The liquor was cheap, too—some taverns charged three cents for a tumbler of whiskey, and six cents for brandy. In some places the water was questionable; in some, there was nothing to drink but whiskey. Not surprisingly, almost every man who worked on the canals was a whiskey drinker.[16]

Garfield, however, may have found this an easier temptation to resist than others. Eliza had succeeded in achieving the great aim of a decent nineteenth-century American mother—instilling in her son a horror of whiskey. No one in his immediate family drank, and the whole neighborhood, as already noted, was unusually abstemious. Even so, he had probably sampled liquor before, at Fourth of July celebrations or raisings, and had apparently decided that he didn't care for it. All the available evidence suggests that it simply did not appeal to him. Plenty of men he knew on the canal drank hard—for instance Harry Brown, a short, stocky, swaggering fellow of twenty-five or so who may have worked on the *Evening Star* for a time—but Jim did not, at least not regularly.[17]

Sex was a very different matter. Sexual freedom for men on the canal was incomparably greater than it was for boys in Orange. There were no neighbors to worry about; on the contrary, one's companions were men, mostly young and unmarried, all interested in pretty much the same thing. Cleveland, as a major port, had an abundance of brothels, high, middle, and low-class. Most of the latter were quite close to the docks, either in Cleveland or across the river in Ohio City, the small suburb of cottages and shanties which in 1849 found it necessary to pass an ordinance against disorderly houses and "any lewd and lascivious behaviour . . . in any of the streets, lanes, alleys, or public places of said city." Jim's sexual appetites were strong. In short, the opportunity and the desire coincided, and there is reason to suppose Jim did not pass up his chance.[18]

Five years later, looking back on his canal experience from the viewpoint of a committed Christian, Garfield reflected in revealing words, "O! at that time I was ripe for ruin, and an active and will[ing] servant of sin. How fearfully I was rushing with both soul and body to destruction."[19] The whole passage, with its mention of "soul and body," is suggestive, especially since the prostitute had been viewed as the classical road to ruin for young men in Western cultures (although from a broader point of view it was debatable who was ruining whom). But doubtless Jim had misgivings. Like many a young man before and after, he found sex at the center of a moral dilemma, intensified by his puritanical upbringing in a house without a grown man. What he was doing was pleasurable and delightful, as even Proverbs 7.18 conceded (". . . let us take our fill of love until the morning: let us solace ourselves with loves"); it was also disobedient, in a Christian view, and wrong. Perhaps he felt that, every time the *Evening Star* put into Cleveland, he was rushing a little farther headlong down the path as he moved into the reeking streets of the waterfront ("not . . . a very safe place after dark," a Cleveland boy recalled), with its muggings and robberies, its dives, and drunken Indians hanging around the distillery. . . .[20]

There were dangers of other kinds. Late one night, the *Evening Star* was gliding noiselessly down a section of the Crosscut, one of the "slackwater" sections where boats used the river itself rather than a canal. According to one account, it was Breakneck Creek, a few miles east of Akron.[21] Jim was the only man awake on board. Apparently he had occasion to go to the bow to uncoil a line. Somewhere in the darkness, the line caught, and in trying to loosen it, Jim gave a vigorous yank. It suddenly came loose, and he pitched overboard into the murky water. This much was not new to Jim, but what happened next was. He felt for the bottom with his toes, and panicked as he realized that in this part of the canal the bottom was not four feet, but perhaps as much as fifteen or twenty. He suddenly recalled that people did drown in the canal, for many men on it like him could not swim at all.[22] Flailing frantically with his arms, he reached the surface and found, as he blinked the water from his eyes, that he had passed under the boat. Beside him was the stern, slowly receding, with a rope dangling from it. He caught hold of the rope and began to pull himself in—but, to his horror, the rope merely paid out as fast as he pulled on it; evidently it was not secured to anything. He sank below the surface again, throat filled with water, the taste of death in his mouth.

Suddenly, for no apparent reason, the rope tightened and held. Jim found himself above the surface again, several yards behind the *Evening Star*, confused and choking, holding on grimly to the line. His feeble cries brought no response from inside the cabin. Finally, when a little strength came back into his arms, he managed to pull himself up to the boat and struggle over the side. There he sat, wet and shaking, on the tiller deck at the stern. He sat there staring and barely conscious for some time.

After a few moments, things began to come into focus again. He noticed the rope lying across the deck, a thin trickle of water snaking beside it, and was curious to see what it had been attached to. He looked. It was not attached to anything, just a coil of rope lying flat on the deck. What had happened, he saw, was that where the rope went over the side of the boat it had caught in a small crack and had become knotted at that point. Idly, he pulled it loose and threw the same length over the side a few times, just to see what its chances were of catching in the crack again. They did not seem good at all.

He tried dully to attach some meaning to his miraculous escape. "I was in a very impressionable frame of mind naturally," he recalled. That the Lord had saved him because of his own worth he doubted. But there was his mother, whom he had not written for weeks, and who perhaps still believed he was working on the lake—possibly her prayers had prevailed. Or perhaps—he hoped against hope, as he sat shivering—the Lord was saving him for something "greater and better than canaling," something socially and morally respectable.

It would be tidy to relate, as in fact some early biographers did, that this incident made him decide to leave the canal. But the relationship between it and his leaving, if any, was indirect. As he remembered, the midnight miracle was not enough in itself to make him quit; there were too many things about canaling that satisfied him. He did not even trouble to write a letter home.

What forced him off the canal was something more prosaic: malaria. They were approaching Cleveland on the fourth trip back from Beaver (possibly the same trip on which the miraculous escape occurred; there is no way of knowing), when he started experiencing the early symptoms—persistent headaches, aching joints, stomach upsets. These complaints, fairly common in rural Ohio, did not define the disease precisely; but when they docked in Cleveland and he began having the telltale chills, it was obvious what was ailing him. He seems to have been feeling miserable by the time they reached the Eleven-Mile Lock on the next journey out. Here Letcher put him ashore and sent word to Uncle Thomas Garfield that Jim was sick; Uncle Thomas sent his son Charles with a team. Letcher paid off his weak, shaking cousin and promised him his place back when he recovered. Charles and Jim headed for Orange in the wagon.[23]

It was 3 October. Jim had been on the canal just short of seven weeks.

9

Convalescence

Fall–Winter 1848–1849

MALARIA, "fever and ague" to most Ohioans, was one of the best-known diseases of nineteenth-century rural America, in fact, the classic disease of the early frontier.[1] Young doctors, who called it an "intermittent fever," learned to treat it sooner than anything else. The symptoms were unmistakable: first came the headaches, pains in the joints, a feeling of general lassitude. What happened after that had been well described earlier in 1848, in a letter to a Cleveland newspaper:

> In two or three days, and usually about 10 o'clock in the forenoon, there is an exceedingly slight sensation of chilliness stretching across the shoulders. In ten or fifteen minutes the air appears to grow cold, although the heat may be at the highest degree. A fire is kindled, and a great cloak is thrown over the shoulders. Anon the teeth click. The fire is increased, and the sufferer draws nigher. His face and arms may burn, while the chills creep through every vein. Generally, in about twenty minutes after the chill commences that singular phenomenon, the shake, takes place. Every muscle is violently agitated and an universal spasm has seized on the citadel of life. . . .[2]

Teeth clicking, limbs shaking uncontrollably, the victim endured the fit for an hour or so; then it passed, to be succeeded by a burning fever, aching back, painful joints, and copious sweat. After an hour or two of fever, the fit was over and the sufferer returned to normal—for that day. The next day he could expect another attack.

This, the "quotidian" ague, was one form of the disease, the one young Garfield had. Slightly commoner, according to Dr. Daniel Drake, a Cincinnati physician who published a cogent and thorough account of the malady in 1850, was the "tertian" ague, in which the chills and fever struck every other day. There were other varieties, too—the dumb ague, the shaking ague, and so on.[3] Sometimes jaundice, an excess of dark pigment in the skin, the whites of the eyes, or the urine, was an early symptom; in almost all cases it existed to some extent, accounting for the unhealthy, "bilious" complexion of Americans remarked by so many European visitors.[4] As the letter above intimates, too, a common feature of the disease was that it came on every day about the same time; thus housewives on the malaria-ridden Michigan frontier could plan their housework around their morning ague fit. One great consolation was that it was rarely fatal, merely incapacitating. But it could go on and on; some people had had the shakes every day for as long as eighteen months, or even two years. And occasionally, for unknown reasons, people did die of it.

No one knew the cause of the disease in the 1840s.[5] The mosquito was not even remotely suspected. There was general agreement that it came from something in the air, some sort of pestilent vapor; "miasma" was a popular word in this connection. Dampness, too, had something to do with it; the unusually wet year of 1846, following the drought of 1845, had seen an outbreak of fever and ague up and down the Chagrin valley, especially in Bainbridge, where Deacon Hopkins had been charged with maintaining a public nuisance because of the noxious vapors rising from his mill pond. As a general rule, however, highland townships like Orange were less susceptible than the swampy, sickly lands of western Ohio and Michigan. By this reasoning, malaria should have been a scourge of the canals, where, as Dr. Drake observed, boats ran "all night, in summer and autumn . . . , through regions which frequently abound[ed] in marshes"; but, for some reason, canalmen did not seem very liable to the ague. The case of a person who came down from the hills to work on the canal might, however, be different.[6]

This was the ecology of malaria; but how, exactly, did one catch the disease? According to Dr. Drake, there were several possible causes: "irregularities in diet, or a debauch; above all, getting wet and cold, or sleeping exposed to the night air." If he was familiar with this list of causes or anything like it, Jim could doubtless come up with several possibilities in his case: the drenching in Breakneck Creek; "irregularities in diet," of which there had been enough, no doubt; "a debauch. . . ." As he lay sallow-faced and trembling on the cornshuck-filled mattress, shuddering under Eliza's solicitude and wrestling with the sexual guilt that was his lot and that of almost all intelligent boys of his time, he felt that the attack was not merely an incident of canal life, but a divine visitation on his rebelliousness and uncleanness.[7]

The general opinion was that one had to suffer through the ague until he "wore it out," although it was also said that it was apt to disappear with the coming of cold weather. In the meantime, Eliza brought out her home remedies; like any good housewife in the Reserve, she had an ample supply. Almost any household in the area had its cupboard of herbs for minor afflictions. In one early settler's home in Bath, near the canal, the specific for every ailment was boneset tea, brewed from the unattractive white-flowered composite weed, called thoroughwort, that grew on all the roadsides. A mother in Hudson treated her youngsters for fever with cream of tartar and pepper tea. Eliza's own preparation for "cleansing the blood" was cold water poured over the pounded roots of burdock and yellow dock and drunk three or four times a day. The treatments seem peculiar and arbitrary now, but behind most there was a long, patient, well-meaning process of empiricism.[8]

After ten days of his mother's care, the chills and fever suddenly stopped—about the time of first frost in Orange. Garfield intended to get back to the canal, but he still felt weak and let himself be persuaded to spend a few weeks longer at home. It was fortunate that he did, for, although he could not know it, another batch of parasites were developing in his bloodstream and, on 3 November, his chills and fever broke out again with redoubled force.[9]

Within a few days, Dr. Butler of Chagrin Falls walked up to the door of the little red farmhouse, medical paraphernalia in hand. Butler was one of several physicians at the Falls, and one of the younger ones, being barely thirty. Why the Garfields chose him is not clear, but he provides a striking example of the uneven spread of medical knowledge in the nineteenth century.[10]

There were several schools of thought about malaria in the American medical profession. Quinine, "Peruvian bark," as it was once called, had been known in America since the 1780s, though by Garfield's time it was usually administered in the form of quinine sulfate, an extremely bitter white powder. Though medical men could not explain exactly how it worked, it was almost one hundred percent effective in stopping chills and fever. Nevertheless, even to eminent physicians like Dr. Drake, it was only one of several possible treatments for malaria. An older school, popular in America since the eighteenth century, probably because its most prominent exponent had been the noted Philadelphia doctor Benjamin Rush, still had its strong adherents. According to it, malaria and all diseases were products of impurities in the blood, and the first line of defense against them, consequently, was bleeding and laxatives like jalap and calomel. Calomel, or mercurous chloride, had the additional property of promoting a copious flow of saliva; these doctors especially liked it because they felt calomel somehow helped dissolve the "ague-cake," or hardening of the left side, another prominent symptom of malaria. (The "ague-cake" was actually an enlarged spleen, caused by the presence of parasites in the blood, but the doctors did not know this.) This latter school was the one Butler belonged to. He bled his brawny young patient and then began pouring in the calomel.[11]

Throughout November and December, Jim lay in bed fighting off not only the disease but the effects of the medication. "I was given terrible doses," he recalled years later. "Only my powerful constitution ever could have saved me." He drooled continually; a slanted board placed by his bedside helped carry off the excess saliva. Probably he remembered having seen or heard of people who had lost all or most of their teeth after calomel treatment—it was not an uncommon happening on the frontier. He could not read, could not work, but only wait for the ague to loose its grip.[12]

There was an irony in the restless young Garfield's being confined to a sickbed at this time, of all times, during his youth. Early in December, while he lay shivering under the bedclothes, President James K. Polk announced, in his official annual message, the discovery of immense amounts of gold in California, thus providing the footloose or adventurous or discontented young men of the Reserve with a perfect excuse for leaving home. "California fever" swept community after community. In nearby Bedford, five young men formed a California party. Newbury, Akron, Farmington, Warren, even "staid, sober, and phlegmatic Cleveland," felt the excitement, which continued full force through the spring; but by springtime, Garfield's energies had been diverted into a different channel.[13]

In December, after Jim had suffered several weeks of Butler's medicine with no effect, the Garfields did what any family of the period would have done—they began "doctoring" with someone else. The new doctor was the best in Chagrin Falls, as he would have told you himself: J. H. Vincent, a portly, fair-complexioned, balding New Yorker who dabbled in local politics on the side. What he prescribed is not recorded; it may have been quinine, for just after the New Year Jim's chills and fever stopped, this time, as it turned out, for good. Jim was weak and exhausted from his ordeal. He had lost weight. Worse, he had had to spend all his canal earnings on doctor's fees and medicines. But at least he was at home, in his mother's care, with a good chance of total recovery.[14]

For a few weeks, his life consisted of nothing but resting, sleeping, and eating, getting reacquainted with the winter fare on the farm. The Garfields probably ate about the same food as any other Reserve farm family—certainly no better than the average, maybe worse. For them, winter was a time of salt rations and cellar vegetables, relieved every now and then by some fresh meat. Since midwinter was the usual time for butchering, there would be blood pudding, fresh sausage, hash, and other meat dishes at times. When these were exhausted, however, the salt pork barrel became, as one old settler expressed it, the "constant reliance" of households in the rural Reserve. On the pewter or blue china plate at most meals there was apt to be either hash or sausage (at breakfast) or boiled salt pork (at other times).[15]

Some families supplemented their table with game. In the early days of Orange and neighbouring townships, venison and wild turkey had been common dishes. But this expedient, with the exception of the wild pigeons in fall and spring, was no longer easy to come by in Orange by the 1840s. The deer had all but disappeared from the woods; one hears no more mention of wild turkey. There was a certain stigma attached to eating raccoon or woodchuck, apparently because people felt that a decent farmer should be able to raise enough food for his family without having to resort to such meat. Moreover, Thomas seems not to have cared for hunting, and Jim was laid up; probably the Garfields ate no game this season.[16]

Meat was not the only item at their meals, or even the main one. The potatoes dug in the fall were a constant part of daily fare—nearly always boiled, not baked, mashed, or fried. (Housewives of the Reserve, in the true Yankee tradition, boiled everything.) Then there were turnips, boiled or mashed, carrots, beets, any root vegetable that kept well, but all increasingly rubbery and tasteless as winter wore on.[17]

After meat and potatoes, the third staple of diet was corn—not sweet corn or corn on the cob, which was unknown then, but dried corn, prepared either as johnnycake (baked corn meal, milk, and eggs) or as mush (boiled corn meal). Mush was sometimes refried, buttered, and served as a supper dish with milk and molasses or maple syrup. Another form was hulled corn, now called hominy: corn kernels boiled in weak lye until the outer covering popped off as the kernels swelled, then drained, boiled again, and served with milk, or butter and salt. Of the three staples, corn was probably the most vital; rare indeed was a day when it did not appear on the plate in one shape or another. One gets the impression that the poorer a Reserve family was, the more it relied on corn for its sustenance.[18]

All these food items could be grown (or, with luck, shot) on the farmer's own land. The only big exception to self-sufficiency made by farm families was in the area of beverages. They drank milk, buttermilk, and water, true—but the preferred drink with meals was either tea or coffee, purchased at the nearest general store. Here again, American tastes were in flux during the 1840s; tea, especially green tea, the favorite beverage of rural Americans for generations, was giving way to coffee. The Garfields drank both, but seem to have preferred tea, which they bought at Chagrin Falls or Bentleyville. They also bought sugar—brown sugar, most likely, since white sugar was a luxury used only for icing cakes and the like. Neither kind was packaged, of course; a quantity was sliced off a loaf of sugar, weighed, and wrapped in brown paper to be taken home.[19]

Almost everything else eaten or drunk on the farm, however, came from the land. Summer brought an enlarged and varied diet, with garden greens, called "victuals,"[20] usually boiled with a piece of salt pork or corned beef and served hot or cold, young fowl, fresh fruits, and, most popular of all, tomatoes.[21] And all year round there was the most savory feature of a Reserve meal: the home-baked bread, wheat, rye, or "rye-and-injun" (mixed rye and corn), served with fresh butter and one or more of the delicious conserves put up by farm women—apple butter, maple syrup, wild berry preserves, strawberry jam, crabapple or plum preserves.[22]

With all its splendors and shortcomings, what the Garfields ate was good plain farm food, probably a rather sharp contrast to what Jim had been having on the canal. There the stress in food preparation was on convenience and quickness, rather than economy. A lot of his diet, probably, had been the popular snacks on the time, easily available in waterfront groceries: crackers and cheese, pickles, dried fish, sausage, fresh fruit. Cooking on board was probably confined to a few easy dishes like buckwheat pancakes, popular in the Reserve, and boiled potatoes with corned beef. In places like Cleveland and Pittsburgh, and possibly Akron, he had had an opportunity to sample imported items that probably got to the Falls rarely, if at all—oranges, coconuts, apricots. As for beverages, a non-drinker on the canal had a limited choice indeed; James must have drunk water or hot coffee to the extent that he could not tolerate beer, ale, whiskey, or gin.[23]

As he recovered slowly from the ague, Eliza was shocked to find that the illness had not convinced him of his folly in going on the canal; on the contrary, he was bent on getting back as soon as possible—not at once, for it was January and all navigation was at a standstill, but in spring. He meant to either return to his berth on the *Evening Star* or try again for a job on the lake. The bustling, sharp-faced little woman probably did not understand the appeal canal life held for her son, but she saw that it was strong, stronger perhaps than she had guessed, and that it would take a really extraordinary effort to overcome it. She did not confront James directly. That was not Eliza's way of handling things. Instead, she prayed fervently and looked for a way to challenge the canal's hold on him. As it happened, luck—or providence—had already begun to supply one.[24]

In contrast to last winter's brouhaha, the district school this year was having a successful session. The teacher was a young student from Geauga Seminary in Chester, named Samuel Bates. Twenty years old, small in stature but enthusiastic in spirit, he was from a rural township like Orange—Hartford, in Trumbull County—bursting with the new knowledge he had acquired at the academy and eager to pass it on.[25]

In addition to the regular reading-and-ciphering curriculum, Bates scheduled extra classes, among them a class in arithmetic, for students too advanced to profit from the regular course, that met at eight every morning in the schoolhouse. There were about fifteen boys and young men in the class, including several friends of Jim's. During December, while Jim was still racked with daily chills and fever, he heard from a friend in the class—Orrin Judd or one of the Boynton boys—that it was good. His chills regularly came on late in the morning, so around eight he was pretty comfortable; in fact, it was his best time of day. He decided to try attending.

Bates remembered vividly, with just a hint of the small man's nervousness, the first time the tall, gaunt Garfield boy, "haggard and forbidding" in appearance, entered his class. He was, Bates recalled, "pale and sallow in countenance, and . . . largely uncultivated in manner." Perhaps the teacher exaggerated slightly; but Garfield's stint on the canal had probably coarsened his manners, which had not been polished to begin with. Moreover, Jim's reputation as a bright troublemaker had no doubt preceded him to some extent. But Bates soon found, like every other teacher of Garfield's, that appearances were misleading; despite his illness, the ex-canal hand was quicker than anyone else in the class. The only problem was that his health really did not allow him to attend regularly; after six days of trying, he gave up and stayed home. But Bates's interest had been aroused.[26]

The little teacher was not only an enthusiast for education in general, but also for his own school, Geauga Seminary, in particular. As he "boarded round" the district that winter, as the custom was, spending several days at a time in each household, he painted a glowing picture of Geauga and urged his students to attend it if they could. He particularly urged Jim to consider the school and even offered to give him private tutoring in arithmetic free to bring his knowledge up to the level of an academy.[27]

Here was Eliza's chance—if she could manage to solve the vexing problem of money.[28] Even in this respect, she learned, the academy at Chester presented less of a problem than many other institutions. It was, one resident claimed, "the cheapest place in the country to get an education." Tuition for a twelve-week term was three dollars for the "common English branches." For fifty cents more one could get instruction in "natural philosophy," for another fifty, Latin and mathematics. Board at the school was seven shillings—eighty-seven and a half cents—per week, but one could board for even less by renting a room and doing his own cooking. (Rent was six cents a week.) It all added up to about sixteen dollars a quarter, not counting books and paper, pens and candles, and other school materials—still a steep sum for a family like the Garfields, who lived on what they raised and sold almost no produce. Eliza and Thomas had small amounts of cash stashed away, however, and by retrenching and planning to do without, they figured that by March, when the spring term began, they could scrape together seventeen dollars.[29]

Getting the money together, however, was only half solving the problem. The other half was convincing the intended student. When Eliza broached Geauga Seminary to her son in a way that let him see what she was getting at (in the kitchen, perhaps, after a meal, Eliza clattering dishes in the dishpan, Jim, tall and wan, listening at the door), she ran into a peculiar reaction. On the one hand, he wanted to go; serious study was what he had always enjoyed. On the other, he savored the free life of the canal and was looking forward this year to realizing his dream of going on the lake. A third reaction, not specifically mentioned in the sources, but not hard to infer from them, may have been the most important of all: he was scared of going to Chester, scared that he might not measure up, that he would waste his family's money and embarrass himself before strangers. He may even have feared that his canal experience had forever incapacitated him for anything higher.[30]

What he needed, clearly, was reassurance, and Eliza sought to provide some by getting two or three other neighborhood boys to go with him to Chester. Their presence would make the whole venture seem more of a lark—and if the work was hard, they could give each other moral support.

Again her idea dovetailed with the plans of Bates, who had already been urging Chester on all his promising students. Together they canvassed Jim's close friends. Orrin Judd was no problem—he was all ready to go. With the Boyntons there was more difficulty. Uncle Amos was convinced that a good command of writing and ciphering, in other words, a district school education, was all a youth needed to be a good farmer, and that any learning beyond that, except the Bible, was unnecessary and possibly harmful. In feeling this way, he was not alone. Excessive reading, in the common opinion of the Reserve, was often either a sign or a cause of mental illness, so that a conscientious father might hesitate to urge study on his son. But Eliza worked on her sister, plump, placid Aunt Alpha, who in turn worked on Uncle Amos, and gradually they persuaded him to make an exception. Henry and William, he decided, could go to Geauga Seminary—but not both at the same time; they would alternate terms. And both would have to pay their own way.[31]

Exactly when and in what order all these pieces fell into place is not clear from the memories of those involved. But when they were all in place, Eliza made her second, more diplomatic approach to her son. James, her argument ran, you are still too weak to go back to boating. The money is available; why not go to Chester until you get your strength back? Two terms at an academy will qualify you to teach school; then you can work on the lake in summer, if you like, and teach in winter. Besides, the mathematics you learn at the academy will help you in navigation. Put this way, the appeal worked. "I really did not feel well," Garfield remembered, "and the suggestion seemed to be just." To his mother's relief, he agreed to go. At once he, Orrin, and William Boynton began making plans for their debut at Chester; the term began 6 March, and there was a lot to be arranged.[32]

At this point, however, one ought to take a last backward look at the whole seven-week-long canal episode. Because of its brevity, most modern biographers have considered it as simply a boyish escapade, colorful but insignificant—in the words of one, "a boyhood rebellion that made no economic sense."[33] Another look, however, makes one doubt that judgment.

At the time he went on the canal, Garfield's life was at an utter standstill; without the money to give his talents the scope they needed, he was sinking, and knew he was sinking, into a pattern of life he detested, in a community that regarded him as a spoiled misfit. Seven months later, his mother and brother were making great personal sacrifices to give him the education he knew he deserved, sacrifices they had not been willing to make before. This is not to say, of course, that Garfield's going on the canal was just psychological blackmail of his family, a way of dramatizing the possibilities of ruining himself so that they would cough up the funds needed for his education. There were many other desires and satisfactions involved. But consciously or unconsciously, he had chosen his gesture well. Had he stayed on the lake or the canal, Garfield would have assuaged his ego with rich draughts of masculine freedom and adventure (as he was later to do, in fact, in the Civil War); by coming home, he gave Thomas and Eliza a last chance to do right by him, to help him develop the talents they had taught him to esteem. Either way he could break the deadlock in his life, and either way achieve something he badly wanted.

Perhaps the real meaning of the canal episode is: once again, when it counted, Jimmy got his way.

10

A Fresh Start

Spring–Summer 1849

BEFORE daylight on the morning of 6 March, Henry Boynton hitched up the team. It felt very much as if they were going to the Cleveland market, though the distance to Chester was shorter, only ten or twelve miles; but there was an extra air of nervousness, of anticipation. William heaved in a couple of mat-

Geauga Seminary. By the 1870s, when this photograph was made, the cupola, the gravel walk, and the picket fence were things of the past.

tresses, the trunk containing his clothes, and some other provisions. The brothers lifted in an old cookstove, intended for the room at Chester. Uncle Amos, Aunt Alpha, and the girls were out to see them off, though probably without any kissing or embracing—public displays of affection were rare in the Reserve.[1] They crossed the road and picked up the trunk belonging to James. (He had been "Jim" in his neighborhood and on the canal; he was going to be "James" in his new identity.)[2] Maybe Orrin and his trunk were there, too; if not, James and the Boyntons drove a mile and a half down the road and repeated the farewell scene at the Judds'. Then they turned the horses' heads to the east, descended the steep hill to the river, sloshed across the shallow Chagrin, passed Bentley's store, rode across the west hill into Chagrin Falls and out the north road into the forested hills of Russell Township.

As the day advanced and they crept northward, it began to seem like a trip to the market in another way; other wagons joined them on the road, churning up the late winter mud, all headed for Chester. An hour more, and they saw it: a settlement of ten or fifteen houses and a store, about the size of Solon Center but probably neater and less rude—Chester, after all, had been settled almost a generation before the Chagrin valley towns. Plainly visible on the east side of the road was the Geauga Seminary building, a massive, rectangular, three-story wooden structure much like the hotels along the canal, with a little square cupola on top, and a confusion of teams, wagons, and people milling about in the road in front of it.[3] James and his companions drew up amid the crowd. The three who would be going to school there went in and paid their fees. They were lucky enough to hear of a cheap room, upstairs in an old, unpainted frame house just across the road from the Seminary, and went to engage it. The lady who lived downstairs, a widow named Reed, contracted to do their cooking and washing for an agreeably small sum. With everything settled, they unloaded their belongings and hauled the stove upstairs. Henry headed back home.[4]

As soon as they had a chance, the boys from Orange went over to the seminary building to look around. It was surrounded by a picket fence in the New England manner; a gravel walk led to the main entrance. Inside was a library containing more books than they had ever seen at one time—about a hundred and fifty, including some printed in strange characters which they later found to be Greek. There was a big room, the chapel, with a lectern and rows of benches, and several smaller classrooms on the first and second floors.[5] On the third floor were two halls, two parlors, and sixteen tiny bedrooms into which fifty-odd students were shoehorned (one hall for male students, the other for females) under the alert eyes of a resident adult couple who must have lived on the second floor. Usually thirty or more students besides these boarded at homes in the vicinity, so that, in any term, the total number enrolled at Geauga was a little under one hundred.[6]

The students, as in most American academies, were a mixed batch. The male students, a majority, ranged all the way from their early teens to their late twenties. The reason was that most came from farms where their labor was more valuable than their education; school was a thing to be squeezed in after the necessities of working on the farm and making a living had been taken care of. Thus it was not uncommon for a young man to attend academy one term, work on the farm the next, and then work at some other job to make money so that he could return to the academy. The process could easily stretch out into a man's middle twenties. There was less variability in the ages of the female students, most of whom were between sixteen and twenty-two. They, like the young men, came mainly from the nearby country townships, although there was a sprinkling of students from faraway places like Iowa, New York, and New England.[7]

By the standards of the Reserve, Geauga was a very ordinary academy, in no way outstanding. "From what I can learn of that school it ant[*sic*] much," a young lady that same spring wrote to a friend of hers who was thinking of studying at Chester.[8] Alumni who went on to other schools often looked back with surprise at how little they had learned there.[9] Like much in Ohio in those years, it was new and ephemeral—only seven years old, and destined to last only three years more. The academy building had been up only five years. Like many academies, Geauga was under the sponsorship of a particular religious denomination, in this case the Freewill Baptists, a small sect strong principally in northern New England and in regions settled from there. Its faculty of four or five included at least one Freewill Baptist elder, and it attracted students like Samuel Bates who thought of going into the Baptist ministry.[10]

But whatever its shortcomings, the academy at Chester meant a great deal both intellectually and socially to the young women and men who came there from their farm homes. It offered not only a basic classical education but also an introduction to respectable living. Students there were addressed, and often addressed one another, as "Mr." and "Miss." They wore Sunday rather than work clothes. They had a chance at such genteel amusements as studying French or going for excursions to enjoy nature—though not, of course, dancing or social drinking, both of which were forbidden at Geauga as at all other academies. Only a few weeks after entering, James sent home in some urgency for the rest of his "respectable" wardrobe—neck handkerchiefs, and a pair of casimere pants. The account book of one male Geauga student shows expenditures for "hair oil" and "Italian soap," items scarcely conceivable for many Reserve farm boys.[11]

James was crossing the treeless seminary grounds one day shortly after his arrival when he was accosted by another student, a stranger as he thought. But then he recognized the dark-haired young man he had last seen on the canal dock at Newport. "I suppose you are one of the b'hoys," he said to

James under his breath. ("B'hoys" was a slang term for rowdy young males.) "Glad to see you. I've spent many a jolly night with canal boys—but a fellow must be mighty pious here if he wants to get into the good graces of Mother Branch." James could not recall having replied anything, perhaps out of surprise. The other boy, he realized, was in an algebra class with him. His name was Albert S. Hall; he was handsome, short but a dapper dresser, and one of the brightest students in the school. His words, and still more his presence, brought home to James the unsettling thought that the respectability he and the others were acquiring at Chester was no more than a veneer; it did not necessarily imply any real change of life. One could not help wondering whether piety and propriety were just a charade in which he and the other male students (at least) were participating.[12]

Fortunately for James's peace of mind, his main interest at Geauga was not social, not that term; rather, he was indulging the intellectual faculties that had been in abeyance for a year or more, reveling in the simple fact of contact with intellectual things. His grammar class, which met when the ten o'clock bell clanged every morning, was a challenge. The teacher was a crusty old woman named Branch, the principal's wife and the "Mother Branch" to whom Albert Hall had referred. She had, it is said, invented her own grammatical system in which "and" was a verb meaning "add" and "but" another verb, meaning "be out." James reacted vocally; in the same letter in which he requested clothes from home, he also sent for his Kirkham's *Grammar*, which he knew almost by heart. From the day he got it, grammar class turned into a running battle between Mrs. Branch and her brightest student.[13] Algebra, on the other hand, was a complete novelty to him; he had only seen one algebra book in his life. But from the time on 14 March when he, as he noted in his diary, began "to see into Algebra," he found the subject more and more fascinating, and looked forward to his 2:00 P.M. class. First Orrin, then William, found the work too hard and dropped out; James stuck with it, making continual progress.[14]

His last class of the day, at three, was natural science (called "natural philosophy" or simply "philosophy"), taught, as it happened, by Daniel Morse's prospective son-in-law, Silas Bigelow, who was finally to marry Zeruiah that summer. James, however, bore Bigelow no grudge for his part in the "servant" incident; as always, he was deferential to his teacher if he liked the subject matter. And what a subject matter it was! The 1840s were an exciting time in science, crammed with new ideas. The science of geology, the idea that earth's history could be read from the composition of its rocks, had aroused wide public interest; to a lad in the Chagrin valley, where even a casual walk could reveal a textbook combination of local strata, it carried instantaneous conviction. In physics, there were the electrical and magnetic forces explored recently by investigators like Volta and Faraday, and utilized in Morse's telegraph, the sensation of the day; no one was quite sure what they were or how they worked. Speculation about extinct animals was puzzling the world of learning, as scholars collected fossils and tried to reconcile the bones and the strata in which they occurred with the pattern of Bible history. How much Bigelow alluded to these topics is unknown, but James found the class enthralling. A fellow student remembered him "sitting at one end of a bench with one foot up and his hands clasped around his knee" as Bigelow explained how water kept its own level, "and suddenly remarking, to the amusement of the other scholars, 'Why, that's why the water doesn't run out the spout of a kettle.'" As always with Garfield, the class was a direct encounter between him and the material—the existence of the other students was peripheral.[15]

Some of the other students in the class illustrate the diversity of types one found at an academy in the Reserve. Twenty-one-year-old Zebulon Sorter, an alert Yankee with a nasal, twangy voice, alternated study at Geauga with clerking at a store in the neighboring township of Mayfield. He was a good student. So was Lucretia Rudolph, a petite, demure, dark-haired seventeen-year-old from Portage County. Then there was John Hodge, twenty years old, sociable and quick-witted, who had returned from the Mexican War only the year before and walked with a cane because of a war injury.[16]

But unquestionably the most unusual student in the class was Garfield himself. Miss Rudolph remembered his "odd remarks" and the fact that the whole class had him "singled out for a prodigy," a sort of rustic wonder. Hodge noticed his clothes, cut evidently "without regard to any particular style; he wore a soft felt hat, and his boots were of coarse and heavy make." But he added that everyone, both classmates and teachers, liked him.[17]

James's scholastic prowess received a severe test this term. Around the beginning of May, halfway through the term, he began feeling sick and unable to study. Orrin took him home to Orange on 7 May, probably borrowing the horse and wagon of their landlady, Widow Reed, who was accommodating in such matters. His illness was apparently not a recurrence of malaria, but something like a severe migraine attack—a "gathering" in the head, he called it. Whatever it was exactly, it knocked him flat for over a week, and left him so feeble that he stayed in Orange, under Eliza's ministrations, for another two weeks. It was not until 28 May that he felt able to ride back to Chester with Newel Judd and William. Despite his absence, however, he was able to resume his work and seems to have had no difficulty completing any of his classes, even the algebra that had given William and Orrin such difficulty.[18]

Geauga, like district school, had regular weekly declamations. Every Saturday, after the regular morning chapel service, students remained in the chapel and read original compositions or declaimed pieces. This was familiar and enjoyable ground to James. His first assignment was a letter; after that, he churned out a composition every week, typically a short inspirational piece in the high-flown language fashionable at the time. There was also a debating society, the Zetelethian, which met in the chapel one night a week. He joined it at the beginning of the term and attended meetings regularly, but does not seem to have spoken much—possibly from diffidence, possibly from a feeling that other debaters would sneer at his rustic manners, country clothes, and canal-driving past. When the Zetelethian split into two societies, late in March, he went with the new one, the Sophomethean.[19]

There were other attractions besides debating. Geauga had a full-time music teacher, a Mr. Wellman, whose singing schools James attended faithfully and with great enjoyment. Toward the end of the term, Wellman organized the students into a Glee Club to sing at the July exhibition at the close of school, and James was an enthusiastic participant. There was also a class that met one night a week to study phonography—shorthand, invented by Isaac Pitman, which had reached the United States in 1844 and was becoming a craze among young people, who saw it as a faster, more rational way of writing English.[20] In May and June, as the weather got better, the school organized or permitted excursions to other schools or nearby beauty spots where students could admire nature and learn to write about it in a tastefully rhetorical vein. ("Cloudless dawned the morning of May 19, 1849," began one of Miss Rudolph's compositions, "and when Phoebus from behind the curtained east, came forth clad in all his glory, and commenced his daily circuit through the azure deep, radiant with joy were our many faces in the anticipation of that day.") Usually students on these occasions were paired off, one young lady to one young gentleman, and behavior was always decorous, although the excursion might last until after dark. An excursion of "five couple of students" to Kirtland Seminary, in the next township to the north, did not return until 11:00 P.M.; next day James, who had been on it, fell asleep in philosophy class.[21]

Finally, for James, there were the experiences inseparable from being off at school, getting used to living in a new place: the time his bed fell in; the time he and William and Orrin heard a cry of "Fire, Fire" outside, and William dashed downstairs and seized the milk pail, not knowing there was milk in it, and dipped it in the rain trough, only to find it was a false alarm. But it was the intellectual experiences he treasured most. Several times that term, he wrote in his diary "Fine times" or "Happy times." As examinations approached, he wrote in what was for him an unwonted burst of emotion, "Feel very lonesome, the prospect of parting is very unpleasant."[22]

At most academies—and Geauga was no exception—it was customary to end the spring term with a certain amount of fanfare, in the form of a student exhibition for the parents and patrons. It usually took place a day or so after the oral examinations which concluded each course. A stage was put up in a grove of trees convenient to the academy and shaded from the July sun, festooned with wreaths and garlands of roses, and there for a whole day the audience sat in its Sunday best, listening to two dozen orations from the best student speakers, male and female, plus musical numbers from the Glee Club and occasional "colloquies," quasi-dramatic presentations in which several students spoke. The crowd brought lunch from home and usually purchased lemonade or sweets on the spot. It was, like most home-grown Reserve productions, a mixture of instruction, entertainment, and uplift.[23]

The exhibition this year was typical. James, with his experience in carpentry, was asked to help in building the stage. The ladies were excused from classes to practice an elaborate colloquy on foreign missions. It was an entire success. The Glee Club sang its numbers, and there were ten orations from the gentlemen, including one on "Our Country's Institutions and Our Duty" from Albert Hall, who had recently begun squiring Miss Rudolph around; other pieces on "The Triumph of Moral Truth," "Common Schools," and "Achievements of Mind"; and a closing salvo from James's former teacher, now classmate, Samuel Bates, on "True Heroism." Then it was all over. James, let down and lonesome, went home to Orange with William and Orrin.[24]

The academy would reopen in a month, and James was determined to get back to the atmosphere he had found so stimulating. In the meantime, however, there was the tricky question of money. Eliza and Thomas could hardly be expected to scrape up another seventeen dollars for his next term; he would have to pay his own way, at least most of it. He was able-bodied now, and had marketable skills. In other words, he had seventeen dollars to earn, and less than a month to do it in. (Of course, as Eliza had pointed out to him, he could obtain over half the money he needed just by selling his rifle, which would bring ten dollars; but he was not yet ready to make that kind of break with the past.)[25]

Carpentry seemed like his best expedient. An average carpenter's hand could earn seventy-five cents a day.[26] Returning to Orange, James found a farmer in his vicinity planning to put up a barn and hired out to him; the day after the exhibition, he was out in the field with his few tools, shaping tenons and joints and pegs for the frame. When that job was done, he found similar work with Zenas Smith, again on a farm outbuilding. It was dull, hot, and often lonesome work. That summer was unusually humid. One day he got off to help Uncle Amos's hands in the hay field for a day, and announced his feelings at day's end in a single word: "Bushed." Except for a few rainy days spent at the Judds' and a few Sundays, sometimes spent at meeting, sometimes at home, that July was mainly work.[27]

Toward the end of the month, apparently concerned that he was not accumulating money fast enough, he left off carpentering and went back into manual labor, where the money was at harvest time. He was now so big and strong that there was no question of his getting less than a man's wages. For most of a week he worked in harvest for a Twinsburg farmer, at a dollar a day, swinging his cradle in steady unison with the other harvesters, drinking cider or honey-and-water from the jug provided for them, the ignorance and profanity of the laborers reminding him by contrast of the refinement and knowledge of Chester. Then he sprained his ankle and had to be carried home. Despite that mishap, he had earned nearly fifteen dollars in a month, if he worked at the going rate on all his jobs.[28]

This hard-earned money went frighteningly fast. Doctors Butler and Vincent had been dunning his mother for the rest of their fees; of course he had to help her out.[29] Then there was the matter of clothes. James's respectable wardrobe had worn very thin; perhaps, too, he wanted something just a little less conspicuous than the shapeless garments John Hodge had commented on. In any case, he had to have something, and on 4 August he and Amos Smith went to Cleveland (Superior Street jammed with wagons; half a dozen near-accidents from careless drivers or pedestrians or runaway teams; tantalizing glimpses of the lake) and he did the necessary shopping, choosing as frugally as he could. There can hardly have been enough money left to cover his tuition and board; he must either have borrowed from Eliza and Thomas again, although it is difficult to see where *they* got the money, or have agreed to pay the academy somehow in installments. One way and another, he was sliding into debt. The life of study was proving expensive.[30]

But it was also joyous. On 8 August, the day after he got back to Chester, paid his fees, and rented a room, he found himself at morning chapel service with his friends and with only six cents left in his pocket. It didn't matter; he was glad to be back. Light-heartedly he threw his six cents into the collection plate for luck, and that night he confided to his diary, "Welcome the day."[31]

11

The Lure of Respectability

Fall 1849

BY August of 1849, Eliza Garfield had every reason to congratulate herself. Her plans for James were unfolding just as she had hoped. He had become so interested in his studies at Chester that he was willing to work long hours at laborious jobs just to go back. To be sure, he still talked and thought of going to sea eventually, but that idea had receded into the background for the moment.[1]

One problem remained, however, potentially serious enough to wreck all her hopes for her youngest son. She must have perceived it, although the sources make no mention of the fact. It was that James was attending Geauga merely because he loved studying, and for no more solid reason. There was nothing beyond enjoyment to hold him there. Given some difficulty with his studies or some new enthusiasm, there was no assurance that he would not be back on the canal next year, or gone to sea, or in California. He still had no long-term purpose in life except to be a sailor.

Attending classes at a seminary of learning, one senses, was respectable, but only provisionally so. One was doing respectable things: wearing broadcloth, singing hymns, writing something more than farm or business accounts. There was no assurance, however, that this behavior would pay off in the form of permanently improved social status. It might, or it might not. A student who was lazy or irresponsible, or simply untalented, might have to leave school, with no useful skills acquired, and go back to working with his hands. Awareness of this possibility was probably the reason why Reserve farmers were cynical about prolonged study, and often thought of it as a dodge to avoid the real challenge of making a living. One can be fairly sure that some of the Garfields' neighbors were still unconvinced that James would ever amount to more than a casual laborer.[2]

How James saw his own situation is problematical. To all appearances, he was having a marvelous time, blithely unaware that his life lacked direction. But this term at Chester there began to be hints in his behavior that, too, was vaguely uneasy, looking half-consciously for some formula, some principle, some activity to organize his life.

His first obligation, making sure he would have enough money to get through the term, turned out to be unexpectedly simple. The new landlord, Heman Woodworth, from whom he and Orrin were renting a room (neither of the Boyntons was able to attend this term) was a carpenter who needed a couple of hands to plane siding for a building he was putting up. James and another student with some experience in the trade, a fellow his own age from upstate New York named Harvey Everest, took the job for seventy-five cents per hundred boards. By working Saturday afternoons, he figured that he could earn five or six dollars by the time the term was over—"which will help some," he wrote Eliza and Thomas.[3]

On returning to the school, James may have been surprised at the changes one month had wrought. Mr. and Mrs. Branch had left during the summer; so had Mrs. Coffin, his algebra teacher, and her husband. Their places had been taken by several new teachers, one of whom was now temporarily in charge of the seminary until a principal could be found. (One constant at Geauga during the whole time Garfield attended was the extreme difficulty the school had, for reasons now hard to reconstruct, in holding on to faculty.)[4] Fortunately, the changes seemed unlikely to affect him. He was taking the most basic courses that fall—grammar, algebra, and geography, of which only algebra promised to be at all challenging. What really interested him that term was not classwork but rhetoric in general—the skill of speaking so as to influence his hearers and convey a wealth of ideas.[5]

The very day he began classes again something seems to have clicked. From 8 August on, his diary entries become longer and begin to express ideas as well as record events. It becomes evident that young Garfield was bursting with opinions. No doubt he had been for most of his adolescence, but now he was beginning to think them worth setting down. His one term's dose of knowledge had given him self-confidence, had made him feel at home in an academy. Now he was ready to criticize as well as to admire and learn.[6]

Public speaking became a passion with James that fall. He took to attending meeting regularly, both morning and evening services on Sunday, not so much to worship as to critique the sermons, which were often delivered by teachers from the seminary, preaching from the pulpit of the Chester Freewill Baptist Church. The first Sunday morning in the term, the speaker was his geography teacher, a young man named Ames, who preached on foreign missions. "He spoke very well," James noted. At evening service, another of the new faculty, John B. Beach, spoke on Job, suggesting that that Old Testament personage was an Arab. "Idea strikes me very favorabl[y]," James commented briefly. There were other sermons he liked during the term—a "good sermon" on Jacob and Esau by a Mr. Nicols, another by Ames on a text from Proverbs.[7]

On the other hand, sermons by Elder George Ball, who taught moral philosophy at the Seminary, nearly always managed to stir up James's critical faculties. When Ball read a sermon at the evening service on 19 August, James listed in his diary reasons why this practice was "a useless habit"—"First, the audience gets tired of hearing that sameness of voice unaccompanied by gesture and their interest relaxes, and it becomes a sure and unerring guide to 'Morpheus.'" (James was, in fact, prone to doze off when he had to listen to something that did not engage his attention.) "Second, it is a studied style and not so easily understood as tho it was spoken extempore." What young Garfield liked about oratory was precisely the dramatic gesture, the intensity, the natural flow of eloquence that extempore speaking offered—a predictable preference in an era of performers like Daniel Webster, Theodore Parker, and Thomas Hart Benton.[8]

But other efforts of Ball's, presumably extempore, met no better reception from James. On 2 September Ball preached on conscience, asserting that a man's conscience would never allow him to do wrong. "But that I consider a flimsy theory," remarked James realistically, perhaps harking back to some of his own experiences. When Ball preached on war, according to James, he "took Ultra ground, and said that there was never a difficulty settled by war." (Ball was perhaps a follower of the American Peace Society, an antiwar movement that won its greatest support from New England.) "I am not decided on that," was James's comment.[9]

The eager young man from Orange did not stop with sermons; he attended other lectures—an "astronomical lecture" where he had "a very interesting time" and picked up some new ideas, and a lecture by one Elder Holmes which elicited a judgment similar to his remark on Ball's: "Good sentiment but I don't like to hear a man read his discourse. There is too much formality about it." He also followed to some extent what contemporary orators were doing, noting 1 October, for example, that the "Immortal" (so he called him) Elihu Burritt, leader of the American peace movement, was "thundering forth the principles of peace" at the Second International Peace Congress in Paris. (It was probably this event that had prompted Ball's sermon on war.)[10]

James naturally wished to do a little "thundering forth" himself, with all the proper gestures and eloquence, and his desire to speak overcame his hesitancy about speaking before the debating societies. There were still two of them, and by the middle of the term he was attending both, wading into weekly debate on a variety of questions. Would the exclusion of foreign articles to encourage home manufacture be conducive to public wealth? Are the causes which strengthen greater than those which tend to dissolve the American Union? Ought secret societies to be tolerated? Are the Negroes naturally inferior to the whites? (The result of this last debate, decided by the Sophomethean in the affirmative, so enraged one student that he resigned and stalked out, an exciting event which James duly recorded.[11] The verdict that blacks were inferior, however, was probably a pretty faithful reflection of majority sentiment in the Reserve.)[12] James spoke in nearly all these debates;

in fact, he became so engrossed that Mr. Beach, the acting principal, had to lecture him about his excessive involvement (though it is not clear from the diary whether this lecture was for a number of students or for James alone).[13]

James's fascination with oratory inevitably raised the question of whether he ought to aim higher in his career. There was certainly little room for public speaking in the life of a sailor or laborer. It was around this time, too, as Garfield later remembered, that he first heard from a faculty member—possibly Mr. Beach, who seems to have taken a certain interest in him—that it was possible for a young man from a poor background like his own to go on to college, if he studied diligently. At college there would be plenty of debating and a wealth of interesting ideas. But the notion may have perplexed James as much as it excited him. A boy could not go on to college simply for the pleasure of cultivating his mind—at least a poor boy could not. Yet he still had no clear idea of a career.[14]

Related to this prospect was another question that was very much in James's thoughts that fall. Intellectually, perhaps, he was up to the demands of a college course, but socially, he was beginning to realize, he was (in his later words) an "overgrown, uncombed, unwashed boy," with no idea how to act in the company of respectable people. Mr. Beach, in the same talk he had with James about debating, had also taken him to task about his eating habits—justly, James thought. His appetites were too strong; he enjoyed food and dug into it with a gusto that matched his size. But if he really aspired to higher things, he had to learn to moderate these appetities.[15]

The appetite that really worried James, however, was not hunger, but sex. The beginning of October found him poring over a bunch of books borrowed from the seminary library, all of them advice to ambitious young men about how to rid themselves of various bad habits. They included all the most popular standard works, like Henry Ward Beecher's *Seven Lectures to Young Men* (Beecher's first best seller) and the Reverend John Todd's *The Young Man.* The one that really riveted his attention, however, was Orson S. Fowler's *Amativeness: Embracing the Evils and Remedies of Excessive and Perverted Sexuality, Including Warning and Advice to the Married and Single*, a tract against masturbation, of which James wished there were "ten thousand copies . . . in every town in the United States." This, clearly, was the area in which he thought his greatest challenge lay.[16]

There had been a horror of masturbation among leading American doctors and divines for almost a century, and a corresponding sense of panic about it among young American males who aspired to gentility. The practice was almost universal and, it seemed, almost universally disapproved. Condemnation of it was linked, historians have persuasively argued, with the rise of the middle class and its vision of the strong, self-sufficient man who controlled all his desires in order to get ahead in the world. Wasting one's energies in sexual activity of any kind was questionable, according to this view; wasting them by the altogether accessible and trivial route of masturbation was not only criminal, but sinful. Masturbators were doomed unavoidably to poverty, insanity, and, worse still, eternal damnation.[17]

Until the appearance of Fowler's book, public mention of the subject in America had been practically taboo. It stood condemned as sinful, being identified (inaccurately) with the sin of Onan in Genesis 38:9. When John Todd included a warning against it in *The Young Man*, he had written in Latin for fear of addressing the subject openly. But public silence did not mean the practice did not exist. On the contrary, Fowler, who dared, unlike Todd, to write about it in English, suggested that nine out of ten boys over eleven indulged "more or less." The estimate, which jibes with twentieth-century studies, seems reasonably accurate. Moreover, masturbation was probably more generally accepted among those elements of the population who were not trying to live up to middle-class ideals of respectability—like the farmhands and casual laborers among whom James had most recently lived. Fowler's first suggestion about where a young boy might learn the habit was from servants. That James used it as a sexual outlet there can be little doubt; but if he wanted to transform himself into a respectable young man, he would have to abandon it.[18]

If he did not, Fowler warned, there were telltale symptoms to betray the habitual masturbator. They included "1. Carrying the hands frequently to [the genital] organs by way of changing their position; 2. Lascivious expression on observing females; 3. Unwillingness to look other people in the face;" and, more seriously, 4. "pallid, bloodless countenance . . . hollow, sunken, and half-ghastly eyes . . . a half-wild, half-vacant stare," and "pain at or near the small of the back." James may have wondered whether he had already given himself away to informed observers.[19]

One can only surmise how hard a struggle he had to master this habit—or, indeed, whether he succeeded. Later in his youth he felt that his sex drives were "perfectly untameable." But being at the seminary may have helped to some extent. At home one could step into the barn, with its maze of lofts, passages, and haymows, and masturbate undisturbed; at school, opportunities were harder to come by. In any case, he felt sanguine about his ability to follow Fowler's advice and "ABSTAIN TOTALLY." Perhaps he was inspired by the book's stirring rhetoric: "Make one desperate stand and struggle. Summon every energy! Stop short!!" and, in a breathtaking misapplication of St. Paul's remarks in Colossians 2:21–22, "'Touch not, taste not, handle not,' lest you 'perish with the using.'" "No!" Fowler continued. "Behold and shout the kindling resolve! See the intoxicating, poisoned cup of passion dashed aside. Hear the life-boat resolution:—'I wash away the stain of the past in the reformation of the future!'" Such exhortations, together with practical suggestions—cold water, brush rubs, and dietary reform, avoiding "ALL STIMULANTS AND IRRITANTS" like tea, coffee, tobacco, sugar, mustard, pepper, spices, and gravies—made Fowler's book seem to James a "very valuable work."[20]

Another probable reason why the book inspired such confidence in James and made him feel that he could indeed overcome his bad habits was that the author's name was already familiar to him in another connection. Like many another young man in the Reserve, he already knew Orson S. Fowler as the chief exponent of a science that held great promise for all mankind, particularly perhaps for young men like him. This was the science of phrenology, now discredited, but in the 1840s at the peak of its influence in America.

Phrenology had an affinity with the very old concept of signatures—the idea that the outside or physical nature of a thing corresponded somehow to its inner properties. But it added a distinctively new idea, that the several functions of the mind were located in different areas of the brain. At the very beginning of the nineteenth century, two German savants, Gall and Spurzheim, had combined these two ideas with some unsystematic observations of their own, and had become convinced that each human character trait had its seat in a different part of the brain, and that the size of that part, as evidenced by the shape of the skull in that area, indicated the strength of that trait in an individual. "Self-esteem," for example, was located on top of the skull, in the front center, "secretiveness," just above the ears; "color perception," in the middle of the eyebrows. An experienced practitioner, by feeling a person's skull, could determine accurately all his character traits.[21]

Half science, half parlor game, phrenology had reached the United States in 1832, and had created considerable stir. Scientifically, at first, it seemed quite plausible. It was logically coherent and could be verified experimentally. Skeptical materialists particularly liked the idea of removing the mental faculties from the airy realm of religion and metaphysics and tying them firmly to the structure of the brain and cranium. If true, to be sure, the system was wondrous, conferring on man a degree of knowledge hardly conceivable before; but the same could be said of electromagnetism, paleontology, and other recent discoveries. After a good initial reception, though, phrenology failed to live up to its promise. Other studies of the brain failed to support its assertions, and by the late forties it no longer carried conviction to American scientists and intellectuals.[22]

With the American public, however, it was another matter. The parlor-game aspect of phrenology—the prospect of having a perfect stranger feel one's skull and deduce all the main features of one's character—had an irresistible appeal, comparable to the vogue of psychological testing in the twentieth century. Two brothers from New York, Orson S. and Lorenzo N. Fowler, took up this aspect in the middle 1830s and began issuing popular books on phrenology, sending out lecturers through the northern states, and making their *American Phrenological Journal* a clearing house for all manifestations of public interest. By the late 1840s, the Fowlers and their lecturers, each with his standard kit—a plaster head clearly marked and numbered with the locations of the thirty-seven faculties, plaster reproductions of the skulls of famous white men like Burr, Voltaire, and Napoleon—and actual skulls of other races—were familiar figures in almost every village in the North, especially in Ohio, Michigan, Wisconsin, and southern New England, areas where the movement was most popular.[23]

For dwellers in the rural North, the Fowlers' brand of phrenology had the enormous spectator appeal of watching Neighbor X, at a local lecture, get his "bumps" felt and hearing the lecturer analyze his virtues and hint delicately at his failings. For a young man like Garfield, anxious to rise in the world, it had an additional appeal—its promise that each individual was endowed with special mental faculties, and that a phrenologist could tell him what they were. Phrenology, in short, became a primitive version of guidance counseling, helping young men find their strengths and warning them what weaknesses to beware of.[24]

James had attended at least one phrenological lecture, the one at Abell's schoolhouse in the winter of 1848, and probably several others. Very likely he had been examined; his huge head was a phrenologist's delight. These readings, with the plaudits of his mother and brother, had powerfully stimulated the "sense of destiny" (as one biographer calls it) he occasionally felt. According to phrenology, he had striking capacities for observation and logical thought; he seemed cut out to be a lawyer or scientist. At the same time, the lecturers told him, his bump of amativeness, at the base of the skull covering the cerebellum, the "organ" that governed sexual desire, was also large; here was a problem he would have to overcome. (As a later phrenologist was to tell him, "[You] should have a wife to keep you in the right place.") Orson S. Fowler had given James confidence that, if he did try to rise in society, he knew what to concentrate on and what to avoid.[25]

James's stirrings toward respectability and his efforts to overcome his improper habits were the main events of his inner life at Chester that term; externally, the main event was certainly the cholera scare that September. The dreaded Asiatic cholera had reached the United States in December 1848, for the first time in seventeen years; in the summer of 1849 it spread rapidly westward from New York. As with malaria, no one understood just how it spread. There were varying opinions: some blamed it on direct contagion from an infected person; others on impurities in the air. Most people saw it as a disease linked to vice, intemperance, and poverty; but for all that, even the respectable feared it. In late June Cholera had broken out in Cleveland among immigrants in the waterfront area; by August it was carrying off two or three victims a day. (Cleveland, at that, seemed to be getting off rather light; farther west in cities like St. Louis, it was killing up to ten percent of the population.) The rural people of the Reserve were uneasily on the watch to see whether the epidemic would spread from the metropolis into the countryside, as was the usual pattern.[26]

Against this background, when Mr. Beach was taken with some sort of gastric upset on 13 September, everyone feared the worst—despite the fact that stomach and intestinal disorders of one kind or another, sometimes called dysentery, sometimes something else, were very common in the rural Reserve in late summer. Cholera was on everyone's mind, and no one was very surprised when Mr. Beach was reported near death. Two days later, Lucretia Rudolph was going into the chapel for Saturday morning declamations when she met Oscar Matthews, another student, who seemed to her to be looking ill. She "was just agoing to ask him if he was not," she wrote her mother a few days later, "when he spoke and said 'that he was taken a few minutes before, and it seemed to him that he could not stand it,' and started strait [*sic*] for the door." Miss Rudolph and another young lady decided to go after him to see if they could help, and found him and two other students outside, vomiting, with severe stomach cramps. The implications were frighteningly obvious, particularly when two more students were found to have the same symptoms. All five were put to bed, under the direction of an older student, while Miss Rudolph and the other girls were set to work picking smartweed and heating bricks for the application of the recommended home remedies. As the news spread, "great excitement," in James's words, pervaded Chester. Perhaps the school would have to be closed; perhaps prudent students ought to leave at once. Fortunately, within a few days Mr. Beach's ailment turned into "chill fever," while the sick students rapidly recovered—their upset was later blamed on the pork they had been eating at the seminary boarding house—and the great cholera scare of 1849 was over.[27]

As the weather grew colder and the end of term approached, James had to begin thinking about what he wanted to do next. All he was sure of was that he wanted to come back to Geauga next spring, with enough money to take the classical course. To do so meant somehow earning enough during the winter to pay off his debts and pay his way through another term. The usual way of making money, for an academy student, was teaching district school, and that was the avenue James and his friends talked over most during the fall.

By now, James had begun to acquire a new set of friends. Orrin had gotten sick early in the term and had had to leave school, so that James was without the company of his old Orange comrades. He and Harvey Everest struck up a close relationship, and he began to make new acquaintances, like Andrew J. Page, one of the boys laid low by the boardinghouse pork, at whose bedside he watched for a night during the cholera scare, and Jackson Bell, a boy from Iowa. He and some of the others formed a semi-secret society called the "Mystic Ten" which met periodically in members' rooms.[28]

There were two possible ways of making money through teaching. During

August and September, talk ran mostly on the first and more exciting one, which allowed a young man to make money and see something of the world at the same time. This was for academy students from the Reserve to go to southern Ohio, southern Indiana, or Kentucky, where there were fewer academies and hence fewer qualified teachers, and where one could supposedly land a teaching job with ease. For a while James was convinced that this was what he wanted to do, and wrote home to Eliza to have his trunk ready; but he probably began to hear conflicting views, to the effect that going south was a chancy venture, that one could easily spend a lot of money and accomplish nothing.[29] By October he had settled for the more prosaic alternative of seeking a teaching job close to home. He joined a class for prospective teachers, taught by an older student with some experience, and in the middle of October went to Cleveland (where the cholera had now abated) to take the examination that would qualify him to teach in a Cuyahoga County school. He passed without difficulty, and was ready to launch into the task of seeking a school for himself.[30]

This turned out to be a painful experience for a young man who hated rejection. He started in the western part of Orange, and had no luck; then worked his way northward, inquiring at country stores for the district school directors (who as often as not were among the crowd around the stove), constantly being turned down because of his youth and inexperience, or because a teacher had already been hired. On he trudged through the rainy October weather, into Euclid, back past the Shaker settlement into northern Warrensville and south into Bedford. By the time he spent the night there with his Uncle Joseph and Aunt Calista Skinner, he had been on the road two days without success. He canvassed Bedford all the way to the county line and was turned down every time—then worked his way back home through Solon. By the time he got home, he was totally dispirited, and still had no job for the winter.[31]

Late that afternoon, only an hour or two after James's return, a man came up to the farmhouse looking for "Jimmy Garfield." He was from across the town line in Solon, it turned out, and wanted to know, on behalf of the directors of District 2, if it was true that the Garfield boy was looking for a schoolteaching job that winter. If so, he should talk to one of the directors.[32] To James, the offer seemed providential, though he did have some misgivings about the school. The neighborhood was a raw, wooded area, settled even later than James's own, mostly by people from Maine, and contained some tough families like the Harringtons and Chamberlains. In past winters, he knew, the school had been broken up and the teacher run out by the bigger boys; he could hazard a guess that the directors had sought him out more for his size and fighting ability than for his teaching skill.[33] And the worst part, from his viewpoint, was that the scholars already knew him as a neighbor; he would have no chance to trade on the mystique of being a teacher. Nonetheless, it was a school. The next morning he talked with Mr. Harrington, one of the directors, at the Falls, and within a few days they had a deal worked out. James would teach four twenty-four-day months for twelve dollars a month, or three for thirteen dollars, starting the first Monday in November.[34]

The prospect of his first teaching job, and the nervousness that went with it, probably overshadowed most other things in his last week and a half at Chester. James did note in his diary that the Zetelethian and Sophomethean societies had met and reunited amid "great excitement," and this event so fired his interest in debating that the first thing he did on arriving home at the beginning of November was to found a proper debating society in Orange. Called the Philomathean, it had its first meeting in the red schoolhouse the night of 3 November, when Garfield and (as the record says) "a company of youth" met to draw up a constitution and bylaws of the usual sort: weekly meetings, Saturday at 6:00 P.M.; officers who served for six weeks—a president, vice-president, secretary-treasurer, and executive committee, whose business was "to purchase candles, and light the room, build fires procure essays, &c. &c." Each side was to have fifteen minutes to present its case and ten to sum up, after which the vice-president would deliver a critique of the whole debate. (James managed to get himself elected vice-president. Amos Smith was president, William Boynton secretary.) There was also a spot on the agenda for essays or declamations. With a good stock of issues for debate, the society was in place, and James could look forward to at least one night a week of intellectual stimulation during his months away from Chester.[35]

But his greatest test still lay before him—seeing whether he was capable of an educated person's work, teaching district school.

12

The Turning Point

Winter 1849–1850

James was familiar with the schoolhouse at the Ledge (the name usually given to that part of northern Solon), where he was to work. It stood just off the Center Road, on the crest of a hill; from the schoolyard one looked down the valley of a brook that flowed between two fairly steep hills into the Chagrin.[1] It was only a mile from the ramshackle farmhouse where Stephen, Hitty, and their brood lived, and less than two miles from his own home. Indeed, he could have lived at home while teaching and earned a considerably larger salary; but the directors, anxious to save their district money, had insisted that he take part of his pay, as the custom was, in the form of "boarding round," enjoying the hospitality of the families of the district. Accordingly, very early on the morning of 5 November, he dropped his trunk off at the farm of Lucian Southwick, one of the directors, received the key to the schoolhouse, and proceeded across the road dressed in his respectable best, black coat and neck handkerchief, to open school.[2]

Despite the anxieties of the fledgling teacher, the first day proved to be an anticlimax. "Had seven scholars," James noted in his diary that night and, addressing his main anxiety, added, "They behave well." As well they might—if James's was a typical school for the region, the younger pupils were the first to report; the older ones and disciplinary problems would come later. Nonetheless, this low-key beginning, with a scattering of small boys and girls, was the start of what was to be one of the decisive winters of Garfield's life.[3]

He ended up teaching the full four months specified in his contract—Monday through Saturday most weeks, with an occasional Saturday off. Week after week he was at the school early in the morning, lighting the fire and bringing his hand-ruled roll book up to date, whether the day was a gloomy, stormy one like 10 November or a clear, serene, Indian-summer-like morning like some later in the month. Actually, the weather that winter was mild, on the whole—Lake Erie remained unfrozen until February, and there was little snow. In February, though, the freezing temperatures and snowfalls finally showed up. A couple of days that month the schoolhouse ran out of firewood, and James had to give the scholars a holiday until he and Southwick could haul some over. When school closed on 2 March, there was snow on the ground an inch or two deep.[4]

Discipline, as with most young teachers, turned out to be James's major worry, particularly in that rough district. The school was never really quiet; there was a constant undercurrent of noise and restlessness, similar to what a classmate of James's at Geauga, Albert Perry, reported to a friend that same winter from an Ashtabula County district that resembled the Ledge, as he tried to write a letter one morning: "I shall have to write what [I] do now pretty quick for the old school house is filling with Scollars—there! one hits me a push and the ink is all over the papers. *Go along and sit down now*! Well Barns if you ever taught School you will know how it goes pull & holl [*sic*]."[5]

James's trials began early. Wednesday afternoon of his first week he found some of his scholars getting "uneasy" and decided "to separate some of the boys so that they would not play so much." This time-honored technique worked for a day or two, but the next Tuesday eleven-year-old Samuel Harrington got so disobedient and impudent that James had to punish him "severely." "He endeavored to fight me," James added, "but he finally gave up and is now a good boy." By this time the school was increasing in size, with as many as twenty-five present on some days, and the incessant whispering was getting on the young teacher's nerves. He tried different approaches to curb it, but eventually had to ferule one boy; he also agreed to punish the next boy that fought at school.[6]

This sequence of events was quite typical of a winter school in the Reserve or New England; if there was a difference, it was that James was slower than most teachers to resort to physical force. Very often, in such a school, the teacher would try to pick out potential troublemakers and forestall problems with them by thrashing their leader, on any or no pretext, early in the term. It was only the slightly-built teachers like Samuel Bates who tried to govern their pupils by "moral suasion." But James was a bit exceptional. He could have used his size and strength to overawe his pupils early on, but was curiously hesitant to do so.[7]

Toward the end of November he noted in his diary, "Large scholars coming in, feel rather dubious." Actually, he already had some older pupils, for on his eighteenth birthday, 19 November, he had noted that he felt "rather Young to have the care of a School consisting of a company of Youth several of whom are older than myself." But his classes kept growing. By 4 December he had thirty-seven scholars, including a "great many large ones." For the rest of the month his school enjoyed an uneasy peace, broken only 24 December when Garfield had to flog a boy of fourteen.[8]

As often happens, it was some time before matters reached a climax; in this case, not until after the New Year. The antagonist was an unnamed boy of sixteen. Friday afternoon, 4 January, the school was having declamations, and the boy was "very saucy" and disobedient. James took him outside, flogged him severely, told him to get back to his seat, and turned to walk back to his own desk. A sudden noise behind him made him turn around, in time to see the boy coming after him with a chunk of firewood in his upraised hand, evidently meant for James's head. Trying to ward off the blow, he caught the full force of the wood on his forearm, hard enough, it seemed to him, to have broken the bone; nonetheless, he managed to knock the boy to the ground, threw himself on top of him, and pounded him repeatedly until he surrendered. "We had a merry time," was James's laconic comment in his diary. The boy left school and did not return, and that was the end of James's discipline problems that winter.[9]

As a disciplinarian, then, James was a success. He had pacified the school, which was what he had been hired for. But what was more gratifying was that he had turned out even better as a teacher than as a disciplinarian. His success was probably due to the same trait that made him reluctant to use corporal punishment—a need to be liked, rather than feared, by his scholars. He taught them almost everything he knew—not only the basics, grammar, arithmetic, reading, spelling, and geography, but also history, which he knew almost by memory, and algebra, which he was just learning himself. He took some pains to make the material interesting to the younger scholars, and discovered, to his delight, that he had a talent for making others understand things. To a degree unusual for any teacher, he tried to monitor where each of his pupils was, intellectually and emotionally. Years later he told a teachers' class that when he first taught district school he had made it a practice, after going to bed at night, to throw back the bedclothes and mentally construct the schoolroom on the smooth sheet, with each scholar in his desk. "I said, Here is John, with Samuel by his side; there are Jane and Eliza; and so on, until they were all placed. Then I took them up in order, beginning next my desk in this manner: This is Johnny Smith. What kind of boy is he? What is his mind, and what his temper? How is he doing? What is he now as compared to a week ago? Can I do any thing more for him?"—and so on round, through all the other pupils. To those who knew the Garfield boy only slightly, it must have been astonishing that this hulking, tousled eighteen-year-old could turn out a sensitive, conscientious teacher.[10]

Besides the respect of his scholars, he had to win the confidence of their families, as he boarded round from farmhouse to farmhouse—with Gilbert Huddleston, a recent emigrant from Ireland, and his family, the widow Short and her son, farmer Harrington, Sylvester Tinker the cooper, and the rest. He did. He did everything a good schoolteacher was supposed to do, praised the food, read aloud to the family in the evenings, kept parents informed of the children's progress, shared the Sunday evening bowl of bread and milk, and put up with his accommodations, drafty chambers, or musty spare beds. From December on, visitors began stopping into the school to observe his classes, including some of the directors and another important personage, the

Congregational minister from Solon Center. By February, the compositions and declamations on Friday afternoon were attracting parents, and when he closed his school 2 March with a small exhibition (a frequent practice in the Reserve), he packed in over a hundred spectators. He had done a good job, and in the process had given a needed boost to his own self-confidence; moreover, there was no question that he would be able easily to get a teacher's position any time he chose from then on.[11]

This success—and it was a great success—coincided with an even more important crisis in his personal life, which was to change the whole direction of his youth, maybe his entire career. To pick it up, one has to go back to the beginning of the winter.

As always in the rural Reserve, winter was a social season, and the young teacher found plenty to occupy him in the evening when school was out. James Hinkley of Chester was teaching a geography school, twelve evenings for fifty cents a head, at a nearby schoolhouse, and young Garfield attended. It may have been one of the new-style "singing geography" schools that were enlivening Reserve communities that winter, where the teacher displayed a set of maps with the names left off, while the students caroled the appropriate nations, cities, mountains, and seas in doggerel verse, singing themselves, as a Chardon lawyer said, "into a knowledge of earth and all that thereon is."[12] There were the more conventional singing schools, too. Mary and Marenus Larabee were apparently in the process of moving, or had just moved, from Independence to Solon, settling in a small house near Hitty and Stephen, and James saw them fairly often. On 1 December, one of his free Saturdays, he drove Mary to town in their wagon, enjoying as always the sights of Cleveland. Near the river, right beside the canal, track was being laid for the new railroad to Columbus, Cleveland's first; the gas works for illuminating the city were almost finished, and the lights would be turned on later that month. After dark, he attended the first in a new series of lectures being given by Mr. Burr of Philadelphia, on the science of Biology.[13]

The subject of the lecture that James attended had almost nothing to do with what is now called biology. Its full name, as announced in newspaper advertisements, was "the newly discovered and wonderful Science of Electro-Biology, or the Electrical Science of Life," and it was, in essence, what the twentieth century knows as hypnotism and the nineteenth century knew as mesmerism. Current in Europe for over half a century, knowledge of the mesmeric trance had reached the United States only around 1838. Like phrenology, with which it was often combined in bizarre and entertaining forms, mesmerism had enjoyed its greatest success in America as a kind of popular amusement, beginning with an extraordinary vogue in New England in the early 1840s. The techniques used were familiar ones. The subjects were asked to fix their attention on some external object as a means of inducing a trance; after fifteen minutes or so the mesmerist selected the most susceptible among them and proceeded to suggest to them that they were hot or cold, in danger or enjoying a delicious meal, or transported to some distant locale and watching what was going on there, while the audience enjoyed the antics they exhibited under the power of these suggestions. It was all immense fun.[14]

What distinguished lectures like the one James attended from mere exhibitions of conjuring or sleight of hand were the lecturers' efforts to link their demonstrations with the physical science of the day. The mesmeric trance, they claimed, was brought about by passage of an invisible "nervous fluid" from the practitioner to the subject, exactly analogous to electricity, which was conceived of as a fluid that passed insensibly from one body to another. Hence the reason that one practitioner had his subjects hold little "batteries" consisting of a copper coin, a silver coin, and a piece of zinc riveted together, to produce their trances; hence, also, the other current name for the phenomenon—"animal magnetism." The trance state induced (in other cases) by repeated downward passes with the hands was called being "magnetized," and one could be positively or negatively magnetized.[15] To skeptics who pointed out that there was a suspicious vagueness about these explanations, the mesmerists replied, accurately enough, that no scientist could really explain what electricity was, although man was acquiring a rough knowledge of how to use it. Their grandiose rhetoric, and the prospect of spiritual communication similar to what the telegraph had brought, but on a spiritual plane, through the "attenuated electricity" of animal magnetism, profoundly impressed young people like James, who came home and noted in his diary, "I believe the science to be a true one."[16]

Back in Solon, the ordinary amusements of winter did not often reach these heights, but there was enough to provide society and some mental stimulation—the various night schools, James's vice-presidential duties Saturday evenings at the lyceum in Orange, and another lyceum that met Wednesday nights at Solon Center. He found himself thrown, to some degree, with a slightly different kind of company, especially at community events like spelling schools. A schoolmaster could not roughhouse with the boys and enjoy their sports as he had once done; district school teachers fraternized mostly with other teachers from neighboring districts—meeting at lyceums, and visiting back and forth at one another's schools on their free Saturdays—or with adults in the community.[17]

Thus his friends that winter came from a somewhat wider circle. To be sure, he saw a lot of Orrin, the Boyntons, and other old Orange chums as he went from country schoolhouse to country schoolhouse on social nights. But he also associated with his old teacher, Harvey Rutherford, who had a school nearby; with a mercurial, profane young man named Henry Deady, the son of the tailor in Solon, who frequented the lyceum there, and particularly with two men whom he may not have known previously, Albert Slade and Oliver B. Stone.[18]

Slade, one year older than Garfield, was from Bedford, the son of a carpenter. He seems to have been teaching in a neighboring school.[19] Less is known for certain about Stone. Apparently he too lived in Bedford. He was married, and may have been considerably older than his two friends. Possibly he was the same silver-tongued Oliver Stone who was familiar to people in Aurora, Bainbridge, and a dozen surrounding townships, a glib shoemaker and jack-of-all-trades with an unquenchable fondness for liquor and a disconcerting habit of turning up at revival meetings full of hypocritical homilies about repentance and salvation. The Oliver Stone that James knew enjoyed debating and hung around the lyceum at Solon Center, and could well have been the same man. In any event, by the end of November James had made the acquaintance of both men, perhaps at the Solon lyceum or at Hinkley's geography school.[20]

From the beginning of December on, cryptic entries of an unusual sort occur in young Garfield's diary. On Thursday evening, 6 December, for example, he went to Solon Center and had "an adventure with Slade and Stone, a discovery." "Adventure" was James's way of describing an incident that was exciting but for some reason not suitable for writing about in detail. What the "discovery" was is a complete mystery.[21] On the sixteenth he spent the night at his home in Orange, where he had been staying less since Thomas's marriage, in October, to Jane Harper, the twenty-year-old daughter of a Maine family recently settled in the neighborhood.[22] Company came that evening, and there was "an incident" involving "T. and S." The "T" suggests Thomas, the "S" one of James's friends, but there is no clue what the incident was. On Monday night, 7 January, there was a spelling school at the center presided over by "Mr. Slade." The quotation marks around "Mr. Slade" were put in by James and might have implied that Slade somehow did not merit the respectable "Mr." Whatever was going on, James was a willing participant in it. Between December and February, he spent at least four nights at Stone's house, though none at Slade's.[23]

Another phrase appeared several times in the diary during late November and December: "Great care on mind." James did not indicate what was causing the care, and several biographers have assumed that his teaching responsibilities were weighing heavily on him; but it is at least worth noting that three of the four times he used the phrase were on Thursday, and that Wednesday was his customary night for visiting the lyceum at Solon Center or the geography school. One of the instances occurs after an evening spent with Stone and Slade, another shortly after an evening at Stone's. On another occasion that month he spent Saturday night at Stone's home and reported Sunday, "At home not well." Beyond doubt, something was troubling him deeply. New Year's Eve he spent at the Judds' house (where he seems to have felt more relaxed than at his own home), waiting up for the old kitchen clock to announce twelve midnight, and scribbling, as he waited, some extraordinarily gloomy verse. One poem, a lament for the passing of the old year, began conventionally enough:

> Old Year! Thy days are numbered
> Thy death is drawing nigh
> And we who long have slumbered
> Awake to see thee die.

But it ended, surprisingly, with the prospect of a new year full of horrors:

> But no! thy Son will proudly
> The iron scepter sway
> And all fears dark and cloudy
> Return with opening day.

The other poem one might call an attempted welcome to the New Year, beginning in gaiety but ending, again, in black, hollow-bellied fear:

> O here you are young fresh and fair
> You're welcome with us here.
> With pleasure rare we'll banish care
> And bless the Infant Year.
> . . . .
> I think and mournfully I think
> That I this year must try
> Perhaps while standing on the brink
> Of endless misery.

This was more than the conventional expression of the uncertainty of life which formed a large part of religious utterance in the Reserve. James was pretty sure that "endless misery," in some form, lay before him.[24]

If his misgivings did relate to his adventures with Slade and Stone, they had no immediate effect on his behavior. In January a lecturer on "biology," probably not Burr, but one of his local imitators, showed up at Solon Center for a week of demonstrations. James and Slade, and probably Stone too, attended several sessions; James volunteered as a subject twice but found he could not be put into a trance. In January he spent a night at Stone's dwelling, in February another.[25]

What Slade, Stone, and Garfield were up to remains tantalizingly obscure. If one considers the reputation of the Oliver Stone from Bainbridge and the morning-after feelings of guilt and malaise recorded in Garfield's diary, the reasonable inference is that Slade and Garfield were leading double lives, teaching their classes in the morning and boozing it up at country barrooms in the evening, and that the nights James spent with Stone were those in which he was in no condition to go back to the home at which he was boarding. But this possibility seems a little out of character for James, who does not seem to have been given to liquor either before or after this winter. A comment made by James on one of the nights he spent with Stone hints at the additional, or perhaps alternate, possibility of a sexual angle's being involved; he noted that Stone and his wife presented "an example of connubial felicity, to all appearances."[26] It is not clear why he was so interested in Stone's relations with his wife. One can only speculate. Perhaps Robert Cottom's conjecture that Garfield was "subject to homosexual feelings" belongs here, if anywhere.[27]

Whatever the precise nature of his activities, at the end of February young Garfield suddenly experienced a violent revulsion against them. "I feel disgusted," he wrote on 28 February, "with low vulgar company and expressions." The turnaround in attitude was rapid, with only a few premonitory signs, barely enough to make it possible to fathom how the change came about.[28]

In early February winter weather set in, and by the third weekend in the month snow had covered the roads. The sleighing was excellent. There was a sort of revival going on at the Disciple meeting house in Bedford—revivals, like singing schools and lectures, flourished in winter when people had time to attend—and a group of younger Disciples from the Boynton neighborhood got up a sleigh ride to go to it. Two of the Smith boys, Orrin, brother Thomas and his wife, and William Boynton were in the party; they were going round by the way of Warrensville to pick up some others. James decided to join them. It turned out to be an especially fervent meeting. A preacher named Harrison Jones gave the message with a smoothness of delivery that met James's oratorical standards, and at the end two Baptist preachers, and some other members from that denomination, joined the Disciples—a dramatic moment, and one that tended to support the Disciple claim that all the older sects were doomed to crumble as the Truth spread. As the sleigh sped home, James's mind was running on religion more than it had for some time past.[29]

He was still in the same frame of mind a week or so later, when he happened to pick up a small book called *The Course of Time*. It is not clear exactly where he got hold of it; probably it belonged to one of the families with whom he was boarding. The Huddlestons, with whom he boarded the last week of his school, were perhaps especially likely to own a copy, for it was the work of a young Scottish Christian poet, Robert Pollok, and was very popular in the North of Ireland, the Huddlestons' native country. It was a pseudo-Miltonic epic, in ten books of flowing, orotund blank verse, on no less than salvation, damnation, and the end of the world, subjects apt to catch James's eye in his present gloomy, apprehensive mood.[30] Its rhetorical power, rather overdone by the standards of a later time, but perfectly in tune with the taste of the early nineteenth century, captivated Garfield. He read attentively of Hell, a "dungeon of unfading fire," in which "there were groans that ended not, and sighs / That always sighed, and tears that ever wept, / And ever fell, but not in Mercy's sight," from sinners tormented by "Remembrance dire of what they were, of what / They might have been, and bitter sense of what / They are, polluted, ruined, hopeless, lost." Counterpoised to this was the heavenly realm, with its "royal city, New Jerusalem," its "bright celestial roads" crowded with beings who rushed to the encounter with their Creator, filled with "love unspeakable, / To God, and to Messiah, Prince of Peace."[31]

Some passages, if James noticed them, seemed to speak straight to his situation. A long paraphrase of Proverbs 7 examined sensual pleasure, personified as a harlot ("Of comely form she was, and fair of face; / And underneath her eyelids sat a kind / Of witching sorcery"), and revealed it as "full of all disease: her bones / Were rotten; Consumption licked her blood, and drank / Her marrow up." Another passage compared intellectual attainment with godliness, and concluded "That not in mental, but in moral worth, / God excellence placed." In all these ways, the poem seemed to be addressing him plainly. "Candor requires me to admit," he confessed to his journal, "that it has a sensible effect upon my feelings and tends to raise my [mind] to nobler and sublimer thoughts than the mean and groveling scenes of Earth." It was here, in a revealing fusion of social and spiritual concern, that he confessed his disgust with "low vulgar company and expressions." *The Course of Time* focused all the vague uneasiness and foreboding that had been haunting him since December; he realized now (a crucial realization for a Victorian youth) that his standing, not only in society, but in eternity, was in peril.[32]

He went home to Orange Friday evening, the day after he made this journal entry, and found a small revival meeting in progress at the red schoolhouse. It was led by a Disciple preacher he did not know, William Lillie, a plain, earnest man about Thomas's age, from somewhere in Geauga County, a straightforward speaker, not fancy, who closed each meeting with the invitation customary at revivals for all to come forward who wished to obey the Gospel and follow Jesus. Snow was still on the ground, and the revival was drawing a good crowd. James decided to attend.[33]

What happened after that was fast and predictable. On Saturday, 2 March, James's time was occupied with the final exhibition for his school, which took place that night. It was a miniature imitation of commencement of Chester, complete with garlands of hemlock draped around the walls of the schoolhouse.[34] But Sunday morning found him back at the revival, at a baptismal service. (Disciples regularly baptized during winter weather, holding their services at ice-covered country ponds—one baptism in Solon took place when the ice was fifteen inches thick, cutting a hole in the ice the size and shape of a grave. The prevailing feeling among them, as recorded by one young Disciple, was that "If the heart is right and warm, Ice and cold can do no harm.")[35] One of those baptized was a young man named Clark, who had been in the Solon lyceum with Garfield, Stone, Slade, Deady, and the others, and this fact conceivably supplied the extra push James needed. After the preaching was over, he stayed to talk with Lillie. The gist of what he said, as the preacher recalled it much later, was that he was not convinced the Bible was true, but that if he could be convinced it would change his life. Lillie, impressed by his sincerity, resolved to preach that night on "What Is Truth?"[36]

Probably James had told Lillie less than was in his mind. He had already decided to make a public profession of faith, and that afternoon he talked it over with Orrin. One would like very much to know what Orrin had been doing that winter—whether he had been running around with James and his friends, or what—but the record is not clear. In any event, the two young men decided that they would profess Christ together. Whether this represented a spiritual crisis for Orrin, as it did for James, or whether he was simply going along with the determination of his old friend, is uncertain, for there seems to have been a feeling among the young men of the district that winter that it was time to be converted. When Brother Lillie concluded his sermon that evening and gave the invitation, not just James and Orrin, but six other young people came forward.[37]

Whatever it may have meant to the others, to James the step was a definite break. The next day when he came up from the freezing waters of some pond in Orange he felt that he had finally left behind "the mean and groveling scenes of Earth," and had been "buried with Christ in Baptism." Now he "arose to walk [in] newness of life."[38]

13

The Young Christian

Spring 1850

JAMES, Orrin, and the others who had been immersed with them were now baptized Christians. The fact held vast implications, some spiritual and eternal, others social and quite immediate.

There was a fairly well-defined set of emotions new converts were expected to feel upon being baptized—a "lively joy," a deep gratitude and sense of brotherhood with fellow Christians, an "unwonted tenderness of manner" toward the unconverted. The exact intensity of these expected feelings varied from one denomination to another. The Methodists, for whom the conversion experience had always been central, were apt to laugh, shout, dance, or thrash around in the first exultation of being saved. "I never in all my life heard such awful holering [*sic*] in my life," one Disciple girl wrote of a Methodist revival in her town. "It almost made me crazy."[1] More staid denominations, like the Presbyterians and Congregationalists, leaned toward tears, embraces, and beatific smiles. The Disciples, at the other end of the spectrum from the Methodists, downplayed emotion as much as possible. All they required of a convert was a simple assent to the truths of the Christian faith—a position that had led critics to accuse them a having a "cold, speculative, philosophical faith" divorced from true Christian experience.[2]

James, by Disciple standards, was a warm, emotional convert—as one might have expected from his personality. In the days after his immersion, as he and the others continued to attend Lillie's meetings, his diary and probably his conversation became filled with outbursts of pious joy: "Still the sinners continue to come to Christ. . . . This is one period when the Lord makes Earth a Paradise, and blesses the labors of his servants. . . . Truth is mighty." Under the strengthening influence of the Holy Spirit within him, he felt able to discard the habits of a sinful past. For one thing, he resolved to give up the profanity he had learned on the canal, and still used occasionally; for another, his long-standing, idle habit of reading novels. Doubtless he swore off other, more serious vices as well; it is noteworthy that nothing like the association with Stone and Slade seems to have occurred again.

Finally, he surrendered, once and for all, his recurring idea of someday going back on the canal and eventually on to the lake. That life, as he now envisioned it, was unworthy of a Christian. In its stead, what he thought he would now do was acquire the best education possible and use it somehow to serve God. In exactly what way is not clear; probably Garfield himself was confused whether he wanted to preach or teach. But he was sure about wanting an education; and either calling was agreeably respectable.[3]

So for James, as for very many other young converts, becoming a Christian was an important step not only personally but socially. It could hardly have been otherwise, considering the frequency of revivals in the Reserve (almost every Protestant denomination had them), the fact that young people tended to be converted in batches of anywhere from a dozen to fifty, as James and his friends had been, and the presence of so many adult spectators. In many churches the revival was like a rite of reconciliation. The young, in laying their sins on Jesus, implicitly announced to their elders that the rebellious dreams of childhood and early adolescence had led nowhere but to dead ends; they were now ready to give them up and abide by the norms of the adults, who of course were ready to embrace them in Christian fellowship. As one early student of conversion observed, it was an "unselfing," similar to a puberty rite in other cultures. For Garfield, with his history of difficult, tense relations with the community, this aspect had to be present, and Henry Boynton's later recollection that word of his conversion ran rapidly through the neighborhood and caused a stir no doubt reflects it. It was a victory not only for God but for community values. George Warren's mother, anxious to clinch the victory, asked for and got James's promise to remain a Christian and not to backslide.[4]

It should be obvious from the foregoing that James's experience was not an unusual one for his place and time. All over the rural Reserve in any given winter, hundreds of young people in Kentucky jean and calico went on their knees to their Creator in repentance. Indeed, it was because conversion was so widespread that backsliding was a problem. Inevitably, in any community, there were young people pressured by family and friends who went into the experience mainly for the excitement of it, saying what they were expected to say and feeling, to some extent, what they were expected to feel, but without any deep sense of inner transformation. John Hodge, baptized at Chester in the winter of 1848–49, inserted a few sentences of fervent exhortation in a letter to a sister in Cleveland: "O Mandanah turn to God before it is everlasting to [*sic*] late we know not when death may come I know you would have many obstacles in your way but never mind them . . . Write when you receive this and tell me if you will not turn to God. . . ." Yet his life and behavior in the succeeding year showed few effects of conversion. Indeed, fifteen months later a friend of his could write him an equally urgent appeal to follow Christ, as though unaware that he had already been saved: "John as a friend if you knew what the love of the Almighty in the heart was you would not hesitate one moment to have it there. May God in his mercy grant it; Think of it!!!" One wonders how many revival baptisms were like these: brief, deep surges of emotion emptying quickly into conventional patterns and then evaporating.[5]

James's conversion, at any rate, was deep and genuine. He looked forward to returning to Chester as the last snows melted from the ground and maple sugaring began, and sharing his faith with fellow Christians there. Money would be a problem as always, but he had enough to get through one more term at least. He would be rooming with two brothers in Christ, Orrin and Cousin Henry. There was another obstacles, however, whose seriousness he may not have realized. He would be going back to Chester not only as a Christian, but as a Disciple.

The Disciples were certainly among the best-known sects in the Reserve and were, arguably, among the most unpopular. Their notoriety did not stem from their doctrine, which was perfectly orthodox. They held, like most Protestants, that man, though created by God, had fallen through Adam's sin and become lost ("nemo est sine culpa"—"no one is guiltless," James wrote in his diary that spring as he studied Latin), but that he could obtain salvation by accepting the redemption God had graciously provided through his son Jesus Christ. Nor were their practices unusual. Like most churches around them, they supervised the conduct of their members and did not hesitate to expel those who drank too freely, cheated in business, or led otherwise immoral lives. Their members, like those of many other churches, often addressed one another as "Brother" and "Sister." The only moderately unusual thing they did was to celebrate Communion weekly, unlike other churches, which preferred longer intervals.[6]

Two things made the Disciples unpopular: their rapid growth and their argumentativeness. The sect, in 1850, was barely twenty years old; its founders, a Scottish-born preacher named Thomas Campbell and his son Alexander, were still very much alive, in Bethany, Virginia (now West Virginia), on the Ohio River. This was the unofficial headquarters of the denomination, from which Alexander Campbell issued his monthly newspaper, *The Millennial Harbinger*, to followers across the land. Their influence was powerful enough to have earned their followers the nickname of "Campbellites" (usually pronounced "Camelites") and the enmity of other, older denominations whose adherents they were winning away. By 1850, the Disciples numbered several hundred thousand followers, mainly in the Ohio valley.[7]

The Campbells' message, simple as it was, had a wide popular appeal. They held that nineteenth-century Christianity needed to recover the sincerity and purity of the early church, and that the way to do so was to discard all the traditions with which it had become encrusted since the Apostolic Age, and to follow only the directives of the Bible as rules of faith and practice. The Bible, therefore, was central to their faith, and knowledge of God's

Word crucially important to living. "Where the Bible speaks, we speak; where the Bible is silent, we are silent," was their motto. James summed up the Disciple position in an impatient diary entry that spring: "I wish that men would let all human traditions alone and take the Bible alone as their guide."[8]

Necessarily, this position involved a criticism, more or less harsh, of all other Christian denominations. All others, according to the Disciples, were wrongly clinging to unbiblical, "sectarian" traditions—infant baptism, robes and vestments, creeds, liturgies. Disciple evangelists spent much of their time attacking such practices and asking their unsophisticated audiences where in Scripture one could find any authorization for them.[9] In thus inviting controversy, they were only emulating their founder. Alexander Campbell was a fearfully skilled debater in an age of great debaters, willing to take on any opponent, Protestant, Catholic, or skeptic, at any time. Indeed, in reading his sermons, one sometimes gets the impression that he valued the cut and thrust of debate quite as much as the doctrines he was supposedly defending. His followers, at least those of an intellectual bent, tended to be cut from the same cloth. "With the constant misunderstanding, not to say misrepresentation, to which the new movement was subject," recalled a young Disciple friend of Garfield's, "almost every member became of necessity a champion, and armed with 'the sword of the Spirit, which is the word of God,' never shunned an encounter with an opponent." In an age when religious debate was almost a spectator sport, Disciples were the semi-pros of their communities, ready to take on the rest of Christendom at any time.[10]

It was with this mixture of sharp-edged zeal and generous, all-embracing joy working within him that James made his way on 12 March through the early spring mud to Chester. Henry was with him; Orrin was to come later. They had their quarters in the front room of a small farmhouse near the seminary. It was, Henry Boynton later recalled, about ten by twelve feet, hardly big enough for their two beds, chairs, and cookstove. Not that they did a great deal of cooking—partly for reasons of economy, partly from idealism, James and Henry had decided to try a diet recommended in one of the advice-for-young-men books James had read the fall before. It consisted mainly of what they called "pudding"—corn meal mush, eaten cold with molasses for lunch, hot with milk in the evening, and for breakfast "a very small piece of meat, potatoes, bread and butter, with plenty of cold water." They bought the molasses by the quart once a week and thinned it with water to make it last; Henry used to complain when it was too watery. But the advantages of the diet were patent. It cost less than forty cents a week; moreover, a light, unspiced diet with little meat was supposed to lessen the urge to masturbate. At night the two young men, new Christians both, read the Bible together; then one would lead in prayer. They alternated from night to night. James still felt a little diffident, he confessed to his diary, about leading a prayer, but it was his duty as a Christian, and he went at it reverently.[11]

The same religious zeal bubbled up in his approach to his studies. As he, Henry, and Orrin (who arrived in April) left their close lodgings and carried their books to class across the new-springing seminary lawn,[12] James would thank God for permitting him "to see the light of another pleasant morning," or ponder "how best to serve the Lord in my daily walk and conversation," or exhort himself to use his time to the best advantage. Two weeks after beginning school, he reviewed his progress in his diary: "This term I have 4 regular studies, viz., Bullions' *Latin Grammar*, Mrs. Lincoln's *Botany*, Robinson's *Algebra and Mental Arithmetic* [These were names of textbooks he used.] . . . They are all very pleasant subjects. Can see many beauties in each, and especially Botany, which teaches us to 'look through nature up to nature's God,' and to see his wisdom manifested even in the flowers of the field."[13] A few weeks later, during an access of tenderness in which he used the word "love" more freely than he ever had, or would again (e.g., "There is a prayer meeting in the Chapel this evening. I love to attend them."), he confessed, "love abstraction, *Amo Libros*." Some days later he added, perhaps unnecessarily, "Love Latin."[14]

Botany was perhaps his favorite class that spring, both because his favorite teacher, Mr. Beach, taught it, and because it afforded room for pleasant little thoughts like "O! How much wisdom of God is shown forth, even in the flower." Toward the end of the term Mr. Beach had each student compile a herbarium, a scrapbook of pressed flowers classified by order and species; so June found James out combing the countryside around Chester, stalking the familiar wildflowers of the Chagrin valley, the little blue spiderwort or showy yellow adder's-tongue, looking for ginseng deep in the woods or wild columbine, a flash of crimson on rocky slopes, and padding the collection with such standards as dandelion and poison ivy.[15]

Algebra was almost as absorbing, in a different way. James found it curious at first to be dealing with mathematics that had no direct application to problems of commerce, land measurement, or time-rate-distance. But as he got into the structure of algebra, the "abstraction" he wrote of in his diary, he found to his own surprise that he understood it and that it made perfect sense in its own terms. By 9 May he could write sanguinely, "We have found a tough spot in Sturm's Theorem but I guess we'll get it strait [*sic*]." This was a term of rapid intellectual awakening for him, in which he realized that he could handle some difficult mathematical concepts that eluded most of his schoolmates. By late May they had finished the algebra text. "It is singular," James reflected, "that so few ever finish algebra. One year ago there were 18 in my class, last fall there were not so many, and now only 3 that went through. They were I. B. Curtis, Z. P. Sortor and myself. I still feel courageous to press on with my studies."[16]

Pressing on meant going to college eventually, though he could not see exactly how this was to be done. But the indispensable requirement was a knowledge of Latin, and preferably also Greek, languages that were still, in the nineteenth century, the passports to any kind of higher learning. This was the term in which James began his lifelong love affair with the Latin language. The idea that English words had Latin counterparts was fascinating, as was the exotic look of the words. It was easy and pleasant to translate simple sentences from one code into the other, and there was a definite proprietary thrill in being able to write "Felix sum" when one was happy.[17]

Joy in his salvation and joy in his intellectual growth were both present, then, in James's heart that spring, often so closely mixed that one could not tell them apart. There was also joy in seeing old friends like Sorter and John Hodge. Of course, not all his friends were back at Geauga that term; that was the way of rural academies. Harvey Everest was somewhere else; so was Lucretia Rudolph. But Albert Hall, dark and trim, was still there. He was keeping up a correspondence with Miss Rudolph; an engagement was presumably in the cards. Samuel Bates was back after a winter teaching in Huron County. And there were some new faces like Symonds Ryder, a fellow Disciple, a tall, gentle, rather morose young man from Portage County.[18]

James saw most of these friends at the Tuesday night meetings of the Zetelethian, which he followed almost as avidly as he had the previous term. He liked the "clashing of sentiment," the hubbub, the drama of standing up amid a welter of opinions to give voice to his own views. At the lyceum, the week after school began, he somehow was assigned to defend a viewpoint that was not his own—arguing against immediate emancipation of American slaves—and found himself on the losing side. But this was uncommon. Most of the time he was battling for his own opinions, as when he delivered an oration on slavery and voting in Saturday morning rhetorical exercises, in opposition to his algebra classmate Israel Curtis; or at the lyceum in May, when he sustained the proposition that the Glory of America was greater than her Shame. (This was a popular question; he had debated it already twice that winter, at the Orange and Solon lyceums.) He really threw himself into these debates; at least once during the term he had to be reprimanded by Mr. Beach for debating too loudly in study hall.[19]

Slavery often figured as a topic. In one form or another, it was a perennial question. James and other young people his age had heard arguments on it since they entered their teens, in the middle 1840s, when annexing Texas had been an issue. Now, with the American victory in the Mexican War, the question had become still more pressing. Should the new territories acquired from Mexico—California, New Mexico, and the rest—be organized with slavery, as Texas had been? Or should the federal government exert its power in behalf of the majority of Americans to keep slaves out? And, more fundamentally, was the slave system justifiable at all?[20]

In feeling that slavery was wrong and that slaves should be immediately emancipated, James was right in line with his neighbors. Slavery was a subject on which the Western Reserve in general was as adamantly moral as New England, the original home of most of its people, and on which Chester was maybe a little stronger than the rest of the Reserve. The Freewill Baptists as a whole were strongly against slavery. The village had supported an antislavery society in the early forties, and Mrs. Jemima Barber, the headmistress of the female students at the seminary, a genial, motherly woman, is supposed to have kept a station on the underground Railroad. Thus it was only natural that a black man, presumably an ex-slave, showed up to lecture on the subject at Chester in early April, or that Garfield and his friends listened approvingly. "The Darkey had some funny remarks," James noted. At the same time, the students' stance on the subject implied no favorable judgment of "niggers," as most white Ohioans called them. The reader will recall that the Sophomethean, in the previous fall term, had put on record its opinion that blacks as a race were inferior to whites; and there were no black students at Geauga.[21]

The one topic for debate at Chester in which there was real dynamite was religion and, fortunately, Garfield managed to stay away from it most of the term, enthralled as he was in the structure of flowers, of theorems and of declensions, and busy with responsibilities he had begun to acquire as an outstanding student. (He and a group of other students, very responsible-looking in frock coats and neck handkerchiefs, began in May to edit a school paper called, oddly enough, *The Human Elevator.*)[22] The subject was dangerous because James was a Disciple, and because the Freewill Baptists were just then sharply at odds with the Disciples. In a way, this was peculiar, for the two sects were doctrinally as close together as any two in the Reserve; both, for instance, believed in baptism by immersion and gave their young people lists of Biblical texts for ammunition in arguing the question with other Christians. But as is often the case with ardent believers, the closer together the two drew in essentials, the more furiously they argued the trivial differences that remained. Disciple students in Elder Ball's Bible classes at Geauga were apt to be singled out for criticism of their doctrinal errors; Lucretia Rudolph and the Boynton boys had already had that experience, and perhaps James had too. The points at issue were trivial indeed. Was it wrong to pray to God to baptize sinners with the Holy Spirit? Had baptism been instituted for the remission of sins, as Acts 2:38 said, or was that verse overruled by Acts 3:19, which mentioned neither baptism nor remission? At the same time that the Baptists were belaboring these points at Geauga Seminary, Disciples elsewhere were striking back by converting leading Baptists to their side. Among the converts at the Disciple meeting James had attended in Bedford in February were several from the Baptists, including a clergyman and an elder.[23]

James, however, mostly stayed away from the strife this year. Unprotestingly he attended Baptist services in Chester; he often did not like what he heard, but apparently confined his criticism to his diary. As the term went on and the weather improved, he and some other Disciple boys at the seminary began looking for different places to worship on Sunday. Sometimes James attended the Presbyterian church in Chester, though he found its preaching little better than the Baptists'. Other Sundays he and his friends walked four miles to Mayfield, where there was a Disciple meeting, or a little farther to Russell, or even nine miles to Chagrin Falls to worship with other Disciples.[24]

Toward the end of May and the beginning of June, he, Orrin, Henry, Symonds Ryder, and a couple of other boys did more; they left Chester two weekends in a row, always on foot, to go to the yearly Disciples' meetings in neighboring counties. These meetings, held annually in each county, were great events in Disciple life, and unforgettable occasions for those who attended. In Cuyahoga and surrounding counties, they were usually held on someone's farm. The huge circular tent, one hundred feet in diameter and capable, according to a contemporary, of holding three thousand people, was pitched in a field near a grove of trees, and believers gathered under it from dawn to dark for sermons, prayers, and hymns. (The tent was quite new; it had been bought from contributions in 1848, and was in the care of Dr. John P. Robison, a prominent Disciple from Bedford, an old friend of Abram and Eliza Garfield. Previous meetings had been held in the open air.) Disciples from all congregations in the county came, and were fed and put up at the homes of fellow believers nearby. To distribute the hospitality fairly, the locale was changed each year. Though the setting resembled that of a Methodist camp meeting, there was little of the drama associated with the Methodists; speakers tended to be logical and undemonstrative rather than vehement and passionate. But for the members of a young and often misunderstood movement, the meeting was a precious time, in which they could share their experiences and receive mutual encouragement.[25]

The two meetings James and his friends attended were about fifteen miles south and north of Chester, in Aurora and in Mentor, respectively. James had a wonderful time. He sang joyfully, listened to at least two long sermons a day, subscribed to *The Millennial Harbinger*, and met old friends and kinsmen in an atmosphere of peace and euphoria. "Such meetings renew my strength," he noted in his diary on returning from Mentor. In addition, while sleeping in Brother Thomas Clapp's barn at Mentor, he and his friends had, he noted, "an adventure" of some kind—this is interesting as the first suggestion that his conversion had not entirely quenched his interest in secret and tabooed activities.[26]

That spring held other notable events: a memorable snowfall on 9 May; an equally memorable flash flood 14 June, when the rampaging Chagrin carried away three dams and "a great many mills"; in April, the arrival of a new president for the seminary, Professor Spencer J. Fowler. In May, James watched enthralled as Mr. Beach gave a series of chemical and physical lectures, including one in which a "mouse was deprived of life by having the air extracted from its cage" with a vacuum pump. In June, Frederick Teale, the son of an immigrant English farm family in Orange, was detected stealing from other seminary students and was expelled. The discovery was regrettable, because Teale had been "lately immersed," conceivably at the same meeting as James and Orrin. His backsliding, however, seems not to have unsettled James, who noted on 25 June, when Teale showed back up at Chester, "I. L. Humiston [a fellow student] used force to obtain his pay from F.J.T. I acted a certain part." He evidently did not want to go into detail about his part.[27]

Also toward the end of the term, James and his roommates gave up their bland pudding-and-molasses diet. It had served a purpose; it had saved them enough money so that now they felt able to move up to richer fare. The change was a relief. Henry vividly remembered James's banging his spoon into the bowl one evening and declaring, "I won't eat any more of that stuff, if I starve!" They switched to hot meals, which they took turns preparing on the stove in their room. The heat of cooking in the crowded little room usually drove out everyone but the cook.[28]

But the overriding theme of the spring term, as clear to Garfield in 1850 as it is to a modern reader of the diary, was intellectual growth—sheer delight in learning and knowing. It culminated fittingly at term's end, when James was chosen by the faculty to be one of the commencement speakers—in fact, the first of the male speakers who made up the afternoon half of the program. His topic, perhaps chosen by Elder Ball, was "The era of universal peace," and from mid-May on he labored at it in a more or less chronic state of jitters. Debate and the rhetorical exercises in the chapel had given him training in the dramatic rhythms and baroque flourishes of oratory as the nineteenth century liked it, and he piled them on liberally; but the piece still left him unsatisfied. He was afraid of getting up on the platform before all the audience and exposing his ignorance. A week before the exhibition he was confiding to his journal, "I hope I shall not break down."

Many of his friends from the Zetelethian were also on the program, a fact which only added to his nervousness. Albert Hall was to speak on "The true way to elevate the masses," an agreeable topic for a young man who enjoyed carousing with the masses in secret. John Hodge had drawn "True dignity" as his subject, and Zebulon Sorter, "The advance of mind—its effects upon Government." Orrin's selection had the somewhat lugubrious title "Passing away."[29]

To add to his labor, James was put on the student committee to make arrangements for the exhibition, responsible for things like choosing a site and building the stage. His committee briefly considered trying to borrow the

Disciples' big tent for the occasion, but that idea was quickly dropped, probably squelched by the faculty or the trustees. Eventually they found a spot in a "nice grove" a few hundred feet south of the seminary building, where the committee put up a stage and seats and hoped for nice weather. James begged off construction so that he could stay home and, perhaps for the dozenth time, practice his speech.[30]

Meanwhile, the other performers for the exhibition were beginning to arrive in Chester, including a singing group called the Spencer Family. It consisted of three male singers, a lady who played something called the Melo-pean, probably one of the portable reed organs then the rage in America, and a fiddler; their repertory of sentimental ballads and light humorous songs, interspersed with an occasional temperance tune, just suited the popular taste. James had seen their wagon a couple of days before, passing through Chester en route to the Kirtland Seminary exhibition. Perhaps he had seen the lady being too familiar with one of the gentlemen, a kind of behavior that bothered him; he noted gravely, "I have not a very high opinion of their moral characters."[31]

Finally the great day, Tuesday, 2 July came, with a threat of rain—it had rained the day before. James was up early, his heart pounding, practicing his piece and "prepar[ing] for the onslaught." Around eight, several wagons rolled in from Orange, with the Judds, Uncle Amos and Aunt Alpha, the Boynton cousins, Eliza Garfield, and perhaps Thomas and Jane too, all in their best clothes. "The teams are continually pouring in from all parts of the state," wrote James, with pardonable exaggeration; then, going off into a rhetorical flight, he continued, "The deep thunder is heard in the dim distance and the dark clouds pregnant with rain are floating lazily along the cerulean. The loud thunder again bursts, and the big drops of rain are hurled from the shivered bolt. The brows of the students contract as they fear for the fate of [the] exhibition."

But in the end, the showers went away and the exhibition went off as scheduled; and early in the afternoon, after some songs by the Spencers, an interminable prayer, and some more music, J. A. Garfield of Orange (so the program had it) got up, perhaps poured himself a preliminary drink from the gleaming silver pitcher in front of him, and began hailing "The era of universal peace." The polished phrases rolled easily off his tongue; his fine, deep voice sounded to good advantage. At the end, he received an unusually loud round of applause; in fact, when it was all over, his fellow students judged that his speech and Albert Hall's had been the two best of the day.

James was exultant. It was the sign he had been waiting for. "The ice is broken. I am no longer a cringing scapegoat but am resolved to make a mark in the world," he wrote in his diary. Possibly recalling that James, the Lord's disciple, had been called in the Bible a "son of thunder," he went on, "I know without egotism that there is some of the slumbering thunder in my soul and it shall come out!" Then, looking back at his castoff career plans, the old desire of becoming a sailor, he added the clinching sentence: "I have fully committed my self to the ocean of truth."

Then he loaded his trunk into the wagon and went home with Frank and Orrin Judd.[32]

14

Disputations

Summer–Fall 1850

WHEN Frank, Orrin, and James pulled up on the dusty, busy main street of Chagrin Falls later in the afternoon of 2 July, they found a phrenological lecture advertised for Champion Hall that evening. The speaker was no less a personage than Nelson R. Sizer of New York City, a principal assistant to Orson S. Fowler himself. James, notwithstanding his conversion, was still a devotee of phrenology, and the Judds were interested too; so they decided to stay, and ended up part of the attentive crowd jammed into the little library under the single homemade lamp. They stayed so late, in fact, that they went on to spend the night at Bayard's Hotel; it is hard to imagine who was responsible for that extravagance.[1]

Sizer's lecture impressed them. So the next day, after dropping James' and Orrin's trunks at home, they returned for the second lecture in the series, in James's estimation a "very interesting one." Again, on Independence Day, he and all the Judds drove in for another. Their keen interest was typical of the Chagrin Falls audience. On 12 July, at the close of the series, a citizens' committee passed a set of resolutions praising the "remarkable and astonishing accuracy" of the character analyses performed "to the amusement and gratification of the crowded audience" and endorsing phrenology as a science. They went on to set up a Phrenological Society of over one hundred members, including the elite of the Falls—doctors, lawyers, and ministers. James and the Judds had not seen the series through to the end, no doubt because of lack of money, no lack of interest, but they would have signed the resolutions unhesitatingly. James very likely bought one of Sizer's advice books for young men, and may have stumped up the aisle, his football-player-cum-plowboy physique bulging beneath work clothes, to have his large skill felt through its mop of stiff light brown hair.[2]

But if he did not, that too was understandable. That summer, of all summers in his youth, James felt confident he knew where he was going and needed no guidance. His way was clear before him—to serve his God by becoming educated enough to preach the Gospel properly. He also needed a way to make a living while he preached, and carpentry seemed like the logical choice. So his other task was to learn that trade, not in a careless, halfway fashion as he had up to now, but really well.[3]

To that end, he spent most of his vacation back in Chester, working on a two-story boarding house for Heman Woodworth. Like all house building, the job was a series of discrete operations—framing the joists one day, raising the frame the next, planing boards for the cornice and putting them on (James called this "getting out cornice"—it took three days), putting on siding (the longest operation, five days). James kept a close watch on his performance, as if he were following the progress of one of his winter-school students. He made two mistakes, he noted, in planning, framing, and raising a chicken coop for a neighbor during a lull in work on the boarding house. When two other hands begged off putting cornice on the gable ends of the two-story part, James (and Amos Smith, who was also working on the job) asked and got permission to clamber up and do it, mainly for the experience. The next week he learned to lay flooring, to his great satisfaction, spacing the broad oak planks on both floors to leave room for winter drying and shrinkage; Woodworth also let him make door and window casings, set the glass, and put in risers and treads on the stairs. The clumsiness of his early adolescence had long worn off; he was now capable of mastering his craft.[4]

Much about the summer was satisfying. He learned his future trade and at the same time earned money toward the next term at Chester. His life as a Christian continued to be richly rewarding. He took part on 7 July in the new Sunday school the meeting at Orange had organized, and recited a lesson. Two weeks later, he came back to the red schoolhouse to hear Lillie preach against the Book of Mormon, and to exult in the "sublime [and] solemn spectacle" as two of his neighbors were baptized. The second week in August he returned for his fourth term at Geauga Seminary.[5]

In sharp contrast to his triumphant finish in July, this was to be a bad term for James. The basic problem was his financial state, which was, if possible, more desperate than at any time previous. He came, as he said, "without a single cent." His wages from the summer barely covered his tuition and board; he could not afford schoolbooks and had to copy his Greek text by hand; and having been unable to get the rest of the money owed him by Solon District 2, he had nothing to buy clothes with.[6] To his embarrassment, he had to forego respectable dress for the clothes of a farm hand—"coarse, striped shirts, patched pants, coarse boots, coarse rye straw hat." He knew some students were "publicly sneer[ing]" at him, and felt that others who aspired to propriety were avoiding him because of what he wore. Fortunately, he did not have to mix much with other students. He had only two classes, Latin and Greek. Orrin and William, his roommates, were supportive; so was his landlady, Widow Morse, a kinswoman of Daniel Morse in Solon. He planned to spend most of his time outside class working for Woodworth, in order to have a little cash in his pocket.[7]

But the term worked out differently. James was too fond of debating, and too good at it, to hold aloof along from the other students. This term, however, conscious of his poverty and his low status at school, he was touchy and combative. Moreover, since his conversion in March he had felt himself bursting with revealed truths which it was his duty to maintain at all hazards. He tried to show Christian forbearance to those who disagreed with him; but imperceptibly, his fall term became a series of clashes with others in the school.

The root of controversy was, predictably, religion. James was hardly back in Chester before he was manifesting his usual irritability at the preaching of Elder Ball (28 July: "G. H. Ball proving the authenticity of the Bible. He had better let that subject alone."); when Ball preached on 11 August, he showed his disdain by dozing off during the sermon.[8] In this and other ways, he tried to distance himself from the Baptists who ran the academy. For instance, Alexander Campbell's translation of the New Testament, often used by the Disciples, rendered the Greek word usually translated "baptize" as "immerse." In accordance with this translation, James took to referring to the Freewill Baptists as "Free Will Immersers" in his journal and elsewhere. Again, in the privacy of his journal, and perhaps also in public, he pointed out that "Baptist" was an "unscriptural name" for a church (so were "Methodist" and "Presbyterian"), and that the proper name for a church building was "house" (e.g., "the Methodist house").[9] His life in "this sectarian place," as he called Chester, became a matter of scrutinizing the errors of those around him as carefully as he studied the classical languages. (Not just religious errors; by October he was so critical that he had taken to grimacing and pulling long faces in class whenever a fellow student said something stupid or erroneous, a fault for which Professor Fowler had to reprimand him.)[10]

As he had done last term, James sought relief in worship with Disciples whenever he could. One Sunday in August, he, Orrin, and Symonds Ryder walked to meeting at Munson; the next weekend, the same three went to the Cuyahoga County yearly meeting at Newburgh, stopping by Orange for James to have a look at his new nephew, Thomas and Jane's first child. They hoped to hear Alexander Campbell himself preach, but the founder failed to appear at the last minute. Nonetheless it was, to James, a joyful meeting.[11]

But where the previous spring's meetings had seemed to reconcile James to living among the Baptists, these seemed to make him more belligerent. The day after he got back to Chester, he got into a warm debate in the Zetelethian, on the question "Do the works of nature teach a correct idea of a supreme being?" (He maintained that they did not.)[12] Next he went beyond religion into an area he had not dealt with much before—politics.

It was apparently that summer that the political world had begun to be a nagging presence in James's consciousness. But no more than a presence; he professed the deepest contempt for it. Early in July he had gone into Cleveland with his mother to sell butter at the market, and had happened to hear the Whig candidate for governor making a stump speech; he was, he said, "perfectly disgusted with the principle."[13] At the same time, the subject had a way of recurring to his mind. Perhaps the reason was that politics, after all, was a likely profession for a young man with debating ability and verbal skills—a sort of diabolical counterpart to preaching the Gospel. It was a temptation he needed to keep reminding himself to resist.[14]

Another reason was that the year 1850 in the Reserve, and in the nation at large, was supercharged with political debate. A national crisis of sorts seemed to be brewing. Leaders of the slaveholding states were threatening to take the South out of the Union unless the territories recently acquired from Mexico were authorized to permit slavery.[15] In northern Ohio, the southern threats evoked jeers, political uproar, and denunciations of slavery which finally impinged on even the apolitical James and prompted his first recorded comments on political affairs. For instance, on 9 July, when President Zachary Taylor, who had opposed congressional attempts to compromise with the South, died suddenly in Washington, James took note of the fact, not because he thought it important but because people around him did. Five days later, in the Baptist church at Chester, Elder Higby preached "Gen. Taylor's funeral sermon or something to that effect" to a congregation that included the impatient young Garfield, who preferred the cosmic questions of sin, eternal justice, and salvation.[16]

Now, at the beginning of September, James suddenly waded into political debate of his own accord, undertaking to support "the following proposition, viz., Christians have no right to participate in human governments!" Coming from someone who only the spring before had been debating "against slavery and in favor of voting" the statement was remarkable. What had happened, one suspects, was something like this: James, in an irritable temper where Baptists were concerned, had heard the Baptist spokesmen at the seminary descanting on the iniquities of slavery and the political duty of a Christian until he was sick of the whole subject. To combat their doctrine, he seized on the perfectly defensible view, held by the Shakers, some Quakers, and one wing of the Disciples, that Christians ought not to mingle with the godless world and its institutions, including government, at all. He knew this argument would cause a stir, and was not entirely unhappy about the prospect. Like a good Disciple, he had already cast himself as the valiant fighter for truth. "I love agitation, and investigation," he wrote, "and glory in defending unpopular truth against popular error. It looks to me like serving two masters to participate in the affairs of a government which is point blank opposed to the Christians (as all *human* ones must necessarily be)."[17] The debate was set for Wednesday, 11 September; his chief opponent was to be the talented, cocky son of one of the leading Baptist elders, a boy named John Miller.[18]

This Garfield-Miller debate failed to take place. James came down with a typical late-summer complaint, dysentery, a few days later, and had to go home for a week. (Dysentery was fairly common at the seminary; Cousin William had contracted it a couple of weeks before and had had to drop out of school. James blamed it on the "impure water" in Chester.) Nevertheless, when he got back, he continued to ponder this new doctrinal error he had caught the Baptists in, and to work out its implications. When the antislavery congressman Joshua R. Giddings, who was a sort of folk hero to his constituents in the Reserve for his unflinching defiance of the South, came to Chester to speak, James dutifully went to hear him and was impressed with Giddings as a speaker, but wondered whether his work as an antislavery crusader was really worth it. "I could not help but consider," he mused, "that the cause for which he was laboring was a carnal one." A few days later, home in Orange for the weekend, he got his Disciples' meeting to consider the question and must have been gratified when they agreed "that we had no right to engage in politics." (Some, even more scrupulous than James, "thought that it was not right to investigate such a subject on the Lord's day.")[19]

Meanwhile, James, still thinking over the Baptists' diatribes against slavery, had come up with an even more provocative idea—that, according to the Bible, there was nothing at all wrong with slavery in itself. This was not original with him either; in fact, it was essentially the position of Alexander Campbell, and James may have picked it up from *The Millennial Harbinger*. It was a strong position, because both Old and New Testaments seemed to sanction the practice of slaveholding. But it ran completely counter to the beliefs of the Freewill Baptists, whose annual conference for some years had condemned slavery as sin, and in a Baptist community would be bound to be considered an affront. When he brought it up as a topic for debate, therefore, he knew he could expect a strong reaction. He got one. Once again John Miller was picked as his opponent in public debate. The choice suggests what Garfield never stated in so many words—that his repeated challenges to debate were seen, correctly, as challenges to Baptist belief. If so, one can imagine the accompanying furore.[20]

One wonders, at the same time, how many of the eighty-odd students then at the seminary were involved in the furore. Most of them, probably, were utilizing the languorous, unusually warm early fall weather for pursuits more traditional and congenial in country academies—socials, visits, writing letters home, and above all, genteel flirtations with the opposite sex. Probably more typical of Geauga than Garfield's fervid arguments on slavery and the Bible were the counsels of a Youngstown student to a couple of friends: "Hodge I want to give you and gilbert [*sic*] some good advice . . . mind and not go to bed with your shoes on and mind and let Jane Morse alone. And tell Gilbert and not [*sic*] to get too samcagious after Maria Dehuff."[21] Garfield's journal for this term, admittedly a partial source, gives the impression that interests like these were completely absent from his mind—that all he thought about were Greek, Latin, and his increasingly active quarrel with the Baptists.

Nevertheless, he did continue to take part in other school activities. For instance, on 9 October, he went to the usual Wednesday afternoon rhetorical exercises in the chapel, with Professor Fowler presiding. The routine was familiar: each student assigned a piece for this Wednesday got up and declaimed it, gentlemen first, ladies second. Usually it was a classic oration or piece of poetry. After each speech, Fowler or another student commented on voice, language, gestures, or anything else requiring correction. James had no assignment. He listened to John Palmer, a twenty-five-year-old Baptist minister, attempt to refute a recent speech of his on God and nature, delivered a brief rebuttal, and stayed to hear the other speeches. There were some funny moments. T. A. Bensley was declaiming a stirring selection called "Fire at Sea" when a prankish student named Aldrich jumped up and shouted "Fire! Fire! Where? Where?" convulsing the audience.[22]

Toward the end of the term, Garfield's journal becomes just a bit spotty, and the sequence of events is hard to follow. It is impossible to be sure, for instance, whether the second debate with Miller came off as scheduled. But for certain, the term ended with a controversy that fittingly climaxed all of James's encounters. Principal S. J. Fowler, not himself a Baptist, had since his arrival in the spring shown himself agreeable to cooperating with other denominations. He had, for instance, tried to introduce the Disciple hymnal, *The Sacred Melodeon*, for use in chapel worship, but had been rebuffed by the trustees. Now, in October, he became embroiled in another dispute with the Baptist directors. The exact issue is not clear, but to young Garfield it was obvious what was going on: "I have ever seen, and still see, a manifest *Sectarian Spirit* in this school, which I fear will eventually destroy the school. I see that the free spirit of S. J. Fowler *cannot* and *will not* brook their restrictions. Nor will I." James at once became a strong Fowler partisan; the principal's difficulties validated all his complaints about "this sectarian place." He boycotted Baptist services, attending Sunday meetings at the Methodist or Presbyterian churches. When Fowler announced his resignation the next week, James chortled in his journal, "He is going to Kingsville [another academy, in Ashtabula County]. Good. Good."[23]

Early in the term, James had had visions of working part-time all fall and earning enough money to continue at Geauga through the winter term. Now his religious combativeness and the upheaval in the school administration made that impossible. He would have to find work for the winter, and hunt around for some other place to continue his education in the spring. The good reputation he had earned in Solon the previous winter made it relatively easy for him to find a teaching job. Probably with a few boosts from some Disciple friends, he rode to Warrensville Center, six or seven miles west of his home in Orange, early in October, talked to two of the school directors, and got the job. His school would begin in November; now he had only to wait for the fall term to wind down.[24]

Wind down it did, amid continuing controversy. Elder Miller, John's father, came into chapel service to discuss rumored charges of "sectarianism" against him and got into an acrimonious debate in which several students accused him of lying. James stood examinations in Greek and Latin, memory exercises, essentially, in which he had to recite material he had learned during the term, and did satisfactorily—in fact, he was the prize student in Latin. But the honor brought no glow of satisfaction as his address in July had done.[25] He was impatient to get out, away from these people who were perverting truth. On 20 October he wrote, "I expect this is the last time I shall attend meeting here." The concluding ceremonies, with music, were the following Wednesday afternoon. He did not describe them, but added only the bare word, "Parting," after which he and Orrin rode home with Reuben Judd, metaphorically shaking the dust of Chester from their feet. It would be years before he saw the place again.[26]

15

Marking Time

Winter 1850–1851

JAMES's teaching job in Warrensville did not start until 11 November, so he had a couple of weeks' free time after getting home from Chester. He spent most of it helping Marenus build an extension onto the Larabee house in Solon; built casings, hung doors, and proudly laid the floor. He also went into Cleveland with Uncle Amos to take the teachers' examination and get a two-year certificate.[1]

The terms of the Warrensville job had been settled earlier when he met with the directors. He was to teach four months, reckoning twenty-two days to the month, for a total of sixty dollars. As in Solon the previous winter, he would board around with the families of the district. At his stipulation, he would not be required to teach scholars younger than ten or twelve, and he agreed to offer algebra, natural philosophy, and beginning Latin in addition to the "common branches."[2]

One of the Smith boys gave him a ride early on the morning of the eleventh and dropped him, with his trunk, at Warrensville Center, a little crossroads about the size of Chester, with a store, a tavern, a couple of churches, a scattering of houses, and the frame, two-room schoolhouse where he was to work. His school would meet in one side; a separate one for younger children in the other. Actually, "trunk" may be an exaggeration for his luggage. The evidence suggests that he was still woefully short on clothes that winter and may have had only one decent suit and a couple of shirts to his name.[3]

After a rather hectic first week in which he had to take care of the younger scholars as well as his own, the other teacher not yet having arrived, he settled into the routine of teaching, familiar from last winter, and found it enjoyable. The school was not very different, except that he knew better what he was doing, and was teaching a more challenging set of subjects. He had five or six students who were reading natural philosophy with him, and three or four who were attempting algebra, out of a total of thirty or so. Discipline was much easier than it had been the winter before, or, to be precise, his discipline problems were of a different sort—gossip and tattling, especially, for his school included a large number of teen-age girls. Once when he and most of the scholars were outside, someone slipped in and "wrote a lot of trash upon the board," evidently about blacks, for in his diary James called it the "black business" and had to give the students a talking-to about it next day.[4]

The fact was that Warrensville was a quite different community from northern Solon, only seven or eight miles away. It had a ten- or twelve-year head start in terms of settlement, which at that point in the two communities' growth meant that Warrensville had fewer woods, fewer rough characters, and considerably more cultivation.[5] There were, to be sure, Gaelic-speaking Manx settlers in the northern part of the town, who could be troublesome on occasion because they were unused to American ways; James noted that he had had to "correct" seventeen-year-old John Kaighan.[6] And there were isolated scenes reminiscent of the Ledge district, as when James had to jerk a fifteen-year-old boy out of his seat and make him promise to be obedient. But by and large things went smoothly, so smoothly that James sometimes felt he unbent a little too much. He left in his journal a verbal snapshot of his class the morning of 13 December: "It is now nearly half-past ten. I am sitting in my desk writing my Journal, waiting for a lesson. There are 17 large girls and 9 boys in school today. They are quite still and studying very well. I have just assisted two boys in Arithmetic, and now the Mental Arith. class's lesson is ready. Thus my school goes today."[7]

Possibly his worst embarrassment of the winter occurred when he was boarding with the family of farmer Hiram Stiles. He was bending forward to do something when his worn, tight Kentucky jean trousers ripped at the knee, almost all the way round the leg. These were his school pants. He had nothing to take their place, and although he could hide the tear to some extent by pinning it, the thought of going to school in that fashion before the probing eyes of his students, who included fifteen-year-old Martha and twelve-year-old Persis Stiles, could not have appealed to him. Worse still, he had no underclothing, and the rent exposed a lot of bare leg. He had no overcoat either—only a wamus, presumably—so that when he walked outdoors the winter winds would have free play through his breeches. It was mortifying. It was also the worst possible luck financially, for he had already had to sell his precious rifle in November to buy clothes for teaching. James spoke to Asa Stiles, who got his mother to darn the trousers. From the standpoint of comfort, darning helped; but as far as appearance was concerned, it was a desperate expedient. As soon as he could, James scraped up the money from somewhere to buy a coat and pants at the general store. Such were the hazards of keeping up a respectable appearance.[8]

Socially it was much the same as last winter. He boarded round, got to know the families of the district, and found them agreeable. There were the same spelling schools, at his school and others', where he presided or pronounced. There was the same visiting back and forth with other teachers on

Saturdays. Twice he looked in on Henry Boynton's school in Solon. Once he went as far as East Cleveland to a spelling school.[9]

In one respect Warrensville was a much better place to teach than Solon. It had a flourishing debating society, the "Warrensville Literary Association," in which a lot of the men in the community took part, like young Dr. Darwin, the local physician. It met on Saturday nights, probably in the schoolhouse. Often the questions were the same ones James had debated at Geauga. At first, it seems, he was a little hesitant about attending, but once he began he was immediately accepted and welcomed into the group. By January he was speaking regularly—an enthusiastic affirmative, for instance, on the question "Is Phrenology a Science?" The same month he scored the personal triumph of debating another question twice, once in Warrensville and once in Orange, taking the affirmative once and the negative once, and winning both times. (One should note, though, that William Boynton, who heard the Orange debate, found his cousin's speech unimpressive. He felt the affirmative should have won.)[10]

Sundays James went to meeting in Warrensville or Orange. For him this was no diversion, but an affirmation of God's guidance. He felt God had led and was leading him, and found himself "much refreshed" by the simple Disciple worship. Once he did attend service, out of mere curiosity, at a strange place, the Shaker settlement in the northern part of Warrensville, with its tidy fields and neat stone buildings. It was not one of the regular meetings, where Shaker men and women entered from opposite sides of the hall and did their odd little dance, gyrating slowly, hands raised to receive blessings and then lowered to "shake the sins from their fingertips"; these were not open in winter. But there was a man there—a "fellow," James called him deprecatingly—who pretended to have the power of the Spirit. He fell on the stove and knocked it over, among other things. Devoted as he was to the Bible and its teaching, James had no patience with these carryings on. To him the man was "a villain," and he saw no need to go back to the settlement again.[11]

In many of the places where he went—Disciple meeting, Saturday night lyceum, visiting in the neighborhood—James was constantly running into the same man, an old friend of his parents, a frequent speaker at the Disciple meeting in Orange. His name was Solyman Hubbell (apparently pronounced "So-*lie*-man"); he was a farmer and carpenter in his middle forties, a tall man with an imposing presence and the gift of cogent speech. His family, like the Garfields, were old settlers in the area. His brother Turner, a successful farmer, was also a leader in the Warrensville meeting; another brother, Jedidiah, was the Chagrin Falls carpenter who had built the Garfields' present house and had taught James; a sister had married into the Warrens for whom Warrensville was named. Solyman lived close to the Center, next to Button's Tavern, so that James saw him often and sometimes boarded in his home. He liked James, in the undemonstrative Reserve fashion; so did his family. Two of the children were in James's school: pretty, talkative, quick-witted Mary, who was eighteen, and her brother Newton, fourteen. They all thought the world of James, as an intelligent, articulate, and above all Christian young man. He responded to their admiration with his usual affection. Their farm, like the Judds', became one of the few places where he felt at home.[12]

Activities, places, people in Warrensville—one can multiply these without difficulty, but one does so with an increasing feeling of impatience, for they seem unrelated to the main theme of James's life at that time, the search for more education. A year and a half earlier, he had first gone to Chester with the idea of getting a higher education; the little he had gotten had notably improved his mental powers; and becoming a baptized Christian had given him a sense of purpose that encouraged him to go on. Now that he had decided not to return to Chester, the overriding question in his mind must have been where to go next.

Curiously, the subject is hardly mentioned in his journals for the winter of 1850–51. From them, indeed, it is not even clear that he meant to continue his schooling at all. An entry written on New Year's Eve, apparently while he was boarding at the Hubbells', mentions his sending a piece of poetry to the *Cleveland Plain Dealer* for publication. It was a rather lame blank verse piece, in evident imitation of Pollok, called "The Stilling of the Tempest," and one can perhaps infer something from it about his literary aspirations.[13] Apart from it, there is nothing until the very end of the winter, when a curt half sentence in the entry of 24 February—"I have given up going to Hiram"—reveals what had been on his mind all the time.[14]

For well over a year, the Disciples of the Reserve had been planning an advanced school, of the academy sort, which would instruct their children in the right approach to religion and remove them from the kind of discrimination practiced at Geauga Seminary. Discussions had begun as early as June of 1849, and in November of that year a special meeting of delegates had chosen the site, at Hiram, a little rural crossroads no bigger than Chester or Warrensville, about twenty miles east of Chagrin Falls. Construction had begun the following March, and young Disciples all over the area followed its progress attentively during the next months, hoping, as one girl put it, for a "seminary where we can enjoy ourselves and have no one to say why do ye so." The actual opening of classes, with 102 students, had come 27 November 1850, and now the school was in full swing, under the name "Western Reserve Eclectic Institute."[15]

This, not surprisingly, was the place young Garfield had in mind for continuing his education. It was not much more expensive than Geauga Seminary; tuition for one term was $5.50, for classical languages and higher mathematics. Room and board charges were about the same.[16] But by 24 February he had, as he said, "given up" going there, and one must ask why.

The answer almost certainly has to do with money. James's eagerness to keep studying, particularly at a Disciple school, was so great that no other motive would have sufficed to keep him away. But his four terms at Chester seem to have followed a consistent pattern: every term he had come back just a little poorer than the one before. In other words, the teaching and carpentry during vacations had not been adequate to get James caught up on his debts; on the contrary, room and board, tuition, clothes, and schoolbooks seem to have been absorbing everything he earned or possibly even forcing him to borrow more.

It seems clear enough, too, that brother Thomas was his main creditor. Writing home in August from Chester, James had asked Thomas to try to collect his remaining Solon schooling money and apply it to what he owed him—this at a time when James was having to wear patched pants and copy his Greek lessons out of a borrowed book.[17] Evidently Thomas needed the money badly. Perhaps things were not going well on the farm. Perhaps the need was connected with Thomas's recently becoming a husband and father; maybe sister Jane was not as easygoing about the debt as her husband. The existing sources give no idea just how much he owed Thomas, but it seems clear that, much or little, a consensual decision had been taken in the slow way such things happen in families that helping Thomas was more important right now than keeping James in school.

The situation with Thomas and Jane may have played a part in the other big decision taken that month. Eliza Garfield had always kept in touch with her brothers who lived in southern Ohio, in the Muskingum valley; now she decided to visit them for a while, leaving Thomas and Jane to run the farm. James no doubt would have preferred to go to school, if he had had the money; as it was, however, he agreed to accompany his mother rather than stay at home. Perhaps he could find work down among Uncle Henry's people and earn more money for Hiram in the fall. In any case, the new surroundings would be stimulating.

Once he had agreed to the plan, there was no delay. He closed his school 21 February, amid good feelings all round. Then on 24 February he went to the Falls and purchased a trunk; on 26 February he retired early to be ready for the long, fatiguing trip in the morning.[18]

16

Outlandish Customs

Spring 1851

From Orange to Blue Rock, Muskingum County, where Eliza's brother Henry Ballou and his family lived, was not a long distance—only 125 miles in a straight line on the map; but the journey between the two points was long and tedious. No main road connected them. In the past, the best way had been to take a passenger packet down the slow windings of the Ohio Canal to Dresden, and from there to catch a boat on the Muskingum River. But this time, perhaps at the instance of James, who thirsted for new sights, he and his mother were going to take a new route: from Cleveland to Columbus on the just-completed railroad, then to Zanesville by stagecoach, and finally down the Muskingum to Blue Rock.

Workmen had been laying track for the Cleveland, Columbus, and Cincinnati Railroad since 1849, and shiny brass-and-steel locomotives had been chugging out of the engine house, which was across the river from Cleveland, to service intermediate points on the line; but only in February 1851 had the connection to Columbus been completed. The line was already built from Columbus to Cincinnati, so that it was now possible for passengers from lake Erie steamers to come ashore at Cleveland and take direct passage to the Ohio valley on fast, modern transportation. The city's first rail connection of any sort was a great event. On 21 February, the week before Eliza Garfield and her son took the "cars" for Columbus, there had been a "jollification" all along the line by a special excursion trainload of state and city officials, starting from Columbus with a sermon by the Reverend Samuel C. Aiken, preaching from Nahum 2:4—"The chariots shall rage in the streets, they shall jostle one against another in the broad ways: they shall seem like torches, they shall run like the lightnings."[1]

James had probably seen locomotives before on his visits to Cleveland. The track ran through parts of the city familiar to him: The new depot was on the hill between the business district and the waterfront, and the railroad crossed the canal near the spot where he had first seen the *Evening Star* loading copper ore, and then cut a straight line across the Flats, the wide, grassy, uninhabited meadows opposite the city.[2] He had not recorded his impressions, which is a pity; but one can attempt to supply a description, for the first sight of the enormous machine seems to have evoked similar reactions from almost every nineteenth-century viewer—awe, respect, and an overpowering feeling of strangeness. "It was no difficult matter," Lucretia Rudolph wrote of her first encounter with one, "to imagine it some monster of an animal, and I must confess I almost felt inclined 'to run.'" To an imaginative German traveler who passed through Cleveland in the early fifties, the locomotive suggested "one of those gigantic many-limbed saurians" of early geologic time. Others saw in it a cyclops, a hydra, or a "dragon with iron wings."[3]

Amid the crowd that waited at the wooden depot on lower Superior Street—gentlemen in overcoats and top hats, immigrants with piles of untidy baggage, women with shawls wrapped tight around them—the Garfields, tiny mother and broad-shouldered young yokel of a son, doubtless drew sympathetic glances. They were a pair straight out of the sentimental mythology of the era. They were overshadowed, however, by the excitement of the train ride to Columbus. Just before ten o'clock, the monster engine drew slowly into the station, its brass trim gleaming, its name shining in gold letters from the side. Behind it and the wood car came the passenger cars—real Currier-and-Ives images, long wooden boxes with rows of fifteen or twenty small windows in the upper half and the name of the company in large gold letters above them. James and his mother climbed on, got their luggage aboard, and settled into the tall wooden seats. The engine gave a shrill, raucous whistle, and the cars began to move.[4]

After they had crossed the Flats, there was not much to see during the ten-hour ride to Columbus—mile after mile of leafless Ohio woods, with frozen puddles and ponds gleaming through the branches; every four of five miles a small, rude settlement. The ride was very noisy, with a constant scraping and banging of metal against metal, and very uneven: smooth stretches would be followed by sudden, violent bumping and bucking of the cars. James and Eliza probably slept now and then. (They had, after all, gotten up at two that morning to ride the wagon into Cleveland, through the frigid winter air.)[5] They were reminded often how new the route was; repeatedly the train stopped for long periods, for no apparent reason, in the middle of the woods. Still, James found it "a very pleasant ride." It was comfortable enough, despite the overpowering heat from the stove in the center of the car. At intervals, a black man came through the cars with a can of free water and a dipper for the passengers, and possibly, even at this early date, there were some of the itinerant peddlers and book vendors aboard who later became such nuisances on this line. Little towns passed by, mere names, heralded by the conductor (who wore no uniform, only a suit)—Wellington, New London, Shelby.[6] The passengers ate food they had brought.[7] As the cars rattled southward and darkness fell, the conductor lighted tallow candles, thick as a man's wrist, in globes attached to the walls. Outside in the darkness, gusts of bright sparks from the engine swirled past like fiery snow. The dark woods slid past at twenty or thirty miles per hour.[8]

It was after eight o'clock when they arrived in Columbus. An "omnibus"—that is, a coach—took them and their luggage through unfamiliar, muddy streets to the Neil House on High Street opposite the State House. It was a veritable brick palace, five stories high with an imposing stone veranda and polished black walnut woodwork. The country visitors were given a room on the fifth story. They took supper in the dining room and arranged to have breakfast on the "American plan." "Good fare," noted James.[9]

James was out early next morning after breakfast, for their stage left at ten and he had only a couple of hours to see the main sights of the capital. It seemed to be about the size of Cleveland, flat and spacious, with broad brick sidewalks. The most imposing building in town, and probably the one he had heard most of during his boyhood, was the state penitentiary, a big, sprawling structure of Ohio marble surrounded by a high wall, several blocks north of the Neil House near the river. He went there first. An admission ticket, he found, cost twenty-five cents at the warden's office. So it happened that he spent most of his morning in Columbus witnessing scenes of guilt and punishment. Doubtless with a suppressed shiver (to be sent to Columbus was the height of criminality in Ohio), he and the other tourists followed the guard who showed them some of the 350 cells.[10] The cells were embedded in the solid wall, he noted, whitewashed, with crude beds, no windows, and a large oaken door with a small opening at the top to admit light, secured by grates and a heavy lock and bolt—fearfully small, too, only seven feet long by three and a half feet wide. They were empty. The penitentiary followed the "Auburn system" in which prisoners stayed in their cells only at night; the rest of the time they worked, forced to march in lock step from work to meals, forbidden to speak. James saw the dining room with its wooden plates and tin cups, and last of all crossed the courtyard to the shops where the inmates, pathetic in their striped uniforms and little caps, worked silently, making such things as shoes, carpets, and farm tools. The guard pointed out some as young as fourteen.[11]

The tour was definitely the highlight of Columbus for James, although when he got back to the hotel he and Eliza crossed the street to visit the State House too. It was an odd little two-story building, brick, quaintly Georgian ("antique," James called it), with a shingled roof and vaguely colonial cupola and weathervane—soon to be replaced; convicts from the penitentiary were already working on the new capitol. Representative Gamaliel Kent from Bainbridge, an old friend of Abram and Eliza from early days in the Chagrin valley, showed them around as the session began. James was unimpressed by the legislators. "Their rubicund, bloated faces spoke plainly of the midnight bowl," he frowned, "and, in my opinion, unfitted them for representing the free people of a Great State."[12]

At ten o'clock they piled into a stagecoach opposite the Neil House for the forty-four jolting miles to Zanesville. In all likelihood, the stage belonged to Neil, Moore, and Company—the same Neil who owned the hotel, whose coaches were reputed the fastest and smartest on the National Road. It was a big, four-horse, nine-passenger affair, lined in faded red plush, supported by thick leather straps that served as springs. They jounced violently as the vehicle rumbled out Friend Street.[13]

It was a cold, rainy day, and a miserable ride. Just as the railroad had represented the newest in the technology of transportation, so the stage and the National Road represented a technology now on the verge of abandonment. Built a generation before, the National Road had been an ambitious government project to link east and west. It started from Cumberland, Maryland—stone markers by the roadside periodically gave the mileage to Cumberland—and ran to Vandalia, Illinois. This section, not particularly well engineered to begin with, had deteriorated under twenty years of neglect, so that the ride was rough, especially as they got out of the flat country around Columbus into the hills of eastern Ohio.[14] At least in this weather there was no dust seeping into the coach from outside, covering everyone and everything, but there was mud in plenty, especially in the tavern yards where they stepped every seven or ten miles, and where the male passengers got out to refresh themselves and returned to breathe whiskey fumes into the close, cold interior. Talk of politics was incessant. The coach splashed on, under the ministrations of the driver, who was required by the company to maintain an average speed of ten miles an hour—ludicrously slow from a twentieth-century viewpoint, but fast, even hazardous, for stagecoach driving. They tossed and jolted and learned for themselves why the stage was nick-named the "shake-guts." Finally, around five that afternoon, they lurched into Zanesville.[15]

Curiously enough, the fare for the two disparate passenges—Cleveland to Columbus and Columbus to Zanesville—had been about the same: four dollars per passenger, fully a third of James's monthly salary as a schoolteacher.[16]

The trip was all but over now. The little pottery-manufacturing city of Zanesville looked unimpressive in the February dusk; James patronizingly called it "nice," but added that it would stand no comparison with Cleveland.[17] The travelers put up at the Eagle Hotel, apparently a pretentious place like the Neil House,[18] and next morning, finding no steamboat to take them downriver, took passage in a skiff and arrived at Blue Rock that afternoon, "weary and worn" with the journey.[19]

They arrived on 1 March, and ended up staying the whole spring. James soon got to know his relatives: Uncle Henry and Aunt Phebe, their married son Jacob who lived nearby, and two other sons, still at home, Ellis and

Orrin. Ellis was about James's age; moreover, he had, like James, taught district school that winter, in fact was just finishing his winter term. He and James became close companions almost at once. They rode horseback together to visit a farmer about thirty miles away—a mode of travel so uncommon for James that he felt it worth noting in his diary. They also shared farm work. James soon found that he was expected to pull his weight on Uncle Henry's farm. Within two weeks of his arrival, he and Orrin were out hauling manure. ("I do not make a very stiff team yet," James wrote.) By the time they left in May, he had also helped clean wheat, stuff sausage, dig limestone for burning, make material for barrels, fill out Uncle Henry's tax assessing papers, chop wood, make wagon tongues, put up a small log building on the farm, and tend several of his uncle's calves that had been poisoned from eating buckeye or mountain laurel.[20]

Though Eliza began getting homesick when they had been there scarcely a month, James did not—probably because he was so busy observing the novel environment he was in, giving it the same critical scrutiny he had applied to the Baptists at Chester the preceding fall. Some parts of the area he thoroughly approved of. The landscape, for instance, was fascinating. Hills rose abruptly from the river valley to summits that seemed loftier, though in fact they were no higher, than the hills of Cuyahoga County. The surface of the land was rolling and broken by rock outcrops. "This country abounds in minerals," James noted at the end of March when he was digging limestone for Uncle Henry. "On this farm there is any quantity of stone—coal and limestone and one mile from here, salt abounds." A few miles downriver, one of his cousins may have showed him the local phenomenon they called the Devil's Tea Table—a thirty-three-foot-long oval slab of sandstone poised on a pedestal of soft shale, overlooking the river.[21]

As the spring advanced and flowering trees, uncommon in the forests of the Reserve, burst into bloom, James was completely captivated. He loved to climb to the top of one nearby hill—it seemed closer to Heaven—for "meditation and communion with the Creator." Now, at April's end, as the hillsides became beautifully soft and clouded with the mauve and pink of redbud, the white of the wild plum, all the way into the blue distance, the whole countryside seemed to him like "one extended orchard." The panorama tempted him to extravagant flights of rhetoric in his diary, concluding with a curious but evocative sentence, composed perhaps on his favorite hilltop: "The whip-poor-will chants her nocturnal orgies as the clear warm vesper hours approach after the retiring sun."[22]

His reaction to the people was not nearly so favorable. The farmers of the Muskingum valley, with their Pennsylvania and Virginia origins, had manners much more open and gregarious than the stiff, brusque style of the Reserve, and their continual socializing got on James's nerves: "In this place the people are of a social nature and have each one a 'Frolic'—husking, loging [*sic*], sawing—and in fact any business which they have on hand. I do not think they make much."[23] His Yankee conscientiousness saw all this frolicking as a waste of time. He was offended, likewise (and maybe alarmed), by the vivacity of the girls, which he mistook for forwardness. He wrote his cousins in Orange:

> Tell your father that I often think of the remark he made to me the night before I came away with regard to the girls here. There does indeed seem to be a want of that modest reserve and retiring deportment which so adorn the character of woman. There seems to be great boldness on their part. It is however customary, but I regard the tendency to be very pernicious in its effect. It is also very customary for young men to spend Sunday evenings with some young lady of the neighborhood, hence, there is hardly a boy or girl 16 years old who are not "shinning" (as they call it) Sunday evenings. Even now Orrin has gone and I presume we shall not see him again before 3 o'clock in the morning.[24]

Now and then his sojourn in Muskingum County gave him a chance to take in something he simply would not have seen at home—a woman preacher, for instance.[25] His reaction to these novelties varied from ironical to scathing. One can sense the horrified fascination with which he described a visit he and Ellis made, once when they were in Zanesville, to early morning Mass at what he called "the Catholic meeting house":

> As each member entered he dipped his finger in the holy water and crossed himself, then immediately kneeled down and those that could read prayers. The others would say them on their amber beads. The priest came in and went into the back apartment and several went in for confession of sins. The priest read in Latin or German, yet his congregation were mostly Germans. He, however, did not read loud or distinct enough to be heard by his audience. He stood with his back to the congregation and made occasional gyrations and genuflexions and changed his garment two or three times. He had two young men to wait upon him and carry his trail (tail). I noticed that the priest (a libel upon the name) seemed the least reverential of all.[26]

On the whole, the short stay in Blue Rock seems to have strengthened rather than weakened young Garfield's religious commitment. Surrounded by shouting Methodists and sinister Catholics with their diabolical overtones, he came to value his plain, rational faith the more. The fact that they did not always go to meeting on Sunday (his uncle, though a Methodist, was apparently a lukewarm one) made him long for the Disciples in Orange, and the weekly fellowship around the Lord's table.[27] He became surer in his own mind that he wanted to attend school at Hiram next term, no matter what effort it took.

The big experience of his sojourn in southern Ohio, one which gave him ample opportunity to observe and criticize the mores of the people, was a two-month stint teaching school. He had been there scarcely a week when his uncle suggested he might want to take over for the spring term at Back Run, where Ellis had just finished teaching. They made inquiries around the district, and apparently no one else was interested in the job, for he got it without effort. On 17 March he went to Zanesville to pass the certification test, and 19 March he opened his school.[28]

James knew before he began that he was not going to like the job. (The money—$16.66 a month—was presumably the reason he accepted.) He would be teaching in a "miserable old log school-house" on the banks of a rocky creek, "as smutty as a blacksmith's shop" inside, furnished with four-legged benches and a tall coal stove. He dug coal for the stove himself from a bank behind the school. The scholars would be mostly small fry, "trying to my patience and also to my stomach," as he wrote.[29] As for educational deficiencies, he was prepared for anything. As school went on, his journal became filled with irritable comments in which one senses the Yankee-educated Reserve boy trying to clean out the Augean stables of ignorance and backwardness in southern Ohio.[30] "The scholars have been allowed to 'go out,' leave their seats when they chose. I must therefore draw the check some. . . . There is one boy in my school that can say his letters down but cannot say them up. It arises from wrong training. . . ." A math problem that had baffled teachers in a nearby county was "no more than a question in Simple Division, and any school acquainted with that rule ought to do it."[31]

Criticism from parents about what he was doing, though he pretended indifference to it, really grated on his nerves. "The people in this district all want to rule," he wrote 21 March, "and because their lordships were not consulted some refuse to send to school, and are trying to break down the school. Go it. I am perfectly willing you should." On 6 April: "Understood that a woman in the district took a boy out of school because I pointed my finger at him. Go it." On 24 April: "Heard tonight that Mrs. Shaw was going to take her boys out of school if I did not make other boys let them alone. . . . Let her drive her team as hard as she pleases. I can stand it." Finally, in mid-May, when parents began withdrawing their children from his school because it was corn planting time and they were needed on the farm, James had had enough. He abruptly closed the school and collected his pay.[32]

By that time it did not matter too much, since his mother was all ready to go home, back to the Reserve where people behaved sanely and predictably, if less colorfully than in the Muskingum valley. After a last round of visits to cousins, and a promise from Ellis to consider coming to Hiram, James and Eliza left Zanesville on 30 May, this time by the old slow route up river and canal, on the canal boat *Sacramento*. Next day they passed through the section (which Eliza duly showed her son) near Newcomerstown, where Abram

Garfield had superintended the digging of the canal. A couple of days after that, the captain of the boat fired his steersman and, hearing that James had some canal experience, hired the nineteen-year-old teacher to steer the boat as far as Cleveland. James was no doubt happy to be able to show off his skills to Eliza.[33]

All the same, his new job of steering the boat down the canal opened up a large area of latent conflict in his thoughts which kept him preoccupied the rest of the trip. It concerned himself, his family, and his future role.[34] Here he was, again working on the canal, part of which his father had helped to build. This was man's work, Garfield work. Uncle Thomas and Amos Letcher and his father and all the Garfields had been men of the same stripe, bullying, tough, capable, with enormous physical strength. (His great-grandfather Solomon Garfield, back in New York, had once carried a five-hundred-pound millstone half a mile, they said. His father had been able to lift a full whiskey barrel by the chime and drink from the bung.) On the other hand there were the Ballous, his mother's family, smart and tenacious, students and teachers, people like Ellis, or Cousins Harriet and Henry, or his mother herself, not domineering like the Garfields but intelligent and persistent. Which was he, a Garfield or a Ballou? Or was he a happy synthesis, a muscleman who could conjugate Latin verbs, a scholar who could steer a canal boat? What was his destiny, if he had one?

These were the kind of thoughts still in his mind 4 June, when the *Sacramento* glided to a stop at Ben Fisher's in Independence, at five in the morning.[35]

17

Reaching Out

Summer 1851

JAMES sat in semidarkness, at a large table in the close, heavily draped parlor of a Cleveland hotel. Around the table he could see the dim faces of fifteen other people, the ladies' faces abrupt above their dark, high-necked dresses, the stiff white collars of the gentlemen faintly luminous in the dim light. He knew none of them. There was breathless silence. The plain, fortyish woman at the head, whose name he understood to be Miss Fish, had finished her preliminary statement; now the group drew their chairs closer and waited for the knockings to begin.[1]

It was, of course, a seance, though James would not have used the word. Some of the paraphernalia the twentieth century associates with such ceremonies were absent: no crystal ball, no bells to be rung, no turbaned gypsy. There were only the bare table and the three ladies at the head, Mrs. (not Miss) Fish and two younger women. This was spiritualism in its earliest, one might say its sincerest, form.

Spiritualism in 1851 was a craze sweeping the Northern states. The two women who had begun it were there at the head of the table, Katie and Margaret Fox. Back in 1848, they had astonished their family in Hydesville, New York, with mysterious rappings that seemed to proceed from the walls and floors of any room they were in. The sounds, they said, were from spirits who wanted to communicate with humans; neighbors came in to hear them, and the noises became a local sensation. Leah Fish, the girls' older sister, who lived in nearby Rochester, had seen the commercial possibilities of the phenomena, and in the fall of 1849 they had begun holding public sessions and charging admission. Success, and the ensuing controversy, were huge and in stantaneous. Everyone in the North wanted to know whether the rappings were a hoax; if so, how did they do it? If not, what did it all mean? The Fox sisters had gone to New York and the other big cities of the seaboard; now they were touring the country with their spirit messages and finding the sensation as great as ever. The Cleveland newspapers were full of their doings, and they continued to make money. James had had to pay one dollar from his canal wages to get in.[2]

He had decided to come on the spur of the moment. He and Uncle Thomas had driven into Cleveland that morning (this was the morning after their arrival on the canal) and, passing the Dunham House on the Public Square, had seen a notice about the "spirit knockings."[3] Uncle Thomas, probably skeptical, had also probably had business elsewhere in town, but James, with cash in his pocket and nothing in particular to do, had decided to try communicating with the spirits. Undoubtedly he had read about the spirit knockings in the papers; the novelty and the sensation sounded exciting. Also, since his journey up the Ohio Canal, his dead father was very much in his thoughts—he had been talking about him to Uncle Thomas—and perhaps his spirit would be among the ones at the session. And more broadly, James, like many another intelligent young person, may have seen in the whole phenomenon a promise of importance for the future.

The twentieth century tends to look at spiritual manifestations as either supernatural or fraudulent. The middle nineteenth century saw them differently. Science and religion, it seemed to many people, had been moving closer and closer, and tending to validate each other as they did so. Geology, for instance, seemed to prove the reality of Noah's flood.[4] Phrenology and hypnotism put humans in touch with the laws of the mind, as physics and chemistry had with those of matter. And there were no real contradictions among the results of these varied inquiries. A vast similitude interlocked all; the world of the Bible and the world of the scientist were the same.[5] Young Garfield, for instance, in common with many educated Americans, felt that the shining planets that moved through the sky, Jupiter, Venus, Mars, and the rest, were the homes of blessed spirits; humans failed to see them only because their instruments were not good enough. Thus it seemed plausible that the Fox sisters had somehow made the final breakthrough between the physical and spiritual realms; men and spirits might now be able to communicate regularly, subject to the Creator's laws.[6]

A communication from Benjamin Franklin, received by the Fox sisters during their stay at Cleveland (a popular feature of their sessions was messages from spirits of the illustrious dead), illustrates, though in nebulous language, the kind of grand synthesis many nineteenth-century Americans were looking for. "Franklin," rapping vigorously and spelling out his message by a prearranged code, stated:

> Spirit is the great positive element of being; matter the great negative. There is an elemental difference between matter and spirit. Electricity and magnetism are intimately compounded with matter, and belong to it. There is a dividing link between matter and mind, compounded of electricity and magnetism, yet finer than either, called vitality or life. . . . Thought is mental motion, and is conveyed from one mind to another by an intermediate medium, which is put into action by the mind. This medium lies between nervous fluid and spirit, and exists in various degrees of refinement in the element of vitality, or life.[7]

Now, at one side of the room, the rapping began—first on the wall, or a settee against the wall, then moving to the table. (Other visitors in Cleveland reported hearing additional sounds, like "sawing, drawing nails, etc." but James and his group heard only raps.)[8] Then, to James's astonishment, conversation with the spirits began. Each person at the table in turn asked whether some spirit wanted to communicate with him; the answer was given by "two or three raps!" The inquirer then asked who the spirit was; "the ladies would call over the alphabet and when they came to the right letter it would rap!" The spirit established its genuineness by answering questions about the number, names, and ages of children or other relatives of the inquirer; it was "infallibly" correct. James called for the spirit of his father.

> It (what professed to be it) responded by rapping. The rapping of no two spirits were alike. I asked my father his name. I called over several names and when the right one was called it rapped! In this way it told me my own name, that I had one brother living, told me his name, said I had one brother in the spirit land, name given, age also, told me how many years he (father) had been dead. There were many other tests and correct answers.

All the questions he remembered asking, one notes, concerned male Garfields—himself, his living brother, his dead brother, his father. The fact suggests that problems of maleness, of masculine responsibility, were on his mind; what he wanted, perhaps, was the assurance that his father would have understood and approved of the course his life was taking.

James left the Dunham House that afternoon bemused, only half believing. Like many others, he had found the spiritualist experience less than wholly satisfying. Perhaps what troubled him, as it did others, was the odd disparity between the cosmic nature of the supposed contact between two worlds and the trivial nature of the information actually exchanged. He was half inclined to conclude that it was a swindle and that the young ladies were making the raps by some device he had not figured out, but could not understand how the "spirits" had been able to answer his questions so accurately. "'Tis a mystery however, and I'll not speculate upon it," he concluded. It would at least be a good tale to regale the family.[9]

This was not the last he was to hear of the spirit rappings, though. For the next few years they were to play a recurrent part in his life and in that of the Reserve.

From a practical standpoint, the next thing on his mind was a summer job to earn money for Hiram in the fall. The sixth day after their return to Orange found James down in Aurora, having dinner at the farm of Worthy Taylor, for whom he and John Rundt had worked back in 1848. Eliza was in Solon, visiting Mary and Hitty and their families, so James had taken the opportunity to go on a few miles to Taylor's. The farmer, a Disciple, was receptive to the young man's questions about a job, but didn't think he would have any work for him on the farm until July first, three weeks away and too long to wait for James, who was eager to start making money. There was always carpentering as an alternative. "Perhaps it would be better if I could work at the joiner's trade," James mused in his diary that night.

By two days later he had made up his mind. He crossed the river and made his way up the steep hill to the Falls in search of his old master Jedidiah Hubbell, to see whether there was any work to be had in building. It turned out there was. Business was brisk, and though Hubbell had one or two hands already, he was not averse to hiring another. He and his partner, George Woodward, took James on at a salary of eighteen dollars a month and board.[10]

"We found him a very good hand for the price," Woodward recalled later; "full as good as the majority even now. He was strong and ready to take hold of anything that came to him, and ever anxious to learn all he could of the trade, although he told me he did not expect to follow the business. . . ." Perhaps, he told Woodward, this would be his last summer in carpentry. But he went with a will at his first job, putting siding and shingles on a half-completed barn in Chagrin Falls. Despite the spring of physical labor at his uncle's farm, it was tiring work. He sweated freely in his work clothes and dropped off to sleep quickly at night, at Woodward's where he was staying.[11]

He worked on the roof, with a good view over the town and the vertiginous slope down to the foot of the valley, the trees in the first full bright green leaf of early summer. It was fortunate James had a good head for heights; nothing seems much higher than a barn roof.

Saturday nights he would trudge home to Orange, and Sundays, in his suit, he partook of the delights of a real Disciple meeting. After his sojourn in Blue Rock, James felt joy in being at home and praising his Maker as he was supposed to be praised. So the affairs of the church were particularly absorbing to him that summer. When Hiram Heath and Joe Cleveland got into a quarrel and had to be rebuked by the church, James was worried that Joe had been guilty of "unchristian conduct." He was even more concerned when Bentley Tinker, extravagant as always, was expelled from the church for false doctrine. "May the Lord preserve the church from apostacy [*sic*]," he wrote in his diary. An odd sidelight to worship one Sunday morning, odd in view of the Disciples' customary seriousness, provided James his most embarrassing moment of the summer. In a parody of the women's rights reformers of the early 1850s, two young men came out dressed in the then-popular Bloomer costume, to the guffaws of the congregation. James, supersensitive to the sexual implications, found the burlesque "shameful in the extreme."[12]

Mainly, though, the center of Christian faith, as it had been from his earliest childhood, was still the fact of death and the promise of resurrection. Viewed one way, death was the question to which Christianity was the answer. From another angle, death was the moment that validated Christian claims; by going forward joyfully to meet it, the Christian proclaimed his faith to those who stood by, especially unbelievers. In the view of early nineteenth-century evangelicalism, the Christian's life on earth was essentially one long preparation for this crucial moment. No wonder, then, that there was in the Reserve as in all America of that era what one student has called the "death cult," a set of customs and rituals surrounding the transcendental event. The dying Christian strove to "fall asleep in the arms of Jesus," with appropriate hymns and prayers; fellow believers watched with interest and concern both for the state of the dying one and the experience that they themselves would have to undergo some day.[13]

Of this struggle at the heart of his religion James was reminded more than once that summer. Periodically he noted deaths in his own neighborhood and nearby, like that of Brother Nathan Robinson of Chagrin Falls, who was harnessing a pair of colts to his wagon when they got away and ran over him. He died two hours later. This was in late July. In June James and cousin Henry had sat up all night, as was the custom, with the corpse of Cotton Harper, dead from injuries received in an accident the day before. This was a tiring duty, but it had to be done. One tried to stay awake and occasionally look at the body, which was sometimes covered by a "dead-cloth," sometimes uncovered. It was a time for serious reflection. In March of next year James, sitting up with the corpse of Edwin Mapes's brother, would watch the "lifeless remains," the "cold marble brow" and dull sightless eyes of the farm lad, and end up writing nine stanzas of verse on the theme of death, ending of course with resurrection. There was also the task of watching with those who were sick and on the threshold of death, as James did that August with old Mr. Paddock in Russell; in July he was watching by the bedside at midnight when farmer Parkman died. All these ceremonial ties kept the fact of death before his eyes and sweetened the promise of Christian faith.[14]

After they completed the barn, the next job they had to do was a new Disciple meeting house right in the village of Chagrin Falls. It would be a simple building, of course—Disciples, at Alexander Campbell's urging, kept their buildings simple, one-story houses, without steeple, galleries, or pulpit. Their only distinctive feature was an inclined floor, "descending from the entrance one foot in every eight or ten" to the Lord's table, and a railing across the interior to separate church members and attenders for communion purposes.[15]

Only a quantity of large logs, the bark peeled off, were on the ground when they arrived at the site. This was to be a job done from scratch; consequently, the workmen's first task was that of scoring the logs so that they could be hewed into the posts and beams that would make up the frame. This operation was most often done with an axe. The log was held in place by a metal "dog" (a sort of giant staple) at each end; straight lines were snapped on it with a taut chalked string; and the workmen who were scoring moved slowly down the log with axes, stopping every few inches to make a deep vertical cut in the side right on the line. This process was repeated on all four sides of each log. The cuts made it possible for another worker to come behind them with a tool called a broadax—a wide axe with a crooked handle, its blade sharpened on one side only—and chop down on the scored sections, hewing the log into a squared timber. The tricky job of hewing, which involved swinging a heavy, sharp tool close to one's legs with considerable force, was done this time by a young man named Uriah Smith—more than likely the Uriah Smith James knew from Orange. His family lived on the Orange–Solon town line near the Judds. He was seventeen in 1851, and the only young man ever expelled from the Philomathean debating society in the red schoolhouse for "bad conduct." James and two other men did the scoring.[16]

Gradually the squared timbers accumulated on the ground at the site. The next step, putting them together into a stout frame, called for two other tools, an auger and a forming chisel. Using the corkscrew-like auger, Woodward's crew laboriously drilled holes near the ends of the heavy beams and then enlarged and squared them with the chisel into deep holes called mortises. Their purpose was to hold the tenons, ends of other beams that had been sawed or chiseled to fit. Woodward drew rough markings to show them where to bore, but measurements did not have to be very exact; in fact, a rough fit might hold together better than a perfect one. Other pairs of beams were joined by an auger hole drilled through both and then plugged with a wooden peg, or trunnel, pounded in with a mallet. All this time, the frame lay flat on the ground; it was not raised until all the pieces were complete. It was rather like a giant, heavy jigsaw puzzle whose solution only the master carpenter clearly saw.[17]

"The large timbers for the Disciples' Church at Chagrin Falls being on the ground July 4, 1851," Woodward recalled,

> Garfield, Hubbell, and myself concluded not to celebrate, but to commence work on that building. So, Hubbell began to hew the rough off, and I began to scratch the timber, while Garfield started the two-inch auger, but by the time he had made one or two mortises for the northeast corner of the house, so that it could be said he had made the first mortise and that in the chief corner, our zeal for labor had gone down and our patriotism had obtained the ascendancy; so we put up our tools, went home, put on our soft clothes and started for the grove about one and a half miles east of the village, where there was a picnic. . . .[18]

Actually, James did not go to the picnic with them; Woodward was wrong there. He went home, feeling satisfied with himself for abstaining from the feasting and drink of the Fourth. "Hundreds are today shouting independence who are slaves to their appetites and passions and sins," Garfield wrote in his diary. Doubtless he felt satisfied, too, that his hand had been the first to work on the frame of the Disciple church. One wonders, in fact, whether it was not James's zeal for the Disciple house that had led him, Hubbell, and Woodward to work on the Fourth at all. He felt proud to be doing the Lord's work, just as much so as when he prayed or preached—for he now spoke occasionally in meeting.[19]

The weekend after the Fourth, he had another gratifying experience in the same vein. He and Henry went to Hiram to see the new Disciple seminary where he was going to enroll in August. It was about a twenty-mile journey, across rolling fields and pastures still interspersed with stretches of primeval forest, with wild chicory and black-eyed susan, midsummer flowers, blooming on the wayside, but well worth the trip to James. He saw the Western Reserve Eclectic Institute (commonly called "the Eclectic"), which was, like Geauga Seminary, housed in a single building. But the Eclectic's building was more striking than Geauga's. It stood on a high hill, impressively isolated from Hiram crossroads, in the middle of a cornfield—a three-story stone-and-brick building, topped with a zinc-covered cupola, with its spacious entrance on the east side ("like the temple on Mount Moriah," as the catalogue carefully pointed out). At some distance stood the few buildings of the hamlet. On the east-west road there was a wooden Disciple church. There was only one other church in town, the Methodist. Truly, this seemed like a place where Disciples could study and worship together in peace.[20]

James and Henry may well have run into problems looking for a room for the fall term. The influx of students in the past year, without a dormitory for them to stay in, had strained the housing resources of the little hamlet almost to breaking. George Udall, whose house was at the foot of the east hill, had seventeen students boarding in his house at one point; Zeb Rudolph, near the college, had ten or eleven in his seven-room house, in addition to himself and his family. Of course the extra income was welcome, and landlords tried to squeeze in as many students as possible. Four to a room was customary; if two double beds would not fit into a room, they were, on occasion, trimmed to fit. James and Henry finally managed to find a room, very near the seminary building, at Cyrus Taylor's.[21]

Then it was back to the Falls and back to work. He did not work on the Disciple meeting house to its completion, only long enough to finish the frame, pounding the timbers, mortised and tenoned, together with the huge mallet, actually a section of log with a handle attached to it, called a commander. (One swung it between the legs, as in croquet.) But before the frame was raised, Woodward put him on another job, out in the countryside of Russell, east of the Falls. This, too, was a labor of love—it was building a house for Brother Lillie, the preacher who had converted him, in a neighborhood much like his own, full of devout Disciples.[22]

Lillie's house was another job from the ground up, so that James, Woodward, Hubbell, and possibly a man named David Burton, another workman, had to go back to the routine of scoring and hewing timber, cutting mortises and tenons, and pounding the beams together. Whether the house was large or small is not recorded. It did have a north wing, which Garfield mentioned several times in his diary. Probably it was a fairly typical Greek Revival house, copied, as was often the case, from another residence nearby or from a picture in a newspaper or magazine. There was no blueprint; the client simply explained to the builder what he wanted the house to look like—often a rough description was written into the contract—and the builder took it from there. By 29 July they had the frame for the main house raised and were working on the north wing.[23]

With the frame and rafters in place (and it now being August: harvest going on in the fields, shadows in the woods deeper and browner, the heat stickier, mosquitoes beginning to be an annoyance), the next step was putting on the roof and its necessary adjunct, the cornice. The cornice distinguished a house from a mere cabin built for shelter only, gave it a certain touch of style and artistry. It was utilitarian in origin, a big rectangular box to cover the exposed ends of the rafters at the gable end of the house. But builders of Greek Revival style, even in rural Ohio, joined this box (technically called the corona) to the plane of the roof and to the siding with graceful moldings modeled on the cornices of classic temples, moldings with classical Italian names like ogee, ovolo, cimarecta and cimareversa, creating elegant patterns of light and shadow above each side of the house. The moldings were made on the spot, at the carpenter's bench, from softwood, with moulding planes whose zigzag blades cut out the right size and shape. A master carpenter might have to carry around twenty to forty moulding planes for us on his different jobs. Thus early August found Garfield and his bosses getting out molding for the cornice at their several benches, carrying on animated discussion as they worked—"litigating disputed points," as James called it. There were about two hundred feet of cornice on this house; they had no small job.[24]

That summer James found a way, after a hot, exhausting day, to get rid of the sweat caked on his body, the sawdust and grime in the creases of his neck and elbows. On the way back from work, he and the other hands would stop at one of the many little mill-dams on the Chagrin river, check to see that no women were about, strip, and take a shower bath under the cascading water. The practice appealed to James not only because it was refreshing; it was also supposed to be healthful.[25] His phrenology and advice-to-young-men books were unanimous in praising the virtues of dousing oneself with cold water.[26] (He liked it so much, in fact, that he built himself a shower bath that fall at Hiram.) In other areas, too, he tried to follow the precepts of modern reform. He avoided harmful foods; when he felt sick, he dieted rather than call in a doctor. The temperance movement, another variety of self-purification, also had his support; he attended a couple of temperance lectures at the Falls that summer and seemed to enjoy them.[27] Presumably he was still also trying to follow the advice books' injunctions against masturbation. All this self-improvement, mental as well as physical (discussing serious topics at work, rather than indulging in dirty jokes and backguard humor), was a supplement to Christian faith. It was not simply a matter of avoiding the sins of the flesh; it was purifying oneself to be able to do God's work on earth.

The cornice was planed and nailed on; roofboards and shingles were in place, as was the siding on the north wing; and it was 20 August, time for James to quit work and collect his pay, preparatory to going to Hiram. Fifteen dollars was still due him. He collected it from Hubbell after the day's work, put it into his memorandum book and stuffed that into his coat pocket. Slinging the coat over his shoulders, he set off homeward—but before he was halfway to the Falls, he happened to check and found that he had somehow lost ten dollars of his money on the road somewhere. In agitation, he turned and began walking back toward Russell. As George Woodward heard the story, he had not gone far before he ran into young Dr. Willard Bliss of the Falls, "and asked him if he had found a certain book, describing it." The doctor had. He handed it down from his carriage, and James, overjoyed by the sudden recovery of his money, like the Ethiopian eunuch in Acts 8:39, "went on his way rejoicing." He was free from manual labor for a year; now it was on to Hiram and learning.[28]

18
The Education of a Disciple
Fall 1851

FROM far away, across the steep hills with their fields of wheat stubble or corn, their pastures of sheep or cattle, arriving students could glimpse the dazzling, zinc-covered cupola atop the Eclectic. One who first came that very month, August 1851, remembered that he first caught sight of it from the hamlet of Troy, no less than five miles away, as he approached down the northern road. To another, the first sight was a startling experience—the building, with its gleaming dome, looked like the allegorical Temple of Fame from his *Webster's Speller*, suddenly materialized in the Ohio hills.[1]

James was approaching on the western road, through Mantua, in a slow, creaky wagon piled with trunks, perhaps sitting with Orrin on the driver's seat, perhaps in the wagon with Phebe, Harriet, William, and Henry (all four Boyntons were entering the Eclectic), when he first saw the cupola. The afternoon sun, behind them but still high enough to be hot, glinted bravely off it in the distance. Harriet and Phebe, encased in the long, heavy dark-red or dark-green or blue dresses necessary for proper young women even in the hottest weather, perhaps commented on the sight.[2]

One can be sure that James's heart beat fast. It was not only that he was going back to school at last, after almost a year, nor even that he was finally in a Disciple-run institution; it was mainly last-minute jitters about his own capacity for learning. "I have not studied in so long I expect I have forgotten a great deal," he wrote in his diary two days later as classes began. "But I must nerve myself up to the task of studying again."[3]

He did not have to face that task for a couple of days. They got in to Hiram late Saturday afternoon, spent the night at Cyrus Taylor's house, where they were to board, and next day went to meeting at the small, plain, frame Disciple meeting house on the southwest corner of the crossroads. On opposing corners of the treeless intersection stood other buildings equally plain: on the southeast corner the little schoolhouse familiarly called the "Stone Jug," on the northwest the simple Greek Revival house and general store of Thomas Young.[4] At meeting the principal of the Eclectic preached: A. Sutton Hayden, a slight, smiling little man with a musical voice, better known as a writer of hymns than as a teacher or scholar. The speaker at the afternoon meeting was the father of one of James's old Chester schoolmates, a carpenter named Zeb Rudolph, a slow, relentlessly logical preacher. That night, doubtless, James and the Boyntons went to bed quivering with anticipation, for the next day was the first of the term.[5]

Registration next morning was wonderfully uncomplicated.[6] All the students assembled at nine in what was called the "Lower Chapel," a large room directly ahead as one entered the imposing doorway, with five long rows of cherrywood desks.[7] After Bible reading and prayer, someone took the names of the students present and began trying to find out what they wanted to study. Though there was a suggested curriculum in the Eclectic catalogue, it was hardly ever followed to the letter—rather, the faculty tried to set up courses to accommodate students' needs. By midday, for example, young Garfield had found out that there were going to be two Latin courses this term, one elementary and the other in Caesar's *Commentaries*. He had not read Caesar at all before but did not want to repeat elementary Latin, so he signed up for the more advanced class and bought a slim school edition of the *Gallic Wars* for a few cents.[8]

Part of the fun of registration was milling around the big room as more students came in their Sunday best, seeing old friends and meeting new ones. James saw several former classmates from Chester—tall, lank Symonds Ryder, little Lucretia Rudolph and a group of her girlfriends. Also there was Solyman Hubbell's daughter Mary from Warrensville. New students kept coming in all morning, and by 2:00 p.m., when they all reassembled in the Lower Chapel, the total enrollment was announced as 114. James and the Boynton boys were also given their room assignment, a small stone room in the basement of the building, under the chapel. They would be sharing it with three other students—enrollment had been unexpectedly high, and space was at a premium. James would share a bed with a boy named Gid Applegate.[9] In the afternoon they moved their trunks over and spent some time helping to clean the recitation rooms on the upper floors.

That evening, still nervous, James started studying his Latin assignment, the first six lines of Book I. He quickly decided that, with five roommates, there would be no place for him to study in his room, so he took his candle, his book, and his notebook to one of the rooms upstairs and spread out the work on a table: "Gallia est omnis divisa in partes tres, quarum unam incolunt Belgae. . . ." He realized with a shock that he had, as he feared, forgotten a lot. He could get the meanings from the glossary, but his memory of the case endings was dim, and he didn't understand the order of the words. In a cold sweat mentally if not physically, he wondered if his worst fears were true after all, if he had lost so much ground staying in Warrensville and Blue Rock that he would have to go back and start over. Grimly he wrote down the English meaning of each word on a separate scrap of notebook paper, then began moving the bits of paper around as if trying to solve a jigsaw puzzle. The idea was helpful to a degree—but there were words that had more than one meaning, and the meanings of the cases were a problem. He kept at his puzzle, he recalled years later, "sullenly and determinedly," in total concentration. Gradually relations between the words became clearer. Some of his grammar exercises from Chester came back to mind, and the passage began to have some significance. Finally he had it translated. For the first time in hours, he looked away from the table and the flickering, nearly extinguished candle, and realized it was the middle of the night. Everyone was asleep downstairs. In the stillness he made his way back to his bed.[10]

The class in Caesar met at nine-thirty next morning, and James recited his lesson. He had gotten it right, but he also learned that the other students—a half dozen or so—had all had some previous experience in reading Caesar, and would have an easier time of it than he. Nonetheless, he felt good enough to go on. The teacher was a tall, wiry, earnest Virginian in his late twenties named Thomas Munnell, dark-haired, with a southern accent and southern manners, whom James immediately liked. Emboldened by his success in Caesar, he also signed up that afternoon for an intermediate Greek class with Munnell. In this class, again, most of the students would be a term or two ahead of him, but he decided to make an effort to keep up or, if he could not, drop out.[11]

The third class James had, if one can call it that, was required of all students. Every weekday morning at eight, the whole upper division of the school assembled in the Lower Chapel—boys on one side, girls on the other—for Bible reading, hymns, prayer, and a lecture, in Brother Hayden's ingratiating manner, on "Sacred History"—that is, the Bible. Hayden began with Genesis that term. James enjoyed the lectures; in the Orange meeting he had never been exposed to systematic exposition of the Scriptures.

One morning Brother Hayden had all the students open their Bibles (a Bible was required at lecture) to the fifth chapter of Genesis, and add up the ages of the Patriarchs before the Flood. His point was that if Methuselah had lived one year longer he would have perished in the Flood; his larger point was that the Bible had an internal consistency most secular history lacked, and that this was a powerful argument for its truth.[12] Other mornings he brought in the latest concepts of science to back up his arguments, in a manner possible only in the middle nineteenth century. One student remembered his pointing out in an exposition of Genesis 1, in opposition to skeptics who doubted the creation of the earth, that "the earth and every thing it contains—the air and the water; are compositions; the elements of which are rarely if ever found uncombined and as the elements must have existed previous to their combination therefore the time must have been when the earth was not."[13] Though the reasoning was perhaps a little shaky, the appeal to chemistry to back up the Bible was bold.

James heard the same blend of science and divinity later in the fall, when Jehu Brainerd, the self-taught Cleveland artist who had done the illustrations for Professor Samuel St. John's *Elements of Geology*, gave a four-part lecture series. He enjoyed the lectures immensely and summarized them in his diary. Brainerd assured the students that the earth had begun as "gaseous matter thrown off the sun by centrifugal force," and had condensed into a basically granite ball, with discernible layers of rock deposited successively at the surface: "Neace" (in James's spelling), then "Mica shiste," then Cambrian, "Celurian," Carboniferous, and so on. The fossils of extinct beasts found in the recent strata did not faze Brainerd; according to him, they were early experiments of the Creator, "[a]s yet . . . unfit for the companions of man." His last lecture was on "the present aspect of our earth, the causes which are now at work to carry out the great design of the Almighty, and the effect now being produced." By Brainerd's count, there had been six major geological eras; the seventh and last, he expected, would be the millennium predicted in Revelation. James was enthralled by this mixture of up-to-date science and sound Biblical doctrine, so much so that he bought St. John's book. Clearly, Hiram was going to be a more stimulating place intellectually than anywhere he had been.[14]

By the time Brainerd spoke, in early October, James had found that he was equal, or more than equal, to the demands of his schoolwork. His Latin class had been shrinking steadily, as one student after another dropped out for various reasons, and by the second week in October he was the only one left. Munnell, on whom the young man's intellect and determination had made quite an impression, gave him extra help with Caesar and lengthened his assignments. James picked up Caesar's Latin so readily that by the end of the term he was preparing as much as 120 lines a night instead of six, and was writing part of his diary in reasonably correct Latin. In Greek he was up with the rest of his class, and in mid-October he judged he had enough free time to start studying geometry, from Euclid, on his own. This was the same sort of rapid achievement that had dazzled people at Chester; at Hiram too it was beginning to make an impression.[15]

Other lectures stimulated him. The Reverend Samuel Ward, a black minister from Boston, spoke at the Disciple house on slavery, always an absorbing topic in the Reserve. The high point for James, perhaps, came in early September when Alexander Campbell himself took the platform in morning chapel—a white-maned man "of dignified sternness" in his sixties, wearing ordinary clothes, with deep-set eyes and a long white beard. He made no attempt at oratory, but spoke in a low, musical voice, with few gestures and without notes, on "Education." The students sat spellbound; though his talk lasted an hour, one called it "short." James, on the alert for transcendental phrases he could use in his own rhetoric, picked up a metaphor Campbell used: "He compared man to a keystone to an arch resting on two eternities, a past and a future. Grand idea."[16]

The progress James was making in his studies was not solely a result of his intelligence. He was working hard at them. Since his near-failure at the beginning of the term, he had resolved not to slack up in any way. He rose every school day at five in the morning or before, not too bad an hour for a farm boy, and regularly stayed up till ten studying upstairs in the recitation rooms. He gave himself little pep talks in his diary. Only courage and perseverance, he wrote, could help him "clamber up the rugged heights" of scholarship. "It is a long road that seems to stretch away in the future before me," he warned himself, "but I have started to tread its winding ways and I must not now turn back."[17]

Somtimes, too, between studies, he wrote verses about the joys of student life, as if to assert the validity of what he was doing. One poem compared study with farming and ended with a pun, surely not original with James, about trying to dig Latin roots and getting stumped. Another began cheerfully:

The rugged path the student treads
O! that's the path for me.
On him the sun of science sheds
No grief or misery.

A third, more serious, concluded that the end of study was eternal life—"To fit the soul, the immortal soul, / For mansions in the skies." These verses helped him to understand why he was pushing himself so hard. They were also genuine expressions of feeling—it *was* good to be back in school.[18]

Even with his rigorous schedule, he enjoyed spending time with other students. Saturdays, in particular, he recorded in his diary, he "played" a lot. This did not mean athletics. The Eclectic had no organized sports of any sort; its surroundings, a cornfield, an apple orchard, a sort of lawn with a few just-planted saplings, suggested its disinterest in sports. But students played the simple games boys and young man enjoy in their free time. On hot days, a group of boys might race down to the creek at the foot of the east hill, strip, and plunge in for a dip, being careful to keep their feet on the bottom. (Few or none could actually swim.) James and his companions liked wrestling matches, at which the big youngster from Orange was good—he nearly always threw his opponent. He could also jump farther and throw a weight farther than most.[19] As for other entertainments, there was a singing school on Saturday night, meeting twice on Sundays, and sometimes a church-sponsored event. On 6 September, for instance, James, Symonds Ryder and his brother, William, Harriet, and Phebe Boynton, and Mary Hubbell set out for the Cuyahoga yearly meeting in Bedford. They stayed at Uncle Joseph Skinner's, heard three or four sermons a day, saw lots of relatives and friends, and had a wonderful time.[20]

Despite all this activity, James often confessed to his diary early in the term that he felt lonesome. What bothered him was not that his friendships were few but that they were shallow; he had no one in whom he could confide freely, not even his Boynton cousins. Rainy days particularly put him in low spirits, and he took refuge in poetry, writing about the coldness of the world and the bleakness of the weather.[21] His thoughts often addressed the fascinating theme of death, and one poem came near confronting a classic Victorian dilemma: since Heaven was so blissful, death so certain, and life so full of cares and sorrows, why should one not wish to die?

Sickness and sorrow reign supreme
In this dark world of ours.
'Tis death alone 'twill change the scene
And give us peaceful hours.

Why do we wish to linger here
And lengthen out our breath?
Is life so sweet: or do we fear
The icy hand of death?[22]

One thing that may have cost James some potential friends was his sensitivity. He was as touchy as ever that first term at Hiram. His diary mentions three quarrels he had with various people, each a brief flareup for which he was sorry later. His warmth and openness and energy, other students learned, overlay a deep feeling of inferiority which could erupt without warning.[23]

That James should have worried about inferiority, in view of the record of achievement he was making that term at the Eclectic, seems incongruous. Actually, his worries had little to do with his performance at any given time; they went much further back. Most of them, one suspects, stemmed from the cause he himself mentioned repeatedly as the great tragedy of his life—the fact of having grown up in a household without a father. He seems to have been desperately unsure of his ability to fill a masculine role in society, having had no one to model himself on. In his relations with girls and in setting himself career goals, the things that really bothered him were problems related to the man's role: aggressiveness versus passivity, decisiveness versus vagueness. When he felt his pretensions to masculinity threatened, he suddenly became combative.[24]

It was natural that his favorite activity, at the Eclectic as elsewhere, should be the stylized verbal combat of debating, and it was fitting that through debating he came to know the student who was to become his closest friend. James had not been at Hiram two weeks before he was heavily involved in the student lyceum. The Eclectic, like Geauga Seminary, had rhetorical exercises one afternoon a week (in this case, Thursday), and James had already head enough speeches to convince him that there was "considerable talent" at

Hiram when he attended his first lyceum on the evening of 12 September, in the Lower Chapel. All the procedures were the same. The debaters were addressing a question left over from the sectional crisis of the year before ("Resolved that the signs of the times portend the speedy dissolution of the American union"), and he joined right in on the negative. The question was strongly contested. "Warm time," wrote James in his diary.[25]

"Warm time" was an entry that was to recur often in his description of debates in the lyceum. The debaters were apt to get passionate. "Don't I remember they were always sissing hot," recalled one early participant years later,"—always under a full head of steam, with many a ludicrous explosion? And I laugh now as I think how enthusiastic, how crude, how conceited, and withal how capable we severally and collectively were." Part of the comedy was the contrast between the country manners and accents of the debaters and their vaulting rhetorical aspirations. This was true even of James, whose diary contained occasional rural expressions—for instance, he described Reverend Ward as "a smart man to speak," and characterized the weather one day as "some rainy"; but when occasion required, as in a speech at the end of that term, he could soar to rhetorical heights like "They sink down into the gloomy caverns of the dead, and are soon forgotten. Shall they there rest while endless ages roll? Shall morning never dawn upon that dreamless sleep?"[26]

The outstanding orator in the lyceum when James began attending, a young man named John Encell, was a virtuoso at this kind of flowery verbiage. He also affected the kind of blunt sarcasm used in legal and parliamentary debates; the combination of the two had gained him a local reputation as a speaker, of which he was proud. James studied his style for some weeks, and then set up a debate with him at a regular meeting, before the usual crowd of academy students and local spectators. Encell led off, concluding with his customary sarcastic challenge. Garfield disposed of that in "a few hot sentences," and went on to a broad, satirical description of Encell's "bombastic eloquence," ridiculing it as "a misty exhalation," and as a sort of rhetorical beanstalk up which Encell hoped to climb. The audience roared. By the time James got to his concluding arguments, he had demolished Encell and was the new uncrowned champion of the Eclectic lyceum. Moreover, he had done so without offending Encell, who joined in the laughter and remained a friend as long as they were at Hiram together.[27]

James's closest friendship likewise began from a competition in debate. Besides their discussions and original compositions, members of the lyceum also declaimed set pieces from great literature. One of James's assignments was Thomas Campbell's "Lochiel's Warning," a dialogue in which he took the part of the Highland chief. His opposite number, who spoke the lines of the seer, was a pale, serious young man named Corydon Fuller. In fact, Fuller seemed most of the time to be on the opposite side of the question from

Garfield, and the two debated warmly; but despite that fact, or perhaps because of it, they came to respect and then to like each other. Talking together after lyceum and sometimes studying together, they discovered they had a great deal in common. Fuller's family lived in Grand Rapids, Michigan, but he was originally from Chardon, only fifteen miles east of Orange. His family were devoted Disciples, and his father was a carpenter. He knew enough carpentry to support himself, and had also, like James, taught district school. Like James, he was strongly religious and intensely ambitious to better himself; he dreamed of becoming a minister in some denomination, not necessarily the Disciples. His gravity gave him the air of a preacher already.[28]

By November, when the lyceum assigned them both to be editors of the newspaper it planned to put out, Garfield and Fuller were close friends. Many an evening Garfield would go to visit his friend, who roomed at Edwards's boarding house, on the east-west road. He would leave the college enclosure, which perhaps had already acquired the yellow board fence that surrounded it in those early years—if so, he crossed it by a step stile on the east side. He came out on the north-south road opposite the big, barn-like Methodist church, walked south to the crossroad, and turned left. Edwards's was the second house on the left; it was opposite a small store kept by a Mr. Bennett who was reputed to sell liquor under the counter to local people. James was proof against that temptation since his baptism, however, and Corydon was almost a fanatic about temperance. After their business for the lyceum was over, they would linger for hours, talking seriously. When the fall term ended and the two young men went their separate ways—both had winter teaching jobs elsewhere—they promised to correspond.[29]

In the same term, at the same time, another important relationship began to develop in James's life, but the evidence on its beginning is fragmentary and tells much less than one would like to know. To explain it, one must suppose that by mid-October most students in the Eclectic knew about Garfield's herculean study habits—how he would come home from supper at Taylor's, take his candle and his books, and go upstairs in the gathering dark to study in one of the recitation rooms. He did not expect interruptions, but late in October he had one—an "adventure," as he described it in his diary. Someone else unexpectedly appeared on the upper floor, and there followed what James cautiously Latinized as a "tener lussus," a tender game, sport, or play—in other words, a flirtation. By chance or by planning, a girl student had happened into the place where young Garfield was studying, and managed to draw him into lively, personal conversation.

The girl was Mary Hubbell, Solyman Hubbell's daughter from Warrensville whom James had taught the winter before—pretty, pert, and intelligent. One may be forgiven for suspecting that she had long admired her teacher from afar and welcomed a chance to get close to him in a different setting, talk with him as a person, and see what happened between them. Probably their first meeting was a little breathless on both sides; James was uneasy with females. But Mary was clever, playful but not bold; besides, she was someone he already knew as a friend. They bantered together, and enjoyed it. When she left, it was understood that she would come again.[30]

To James it was novel and exciting to be seeing a girl like this. He used his newly acquired command of Latin to hide the affair in his diary—"Ten. Am. cum pu." (Tender friendship with girl), he wrote next week, after they had seen each other again. But beyond his obvious excitement, it is not really clear how he felt. Nothing suggests that he found himself in love; rather, like many an introspective young man in a comparable situation, he may have felt confused, even apprehensive about what might develop. One evening when Mary came he brought Henry Boynton upstairs to study with him, perhaps to avoid a tête-à-tête. Another evening—or perhaps the same one—he took her outside and gave her a basic lesson on the constellations.[31] He enjoyed a buggy ride with Symonds Ryder and two girls, of whom Mary was one, to a nearby Disciple meeting. Perhaps he felt there was safety in numbers, or maybe he wanted to think of Mary as one good friend among several—"one of the boys," so to speak. She had different ideas, as will be seen.[32]

Amid the dawning of new friendships and the excitement of the classics, the end of the term came too soon—Friday, 14 November. It was an exciting time at the Eclectic; the last few days of the term students rushed around the boarding houses and the campus calling at each other's rooms and sharing sentimental farewells. Selected students had pieces—songs or original speeches to prepare for the final ceremonies. For James it was especially busy. Brother Hayden, impressed by his scholarship, had asked him to give a valedictory, and James duly wrote one, heavily rhetorical, centered on the fascinating themes of parting and death.[33]

The ceremonies took only a few minutes, and after them was the time of final parting. Corydon and his friend from Chardon, little Amelia Collins, came over to James's room to say goodbye to him and his roommates. Most of them would not see one another again until March—they all had teaching jobs lined up for the winter. Corydon would teach in Chardon, Henry Boynton in Russell. James felt certain he could get his Warrensville position again. In the morning he and the Boyntons and their trunks were rolling home through the mud.[34]

Sure enough, the Warrensville job was easy to get. He went over there a week after returning home and found Mr. Stiles and Mr. Gleason, two of the directors, entirely agreeable. They and the other directors had almost been holding the slot open. They were glad to see young Garfield, and bantered with him. Solyman Hubbell was particularly cordial—a fact into which James apparently read nothing. At the same time, there was other welcome news. James found out one morning while he was helping his brother butcher that Thomas had gotten some long-awaited money from the Rundts across the road. His own winter earnings would not have to go to help Thomas out, then; they could all apply to his tuition and board next spring. In anticipation, James had already bought himself a gold pen and a pocket watch for his teaching job. "May he that rules the destinies of the Universe support me in my responsible labors," he wrote.[35]

Brother Lillie was holding another series of meetings in the schoolhouse when James returned home, and for several days he attended them faithfully, thrilling as some of "the hard cases of the vicinity" turned to Christ and received baptism for the remission of their sins, just as he had done. It was a solemn spectacle, made more solemn by a milestone of his own: 19 November was his twentieth birthday.

O pleasant teens sweet days of joy
I've journeyed through your whole domain
You found me when a sportive boy
But now you'll ne'er return again,

he wrote in his diary. His teens, actually, had not been very joyful, but on a muddy, dismal November evening it was easy to look back and pretend they had. But the real concern of the poem lay some stanzas farther on:

But Time with swiftest wheels has sped
And I upon his mighty car
Have neared that "city of the dead"
Where ends all strife and raging war.

For a pallid Corydon Fuller, a gloomy Symonds Ryder, or a sickly William Boynton to be preoccupied with the next world was not astonishing; but for James, with his vitality and ambition, it was. Or rather, it would have been surprising in another time. In middle nineteenth-century Ohio, with the rhetoric of the "death cult" at its lushest, it was a sign of energy and high aspiration. Death was the ultimate adventure that gave meaning to the rest of life; it was also the portal to the glorious world where treasures were laid up for Christians like James. Life was a celestial railroad hurtling toward this fascinating destination. When would he arrive? In fact, would he live to see another birthday?

With him alone who reigns above
And rules the armies of the skies
And binds creation with his love
The answer to that question lies.[36]

19

Mary

Winter–Spring 1851–1852

DECEMBER 1851 at Warrensville was very different from the December before. To begin with, there was the weather. It was the coldest winter in sixteen years. There had been snow already in October; by the tim^ James began teaching on 1 December, there was enough on the ground for good sleighing. Both December and January were uncommonly cold, and in the latter part of January the temperature once got down to eighteen below zero. James was lucky not to have the wind whistling through his trousers this year as it had last. Sometimes he was out afoot, well wrapped up, when nearby farm buildings were just blurs behind an attacking host of snowflakes; one Monday morning, he had to walk from Orange to Warrensville in "a violent snowstorm," to open up school at nine. One night his ears froze.[1]

Continued brisk weather and deep snow meant good sleighing, and good sleighing meant an explosion of winter social life. Warrensville suddenly turned out to be a much more social community than it had seemed the winter before, teeming with balls, dances, and other parties at every little country crossroads, and James's students, healthy country youth, were eager to attend them all. Coming from a different sort of neighborhood, he had little sympathy for them. "*Saltant hac nocte*" (They are dancing tonight), he noted one evening unenthusiastically.[2] Their dullness and lack of interest in class, he thought, were due to these late-night entertainments. Occasionally he did a little partying himself; on 14 January, rather surprisingly, he and several other young men slogged through the snow to an oyster supper at Chase's tavern—surprisingly, because Fowler's *Amativeness* had warned him against such events, too often given, Fowler said, "expressly to beget unhallowed desires." More often, however, he spent the evening in his room, catching up on schoolwork, reading improving books, and pondering the apathy and "rowdyism" of his students.[3]

Part of James's problem seems to have been that his own attitude toward learning was changing, thanks to his success in mastering the classics and his contact with people like Professor Munnell. Learning now was no longer just fun, nor even just a tool one could use to serve the Lord better; it was something that could lead to earthly accomplishment, that could change one's whole life. He could use his learning to raise himself in people's estimation; so could others. Unrealistically, he wanted his students to realize the importance of the gift he was offering them. A few did respond to his enthusiasm. He had one group going through a Latin reader under his direction—fables, mythology, and Roman history. A couple of others wanted to study Legendre's *Geometry*, and he was teaching them although he had not yet formally studied the book himself, and had to read carefully every night to stay a page or two ahead. But he could not give these scholars all the attention they needed. He had too many others to teach—thirty-two subjects, he calculated one day, fifteen before lunch and seventeen after. He was continually switching from Latin to writing to botany to geography to arithmetic, at ten- or fifteen-minute intervals.[4]

This exertion was enough; but to be working with an advanced class and to have others in the room break out into noisy quarrels and horseplay was just too much. Several times he almost lost his patience; he took to writing cutting comments about the school in Latin in his journal; on one occasion he told someone that he disliked teaching where there were so many "frolickers." The remark got around and caused several students to feel insulted and quit the school. "Go it," was James's only comment, in his journal. To Corydon he wrote that at the end of school he intended to give a long talk "to some of them on the subject of rowdyism. I intend to do it up in as *brown a rag* as I am capable."[5] Sometimes he reflected that others were having similar problems; that John Smith, who was teaching in another of the Warrensville districts, had told him his school was in the same condition; that Corydon had written from Chardon that his students too were noisy and sluggish; that Orrin, in the home district in Orange, was having problems with student noise. Then he was inclined to blame their slackness on vague general causes, like impurities in the atmosphere. More often, however, he blamed it on them. "Oh! that I possessed the power to scatter the firebrands of ambition among the youth of the rising generation," he wrote Corydon in February,

> and let them see the greatness of the age in which they live, and the destiny to which mankind are rushing, together with the part which they are destined to act in the great drama of human existence. But, if I cannot inspire them with this spirit, I intend to keep it predominant in my own breast, and let it spur me forward to action.[6]

A month earlier, he had sent Corydon a wry little poem about his trials as a teacher:

> Of all the trades that men pursue
> There's none that's more perplexing
> Than is the country pedagogue's

In every way most vexing.

Cooped in a little narrow cell
As hot as black Tartarus
As well in Pandemonium dwell
As in this little school house.

Which was substantially true; his classroom, all of eighteen by twenty feet, probably did seem a little like Milton's Hell when he had thirty talkative students in it, the stove in the middle going full blast, and snow swirling outside.[7]

Of course he had the same consolations as last year: debate at the lyceum with Dr. Darwin, the Hubbells, and other good speakers; prayer and worship with the brethren; visiting other teachers' schools and talking shop; the conversation of the families he boarded with, the Stileses, Adamses, Hubbells.[8] Most of all, perhaps, there were poetry and prayer. He felt he ought to read the Bible more. "I need more faith," he wrote. "Faith comes by hearing and it by the word of God." But poetry could strengthen his faith by portraying the world as faith saw it, a world in which good and evil spirits fought one another, in Warrensville and everywhere else, for the souls of men:

In the dark watches of the night,
When earth's vast realm is still,
Thousands of winged seraphs bright,
These earthly regions fill.

And Satan's host—a numerous band
From dark Tartarus come,
And strive to gain the full command
Of man's eternal doom.[9]

One other difference probably caused him more anxiety than anything mentioned so far: the presence of Mary Hubbell in his classroom. Mary, home from Hiram, had lost no time in signing up for his school. In some ways, the fact was flattering; it added to a young man's status to have a young lady in whom he was especially interested. (The term "girl friend" was not then in use, at least not in the Reserve; there were only indirect and awkward equivalents like "particular friend" or "chosen one." If there was a shorter term in common use, I have not found it.) James had never had such a relationship before, though many of his contemporaries had; consequently, he did not mind his friends' delicate banter about his "attentive student."[10]

But the attentive student herself was a problem. Other teenagers in the classroom suspected her feelings about the brawny, brilliant "Mr. Garfield"; whenever she and James exchanged a look, James felt as if a dozen pairs of eyes, male and female, were watching. He did not particularly want to become a subject of local gossip; in Warrensville, as in any rural community, while the elders were talking of cattle and hog raising and the foibles of their neighbors, the young discussed the attractions of members of the opposite sex ("I must tell you John that I think a dam sight of Olive Juliet is a mighty slick girl but she can't shine with Olive"), who was sweet on whom, and what boy had recently gotten what girl in trouble ("You say you do not know how Orlando H has distinguished himself I will tell you he is '*papa*' and Julia Soule is '*mama*'").[11] He did not want to seem cold either, but he could not do or say a thing without adding to his discipline problems; and with the winter winds piling up snow around the schoolhouse and everything else in Warrensville, there was no place for a tryst. Nor was there time for them to converse while he was boarding round with the Stiles and Adamses, singing at singing schools, or writing names on an album quilt in the evening for Dr. Morrill's wife. He had to pick his steps with care socially.[12]

This caution was not enough for Mary. She wanted at least the same degree of closeness she had had at Hiram, as an incident one evening while he was boarding at Dr. Morrill's suggested. He jotted its nature down in cryptic Latin—"Epistolae ignotae ad puellam," The "puella" was certainly Mary, as his care to put the incident in Latin shows, and she evidently brought him anonymous letters of some sort she had received. Whether he read the letters and what he did about them are not recorded. But within a week or two, circumstances gave Mary a much better chance to get her message through.[13]

It was the week before Christmas. The weather remained frigid. James, boarding with the Hubbells, caught a bad cold and by Wednesday the twenty-fourth was too sick to keep teaching; he closed the school early and went back to the Hubbells', where he stripped, lay in some unheated back room, and got Solyman or Newton to wrap a cold, wet sheet around him. This was the standard treatment for fevers, the idea being to counteract the fever with a stronger chill. James lay there for over two hours without feeling better, so he put his shirt back on and got into bed while the family sent for Dr. Morrill, who took a look at the sufferer and diagnosed "lung fever, caused by a very bad cold"—in other words, pneumonia. Morrill prescribed cold cloths on the chest and (he was evidently a homeopath) "infinitesimal doses" of medicine.[14]

Christmas Day found James in bed, coughing, feverish, and unable to get up. Mr. and Mrs. Hubbell had been planning to visit Mr. Hubbell's father that day for a family gathering, and decided to go ahead, taking their younger daughter, Augusta. They left Mary at home to tend the sick, apparently figuring that there was no risk in leaving their daughter in the house with a young man who was bedridden and was in any case practically a member of the family. So all that day Garfield had an attentive, attractive, bright-spirited angel of mercy by his bed, talking when he felt like talking, watching silently, cheerfully doing all the menial things one has to do for the sick. It was a moving experience. Probably no one but his mother had ever done as much for him. Imperceptibly, wonder and gratitude blended into an emotion very much like love.[15]

James remained in bed two more days, with Mary still caring for him. Friday he was able to sit up, though he had a racking headache. Sunday he got out and went to meeting, still rather weak, and Thomas showed up, having heard from the Hubbells that James was ill and driven over from Orange to see how he was. Sunday, too, James put down in his diary the same notation he had used at Hiram in the fall: "*Ten. Am. cum pu.*"[16]

From his illness on, there was a definite change in James's behavior toward Mary. He found more and more excuses to be together with her alone—moonlight walks, rendezvous at the schoolhouse in the evening, moments discreetly snatched during the noon recess.[17] None of this, one can be sure, was at all physical; it was just serious conversation, but sweet and significant for all that.[18] It seems likely that Solyman and Mrs. Hubbell knew and approved of these meetings. Little by little the affair advanced. By late February, when his school ended, Garfield could refer in his diary to "*meam puellam*"—my girl. When he next went to Cleveland in March, he had two daguerreotypes taken of himself, one for her. When he returned to the Eclectic later that month and she remained at home, they promised to write often.[19]

(Curiously, amid all this excitement of first love, there is a cryptic Latin note in the diary in February: "*Ad Oliverumque hoc vesperi*"—to Oliver also this evening. One wonders why the entry was in Latin—whether this was the same Oliver Stone whom he had known two winters before, before his conversion, who lived about five miles away—and why, at this time, he bothered to visit him.)[20]

The many varieties of love are hard to analyze, but on the showing of the evidence it seems unlikely that James felt the urgency or the giddiness of adolescent love. There is no passionate poetry in his diary, no flowery description of his feelings in his letters to her—not even a mention of her on Valentine's Day when it was customary to send notes to one's sweetheart.[21] He was not infatuated with Mary as she, apparently, was with him. Instead, he was simply, after a tentative beginning, enjoying the warmth and intimacy of a close relationship with a girl his own age, with whom he could share some of his deepest feelings. It was a sort of lovely narcissism. He was in no hurry to have the affair develop, and seemed studiously unaware of any long-term implications.

That was not the case with Mary's family. The Hubbells seem to have thought—and one can hardly blame them—that they were seeing the early stages of a courtship. And indeed it did resemble the beginning of courtship as that process was practiced in the Reserve. A young man became particularly attentive to one young lady; he spent a certain amount of time alone with her; they wrote letters to each other; sooner or later, as custom demanded, he asked her to marry him, and she assented or refused. If she assented, there might be an engagement of several months, even years, if the young man had some schooling left to finish. But once the engagement began, the prospective husband was locked in. The girl, it was understood, could break the engagement at any time should she develop scruples about the character or (quite often) the religious soundness of her suitor; the young man could not, not without incurring the reproach of being a deceiver of helpless womanhood, a "rake," as Garfield was later to put it.[22]

The Hubbells were probably delighted with Garfield as a prospective son-in-law, and had perhaps been giving Mary tacit assistance in her efforts to snare him. He was an intelligent young man with two reliable trades—an excellent schoolmaster and a decent carpenter—strong and able to support a family, with no obvious bad habits. He came from a good background, even though some parts of his early upbringing had been questionable. Most important, he was a Christian and a devout Disciple, who planned to serve the Lord. At a guess, the Hubbells expected that after another term or two at the Eclectic, James, who obviously had mastered all the book learning he needed, would put the question to Mary. He would finish school, they would get married and settle down, and he would begin either carpentering or preaching full time. It seemed a bright future for them both.

Garfield did not see it that way. In the brief review of his plans for the New Year that he wrote in his diary on New Year's day there was no mention of Mary, of marriage, nor of leaving school. He assumed that he was going to school two terms and would teach again next winter, to make money to pursue his still unfinished education.[23] He was aware, barely, of his obligation not to mislead Mary, and was careful to avoid mentioning marriage in all their sweet, companionable conversations.[24] Marriage was, after all, a serious transaction, not a "mere joke, or frolic, to be engaged in at any moment, without forethought or preparation," as one of the books he had been reading that winter, *Golden Steps to Respectability*, reminded him. It was something he did not want to get into "without," as the book said, "viewing it in all its bearings." Perhaps the memory of his mother's failed marriages bothered him. At any rate, he was determined not to propose. His position made sense, but it did mean that he and Mary were at cross purposes in their relationship, and were to become increasingly so.[25]

This was the situation as James finished his teaching at Warrensville in February, with the customary exercises, "compositions and declamations," and a paper called "The Student's Repository," all delivered in front of a large and appreciative crowd of spectators packed into the little school. Then he went home through the mud to Orange. He did not stay there long, however; he had plans for the four weeks before the spring term began.[26]

That year, apparently for the first time, young Garfield had given some concentrated thought to the problem of financing his studies, an area in which he had always fallen slightly short before. What he really needed, he concluded, was a way of making money during the school term, to cover at least some of his debts as he incurred them. One way was to teach penmanship. It was a subject steadily in demand, and not hard to learn. Dr. Alonzo Harlow, one of the six or eight doctors at the Falls, who had his office in a new brick building called the Philadelphia Block, taught "Penmanship, Drawing, Mezzo Tint painting and a variety of useful and ornamental arts" as a sideline, at ten dollars for a four-week course. Harlow was a fortyish Vermont Yankee, smooth-tongued and something of a quack, but adept at making money. To him James decided to go. Armed with a certificate in penmanship, he would be able to pick up more money toward acquiring the learning for which he so desperately thirsted.[27]

It turned out to be a delightful experience. For the first time since his canal days, Garfield was associated mostly with adults—but with a very different sort. At his Chagrin Falls boarding house, he wrote, he could "enjoy intelligent conversation which is a rare jewel." One of his fellow boarders, C. T. Blakeslee, was an opinionated, articulate village lawyer with whom he had several good discussions. Others were fellow students of Dr. Harlow's, including some Universalists, always up for a good round of theological discussion about whether all, or only some, would be saved. The Doctor himself could generally be counted on for a bit of uplifting bombast.[28] Not only that, his writing class was in some ways conducted like an overgrown debating society. The students would practice writing for two hours, then take a break and entertain each other with impromptu speeches on topics proposed by the Doctor, for example temperance. Local citizens sometimes stopped upstairs to listen. On occasion they constituted themselves a model U.S. Congress, each student representing a different state, and argued current political questions—the annexation of Canada or Mexico, or the abolition of slavery in the District of Columbia. Garfield represented New York, and was clearly, Dr. Harlow claimed, "the best speaker in the school." He may have been; he had certainly had the practice. The Warrensville debaters had done the same thing during the winter, with Garfield as a representative from South Carolina, devoted, as he said, "to the interests of my nullifying constituents."[29]

As the class progressed from simple script letters to elaborate eagles and scrolls in script, and on to rather clumsy copies of newspaper engravings in drawing class[30] (Dr. Harlow was something of a humbug in art as well as medicine), Garfield heard of another good way to make money. This one was to capitalize on the public excitement over Louis Kossuth. Kossuth was a former "Governor of Hungary" (so James had it) who had led his people in a revolt against their Austrian overlords in 1848, had been defeated and exiled, and was now touring the vast western democracy to raise money and support for a European democratic revolution. Public interest was immense, and a New York publisher had just brought out a potboiler called *Kossuth and His Generals*, which in the literate, book-oriented Reserve ought to sell splendidly, particularly as Kossuth and his party had just passed through Cleveland. (Garfield had nearly seen them. He had been visiting Uncle Thomas in Newburgh one rainy Saturday in February and had crossed the new Cleveland and Pittsburgh tracks a few moments after Kossuth's train left. A hundred citizens and a brass band were still at the station. They had taken up twenty-five dollars in contributions at that one stop.) James decided—he may have gotten the idea from Harlow—to try to sell a few dozen books.[31]

Friday afternoon, 12 March, he walked home, and thence to Warrensville, where he spent the night with Mary's family. Next morning, with a horse borrowed from Mr. Hubbell, he was off to Cleveland. The books were to be ordered from the *Plain Dealer* office downtown, a fascinating location for country people like James, who found the arcane processes of typesetting and printing endlessly intriguing. The new office was at the lower end of Superior, on the corner of Vineyard Street, across from George Worthington's hardware store with its collection of huge, rusty potash kettles, anchors, and chains on the sidewalk out front. Inside James found his old friend from Chester, John Hodge, in charge of the book operation. He ordered three dozen books, to be sent to the Falls by stage, and also used the opportunity to get a daguerreotype made for Mary. He gave it to her on the way back, when he spent the night again and returned Solyman's horse.[32]

How well Garfield came out financially from the book business is far from clear. When the books arrived he sold about a dozen before leaving the Falls, and seems to have taken the rest to Hiram with him, where he may have sold more but made no mention of it. One can say confidently that it was not a lucrative business for him, and he may have taken a loss.[33]

Enjoyable as his stay at the Falls was, Garfield was fairly panting with eagerness to get back to the Eclectic. He had been back once during the winter, to engage a room for the spring term, and had savored the trip. "It seems some like old times to be here and see the students," he had written. Then in March, he, Orrin, and Corydon, who was visiting, had run into a bunch of Eclectic students at the Falls, returning from the winter term. He went into rhapsodies—"fine sing . . . first rate times," and so forth. They had all put their heads together and sung the "Eclectic Farewell," with, one gathers, much pathos. To James it was thrilling.[34]

So 22 March was a blithe day for Garfield. With his diploma from Harlow in hand, with his trunk all packed, he returned to Hiram. His ride was with Charles Kilby, a young carpenter who had recently married Mary's sister Leora and was moving to Hiram, doubtless to take advantage of all the new construction.[35] Kilby let him off at the Eclectic building, where he was delighted to find Symonds Ryder rooming in the basement, where he and the

Boyntons had roomed in the fall term. Symonds had a good arrangement: his room, including board, was \$1.50 a week, but in return for acting as janitor—building the fires, sweeping the upstairs rooms, and ringing the bell to signal rising (at 5:00 a.m.), curfew (at 9:00 a.m.), and the change of classes—he had seventy-five cents knocked off his bill. That was a real bargain, even by Hiram standards. Symonds wondered if James would be interested in sharing the janitorial work, if Mr. Udall, who had charge of the building, was agreeable. James accepted with alacrity, Udall was persuaded, and Ryder and Garfield were officially installed as janitors. It was fairly hard work, chopping and bringing in wood for four stoves, hauling out the ashes, sweeping the rooms every day, and ringing the bell in the cupola, the rope from which hung in the hall just outside the Lower Chapel, but they were both young and strong and up to it. Except for the bell-ringing, which the slender Ryder soon yielded to his more robust partner.[36]

This James Garfield, the bell ringer, was the one who stuck in the memory of almost all who attended the Eclectic with him. "His clothes had a poor-student look," one girl recalled. "At the close of the morning lecture, before the students left the room, he would leave the chapel, and ring the bell. His tread was firm and free. . . . He was modest and self-possessed, and then and always absolutely free from any affectation whatsoever." Corydon Fuller remembered the image vividly, though he displaced it to the previous fall, before Garfield had the job: "a broad-shouldered, powerfully built fellow, nearly six feet high; his hair cut rather short and standing almost erect; his eyes blue; his clothing was of material then known as Kentucky jean, and his arms to the elbows were protected by sleeves of calico. There was a genial, kindly look in his eyes. . . ." Day in, day out, James Garfield was always at his post, pulling away at the bellrope, big and friendly.[37]

Almost always, that is. Two weeks into the term, Garfield caught what he thought was a cold. Fever and headache supervened, and it turned out to be a virulent attack of measles, which laid him flat on his back, with sore, bleary eyes and fever, for over a week. Symonds took care of the janitorial duties, and William and Henry Boynton and Corydon, who was rooming at Rudolph's that term, came over and watched with him at night through the worst of the illness. As with most diseases at the time, there was nothing medicine could do; one simply rode it out. The fifth day the measles turned; "I am perfectly pied," James wrote. And even after he felt better and the rash was dying down, his eyes continued so weak that he could not study for five or six days. One way and another, the attack kept him out of action for over two weeks.[38]

But, in what was becoming a pattern with him, the illness had no effect whatever on his schoolwork. He was taking Greek again, Latin prose (Sallust and Cicero this term), and geometry, which he had been hankering to take since he first came to Hiram, and in all three his work went on without difficulty. Indeed, he had just gotten over the measles when Brother Munnell, one Saturday evening as they rode to Ravenna in a buggy, asked him to teach the class in Caesar while he, Munnell, visited Bethany College for a week. The request was, as James appreciated, an honor; moreover, Munnell, conscientious Virginia gentleman that he was, probably paid Garfield himself or arranged for him to be paid.[39] At the same time, Garfield began giving lessons in penmanship, drawing, and mezzotint at three dollars for a week's instruction and, as soon as he was well, took on a full schedule debating in the college lyceum. It was a heavy schedule, as he was entirely aware; more than once he exulted to his diary about the heavy load he was carrying: "I can feel hard study drawing up on my nerves and making my physical system tremble in unison with that thinking, acting, living principle called the *Mind*." It was glorious to be twenty, strong, ambitious, and capable. Perhaps for the first time in his life James was tasting the satisfactions of hard work.[40]

It was in this mood of young masculine well-being that Garfield sat down on 10 April, after a half day cleaning the upstairs rooms, to begin the first letter he had ever written to a young lady—directed, of course, to Warrensville Center. Much of it was the chatty, comradely letter of one student to another, about what students were back that term, how classes were, what her brother Newton was doing, and narrating the stoicism of Symonds, who had been disappointed in love (tall, woebegone Symonds was continually disappointed in love). But the last part was what Mary (and probably James) was waiting for. It gushed with all the cliches of early Victorian sentimentality:

> Mary you know the affections of my heart. They are still unchanged, unless it be indeed that they are strengthened by absence. To no other being but yourself is the fountain of my heart unsealed, and gushes forth with all the ardor of youthful affection, and it causes my heart to thrill with emotion that she, upon whom I lavish my fondest affections, bestows her warmest love upon a poor, penniless, orphan-boy like myself.

Despite the attempt at fancy writing, there is, one suspects, a solid core of truth in the passage. He was proud and thankful to be loved by an attractive girl, and he did care for her. But he was very scrupulous about not committing himself to either love or marriage. The situation is not uncommon. If what he said misled Mary—and it did—it was not that he intended to deceive; simply that he was too much wrapped up in his own dreams to be aware of hers.[41]

The vision of the absent loved one was perhaps a sort of catalyst by which the beauties of that spring came into magical combination. For the first time, James began to be acutely aware of nature. His diary, up to then dependably concise, swelled with apostrophes to spring days and evenings—"the vernal Zephyrs" that kissed "the face of Nature and fan[ned] the ruddy cheeks of many a glowing youth," or, late at night, the moon and stars shining "down from their cloudless homes and light[ing] up a mellow landscape." Beauty and contentment seemed to shine from everything. That twentieth spring James felt as if he were rising on a tide of achievement, beauty, and love, quiet but irresistible.[42]

20

Pressure

Spring–Summer 1852

It may have meant little to Garfield when Joseph Treat announced that he was giving a set of talks on the spirit-rappings at the Hiram Methodist church in May, and that he would welcome debate with those who held contrary opinions—but there were probably some in Hiram who suspected what they were in for. Treat, a son of the Congregational minister in nearby Garrettsville, had perhaps spoken there before. He was a fiery, vehement individualist, insatiably curious about spiritual phenomena, and with his own theories about nearly everything. He was also a fluent speaker, well-versed in the Bible and deft at handling the nebulous concepts that made up so much of nineteenth-century religious and scientific thought. His ideas were anything but orthodox; recently he had been flirting with, if not actually preaching, atheism. But since his announced topic was the spirit-rappings, he was guaranteed a good audience.[1]

The spirit-rapping craze had come a long way in the Reserve since young Garfield first encountered it in Cleveland, nearly a year before. Interest in the spirits had spread from Cleveland into the countryside with the rapidity of a chemical reaction. Evidently, there was something powerfully gripping to the imagination in the idea that the spirits of the dead were nearby, willing, and indeed eager to converse with the living. Perhaps it was that it fit in so perfectly with the superstitions of many rural people. For the Reserve, despite its literacy, was an oddly superstitious area; its early settlers had brought from New England a full complement of beliefs in things like headless monsters, haunted treasures that suddenly sank into the ground, witchcraft, and spells. The exploits of the spirit-rappers seemed to some country people, no doubt, to validate the reality of some traditions they had half believed, half doubted, all their lives.[2]

They wanted not only to talk about the phenomenon; they wanted to experience it. From around the beginning of 1852, almost every one of the proper little Greek Revival villages of the Reserve had been infested with a host of spirit-rappers, spiritual mediums, automatic writers, and table turners, practically all of them local people bent on opening a pipeline to the spirit world. Teenage girls were particularly apt to be involved. In Ashtabula Country, where, by one account, "nearly every household had its medium, and the tables that tipped outnumbered the tables that did not tip," the psychics were "oftenest the young girls one met in the dances and sleigh-rides," young people "of a nervous and impressionable temperament" who believed implicitly in what they were doing. The breadth of the interest was surprising. Two adjacent towns in Ashtabula claimed to contain "fifty mediums and more." From Columbiana, just below the south line of the Reserve, a friend of John Hodge's wrote, "We have any amount of 'Spiritual Rappings' in this village. There are more than a dozen writing mediums and twice that number of rapping mediums here."[3]

Garfield's debating companion of the spring, the lawyer Chiles T. Blakeslee, years later wrote an account of the progress of spiritualism, which he called "a kind of mental epidemic," in Chagrin Falls. The Falls was an intellectually volatile little place to begin with, as witness its reception of phrenology two years before; but its residents' reaction to the new excitement surpassed even that. "Nothing was talked of but spirit rappings and spirit manifestations and spirit communications, at every gathering among neighbors," Blakeslee averred. Seances were almost nightly affairs. At some, "tables were tipped, chairs thrown about the room, and bedlam let loose generally. The only condition necessary to get these demonstrations, being a dark room and a man to play the fiddle."

As the craze went on, the spirits became less shy and identified themselves to astonished spectators not only as the dead from local families, but also as illustrious spirit visitors to the Falls, greats from the Bible and the New England pantheon like "Adam and Noah, Abraham and Melchizadec, Sampson and Delilah, Deborah and Barak, Zoroaster, Solomon, Byron, John Westley [*sic*], Daniel Webster and Dr. Edwards," plus number of dead Indians whose biographies had captured popular fancy. Other spirits turned out to be those of deceased oxen or horses who wanted to speak with their former owners. The communications varied in quality as well as origin. One of the first mediums in the area was a Bainbridge girl

> brought up in ignorance without education, possessing a mental capacity below that of ordinary females of her age. Now in her early teens, she thought it a very fine thing to become a "medium," and have all the boys in the neighborhood come to see her. Many went, perhaps mainly from curiosity to her sittings, and were treated to the most vulgar and profane nonsense that ignorance and profanity and vulgarity can invent. . . .[4]

But spirit-rapping was not just a game for sensation-mongers among the ignorant country folk. It also appealed to the intelligent. In Chagrin Falls, Blakeslee recalled, the first excitement about the movement was among the "reading people." In Ashtabula, "the mediums and the believers belong[ed] to some of the best families in the vicinity." To an educated person, the phenomena might well seem linked to recent scientific discoveries, especially in electromagnetism; one believer at the Falls was sure he saw electricity darting about the room where a sitting was held, "making thousands of acute angles." The movement also had a strongly reformist cast. Many of its supporters were also devotees of phrenology, animal magnetism, health foods, phonography, or antislavery; it was no accident, for instance, that the Fox sisters had held forth at the Dunham House, the best-known temperance hostelry in Cleveland.[5] The idea that the earth was full of wandering spirits was no bar to belief by the educated. Most educated people were Christians and believed, like James, that hosts of invisible spirits both good and evil haunted the earth. Some held (the Bible was not crystal clear upon this point) that spirits of the departed might be among them. James himself sometimes referred to dead friends as being, not in Heaven or Hell, but in "the spirit land."[6]

The spiritualist movement, however, had unsettling implications for Christian faith. Spirit communications, if one accepted their reality, seemed to portray a harmless, nebulous afterworld, a sort of denatured version of everyday existence, vapid in all senses, certainly far from the more dramatic Christian belief in Heaven and Hell. They undercut, and sometimes directly challenged, Christian doctrines about life after death. For this reason, the rappings were a continual topic of discussion in many little rural churches of the Reserve.[7] For this reason, too, some of the strongest adherents of the movement were people already alienated from Christianity who hoped that the spirit messages would win people to their views. And in fact, the movement in the Reserve was having just this effect. Many people found the spirits' message more satisfying than their preacher's, and abandoned the latter. "Churches," a spiritualist newspaper triumphantly reported from the Reserve a few years after 1852, "which have heretofore been filled to overflowing with orthodox worshippers are now deserted. The altars where priests thundered forth the terrors of 'hell fire, infant damnation,' and the doctrine of 'an angry and revengeful God' are now silent." Spiritualism in Ashtabula County, according to one witness, "left behind a great deal of smoke and ashes where the inherited New England orthodoxy had been."[8]

This version of spiritualism, as a vehicle for attacking Christian dogmas, was essentially what Treat was preaching. But Hiram students did not shun him as an atheist. On the contrary, there was a feeling—one could call it an example of the Yankee taste for intellectual sensationalism—that the rappings were a reality that needed to be investigated, and that Treat's anti-Christian arguments only made the need more urgent. His lectures drew large audiences to the Methodist church, and one evening, after several in which no one had accepted the challenge Treat flung out at the end of every lecture, the students prevailed upon Professor Munnell to do battle for the Christian side.

This was where Garfield came in. Munnell was his idol at that time, and he was in the crowd that gathered on the evening of 5 May to hear the debate between him and Treat. It was heavily oratorical; the contestants alternated with half-hour speeches, and the whole thing went on until eleven. As far as Garfield was concerned, Munnell won hands down: "Mr. Treat did not prove a single point in dispute, nor bring a shadow of an argument to establish one." Not everyone in the audience was so sure. Corydon, who was probably with James, felt that Treat's sarcasm and his broad, abusive attacks on Christian tenets had scored a lot of laughs at Munnell's expense. And Garfield himself was not too sure that Munnell had taken the right tack on the spirit-rappings; he had contended that they were real, but were the work of evil spirits. Treat, in any event, was undaunted; he continued his lectures and challenges.[9]

In the next few days, students started coming to Garfield and suggesting that he ought to respond to Treat. Munnell's southern smoothness and courtesy, they argued, had made him a bad choice to oppose Treat; what was needed was someone who could press the counterattack vigorously, as James had done against Encell the previous fall. Some of his teachers seconded the idea—Hayden, perhaps, or Munnell himself. James was uncertain. Tuesday, 18 May, Treat spoke again; Orrin happened to be in Hiram for a visit, and James took him to the lecture, along with Symonds and Corydon. "I consider him a perfect fanatic, and injurious to society," he wrote afterward in his diary; one senses that he was bracing himself for the confrontation. Two days later, he replied.[10]

The church was packed, Corydon Fuller recalled later, as word had gotten around that Garfield was going to take up Treat's challenge. He went on to relate how James came out swinging:

> Mr. Garfield arose and said that he had listened with great attention to the gentleman's speech, and hardly knew what to say in answer, but he would like to ask him one question. Would he be so kind as to tell the audience what was the present participle of the verb *to be*, in Greek, or in other words, the Greek word to correspond with the English word 'being'? Mr. Treat made no answer, and Mr. Garfield repeated his question and challenged him to answer, but *the poor man did not know*. Then, turning to his audience, he asked them what they thought of a man traveling over the country criticizing the work of the world's great scholars, when he did not know the very first thing the school-boy learned in his Greek grammar.

To fully appreciate the scene, one should imagine the husky young Garfield, all of twenty and a half, in his worn gray suit and cambric oversleeves, brandishing at Treat the rudiments of Greek grammar which he himself had learned only the previous fall. It was a solid debater's point, no doubt of it; Treat was caught. But the atheist came back quickly, and for the rest of the evening they had what Garfield described as a "warm time," ending at 10:30

with a promise to continue debate the following Monday.[11]

Garfield felt good about his effort. A euphoric mood surrounded him all weekend; everything was beautiful—debates in the lyceum, Disciple meeting, a visit from his mother and Hattie Boynton (with whom he proudly shared, no doubt, what he had been doing), the "living green" of the fields around Hiram, the spring flowers. At times bits of soaring rhetoric and thunderous anathemas against Treat's views crept into his diary, suggesting the highly rhetorical character of their debate: "Let him raise his insect arm against infinity, and the Almighty, but truth is mighty, eternal, and the Bible firm as the Throne of God shall stand when kingdoms crumble and the planets crash," and so forth.[12]

By the time the debaters met again on the twenty-fourth, their topic had veered round to the basic argument of Christian polemic: the authority of the Bible. Treat went after the Bible on a variety of grounds: it disagreed with scientific fact; it was full of trifling and temporary things; it made no claim to be inspired by God; in some parts it contained bad commands and encouraged wickedness; it countenanced slavery and degraded women. Garfield countered him point by point, in half-hour speeches. Again the discussion was warm, and neither side conceded defeat; but Garfield felt satisfied with himself. One hears no more of Treat lecturing in Hiram. It would be too much to say that these debates made Garfield a celebrity in the village—to some extent, he was already that. But they did confirm his status as a leader in the college community; more importantly, they reinforced his belief in his own intellectual powers.[13]

Oddly enough, his letters to Mary, who was teaching at Chagrin Falls, said almost nothing about the debates. He told her how her brother Newton and sister Leora Kilby were doing in Hiram; he thanked her for the miniature she had sent; he apologized for not writing sooner, citing all the business he had had for the lyceum. (Because of his skill in penmanship, he had been asked to make the official copy of the lyceum's "Literary Offering" for the 28 May meeting—twenty-seven pages in longhand, over which he toiled for five or six nights.) But he told her much less about what he had been doing at school than he had in April.[14]

Part of the reason for this close-mouthedness, no doubt, was a vague awareness that Mary would not approve of everything he was doing. The rosy glow that hung over everything else that spring also surrounded his social relationships. He, Symonds, and Corydon were almost an inseparable trio that term; they boarded together, debated together, studied together, and often stayed up late talking together of their plans. In Latin, the only class all three shared, their progress was, according to Munnell, "rather extraordinary"—they finished both histories of Sallust and six Ciceronian orations. In geometry, James and Corydon, though beginners, soon outdistanced the rest of the class. "James is a perfect giant," Corydon wrote his parents. "We get along first rate. He sometimes says he wishes we were in a class by ourselves." The story was the same with James and Symonds in Greek. After classes most afternoons, Corydon would drop over from Brother Rudolph's, where he boarded, to the basement of the Eclectic building, and the three would start studying.[15]

And later, around suppertime, Corydon and James, often joined by Henry Boynton, who also stayed at Rudolph's, would amble down to Raymond's boarding house about a mile south of the college on the north-south road, where several of the female students lived, and where there was a melo-pean.[16] (The misogynous Symonds usually steered clear of these excursions.)[17] James still loved singing, and would break into song on any occasion; so the boys would gather round the instrument with the girls and begin the soft, sentimental songs popular at the time—"Ben Bolt," "Blue Juniata," "Tell me, ye winged wings," and the rest; James, as one girl remembered, throwing himself into it with gusto, head flung back, chest expanded with a "free" and "joyous" air.[18] Afterwards, often, they would go for a stroll around sunset, usually with the same three girls: Laura Stiles, Corydon's cousin Susan Smith, and Hattie Storer of Akron. The Raymonds, comparatively lenient where young people were concerned, let them stay out after dark, a thing Brother Hayden would never have allowed.[19] Their destination was generally some nearby spot like the graveyard. As dusk fell, they traced the constellations, as James and Mary had last fall, and sang some more. It was all very quiet, low-key, and blissful. At one point in the spring, James briefly thought he was in love with one of his evening companions, but evidently changed his mind. As for the girls, they probably did not get their hopes up about James; the general understanding around the school, though James was unaware of it, was that he and Mary were engaged to be married. But one sees why he did not write Mary about these visits.[20]

The fact was that since Mary had unsealed the fountain of his heart (as he put it in his letter to her)[21] he had become much more relaxed with young women in general. He enjoyed their company, and did not mind showing it, in conversation and even in physical contact—at least, in shaking hands. One female student remembered his cordiality; he "had a happy habit of shaking hands" with men and women alike, with "a hearty grip, which betokened a kind-hearted feeling for all." This physical demonstrativeness, rare in the stiff Reserve, was possibly what caused a fellow student a few years later to write of his "disposition to cling to and love some one."[22] His affections were generously distributed. One of four young women who rode with him in a buggy to the Portage County yearly meeting in June remembered with delight how he kept them all entertained en route with apostrophes to the beauties of nature, appropriate bits of poetry, and snatches of song. No one seems to have thought these displays excessive; on the contrary, they seemed to go well with Garfield's sincere and well-known piety. "I suppose he will be a preacher," Fuller wrote his parents, "and if so he will be a superior one."[23]

But despite the general warmheartedness he showed young women, Garfield remained convinced, most of the time, that there was only one real love in his life. Around the middle of June a traveling phrenologist turned up in Hiram who, somewhat unusually, seems to have spiced his presentation with a dash of astrology. At any rate, he associated each of his audience with a constellation, and paired some of the boys and girls off together. To James he gave the constellation Leo, but said there was no girl at Hiram for him. James dully passed this information on to Mary, adding, "Don't that make it bad?" He concluded with a few lines of doggerel, including "I trust that the love that binds two young hearts / Will never, never cease to be true."[24]

The association with Leo turned out to be apt, too, in quite another way. As the end of the spring term neared, amid "glorious" days, with "pure and bracing" air, the faculty began thinking about the commencement exhibition, which was to be held 25 June in the apple orchard behind the Eclectic building. Garfield was asked to give an oration, of course;[25] he was also asked to be on a committee to write a "colloquy" for presentation, with Corydon, Susan Smith, and a somewhat older woman, Almeda Booth, who taught in the primary department. The colloquy was to be, essentially, a short play without scenery or costumes, on an uplifting subject; it was understood that the writers would take the main parts. Guided, probably, by Miss Booth, who had read widely, the committee settled on the persecution of Protestants in Italy as its theme, and ended up with a fourteen-page drama entitled "The Heretic," in which Miss Booth portrayed Madame Varrencia, the Protestant martyr; Corydon, the wily Cardinal Claudius; and Garfield, no less a personage than Pope Leo X.[26]

As commencement day neared, an air of purposeful abstraction settled over the Eclectic. Students walked around preoccupied, mouthing half-memorized sentences from their speeches for the exhibition; in a corner of the orchard, other students worked on the "bower" for the performance; Thomas Young, the innkeeper at the corner, got his rooms ready for guests; and the participants in the colloquy worked on their lines. Finally the day came, cool and pleasant. At nine-thirty the students assembled at the Eclectic building, and Corydon Fuller and Edwin Hathaway, marshals for the day, paired them off and marched them down the hill in double file to the stage where the "literati," the faculty and visiting preachers, were already seated. As the students passed around behind the stage, little Lucretia Rudolph stepped in a hollow in the irregular ground, lost her balance, and then found herself, to her sudden, inexplicable delight, caught in the arms of Garfield, who had been walking behind her. It was a small incident, which neither party thought of again until some time later.[27]

Garfield had seen surprisingly little of Miss Rudolph since he had been at Hiram. During the spring term, she had been teaching in a rural district a few miles to the north, coming home only on weekends; Corydon, who stayed at the Rudolph house, had seen more of her. In fact, it was Corydon who was escorting her to the Spencer Family concert that night after the exhibition. Corydon approved of her in his terribly earnest way: she was "dignified," "intellectual," "tidy in her dress," and a true Christian. The only thing that put him off was that she seemed rather cold and standoffish. This behavior, however, was easier to understand for those who knew, like James, that she had broken off her long-standing engagement to Albert Hall that winter, after much heart-searching, over a question of religion; her parents did not think Albert was a good enough Christian. And indeed he was not, Garfield may have reflected.[28]

The exhibition went beautifully. There were a few weak spots, some essays, supposed to be original, in which the quick-eared, critical Garfield caught hints of plagiarism; but most of the pieces were good. Little, smiling Charley Foote gave a fine oration; so did Calista Carlton, Lucretia's merry, witty friend; and the colloquy was "highly applauded" by an audience of fifteen hundred, especially Garfield's commanding portrayal of Pope Leo. His own oration, "The Student," was, as usual, one of the standouts. The Spencers sang pleasingly.[29]

After it was over, James went over to Charles Kilby's house, where the Hubbells were staying. (They were the nearest thing to family he had at the occasion; Eliza and Thomas had been unable to come.) Mary, of course, had come with them. "I took supper at C. Kilby's, then took a walk with 'A Friend' (if no more)," he wrote. Later they went to the Spencers' concert, which Corydon pronounced "very fair," though he thought too many pieces were "of a trivial character." Still later, James and Mary went back to Kilby's, and retired late—as James put it, "after *some* conversation."[30]

One wonders what they talked about. It seems likely that the Hubbells were becoming increasingly impatient for James to make some move—if not to marry Mary at once, at least to propose to her formally and set a date, or leave school and get a job, or do something to make his intentions clear. The problem for James was that his intentions were not entirely clear even to himself. The one thing he knew for sure was that he wanted to stay in school as long as he could and get "a *thorough, classical* education." He had tried to explain his determination in his letters to Mary that spring. Education, he wrote her shortly after his debate with Treat, was "a path by which young men, and young ladies can rise above the groveling herd 'that scarcely know they have a soul within'. . . . The thought of dying as the ox, of leaving behind no monument for good, and of having elevated no mortal in the scale of human existence, freezes my soul. . . ." Here he attempted to justify his quest for further education on the plea of doing the Lord's work, or at least doing good on earth; later, in July, he rested his case on the ground of sheer personal need and an appeal to Mary's vanity: "Can the soul that yearns for knowledge, enjoy life, to grovel in ignorance? I feel within me that it is necessary to my happiness that my mind should be cultivated, and may I express, without flattery, the conviction, that you, dear Mary, have an intellectual diamond implanted within you, which needs only the polish of cultivation, to render it conspicuous in the literary world." This was apparently his plan, to the extent that he had one: he would go somewhere to get a thorough college education; Mary would stay at home and improve her mind; and when they were both completely educated, they would get married and become "conspicuous" in their separate spheres.[31]

This was all much too rarefied for the Hubbells, who simply wanted a good husband for Mary. Several bits of evidence suggest that during the spring Mary and her family had been trying hard to dissuade him from his endless commitment to education. Scattered allusions in his journal give some idea of the arguments they were using on him. There was the idea, widely held in the Reserve, that prolonged study could be fatal to even the strongest constitution; by persisting in study, he might be menacing his own life.[32] This notion seems to have had some validity for Garfield, and there may have been something to the rumor, current in Hiram around this time, that he had asked Dr. John Robison (whose daughter Janett was on the commencement program and who had been in town for the exhibition) to give him a physical examination and assure him that he was fit to undergo several more years of study. It sounds like the kind of problem that would have worried him, despite his flat denial of the rumor to Corydon.[33]

Another bugaboo was the argument that what God wanted was not mental excellence, but faith and a moral life. The image of Byron, who to Christians of the early nineteenth century represented a horrifying example of genius and knowledge being used for corrupt purposes, haunted James as he grappled with this problem. Was it possible that he could become a Byron if he pushed his studies too far? He doubted it; mental culture presented no danger as long as it was restrained by morality. But the way he kept recurring to the point suggests that it was a tender spot.[34]

In the end, the efforts of Mary and her family were futile, and James remained unswayed. In his long conversations with her at commencement, and later in Warrensville, in the starry and moonlit nights of late June, he held firm to his point: he was going back to Hiram for the fall term, and probably for several terms after. He very much wanted her to attend in the fall and winter terms, too, and continue cultivating her own mind. As for the summer, of course, he would have to work and make money for the fall. The job would be carpentry again—the employer, Mary's brother-in-law Charles Kilby. As for definite commitments to Mary, he could make no promises. Perhaps his plea was to let matters ride for the summer; in the fall, they could come to some firm decision.[35]

Just after the term was over, he discovered that his affair with Mary was going to mean trouble not only with her family but with his own. Home for a brief weekend before starting work with Kilby, he attended meeting with his mother, Thomas, Hitty, Mary, and their families and, after a long day of conversation, confided to his journal that he felt "rather downhearted for certain reasons." He added a cryptic note, "M. adv. *M," which it is not too far-fetched to interpret as "Mother adverse to Mary"—the asterisk seems intended to show that the second M refers to a different person from the first. He had evidently told Eliza about Mary, and she, for whatever reason, had expressed disapproval. As usual, however, she did not try to oppose her son openly. She did not try to break up the relationship; on the contrary, when James left Orange that afternoon he went on to the Hubbells'. But knowing his mother's capacity for persistent, indirect pressure, he could be more certain than ever that it was going to be difficult to plan a future with Mary.[36]

Or did Mary actually figure at all in his plans for the future? An incident later that summer makes one wonder. The third weekend in July, Garfield came home. He spent Saturday night at the Hubbells', where he and Mary read a hundred pages of the current bestseller, *Uncle Tom's Cabin*, and discussed it, themselves, and other equally fascinating topics until four in the morning, evidently with the elder Hubbells' consent. The next day, before heading for Hiram again, he attended meeting in the old red schoolhouse (Brother Lillie was preaching on the divinity of Christ) and then walked into a spirit-rapping session in his own house. Thirteen-year-old Eliza Trowbridge, Stephen and Hitty's eldest daughter, was the medium. That two such devoted Disciples as Thomas and Eliza Garfield would allow such a proceeding in their own home shows just how pervasive the spirit mania was around the Falls. (The Garfields, to be sure, were no less superstitious than the average Reserve family, perhaps more so. Eliza's father had dabbled in astrology back in New Hampshire, and James's sister Mary Larabee had perhaps already developed the psychic powers she was to claim later in life.)

Young Eliza and the family, including Corydon, who was there on a visit, had been conversing with the spirits for some time before James's arrival, it turned out. Revealingly, one question they had asked the spirits was about James's movements the preceding night—where he had been, who he had been with, what he had done—and when he came in, they greeted him with jokes. James thought it was a lot of claptrap, but he and Corydon were no more immune to the fascination than the rest of the family, and presently James found himself in a long rapping conversation with his father's spirit, conjured up by his niece.

The spirit announced itself pleased with the course of study James had pursued so far. It "told past events correctly," he noted, "but I have no confidence in the prophesies." Two prophesies stood out: one, that he would attend school four more terms, the other that he would be married in a year. Garfield's comments were revealing. "With regard to the first, I hope to go more than four terms. The second must not be true."[37]

21
Up from the Herd
Fall 1852

It was not until that fall, when he was reading Horace's *Satires*, that Garfield actually found the quotation. But the thought had been trying to take shape in his mind for some time, at least since the spring and his letters to Mary about the frightening thought of dying as the ox, and "the groveling herd 'that scarcely know they have a soul within.'" Now here it was in cold type in his school edition—in the Third Satire, where the poet was discussing the evolution of human society and law:

> Cum prorepserunt primis animalia terris,
> Mutum et turpe pecus. . .
>
> (When the first living creatures crawled forth on the primeval earth,
> The dumb and filthy herd. . .)

This last phrase seemed to crystallize everything James had been thinking about. It stuck fast in his mind: he himself, with his background of crudeness and ignorance, log cabin and canal, had been one of the "mutum et turpe pecus." His family, Eliza, Thomas and Jane, Hitty and Stephen and their offspring, were still part of it. He was out, thanks to God, thanks also to himself. He could read Latin, wore a suit, debated in public, had obvious talent and industry and energy. He was respectable. Mary was somewhere in between.[1]

Yet all the phrase from Horace had done was to paste a classical label on a collection of thoughts already there. One can see them accumulating during the summer he spent working in Hiram. During summer vacation, Hiram was, like any small college community, a ghost town. "The Eclectic is dumb as a churchyard, and her halls are silent," lamented Garfield. Yet the little settlement was changing, had changed since he first saw it barely a year before. The college was attracting residents; people were moving in and changing the geography of Hiram Hill. Around back of the college building there now ran a little dirt lane called West Campus Street, where Charles Kilby was building the two-story house that Garfield would be working on. On the same side of the campus were five little white houses that the college had erected the previous year, in appearance somewhat between barracks and Greek Revival farmhouses, for students who wanted to "board themselves"—cook their own meals. A man named Buckingham, from Howland, was building a house at the bottom of the hill on the north side—Corydon had found summer work with him. And there were other building projects under way.[2]

Manual labor, after so long a period spent in study, was at first numbing. "Arose this morning about 5 o'clock and feel about 4 years older than I did two days ago," he wrote his second day on the job. He told Mary that his fingers felt "more like sled stakes than writing members" and observed in his diary—a deeply felt though unoriginal observation—"The sleep of the laboring man is truly sweet, and if Morpheus loves to clasp any in his drowsy embrace, it is him who has earned a sound night's rest by honest toil."[3] But as he became inured to physical labor, he and Corydon fell into the habit of visiting each other. Many evenings, at quitting time, Corydon would trudge up the hill to spend the night with James, and they would lie awake in bed for hours talking, sharing their views, their hopes, their experiences. Other evenings it was Garfield who visited, but the conversation was the same: "talk of the past and future," "air-castles." "With no other man was I ever so intimately associated," Fuller remembered later.[4]

The two had so many views in common that they reinforced each other constantly in these late-night conversations. In particular, both had an urgent desire to succeed, to make something of themselves; they spoke to each other of the "fires of ambition" raging inside them almost like a physical affliction.[5] This intense ambition seems to have been less economic than visceral, a desire not for money but for recognition. Corydon, who though he talked sometimes of becoming a Methodist minister, did not have James's warm faith—in fact was much more a skeptic than his friend—wrote (and doubtless shared with James) a blank-verse poem that summer called "Ambition's Dream," in which, with a remarkable absence of Christian imagery, he expressed the hunger both of them felt:

But oh! to die and be forgotten! this
Is tenfold death! to pass away and leave
No mark to tell the world that I have lived!
I could not sleep in peace even in the grave,
Were I to know that none remembered me.
Then grant, O Ruler in the heavens above,
That I may live till I have done some deed
To clothe my name with immortality.[6]

Corydon had another thought he shared with James, doubtless with some diffidence at first. It was about Mary Hubbell. She was bright and sprightly, he conceded, but her performance in school was in no way outstanding, her ability was only "fair," and her approach to life was noisy and shallow. Corydon and a number of others had long thought she was unsuitable for James—that he could and should do better.[7] James, disturbed already by the direction his relationship with Mary seemed to be taking, was probably more receptive than Corydon had expected. He had been thinking specifically about colleges, Bethany College in Virginia, at Alexander Campbell's headquarters, and even some of the older New England institutions. Indeed, a "friend," tantalizingly unidentified (but possibly the blustering Dr. John Robison), offered that July to pay Garfield's way through college. James did not feel he could accept that offer, but however long it took him to raise the money, he was fairly certain he would go; and if that was the case, what would become of his understanding with Mary?[8]

Garfield was reticent even with his diary, and also, with his workstiffened fingers, probably did not feel like writing at length, but scattered entries that summer suggest the tempest bubbling underneath; on 10 July he wrote, "A great question is being agitated in my mind about my future course. Let me reflect seriously." He rebuked himself on 8 August for speaking evil of others "when I am abounding in faults and misdemeanors myself. Mary." At summer's end, 26 August, he noted again, "There is a question weighing upon my soul of the greatest earthly importance which must be settled before long."[9]

Mary, warned perhaps by some sixth sense, was no more complimentary about Corydon than Corydon was about her. When Garfield and Fuller went on a visit to Orange one July weekend, Garfield left his friend at home when he went over to Warrensville. In August, when he told Mary of his plans to room with Fuller the coming term, she objected vigorously, prompting Garfield to an immediate defense of his friend: "Corydon E. Fuller, notwithstanding his exceptionable features, is a firm & unswerving friend, and such I have ever found him."[10]

These worries must not obscure the daily events of this laborious summer: grinding tools, digging cellar; getting out stone for the cellar wall in the seminary quarry, with aching limbs and annoyed by mosquitoes; putting in the kite-shaped piece at the ridge of the front cornice; watching a man in a balloon go up from Ravenna and stay visible most of the day as he worked putting a cornice on the south side; writing ornate paragraphs in letters late at night, as the cricket chirped and the tree-toad croaked outside and the Kilbys' clock chimed the hour; watching the ample two-story house, with its L shape, its simple cornice, and its six large windows facing the street, take shape under his and Charles's hands.[11]

By 23 August, when the Eclectic reopened for its fall term, he had all his arrangements made. Corydon's brother Ceylon ("an intellectual looking young man") was entering the school, and Garfield had decided, despite Mary's objections, to room with him, Corydon, and their cousins, Sophronia and Maria Smith, in one of the college boardinghouses. Cousin Ellis Ballou was also coming up to Hiram from Blue Rock; Garfield had engaged him a room at Rudolph's, and went to meet him in Cleveland the week before school started. If he had planned to have a frank talk with Mary before the term began, however, he was frustrated. Coming back from Cleveland with Ellis and Symonds, he had an attack of stomach virus or food poisoning that left him weak and exhausted the first day of school. He took to bed at Kilby's, with Mary, who had come to enroll for the fall term, keeping watch beside him, in a replay of last winter. It was no time to speak frankly.[12]

A few days later, however, he did get to talk with her. "Habueram conversationem cum *una*; ad varia negotia," he wrote. "Dici clare." [I have had a talk with *the one*; on various matters. I spoke clearly.] He may have spoken to her clearly, but if so, it is hard to imagine what he said. He certainly did not tell her everything that was on his mind, for their relationship persisted unaltered through the rest of the term. They had several evening visits together; he could write (in Latin, backwards) of "an adventure with the girl I love." Yet almost certainly he remained, deep inside, more ambivalent than ever.[13]

It was a busy term. He studied Xenophon and trigonometry in addition to Horace; "We are going more critically this term than ever before in all departments," he wrote. In the Eclectic lyceum, he became disgusted with the low quality of debate and led a secession, with nine other members, to form a new, more serious society called the Philomathean, for which he wrote much of the constitution and bylaws.[14] He attended Disciple meeting regularly and, as always, noted the subject of each sermon preached. He taught two more classes in penmanship and mezzotint, making at least twenty dollars, probably more. These were part of his campaign for keeping up with the costs of his studies. He still owed twenty-one dollars on the previous term, a debt he was anxious to liquidate, so much so that he passed up buying new clothes for the term and simply asked his mother to patch his old ones.[15]

The experiment in self-boarding with the Fullers and their cousins had mixed results. At first things went very well, the girls tending to the cooking and Corydon and James building furniture for the rooms, but in September, when first Maria Smith and then Corydon became ill and had to leave school for some weeks, they were a little more complicated. Eventually James and Ceylon decided to begin taking their meals at the Raymond house, as "our girls have rather too hard a time." Corydon apparently joined them when he got back.[16]

By and large, Garfield's friends and associates this term were the same as in previous terms: Fuller, Ryder, Henry Boynton, first of all; then Charley Foote; an even-tempered, perceptive young Disciple from Canada, with a mild, open face, named Philip Burns; and John Harnit, a clever, quarrelsome young man from Pennsylvania whose ability Garfield respected but whose personality he detested, and toward whom he felt intensely competitive. All these had joined him in the Philomathean.[17] But this term, in addition to them and the young ladies at Raymond's boarding house, he began developing two relationships with members of the faculty that were to become very important in his life. One was with Charles D. Wilber, who taught mathematics.

Wilber was only a year or two older than Garfield. He came from a Disciple family in Newbury, seven or eight miles to the north. Like Garfield, he was intelligent; unlike Garfield, he looked it, with a pale face and what one acquaintance called an "intellectual cast of countenance." He limped badly, and had to walk with a cane. Garfield had already gotten to know him the previous term; this term, he lived in the lower end of the same boarding house, and Garfield saw a lot of him. Essentially he was cut from the same cloth as Garfield and Fuller—a boy from the rural Reserve, very ambitious to distinguish himself, but two or three years ahead of either of them. He had already spent part of a year at Bethany College (which he disliked, although he admired Alexander Campbell) and wanted to continue his higher education. He had been a teacher at the Eclectic since its opening.[18]

In some ways Wilber seemed much more sophisticated than Garfield. He had a quiet, puckish personality, with a flair for the original word and the sardonic turn of phrase that Garfield admired. Moreover, to add to his air of worldly wisdom, he was just getting over a very difficult experience in his own life—extricating himself from an engagement with Laura Ann Clark, the attractive young woman who taught the lower school at the Eclectic. The facts of the case are hard to recover at this distance in time, but it appears that it was Wilber who had broken the engagement, and that Miss Clark felt herself wronged. To society at large, according to Garfield, Wilber's conduct had been "almost criminal"; but that did not prevent James from seeing a good deal of him that fall.[19]

Garfield's other developing relationship was with perhaps the most remarkable member of the Hiram faculty, Almeda Booth, who roomed in President Hayden's house. Eight years older than he, she possessed most of the qualities he fervently wished Mary had—a calm seriousness, intellectual acumen, and an incredible ability to study—everything, in fact, but beauty. She was overweight—as Corydon delicately put it, "rather above the medium size"—and exceedingly homely. Her dress was aggressively plain, at times untidy. Her appearance suggested that she had no taste for feminine fripperies and preferred to adorn her mind. This impression was generally correct. She was interested in women's rights; she was reading Margaret Fuller's writings that fall and urging them on the brighter female students, to whom she served as a sort of mentor.[20] But her main interests were science and mathematics, considered unfeminine subjects. Garfield had first seen her the day he enrolled at Hiram in 1851, studying in a geometry class in the Lower Chapel. Now she was a member, with him, of the small Xenophon class taught by Munnell, and he was discovering with a delighted shock that they shared the same "natural turn of mind" and that she had a benevolent, protective, almost motherly interest in him. Impressed and flattered, he added her to the circle of pious, intelligent, ambitious young people who increasingly made up his friends.[21]

That fall he met with what one could call a typical Garfield accident, a throwback to the days of his early teens. He was out in the woods west of the seminary in the mild mid-October weather, gathering chestnuts. He leaped over a log, struck his foot on a smooth stick on the other side, lost his balance, and fell heavily. Having limped back to his room, he discovered his ankle swelling badly; Dr. Trask, the village physician, called in next day, confirmed that it was a sprained ankle and warned him to stay off it. The bones were separated about three-eights of an inch, and recovery might be slow.[22]

It was an intensely painful injury, and the thought of being disabled was unpleasant, but he tried to make the best of it, keeping up his studies and reading *The Millennial Harbinger*. Brother Munnell brought the Latin and Greek classes up to recite with him; numerous students stopped by to visit; Corydon and Ceylon ran his meals up from the Raymond boarding house. And in what was becoming almost comically repetitious, Mary came over and sat with him in the evening and during morning lectures. Restless as ever, James tried to get around on crutches, and only succeeded in aggravating his injury. "I never knew the value of an ankle before," he observed wryly.[23]

During his convalescence he saw Mary almost daily, for long periods of time, and enjoyed it—yet there was something, perhaps a certain possessiveness she felt entitled to show toward him, that he found troubling. After one long visit with her, he noted in his diary, in Latin, "This is a sign (beware)."[24] He cannot have been looking forward to teaching at Warrensville Center again that winter, and some evidence suggests that he was trying, through Corydon, to get a teaching job in Michigan, as a relief from his confining dilemma.[25] But at the end of October circumstances suddenly worked out the problem for him in an unexpected way.

Charles Wilber had been seriously ill with typhoid fever earlier in the fall and had had to leave school, but in late October he turned up again in Hiram. The only problem was that he was raving, perhaps from the effects of the fever. He was manic and talkative; he thought himself immensely rich, and tried to buy almost everything he saw. Fittingly for a school where classics were so important, he went around caroling an original version of "Old Grimes is dead, that good old man," which began, "Old Grimes est mortuus, / That agathos old anthropos." His friends were sympathetic, but no one got unduly upset; the age accepted temporary insanity as a side effect of fever. Garfield, despite his sprained ankle, escorted him home to Newbury one chilly October night.

Of course Wilber would not be able to teach the next term. The same day

Garfield took him home he was approached by Brother Hayden, who asked whether he would be willing to stay in Hiram over the winter and pick up the elementary grammar and mathematics classes Wilber had been teaching. Initially the offer staggered Garfield, who was perhaps already far along with his plans to teach in Michigan. But it was logical; he was, after all, the brightest student on campus and an acknowledged leader. The more he thought it over, the more he saw the hand of God in it, shaping a special providence for him. Now he would be able to forward his classical studies at no cost and at the same time make the money he needed to go off to college. He had no doubt he could handle the teaching. It would be essentially the same as district school, only with older and better behaved students. He had already taught a few classes for Brother Munnell; this term he had taught a class in penmanship at Brother Hayden's request. Once he had established himself as a full-time teacher, it was only a step to becoming a regular member of the faculty. No doubt of it, this was the next step in his escape from the *mutum et turpe pecus*, and the full development of his talents for God.[26]

Once he had accepted Brother Hayden's offer, the last two weeks of the term flew by. Fall term was informal anyway, compared with the spring; there was no commencement program, only an assembly of students in the Lower Chapel with a couple of short addresses. He delivered one ("The Bible") that year, Lucretia Rudolph the other ("a fine piece, full of good, practical, sound common-sense"). There were a couple of ladies' lyceums too, with "first-rate" speeches by Almeda Booth and others, and the usual gatherings in students' rooms, with the usual goodbyes. Corydon, Henry, and most of James's other friends would be off teaching school during the winter; only Philip Burns and John Harnit planned to stay. Mary would be there, however, as a student. (Her decision to attend was perhaps the result of a sudden change in plans.)[27]

It was a time for looking back on the term, which that year had coincided with a heated presidential campaign between Franklin Pierce and Winfield Scott. Garfield had felt again the simultaneous attraction and repulsion politics had for him. Political debate, he wrote in his diary, was "miserable, low, ungentlemanly trash" of which he desired to remain ignorant; nevertheless, he could not help noticing it from time to time. He was not sure whether he would have voted if he had been twenty-one; a respectable body of Disciple thought held that Christians should not corrupt themselves by contact with politics. He was glad, he noted on Election Day, to be seventeen days short of twenty-one and not have to make that decision. "I think however," he went on, "I should not have voted had I been 21 years of age."[28]

He and Ellis Ballou rode home in Solyman Hubbell's wagon under cold, stormy skies. Neither carried much baggage; both had left most of their things at Hiram, since they expected to return in a few days. Hiram was now Garfield's real home; he had already acknowledged the fact by having his church membership transferred there from Orange. The little red farmhouse in Orange was only a place to visit.[29]

The following Tuesday James and Ellis drove on to Cleveland, in somebody's wagon—maybe they borrowed Uncle Amos's, or perhaps Thomas owned one by this time. The purpose of the trip was to buy clothes suitable to James's new job, to see the sights a little, and to visit other nearby kinfolk—Uncle Joseph and Aunt Calista Skinner in Bedford, Uncle Thomas Garfield in Newburgh. Their first stop was for dinner at the Hubbells' in Warrensville. It can only have increased James's perplexity. Now he had a better chance than ever of going to college someday; but what of his intimacy with Mary? Garfield was beginning to realize that, without making specific promises, he had led Mary too far. Was he now committed to her, even at the sacrifice of his ambitions? If not, how could he break off the relationship without hurting them both and bringing scandal upon himself? Was his Christian duty to her or to himself—to her affection, or to his own talents? Did he need to get married to tame his sexual desires? As he and Ellis sat there enjoying the rural hospitality and piety of the Hubbells' table, questions like these must have assailed him. It was more comfortable not to think about them and to hope that God would take care of the problem somehow, Resolutely he put them from his mind.[30]

He and Ellis were to head back to Hiram on Saturday, 20 November. Orrin Judd was giving them a ride. On Friday, his twenty-first birthday, he packed his belongings under a lowering sky. Winter had held off long that year; now, it seemed, it was really approaching. He and Harriet Boynton spent a lot of the day together, reading a novel—the first he had read since before he went on the canal. He left a vague uneasiness about slipping back into his old reading habits this way; but then he felt a little uneasy in general. Life was too full of problems and uncertainties—problems of being a Christian, problems of being a man. Maybe the songs and hymns were right. Maybe death was indeed preferable.

In this cheerless mood he summed up his thoughts on the day:

> This is my birthday; a date when young men usually "*commence to be men*," as they say. It is, however, to me, but another milestone on the great highroad of my earthly existence, bringing me one year nearer the "Silent City," where end all strife and raging war. Where will my next natal day bring me? I cannot prophesy. It is a time in my life when I know as little of my future as any other since reason first dawned in my mind.

Afterword

WITH this flash of insight into young Garfield's thoughts on his twenty-first birthday, this story ends. The reader, however, is entitled to know what became of the people mentioned in the main narrative, and how Garfield rose from Hiram to the Presidency.

In January 1853, after months of hesitation, Garfield finally got up the nerve to break with Mary Hubbell. The results were fully as messy as he had feared—tearful letters from, and tearful interviews with, Mary; rumor-mongering and scandal among the Hiram students. But the scars healed eventually. Garfield stayed at the Eclectic as a teacher five more terms. In 1854 he enrolled as a sophomore at Williams College in Massachusetts, where he attended with Charles Wilber. He graduated in 1857 with a distinguished record. By that time he had become engaged to Lucretia Rudolph; they married in 1858. He became president of the Eclectic on his return to Ohio and then, in 1859, yielded to the temptation that had tugged at him for so many years and ran for the Ohio Senate as a Republican. He was elected; but it took the Civil War to launch him on his rise to national prominence as a general and a U.S. Congressman. The rest of his story can be followed in the biographies by Leech and Brown, Peskin, or T. C. Smith.

Garfield's story at Williams was financed mostly by his Uncle Thomas, whose contracting business had been going well and who, in fact, became a rich man and one of the leading citizens of Newburgh. The destinies of the rest of the Garfields, however, sufficiently indicate the kind of life James had broken away from. Thomas and Jane farmed all their lives, first in Orange and then in Jamestown, Michigan, and never made enough money to live comfortably. Both Hitty and Mary, with their husbands, lived out their lives in the Orange–Solon area, on the edge of poverty. Uncle Amos lived to 1866; Henry took over the farm after him and ran it with fair success. William died only a few years after the close of this story. Silas was the most successful of all the Boynton children, becoming a prosperous doctor. Eliza, as she grew older, lived increasingly with James and Lucretia and shared in their rise to fame; in fact, she outlived her famous son.

None of Garfield's early friends had a career anywhere near as successful as his. Perhaps Charles Wilber came closest: he published some books on the geology of the Plains, became state geologist of Illinois, and had a town in Nebraska named for him. Albert S. Hall attained another kind of fame: he was the dashing captain of an Ohio regiment during the Civil War, and died with a bullet through the head at Murfreesboro. Corydon Fuller led an up-and-down life all over the Midwest, but ended on the upswing, as the president of a bank in Des Moines. Orrin Judd ended up farming in Nebraska. Symonds Ryder stayed around Hiram all his life and died of tuberculosis in the 1870s. Mary Hubbell married a farmer named Bill Taylor and died young, in the 1860s.

Finally, three features of Garfield's adolescence deserve special comment. The first is the extreme instability of the environment he grew up in. Collectors of presidential trivia point out that Garfield was the last American president born in a log cabin. The fact is true, but one wonders if the people who cite it sufficiently appreciate how significant it is. Northeastern Ohio in 1831 was not a classic, isolated, pioneers-and-Indians frontier; instead, it was an area about to pass turbulently out of the frontier stage into a modern, multiethnic, urbanized manufacturing area. The Garfields' log cabin still standing on a main road in 1845 was a relic of a rapidly dissolving past. The society, and the institutions through which James moved as he grew older, share this evanescent quality. He worked on a busy canal that had been open barely six years and would be out of business in five years more; he attended an academy that had opened in his thirteenth year and would close before he was twenty-three. The Cleveland he knew at the beginning of his adolescent years was a bustling transplanted–New-England town of basically Early American character, without docks, railroads, gas lighting, modern communication, or paved streets; Cleveland at the end of his adolescence was a small but dynamic urban metropolis, with all these amenities. By the time he was an adolescent, the home of his boyhood had been destroyed. By his early manhood, the home of his adolescence was not standing either. Short of war, it is difficult to imagine a society more in the throes of rapid change than this one.

What this meant for young Garfield in practical terms was that there was no established road to success. A poor young man like him had almost the same chance as the child of a much richer family—which is to say, not much chance at all, since the ladders to riches and fame were so violently mobile, their rungs appearing and vanishing like images from a video game. In this seething society, the path to success was not through conformity to an external set of rules and institutions, but through a transformation of self into an adaptable, determined, protean person bent on success. Hence the importance of phrenology, temperance, and the other reform movements that stressed self-control. Any of them, followed faithfully, could give a young man confidence that he knew what life was about and that he was capable of meeting its challenges. The confidence might be unjustified, but its very existence gave its possessor an advantage in the race for success.

If Garfield's adolescence proves anything, it proves the power of the

Christian conversion experience as an engine for accomplishing this self-transformation. Garfield's background was unpromising, to say the least: poverty, indiscipline, instability ("chaos," to use his own word), traumas at which one can barely guess. At eighteen, thanks to the maneuvers of a fond mother, his own penchant for reading, and a good deal of luck, he was attending school, but still unfocused, without a goal in life beyond acting out boyhood fantasies. Then his conversion in March of 1850 reorganized his life substantially and brought into play abilities he hardly knew he had. He changed his goals, his friends, his amusements, his attitude toward work, everything. He felt freer to take risks like speaking in public and studying difficult subjects. For a boy who had been haunted by the fear of failure and his own sensitivity, the promise of divine help brought a new sense of adequacy. Most important, he gained a sense of mission in his life and a charter for transforming himself.

The quest for knowledge as a means to serving God carried him far, indeed far beyond his original vision. Like his friends Wilber and Fuller, Garfield lost much of his fervor and orthodox faith as he grew older and more successful. For him as for them, one might almost say, the Christian experience was a sort of booster rocket, powerful in enabling him to shake free of the early forces that held him down, jettisoned when it had served its purpose. This may have been the case with many nineteenth-century Americans, for whom the Christian message restated the ideal of respectability in symphonic, cosmic terms capable of luring young men but less and less convincing as life wore on.

When one had given credit to the power of evangelical Christianity in providing young Garfield with a model of respectability and giving him an opportunity to attain it, there remains, larger than any other single factor, the element of luck—or providence, as James would have called it. If the rope on the *Evening Star* had been a few feet shorter; if his malaria attack had not coincided with the outbreak of the Gold Rush; if a different ship had been in port at Cleveland on the morning of 16 August 1848—then in all likelihood Garfield would have been dead, or a California pioneer, or a lake sailor, and there would have been no occasion for this sketch. The facts serve to remind one of the importance of pure chance in life. There was no sure road to respectability; for a young man of Garfield's class, there were dozens of wrong turnings and only a few right ones. A whole array of circumstances had to fall into place, like the tumblers of a vast lock, for a youth of the laboring class even to think of becoming "respectable." For Garfield they all somehow fell into place. This tall, burly, bushy-haired youth, hesitant and self-absorbed, enthusiastic and eloquent by turns, can stand as a representative of the thousands of young men whom the open-class society of nineteenth-century America permitted to rise out of privation and ignorance to responsible positions in society—and occasionally, by chance, to leadership of the nation.

Appendix

1880 Campaign Biographies as Sources for the Early Life of James A. Garfield

Seven biographies of Garfield were published in 1880, the year he first ran for the presidency. All could be described as campaign biographies—books designed to present their subject to the public as an interesting person, worthy of the office he sought; but all were factually based. Subsequent historians have tended to minimize the factual element in them and class them as unreliable sources because of their dubious origin and evident partiality. With a little effort, however, it is possible to determine where each biographer obtained his information, how well it agrees with the records of Garfield's life in written sources, and, consequently, how reliable each biographer is on the events of his early life.

A review in the book columns of the *New York Times* for 23 August 1880 considered the merits of the six Garfield biographies issued since the nomination in June. With one addition, the books from that list will be the ones dealt with here, in alphabetical order by author.

James S. Brisbin, *From the Tow-Path to the White House: The Early Life and Public Career of James A. Garfield*. Of all the early Garfield biographers, General Brisbin is the most obscure. A professional military man in his early forties, he had been stationed on the western plains with the cavalry for several years. No novice as a writer, he had already edited the memoirs of a western Indian agent, and was preparing a book on the cattle business on the plains; more to the point, he had written a biography of Grant for the 1868 presidential campaign. But it is not clear what in particular moved him to write a life of Garfield. He was a Pennsylvanian by birth and seems to have come from a farm background; possibly he felt some sympathy with General Garfield's origins. But one would like to know why the title page of his book says that the work was "prepared," rather than written, by him, and why Hubbard, the publisher, reissued the book the following year, after Garfield's assassination, under the name of William R. Balch, a local writer. The book is hefty, over 500 pages, and not badly written, although at times given to vivid and probably fictitious dialogue. It cites a good deal of matter from other sources, such as newspaper interviews.

Jonas M. Bundy, *The Life of Gen. James A. Garfield*. Bundy, an editor of the *New York Evening Mail*, was Garfield's own choice for a campaign biographer—exactly why is not clear, but the choice was a reasonable one. Born in New Hampshire, raised in Wisconsin, Bundy had come to New York at the close of the Civil War and had made his name as a good journalist and practiced writer on a variety of subjects.

Russell H. Conwell, *Life, Speeches, and Public Services of Gen. James A. Garfield of Ohio*. Conwell, pastor of Grace Baptist Church in Philadelphia, had any number of good reasons for wanting to write Garfield's biography. The General was, by all accounts, a good Christian man, and his remarkable rise was an inspiring story, especially meaningful in that it resembled Conwell's own. The minister had been born into a poor, ill-educated farm family in South Worthington, Massachusetts, had left home and put himself through college, and had fought in the war—all very much like Garfield. He had a ten years' successful career as author and lecturer behind him, and had written lives of Republican presidential candidates (Grant had been his first); but one can guess that Garfield had a special attraction for him. A fast, workmanlike writer, he brought out a 300-page book in August, with prefatory apologies for the "difficulties" and "haste" with which it had been composed.

In the preface to his *Life of James A. Garfield*, James R. Gilmore of Boston, a widely known author who published under the pen name of Edmund Kirke, told a remarkable story of his acquaintance with Garfield. He had first met the General, he said, on the battlefront in Tennessee in 1863, where he was collecting material for a book about the war. Circumstances had detained him in General Rosecrans' camp for several weeks, and during that time he had talked a good deal with Garfield, learned the story of his early life, and recognized in it a fascinating account with obvious commercial possibilities. Gilmore, who was then in his forties, was just beginning his writing career, having spent the prewar years working in the family mercantile house in Boston, and decided he could use a story like that. So, according to his account, he took notes of his conversations with Garfield, did some research among his Ohio friends, and had a book written by 1864—but then, for some reason, he decided not to publish it. When Garfield won nomination in 1880, however, Gilmore brought his book out, rapidly rewritten in parts, but based mainly on his earlier account. If any book can be said to be the standard campaign biography, it is probably Gilmore's, not Bundy's. Gilmore had a better publisher, Harper and Brothers of New York, and his version was probably the most widely distributed. It was also among the earliest to appear, and one of the shortest.

Like Gilmore, Albert G. Riddle of Cleveland did not have to start completely cold in 1880; only three years before, in fact, he had written a biographical sketch of Garfield, a friend, neighbor, and fellow Republican. Like Gilmore, too, Riddle was a prolific writer, but the backgrounds and literary styles of the two were dissimilar. Gilmore's interests ran to political, military, and historical questions; Riddle, though a lawyer by profession, preferred fiction. His *Bart Ridgely* had been acclaimed in some quarters as the best American novel of 1873, and by 1880 he had three or four other fictional works to his credit. In addition, in 1877 he had taken the assignment of writing a local history for Geauga County, where he had been born, and neighboring Lake County, where Garfield lived; and it was in connection with that history that he wrote a sketch of Garfield's life, based on notes Garfield furnished him and the recollections of his own long acquaintance. When his friend unexpectedly won the nomination, it was only natural for Riddle to take out his "life," make a few additions, and go looking for a publisher. By August he had one—William Flint of Philadelphia, who brought out Riddle's *Life, Character, and Public Services of James A. Garfield.*

The sixth biography mentioned in the *Times* review, Burke A. Hinsdale's *Republican Text-book*, in other circumstances might have been the best of the group. Hinsdale was a close friend of Garfield's, had succeeded him as president of Hiram College in Ohio, and was a historian by training; but he was so close a friend, apparently, that he felt uncomfortable writing at length about Garfield's personal and family history, and confined himself largely to the political career. For this reason I have not included it as a source.

One another book, which came out later than August, is useful because it seems to rest in part on original research; that is *The Life of James A. Garfield* by Charles Carleton Coffin, published by James H. Earle of Boston. Coffin was a New Hampshireman who had begun writing for various Boston newspapers on the war and was known for his battlefront correspondence. Like Gilmore, he had met Garfield during the course of the war, but had not had the idea of doing a book on his life; in fact the 1880 life appears to have been his publisher's idea rather than his own. Once he accepted the assignment, however, he went at it with the same professional skill and good humor that characterized all his work, and produced a solid, well-crafted 400 pages amid the pressure of other concurrent assignments.

What sources did these authors use? And how trustworthy were the accounts they produced?

To begin answering these questions, one had to consider what sources were available for information about the General's early years—up to 1854, when he left for Williams College in Massachusetts at the age of twenty-two. First, there were a few sources in print: Riddle's printed biographical sketch; a memorial address Garfield had delivered at Hiram College in 1875 in memory of Almeda Booth, in which he talked a little about his own college experience; and a letter he had written to the Trustees of Geauga Seminary, relating some of his experiences, as part of a commemorative occasion at the school. And there were, of course, scattered references to his early years elsewhere in his public speeches and papers.

Besides these sources, as the election year wore on, there appeared in newspapers all over the North an increasing number of interviews with people who had known, or claimed to have known, Garfield as a young man.

Not printed, but in writing, and very important to any potential biographer, was a copy of some recollections the General had dictated in 1877, probably to Albert Riddle. Riddle had used the manuscript freely, but had not reprinted it verbatim. To Garfield, it was no doubt a handy document to have, as he could furnish it to aspiring biographers, without having to make any extra effort of his own.

Then there was a host of potential interviewees, especially in the Reserve. The General was a relatively young man, and most of his childhood acquaintances were still living, as were some of his teachers and employers. And above all there were family members—his mother, his aunt, and numerous cousins, including one who lived on the property adjacent to the old Garfield farm. There was, in short, wide field of source material for an assiduous biographer—but of course, all the biographers of 1880 were under time pressure to get their accounts out well in advance of the election.

A fairly easy way exists to establish whether Brisbin, Bundy, and the others used the recollections of Garfield already available—the 1877 notes, the letter to the Trustees of Geauga Seminary, and the eulogy of Almeda Booth. Each of the three printed source documents contains distinctive features which, if reproduced in another account, constitute strong evidence for the use of the corresponding source document in the writing of that account.

The dictated manuscript autobiography of 1877 contains the only detailed version of the six weeks Garfield spent working on the Ohio canals, and includes certain pieces of information only the General himself could have furnished: A fight he had with another deck hand named Dave; the fact that he fell into the canal fourteen times; a miraculous escape from drowning one night when he was the only person awake on board.

The letter to the Trustees of Geauga Seminary contains a tribute to Samuel D. Bates, the young schoolteacher who urged him to attend the seminary, with mention of the fact that Bates was now a Baptist minister at Marion, Ohio. Bates was indeed in Marion in 1877, but by 1880 he was president of a college in Indiana. Any account in 1880 which identifies Bates as living in Marion, thus, is almost certainly drawn from thc letter to the Trustees. Another identifying feature is the mention of the sum Garfield took to the seminary when entering in 1849—seventeen dollars; another the fact that he roomed the following term with a family named Woodworth for $1.06 a week.

The eulogy of Almeda Booth, likewise, has some quite distinctive marks: A comparison of Booth with Margaret Fuller, an account of a New Testament translation they undertook jointly, and a mention of the first time Garfield saw her, in a geometry class at Hiram College.

Armed with these guidelines, one can proceed to analyze each of the 1880 biographies in terms of the author's sources and methods.

The Riddle biography, the first (in its 1877 incarnation) to be written, is the easiest to characterize. It followed very closely the manuscript autobiography Garfield furnished Riddle. It contains, to be sure, a few other anecdotes that do not appear elsewhere in the biographies and that may not have come from the 1877 manuscript, like the tale of the boys breaking the lock on the schoolhouse door. This sounds as though Riddle had gotten it from conversation with the family. It is a bit curious that no later biographer reproduced this appealing story; the omission suggests to me that none of them read Riddle's printed account, although some certainly used the manuscript on which it had been based. In the 1880 version, Riddle updated his sketch very little concerning Garfield's early life, adding only an account of Garfield's request that Dr. Robison give him a physical—this story is taken, presumably, from Gilmore's account.

Gilmore's account of Garfield's life, according to its author, was the result of "a careful gathering and sifting of material" that had begun seventeen years before. It seems certain that its nucleus consisted of Gilmore's notes on his conversations with Garfield in 1863, with perhaps a little other exploratory research he had done at the time. In 1880 he had added an unspecified amount of material.

From internal evidence, it is clear that Gilmore used the letter to the Geauga Trustees and, in fact, depended almost entirely on it for his account of Garfield's years at Geauga Seminary. On the other hand, it is questionable whether he had access to the manuscript autobiography of 1877. His account of Garfield's canal experience, though strikingly similar in broad outline to the story given in Riddle, often differs in important details. Gilmore says Garfield spent four months on the canal; the actual time, as stated by Riddle, was six weeks. Both men recount a fight on the canal, but Gilmore's version differs as to the name of the other man and the sequence of blows. His account of Garfield's looking for work in Cleveland has no parallel in Riddle. My guess is that this section was based on Gilmore's 1863 notes, and that some of the difference between the two versions stems either from his lack of skill at note-taking or the fact that Garfield, like most good storytellers, rarely told the same story exactly the same way twice. Wherever comparison is possible, Riddle's account corresponds more closely with Garfield's boyhood diaries than does Gilmore's—as is natural, since Garfield no doubt read through his old diaries before dictating his 1877 autobiography. In general, then, Riddle's version is more factual than Gilmore's. It is possible, but unlikely, that some of Gilmore's variants not contradicted by the diary preserve actual memories that Garfield had forgotten by 1877.

In writing up the Hiram years, Gilmore again apparently relied on his 1863 notes. He duly records Garfield's great admiration for Almeda Booth, but in language that does not seem drawn from the printed eulogy. Most likely

Garfield had mentioned her name in their wartime conversations.

So far, then, one can identify just two sources for Gilmore's work: His own 1863 notes and Garfield's letter to the Geauga Trustees. But there were obviously others, for Gilmore quotes from other people's recollections at several points in his account—Dr. J. H. Robison of Bedford, who is mentioned in the Diary; Amos Letcher, Garfield's cousin; Frederick Williams, a trustee of Hiram College; a Mrs. Stiles, with whom Garfield once boarded; and a lady not identified, an ex-Hiram classmate, described as living in Illinois. How did Gilmore come up with this wide and interesting collection of sources?

There is good reason to doubt that Gilmore was in Ohio at all during the summer of 1880; if that is so, he cannot have interviewed these people personally then. Yet the reminiscence of Mrs. Stiles, in which she is identified as the mother of the present sheriff of Ashtabula County, seems to point to an 1880 date. My hunch is that Gilmore collected all these interviews from newspaper clippings in June and July 1880, and wrote them into the account he already had.

If this conjecture is right, his *Life* is a rewrite from a combination of sources: current newspaper interviews, one document, the Geauga letter (probably also reprinted in some newspaper), and his own early notes.

One needs to ask how good Gilmore's notes were. First, Gilmore makes no mention of the Boynton family, Garfield's neighbors and cousins with whom he was intimate during his youth. Every other biographer does so, for the simple reason that Henry Boynton, Garfield's cousin, and his mother, Garfield's aunt, were still living in 1880 on the farm next to the site of the candidate's boyhood home. Any inquirer in the neighborhood was sure to run into the Boyntons and avail himself of their reminiscences to some extent. There is no good reason why Gilmore would have left their material out if he had had it—it was an important part of the story, and was the sort of homey stuff Gilmore liked to use. The clear inference is that he had never done any research in the vicinity when he wrote his book.

Equally suggestive is his treatment of Garfield's family. He frequently mentions the General's oldest sister, Mehetabel, and makes mild fun of her unusual name, but he never mentions the name of the other sister, Mary. Indeed, from the awkward way in which he writes around it, it's clear that he doesn't know Mary's name. Had he been in Ohio in 1880, he could have found out her name without difficulty; presumably, however, he was in New York, writing from his 1863 notes, which were detailed in some respects but scant of detail in others, and didn't feel he had the time to check the missing data. As he conceded in his preface, he wrote in haste. But his speed, at least, was creditable; by 30 July his book was on sale, probably the earliest of the lot.

The biographies by the two journalists, Coffin and Bundy, present a less confusing picture. Both relied on a mixture of sources, but in both cases it is fairly simple to infer what was in the mix.

From textual similarities, it is evident that both Bundy and Coffin used the 1877 autobiography, the eulogy of Almeda Booth, and probably the letter to the Geauga Trustees. Both, moreover, mention that they had had interviews with the General—likely enough, as Garfield was a very approachable man. Both did workmanlike jobs of putting all this material together, though Coffin apparently made a slip of the pen and wrote the figure 11 for 17 in noting how many dollars Garfield took with him to Geauga Seminary. Basically, however, both writers were working from the same sources, a package of material provided by the candidate himself.

There are, nonetheless, some interesting differences between the two accounts. Bundy's contains a story found in no other biography of Garfield's struggle with his first Latin assignment at Hiram. He also mentions Garfield's reputation as a fighter in his youth, and reports by far the most psychologically detailed account of his conversion experience. All this seems likely to be material obtained from interviews with either Garfield or his mother. There is also a quantity of letters included from the General's ex-classmates at Williams. These are sources of the sort one would expect an official biographer to have access to.

Coffin seems to have researched more widely, if somewhat spottily. He knows about the Boyntons, though not the names of Garfield's siblings. He has a story about Garfield's Hiram days, and his willingness to let the younger scholars take part in games, probably from some printed source, and also the same Frederick Williams story Gilmore uses. His write-up of the letter to the Geauga Trustees is quite careless in spots. Finally, he includes two letters to him from figures in Garfield's early years, S. D. Bates and Dr. Alonzo Harlow.

In Bundy, then, one has probably the fullest account of Garfield's youth from Garfield's own viewpoint, based on his written recollections supplemented by interviews, without contributions from other sources except possibly Eliza Garfield. In Coffin, one has an interesting collection of material, unsystematically collected and incomplete, and varying, alas, in accuracy.

There are puzzling features about the Brisbin biography. Brisbin quotes at length and almost verbatim (though without indicating sources) from both the Geauga letter and the Booth eulogy, and gives some indication of having had access to the 1877 autobiography. He uses, in other words, essentially the standard package of sources that Garfield made available to Coffin and Bundy. Like Coffin and Gilmore, too, he uses interviews that seem to have come from newspapers or some similar contemporary source, notably an interview with Amos Letcher which is verbally close enough to the one quoted in Gilmore to show that they came from the same source, but also substantially different in its coverage, containing material omitted in the Gilmore version and omitting material that Gilmore contains.

There are, however, some odd differences in nuance between Brisbin and the journalist-biographers. Almost alone among the biographers, Brisbin takes a rather critical attitude toward Garfield's older brother Thomas, describing him only as quiet, unambitious, and limited in his aspirations. This stance contrasts sharply with the one manifest in Gilmore's and Conwell's books, particularly; both these writers praise Thomas for the self-sacrifice that made it possible for the family to stay together after Abram Garfield's death and for James to begin getting an education. The latter stance was Garfield's, as is evident from letters he wrote to his friends in the 1870s, in which he expressed his high regard for Thomas and his feeling of indebtedness to him. Gilmore doubtless got his perception of Thomas from talking with Garfield; Conwell, I suggest, probably had it from Eliza Garfield. Perhaps Brisbin failed to get it because he did not talk with Garfield or any other member of the family.

This conclusion has some support from a series of odd minor discrepancies throughout Brisbin's book, hard to account for except by honest ignorance of the facts. Garfield is described as getting from his home to Cleveland "after a tramp of several days"; yet he lived only seventeen miles from the city and frequently walked there in one day. On his return from the canal, Brisbin avers that he talked his mother into letting him go back to it and was about to set off again when he came down with the ague; but the diary, as well as the versions given by Gilmore and Riddle, state that Garfield came home from the canal because he had come down with the ague. These variants are inexplicable if Brisbin was working from the manuscript autobiography or from interviews with Garfield himself; apparently he had access to the 1877 autobiography, or Riddle's version of it, at second hand and in incomplete or garbled form.

Alongside these flaws, however, Brisbin includes a number of stories which have no counterparts elsewhere in the Garfield lives and several quite detailed accounts of the General's school days at Chester and Hiram. All of these, when they can be checked against the diary, turn out to be substantially true and usually more accurate than the accounts of other biographers. Some, of course, cannot be checked, but they sound likely: Garfield and his Bible disputation; Mrs. Branch and her eccentric grammar; the tutorial in geometry at Warrensville; and the way in which he got his first teaching job. Brisbin, it seems, had a source or sources of information in the neighborhood of Orange, Garfield's boyhood home, which no other biographer managed to tap. Possibly it was a Boynton cousin, maybe Henry—in view of Brisbin's including an account of the semester at Chester when Garfield and his cousin went on a special economy diet—but this is only a guess. It may well have been some neighbor who did not share the Garfield family's high estimate of Thomas Garfield.

In sum, Brisbin's book, possibly the work of several hands, embodies a variety of sources: generally accurate reproduction of some available printed material; a fair amount of careful interviewing in the area where Garfield spent his youth; and careless use of the 1877 autobiography, used to better advantage by two or three other biographers.

R. H. Conwell dedicated his biography of Garfield to Eliza Garfield and Alpha Boynton, the candidate's aunt; and although he did not say so explicitly, these two women seem to have been the chief sources for his work. It certainly bears every mark of having been drawn from some source, not Garfield himself, but someone very close to the family. The family history is uncommonly detailed and accurate, including full data on all the General's siblings; the attitude toward Thomas Garfield is notably warm and commendatory; and there are numerous details about the Boynton family, especially Amos Boynton, Garfield's uncle.

Conwell uses few other sources. He does not mention Almeda Booth and, in fact, skips over the Hiram years as quickly as he can. His account of the canal experience is very much from the mother's viewpoint, accurate as to the beginning and ending of it, but as to the canal work itself dependent upon an inaccurate story by a Captain Jonathan Myers of Jersey City, New Jersey, which had appeared in the newspapers just after Garfield was nominated and is flatly contradicted by the diary and all other available sources. It is clear, thus, that Conwell did not use the 1877 autobiography or the Riddle sketch.

It does appear, however, that Conwell visited Geauga Seminary in preparing his work. His descriptions of the place are full, and he had a better grasp of the rivalry between the Freewill Baptists and the Disciples than any other writer. But it does not seem likely that he used the letter to the Geauga Trustees; his account of Garfield's school days there, for which he names Henry Boynton as his main source, departs from it in many details.

With these data in hand, it is possible to make some generalizations about the usefulness of the six biographies as sources for Garfield's early life.

Bundy probably had the fullest access of any writer before or since to Garfield's own recollections of his youth. He was an honest writer, who did not hesitate, for instance, to record that Garfield had had a reputation as a "fighting boy" in his early teens, or that he had been a bit "offish" on the subject of religion about the same time. He seems to have been careful in transcribing his material. All in all, his work is about as trustworthy as any contemporary biography can be.

Most of Riddle's account came from the manuscript autobiography to which students now have direct access among the Garfield Papers in the Library of Congress. For many purposes, his book has been superseded. But the small amount of material he added from his own knowledge and investigation seems worthy of credence. Riddle was, after all, a friend and neighbor of Garfield, with a wide acquaintance in the area and without any discernible axe to grind. His only fault seems to be a slight tendency to embroider his stories; with that allowed for, his biography is trustworthy for the small amount of new material it contains.

The bulk of Conwell's *Life* is very useful. The sections on the Garfield family and on Garfield's early years reproduce the recollections of Eliza Garfield, Alpha Boynton, and Henry Boynton, and seem to do so fully and honestly. Conwell concedes, for instance, that Garfield was rather lazy as a young man and somewhat accident-prone as a laborer, both points which can be corroborated from other sources. For this material the book is valuable; the rest of it can be ignored.

As for Coffin and Brisbin, both seem to be combinations of material of varying reliability, and should be used with care. Some of the neighborhood anecdotes in Brisbin's account are probably quite true, but they would be easier to assess if it were known exactly who furnished them. The letters from Bates and Harlow in Coffin's book both seem a little overdone but may contain some truth. There are factual slips in both books.

Gilmore's book is probably the least reliable. It seems to rest on notes of uneven quality, seventeen years old, and newspaper accounts that were incorporated into the narrative without much, if any, attempt at verification. Certainly some, perhaps a good deal, of the material in the notes comes from Garfield's memory and is reproduced authentically, but it is almost impossible to tell which. Gilmore seems to have had the knack of slightly distorting any story he touched, and it is hard to tell, unless a parallel source exists, where the distortion lies. Although it was, ironically, the most widely distributed of the six, the temptation to depend on Gilmore's book is one for a modern biographer to resist as energetically as possible.

Notes

Abbreviations and Short Titles

List of abbreviations and short titles used in the Notes and Sources.
Short titles are given when their initial letter differs from that of the full citation in "Sources."

JAG: James A. Garfield

LC: Library of Congress

WRHS: Western Reserve Historical Society, Cleveland, Ohio

Diary: James A. Garfield, *Diary*, ed. by Harry James Brown and Frederick D. Williams

Early Settlers: *Annals of the Early Settlers Association of Cuyahoga County*

Eggleston: "The Personal Reminiscences of General Chauncey Eggleston"

Geauga Seminary catalogue: *Catalogue of the Officers and Students of the Geauga Seminary* . . .

Rudolph: *Pickups from the "American Way"*

Western Reserve Eclectic Institute catalogue, 1851: *First Annual Catalogue* . . .

Western Reserve Eclectic Institute catalogue, 1852: *Second Annual Catalogue* . . .

Chapter 1. The Black-Salter

1. Several sources provide data on the extent of settlement in Solon in the 1840s. The central part of Solon was unsettled in 1835; Seymour Trowbridge had to have his uncle's help that year in locating his 200-acre lot, in an area where not a tree had been cut (Trowbridge, p. 305). A description of lands in southern Orange, the next township to the north, dated 9 October 1841 (in the Perkins Papers, WRHS), shows that of sixteen lots listed five were still unoccupied; and one can assume that the others were only partially cleared. Farms quite close to Cleveland were less than half cleared even in the late forties; see advertisements in the *Plain Dealer*, 16 February, 15 March 1848. Garfield's friend Orrin Judd, in a letter dated 19 November 1855, recalled that when he and his family moved to the area in 1842, settling right on the town line, in Orange, it was heavily timbered and the roads only partially cut through. Johnson, p. 518, states that the deer disappeared from Orange and Solon in the course of the 1840s, though from the Perry Mapes autobiography in WRHS it is evident that there was one wolf that passed through as late as the 1850s. During the 1840s, in other words, Orange and Solon passed from frontier to farmland; it seems reasonable to

consider 1847 as about the turning point. On wild animals in the forest, see Henry, pp. 45–46.

2. Trees of the forests: Cherry, pp. 141–42; W. A. Knowlton, p. 12; personal observation. Fall foliage: Henry, p. 24; *Diary*, 2:227.

3. Dickens, p. 223. Cf. also pp. 178, 215; Van Wagenen, pp. 31–32; Schob, pp. 15–19; Henry, p. 45; Dickinson, p. 60.

4. Riddle, *Ansel's Cave*, pp. 90–93.

5. Black-salting generally: Van Wagenen, pp. 166–67; Carson, p. 10; In the Reserve: *Lake County*, pp. 701–71; *Geauga County*, pp. 233, 235; Dickinson, p. 87 (ashery in Randolph); Riddle, *Ross*, p. 383 (ashery in Munson). These sources suggest that there was no accepted division of labor in the potash business in the Reserve. Some farmers may have made their own black salts and sold them to local asheries, as Van Wagenen describes. Others, as in Riddle (*Ansel's Cave*), sold the raw ashes. Some asheries made potash as well as pearlash (*Geauga County*); others made only pearlash (Johnson, pp. 517–18). It is not wholly clear whether an operation that went no further than black salts would qualify as an "ashery", but it probably would.

6. I know of no work that discusses satisfactorily the process of settlement in the Reserve. Milton C. George, "The Settlement of the Connecticut Western Reserve of Ohio," (Ph.D. diss., University of Michigan, 1950) is wholly inadequate in concept and execution, and I have had to go over the data myself to get some feel for the process.

Certain broad patterns are obvious. The general thrust of settlement was from the Pennsylvania border west and from the lake shore south. Another area of early settlement lay along the Cuyahoga west of Orange and Solon.

One can construct a rough timetable of the process by combining, for each township, the traditional dates for the first settler, first school, and first church, as given in county histories. If one does this for the central Reserve, it is at once obvious that a cluster of three townships in the Chagrin Valley—Orange and Solon in Cuyahoga County, Russell in Geauga—were settled much later than any of their neighbors. Early population figures reinforce this pattern. From 1830 to 1850, Solon was the smallest township of Cuyahoga County in population, i.e., it was less fully settled than the others, since all the townships were roughly equal in area. Russell was among the smallest townships in Geauga, and Orange, after a fairly impressive start, lagged behind its neighbors and by 1850 was a relatively underpopulated area.

Several factors account for this late settlement: the rough terrain, the difficulty of transportation, and the mediocre soil. They combined to render the Chagrin Valley in, say, 1840 a little island of frontier surrounded by areas that were ten or fifteen areas ahead of it in the settlement process. Its inhabitants were, and felt, poor and backward relative to their neighbors. For an example of a town in neighboring Geauga County settled relatively late, an isolated community ridiculed by people at the county seat, see Riddle's discussion of Munson ("Monson") in *Ross*, pp. 380–381. It is part of my thesis in this book that people at the time were quite conscious of the difference—also that, during the 1840s, the later settled townships began catching up with their slightly older neighbors, so that by the 1850s the difference was much less marked.

7. Wickham, I, 489; Johnson, p. 518. On Hampshire Road, see Coates, 1:214, 219. I infer the social pretensions of these families—the Cloughs, the Gerrishes, the Patricks, and the Morses—from several small bits of evidence: first, their forming a Congregational church, Congregationalism being the most prestigious and formal of the sects favored by New England settlers; second, the Morses' treatment of Garfield, described in this chapter; third, the early eminence of Joseph G. Patrick as president of the county's Total Abstinence Society (*Plain Dealer*, 16 October 1844).

The only concrete evidence I have that Daniel Morse ran an ashery is the recollection of Henry Boynton discussed in the next note, but there is no evidence whatever to connect him with any other business. His occupation, oddly, is not given in the 1850 U.S. Census, which shows him living with his wife, Lucretia, 53 (Morse was 54), his daughter Zeruiah and (by then) son-in-law Silas Bigelow, his daughter Eleanor, 15, and a thirteen-year-old boy, William Ferris, born in England, who probably was filling the same position Garfield had had. Possibly Morse ran a small store and operated an ashery as a sideline.

8. Almost all the early biographies mention JAG's early employment in black-salting, beginning with Gilmore's reference to a "dry-saltern" in *On The Border*, p. 222. They differ, however, as to his age at the time, the location of the work, and the nature of his job. Not all include the story, recounted in this chapter, of how he left the job; it is discussed in a separate note below. Here it will be convenient to compare the early versions briefly.

Riddle (*Life*, p. 37) says that JAG worked for a "merchant," and implies that he did the actual, physical, dirty work of boiling the salts. He gives no particular indication of the time—only that it was before he entered Geauga Seminary in 1849. He does not say where the ashery was.

Gilmore (*Life*, p. 6) seems to place the work around 1847, after JAG had been working at carpentry two years. The ashery, according to him, was ten miles from the Garfield farm, in the direction of Cleveland. He has JAG working as a bookkeeper for fourteen dollars a month, and says that he had first encountered the place in the course of doing some carpentry there.

Bundy's mention (p. 15) is brief and does not give the location of the place. JAG, he says, was 14 or 15 (that is, the year was 1846 or 1847); he received nine dollars a month and board.

Conwell's account (pp. 67–68) places the work somewhat earlier than the others, in 1844 or 1845. Writing, as always, from the mother's point of view, he stresses the dirtiness of the work and the long hours. He gives no hint where the ashery was.

Coffin (pp. 44–45) suggests that it was before 1847, and says that the place was in Orange. Like Conwell, and Riddle, he stresses the hard and disagreeable nature of the work.

Only Brisbin, of the early biographers, fails to mention the episode at all.

None of these accounts names JAG's employer. William M. Thayer's fictionalized biography, derived largely from the Gilmore version, calls him "Barton" (pp. 156–70); but this name, like most of the others in the book, is pretty evidently Thayer's invention. There is, however, an interview with JAG's cousin Henry Boynton, from an unidentified newspaper dated 22–23 September 1881, in a Scrapbook in the JAG papers, which contains more information. Boynton was a little unsure about the time JAG went to work black-salting; he said that it happened when JAG was fourteen, and that he "immediately . . . left Mr. Morse's employ, and went on the canal." This sequence of events is clearly impossible, for the *Diary*, which begins 1 January 1848, shows what JAG was doing for the seven months just before he went on the canal—and he was not working at an ashery. Probably Boynton telescoped two events in his recollection, and this episode really took place in 1847. But he was definite about the name of JAG's employer—Daniel Morse, who, according to him, lived about four miles away. The distance is correct, and says something for the accuracy of Boynton's memory.

It may seem unlikely, at first blush, that JAG boarded with a family living only four miles away—as most of the accounts, Gilmore's, Riddle's, and Bundy's, imply that he did. Bundy, in fact, states expressly that he received board as part of his wages. But the long hours of his employment, alluded to by Conwell, probably required it; if he was to start the fires early in the morning, his employer could not afford to wait for him to walk over.

There seems to be no other reason to reject Boynton's identification. He was clearly in a position to know the employer's name, and several details in his story of the incident with the employer's daughter coincide with other information about the Morse family. I have therefore accepted the identification.

One other discrepancy remains to be settled. Conwell, whose account is usually accurate, maintains that JAG worked at black-salting when he was twelve or thirteen, no older—that is, in 1844 or 1845. An entry in JAG's diary for 1875, referring to "Stephen Mapes's ashery, where I worked 30 years ago," squares with this assertion. JAG's memory was good, and I think it true that he worked black-salting in 1844–1845 for Stephen Mapes, a neighbor who lived about a mile away. But I cannot identify this job with the black-salting mentioned in the other accounts, for the following reasons:

A. Most accounts, including the very trustworthy Bundy, state that he boarded with his employer while black-salting. He did not board with Mapes, for in his reminiscent letter of 19 November 1855, he remembered that he had never been away from Eliza for any length of time before 1847.

B. All other accounts put his black-salting later in time, and Henry Boynton, as noted, connected it in his mind with JAG's going on the canal in 1848. A three- or four-year lapse between these events seems too long to be plausible.

C. The incident of the employer's daughter, very possible with the Morse family, would have been impossible with Mapes. He married in 1832 (Ham, p. 178); his oldest child would have to have been at least a year younger than JAG.

D. Mapes disappears from the county tax records in the middle 1840s; he could not have been the employer if the affair took place after that time.

I conclude, therefore, that JAG worked for Mapes a month or two in, say, 1845; that he came home late every night, black from head to foot, and that his pathetic appearance impressed itself on his mother's memory. Later, probably in 1847, he went to work at Daniel Morse's. His previous experience in the business was probably one of the reasons why Morse hired him.

As to the nature of the work, it seems obvious that here, as often, Gilmore was in error. JAG's work was thoroughly manual, and Bundy's quoted salary of nine dollars a month seems altogether plausible. Gilmore, wishing to stress his subject's intellect and innate respectability, jacked up both the figure and the job.

9. Reserve farmers' clothing: Welker, p. 38; Carter, p. 33; Dickinson, p. 59. JAG's appearance: Bundy, p. 14; Conwell, p. 67; interview with Lucinda Gould, Cleveland *Leader*, 15 July 1899, in scrapbook at Lawnfield; clipping from *Tribune*, 4–5 July 1880, in scrapbook 39, JAG Papers.

10. The Morse household, Morse's wages, and hired boy: See previous note on "Garfield and black-salting." Details of black-salting: Van Wagenen, pp. 166–67.

11. "Gaffield": Leech and Brown, p. 9; Brisbin, p. 64; Hinsdale, *Life*, p. 48; Riddle, *Life*, p. 38. The last three citations suggest that the New England pronunciation was more common in the area than Leech believes. Note that the name of the Garfields' neighbor Daniel Partridge was commonly written "Patridge," as on the county tax record for 1848; and cf. Kenyon, p. 397.

12. JAG's previous experience: See note on "Garfield and black-salting". JAG as a worker: See chapter 4, *infra*, and notes.

13. The Morse home: Probably the best way to get a feel for the homes of the early Reserve before 1850 is to visit the Hale Farm at Bath, Ohio, maintained by the West-

ern Reserve Historical Society, where several such homes have been restored. There is also a large body of literature on the subject. My description here is based on a visit to the Hale Farm and on Davis, *Hinsdale*, p. 11; Carter, pp. 30–33; Frary, pp. 127, 239, and *passim*; and Dickinson, p. 60. On the sitting room, Cf. Riddle, *Ross*, p. 161; "They entered the front door (not the rule in the country) and found the parlor empty."

14. JAG's leaving Morse's: Three sources, two of them quite trustworthy, give this story in one version or another: Riddle, *Life*, p. 37; Gilmore, p. 6; and the newspaper interview with Henry Boynton in the JAG Papers. All agree on the essential points: the suitor, the use of the word "servant," and JAG's immediate reaction. The Boynton interview stresses JAG's lasting indignation. The story seems entirely consistent with what is known of JAG, is vouched for by two credible sources, and squares with all the facts available about the Morses. For these reasons I have accepted it.

Riddle describes the suitor as a teacher from the Geauga Seminary; Boynton remembered him as a teacher in the Cleveland schools. It is pleasant to relate that the man who actually married Zeruiah Morse on 31 August 1849, fills both descriptions. Silas Bigelow taught at Geauga from the middle forties to 1850, and later in the Cleveland schools. Howe, p. 452, gives these and other essential facts about him. He was JAG's teacher at a later period, and the two remarks JAG made about him may have special meaning in this connection. On hearing of Bigelow's marriage he wrote (*Diary*, 1:23), "Peace and long life to them and then 'peace to their ashes'." Several years later he stopped in Solon to visit Bigelow and commented: "Our circumstances have been reversed . . . Marriage has upturned his calculations with respect to college, and real life has taken away some of his haughtiness." (*Ibid.*, 1:239). The mention of ashes and haughtiness in these passages is at least suggestive, and tends to support the story as told by Riddle and the others.

For the implications of the word "servant" on the Michigan frontier, which was settled by the same kind of people as northern Ohio, see Osborne, pp. 75, 84. Riddle's account of the frontier township of Munson ("Monson") in Geauga County shows how misunderstandings might arise when a new settler came from a community where there was "a marked difference" between members of the family and the hired help (*Ross*, p. 385).

Chapter 2. James and His Reveries

1. There are many good descriptions of the Chagrin valley in the local literature, e.g. Riddle, "55 Years," pp. 127–28. For its similarity to New England topography, see Cleveland *Daily True Democrat*, 23 July 1852, quoted in *Annals*, 35:109.

2. Climatic differences: Alexander, pp. 113–16. Pine and hemlock: *Ohio Railroad Guide*, p. 82, on pine. There was no hemlock in Royalton, in western Cuyahoga County (W. A. Knowlton, p. 12), but it is abundant in the Chagrin valley and the eastern Reserve (see, e.g., Howells, p. 71).

3. JAG's roaming in the woods is mentioned in Lucretia R. Garfield's "Rough Sketch," p. 9. The description is a composite of three rich sources: Charles Henry's remembrance of his pioneer boyhood in Bainbridge, the township east of Solon; Albert G. Riddle's descriptions of his boyhood in Geauga County, ten or fifteen miles to the east; and the autobiography of Perry Mapes, the Garfields' neighbor. The source of each detail follows.

Fear of the woods: Riddle, *Old Newbury*, p. 71; strayed cattle: Henry, p. 46; wild berries: Mapes, p. 6; Riddle, *Bart Ridgeley*, p. 68; chill east winds: Henry, p. 335. loon and whippoorwill: *Ibid.*, p. 46. spring flowers: *Ibid.*, pp. 336–37. bees in basswood: *Ibid.*, p. 46. creaking of branches: Riddle, *Old Newbury*, p. 10.

4. Mapes, p. 3; Riddle, *Bart Ridgeley*, p. 68; Thomas Garfield to JAG, 1 April 1855, JAG Papers, LC. JAG's letter to his mother, 19 November 1855, also in the JAG Papers, mentions his "playing on the *rocks*" when he was younger; Mapes's account stresses the fascination they held for him even as a college student. His naming the rocks is from Conwell, pp. 60–61. "up west": *Diary*, 1:33 (9 January 1850).

5. JAG's early preaching is mentioned in Conwell, p. 65; Patterson, "Recollections." Books were important to JAG from a very early age; some Orange neighbors told Conwell (p. 63) that they thought he had learned more from his reading than from attending school. One main aim of this chapter is to survey his reading through early adolescence and try to pick out the major themes in it, so a brief note on the sources follows.

Four sources discuss JAG's early reading habits with some specificity: Bundy, p. 13; Conwell, pp. 60–64; the biography from the *Tribune* in Scrapbook 39, JAG Papers, LC: and an article by Henry Boynton in the *Hiram College Advance*. (In addition, JAG's autobiographical letter of 19 November 1855, mentions a few other things he read in his boyhood, like the tale of Putnam and the wolf.) Bundy's list, which was based on an interview with JAG, is no doubt the most trustworthy. It mentions Josephus's *Histories* (cited also by Conwell and the *Tribune* biographer), *Robinson Crusoe*, the histories of Goodrich and Eggleston, *Alonzo and Melissa* (which the *Tribune* biography also mentions), and a story, without title, of a man traveling down the Mississippi.

The *Tribune* biography adds two more titles. "Tom Halyard," which I have been unable to identify, was presumably a sea story. *The Cow Boys of the Revolution* was another American historical novel.

Conwell's account names fewer specific titles. Of course, *The Pirate's Own Book*, named by all biographers (see below); something called "Tales of the Sea" which may be identical with Sleeper's *Tales of the Ocean*; and a book called "Indian Tales," too vague a title to identify, but one that supports JAG's early interest in the Indians. Conwell also mentions his reading a lot of history, and narratives of scientific discovery.

Boynton's account, the most inclusive, is probably also the least reliable; this article was the last of the three versions Boynton gave on JAG's early life, and the least in harmony with other evidence. It cited a general and undistinguished array of works: Webster's Speller, Scott's novels, histories of England, Rome, and the U. S., and *The Pilgrim's Progress*.

All sources seem to agree on the four main categories of JAG's early reading: religious works, histories, nautical books, and novels. Gilmore's statement (p. 6) that JAG first ran into nautical stories and novels while working at black-salting conflicts with all the other evidence and can safely be dismissed.

Lucretia R. Garfield, "Rough Sketch," p. 7; and Cottom, p. 48, comment on JAG's memory. For his naming the trees, see Conwell, p. 61, and clipping of 22–23 September 1881, Scrapbooks 39, JAG Papers, LC.

6. *Early Settlers*, 8: 4, 43.

7. American attitudes toward Indians are brilliantly discussed in Slotkin, especially pp. 354ff. and 427–29. The quotes are from Goodrich, pp. 14–15, 17.

8. Bundy, p. 13, says that he read this when he was about fourteen. The quotes in the paragraph are from pp. 22–28 and p. 4.

9. Benjamin Eggleston's *An American Field of Mars* was published in Cleveland in 1839; that JAG read it in his early teens seems entirely plausible. The quotation is from p. 410.

10. William Cutter, *The Life of Israel Putnam* (New York: George F. Cooledge and

Brother, 1847), is probably just too late to be the account JAG read, but it is representative of the genre and in fact was compiled from several previous lives of Putnam. Pp. 35–41 tell the story of the wolf. Another exploit of Putnam's appears in Goodrich, p. 204.

11. Garfield's ancestral background: Johnson, p. 495; *Diary*, 1:9–14. Goodrich on New Englanders: p. 63.

12. Clipping of 22–23 September 1881, in Scrapbook 39, JAG Papers, LC.

13. Fuller, p. 48; clipping from Cleveland *Leader*, 15 July 1899, in scrapbook at Lawnfield. For her voice and repertory of songs see Bundy, p. 13.

14. Henry, pp. 28, 236.

15. JAG to Phebe Boynton, 30 May 1854, JAG Papers, LC. For his knowledge of the constellations, see *Diary*, 4:466 (10 October 1880).

16. Bundy, p. 10, is one of several writers to assert that he had read every book in the neighborhood by his early teens. His brother Thomas, in an interview in the Cleveland *Leader*, 25 April 1891 (clipping in scrapbook at Lawnfield), recalled that the whole family talked of his going to college. "Little head, little wit": Patterson recollections, Hinsdale Papers, WRHS.

17. Conwell, p. 64. Riddle, *Life*, pp. 25–26; Cleveland *Leader*, 25 April 1891, clipping in scrapbook at Lawnfield.

18. "Our days are as the grass": The hymn tune, "Boylston," is mentioned in Henry, p. 36; the text is from *Sacred Songs for Family and Social Worship*, p. 233.

19. Bundy, p. 14; cf. Davis, *Hinsdale*, p. 20.

20. JAG to Lucretia Rudolph, 21 April 1855, JAG Papers, LC.; W. A. Knowlton, p. 23; Beecher, p. 210; Bundy, p. 13.

21. The quotations are from Jackson, pp. 101–103, 49.

22. As mentioned above, this book could have been the "Tales of the Sea" cited by Conwell. Printed in Boston in 1843, it was doubtless available in the Reserve by the middle forties. The quotation is from p. 10.

23. This work is cited by almost every biographer, largely because JAG mentioned it in his 1877 autobiographical sketch and credited it with luring him onto the canal. For example see Riddle, *Life*, p. 24, and Brisbin, p. 45. The book, by Charles Ellms, was first published in Boston in 1837. For the quotes, see pp. 82, 31.

24. "A kind of Bible": 1877 autobiographical sketch, JAG Papers, LC.

25. *Diary*, 1:257 (29 June 1854), 372 (17 July 1867); Conwell, pp. 60–61; Ellms, pp. 97ff.; Phebe Boynton to JAG, 31 [*sic*] April 1853, JAG Papers, LC. (The exact wording is "O James! Do you visit with yourself as much as you used to?")

26. Kenyon, p. 391, lists "horse-dirt" and "cow-dirt" in a glossary of "Western Reserve Expressions." JAG used the phrase "hen park" in his diary 9 July 1850 (1:51).

27. Description of the Garfield farm and its environs come from Conwell, p. 60; Brisbin, p. 31; Conwell, pp. 43–44; Thomas Garfield to JAG; 1 April 1855, JAG Papers, LC; Coppess, p. 96 and personal observation.

Chapter 3. The Garfields

1. Lucretia Garfield's brother Joseph Rudolph began his memoir with the statement (p. 1) that he was born in 1841, "just at the turning point marked by the clearing of the original forests and the change from the log house to the somewhat primitive frame house and barn." A. G. Riddle (*Riddle*, p. 44) put it this way: "The most marked events in pioneer life are the erection of nice framed buildings to take the place of the primitive structures of unhewn logs." Cf. Coates, 1:218. Hutslar, pp.

201–3; on p. 208 is an admirably thorough treatment of the steps in replacement. Dickinson, p. 66, has a good description of an early frame house.

Windows that opened and shut were a feature of the most pretentious early house in south Orange, that of John Mapes. (Wickham, 1:598). Some examples from around this time period of families' moving from a log house to one of frame or brick are in Benjamin Wood diary, entry of 14 January 1847 (Independence township); Erickson, p. 108 (Newburgh, 1842); and Carter, p. 30 (Twinsburg, c. 1850). Riddle, *Riddle*, p. 44, is the authority for the barn's being built first.

2. Johnson, pp. 493, 518. Bard, pp. 24–25, includes a fairly detailed description of the log house on a side road in northern Solon where the Chamberlain family lived until 1850. Corlett's cabin: Erickson, p. 105. Burgess's cabin: *Early Settlers*, 6:1, 46. Another cabin, in Bainbridge, is mentioned in Henry, p. 43.

3. This 120-acre property, Lot 14 of the Middle Division of Tract 3 in Orange, was sold by the Perkinses quite early. It is shown in the 1841 "Notes and Descriptions" as deeded to E. Morgan. According to Cuyahoga County tax records (microfilm, WRHS) Elias Morgan paid taxes on it through the forties, but the U.S. Census manuscripts of 1840 and 1850 show no person of that name living in the neighborhood. By 1874, according to Lake's atlas, it belonged to Calvin Gilbert and is presumably the unoccupied "Gilbert farm" referred to by Perry Mapes in his autobiography, on which the standing timber was cut down in the 1850s. "Pulpit Rock," from which JAG was supposed to have practiced oratory as a boy, was on this property, which now belongs to the Chagrin Valley Country Club (clipping from Cleveland *Plain Dealer*, 21 October 1918, in Henry B. Boynton Papers, WRHS).

4. Wickham, 2:595; Henry, pp. 18–19, 25–26; Welker, p. 21.

5. Three sources give approximate dates for the building of the frame house. Gilmore (p. 6) is, as usual, the least credible; he suggests that it took place when JAG was eleven or twelve years old, that is in 1842 or 1843. This is the period of Eliza's marriage to Alfred Belding, when the family was not even living in Orange (see below). Conwell, p. 69, and the *Tribune* biographer, whose account is reproduced in Coates, 1:199, agree on the summer of 1846, when JAG was fourteen.

The house itself ceased to exist long ago. When Eliza moved out in the early 1850s, she sold it to Henry Boynton, who moved it across the road. It was destroyed by fire shortly afterward. The historian who wants to describe it, therefore, has only recollections to go on.

Thomas Garfield's letter of 15 April 1854, to JAG (JAG Papers, LC) makes it clear that the house was painted red, as the *Tribune* biography states. The *Tribune* biography also states that the house had five rooms, three below and two above; Conwell, however, says it had four rooms. It is not clear where the *Tribune* writer got his information; Conwell, on the other hand, interviewed both Eliza Garfield and Alpha Boynton, and visited the site of the house; I am inclined to accept his version.

6. Carter, pp. 30–31, explicitly notes the transition from fireplace to cookstove as a feature of pioneer life in Twinsburg. That there were cookstoves in use in the area is clear from an entry of 26 August 1842, in the Luther Prentiss Docket Book (Warrensville); from the Perry Mapes autobiography; and from Grismer, *Kent*, p. 34. Rose, p. 219, notes an advertisement for cookstoves in a Cleveland newspaper of 1849. But fireplaces were still in use for cooking, too: see *Early Settlers*, 1:3, 69; Erickson, p. 498; and Susan Thomas to Mary T. Roys, 21 August 1846, Thomas-Wilson-White Family Papers, WRHS.

The Batsdorff reminiscences describe "Grandma Garfield" engaged in making yarn for a rag carpet. Other Garfield household items are preserved at Lawnfield, the Garfield mansion in Mentor.

7. The minute description of bathing in Damon, pp. 26–30, comes from an old-

fashioned Connecticut home of the late 1800s but no doubt applies equally well to the Reserve in this era.

8. JAG to Mary G. Larabee and Eliza B. Garfield, 2 April 1854; JAG to Lucretia Rudolph, 2 March 1854, JAG Papers, LC; Perry Mapes autobiography, p. 2; Sloane, *Diary*, p. 10; Hutslar, p. 175 (several varieties of stairs are illustrated in Sloane, *Diary*, p. 11.); Henry, p. 26.

9. Description of cabin: Attempts to reconstruct what the original Garfield cabin in Orange looked like do not entirely fit together. Null's description, detailed and plausible, seems based on solid research, though it gives no sources. According to it, the cabin was of unhewn logs, twenty by thirty feet, with a slab roof, a cat-and-clay chimney, a loft, a floor of hewn logs, three windows, and a plank door (p. 2). Two usually trustworthy early sources, however, show peculiar differences in detail from this description. According to Conwell, p. 44, the cabin was nearly square, with windows in each end. According to the *Tribune* biography, the roof was of split shingles and the floor of puncheons. Only the log construction, the fireplace, the loft, and the single door are agreed upon by all. Accordingly, I have been vague in my description, though I have accepted Null's figures as to size.

On the purchase of the schoolhouse and the deterioration of the old cabin; see clipping from the *Tribune*, 4–5 July 1880, JAG Papers, LC.

10. A good genealogical chart of the family is in Leech and Brown, facing p. 1. Mehitable was born in 1821, Thomas in 1822, and Mary in 1824. A fourth child, James B., was born in 1827 but died young.

11. There is no real question about the size and location of the Garfield farm in Orange; an unfortunate mistake by Bundy, normally one of the most reliable of JAG's biographers, has, however, confused some later writers.

Bundy, p. 10, apparently misread his notes when he wrote that the Garfields bought eighty acres, later sold fifty, and kept thirty. They actually bought fifty, later sold twenty, and kept thirty. The true account is given in the interview with Thomas Garfield (clipping from the Cleveland *Leader*, 25 April, 1891, in scrapbook at Lawnfield) and in the introduction to the printed *Diary* 1: 10.

The "Notes and Description" of Orange lands in the Perkins Papers, WRHS, shows that Lot 10 of the Middle Division of Tract 3 had been deeded to "Byington [Boynton] & Garfield." Evidently the two brothers had purchased the 120-acre lot together and divided it between them. One would expect a roughly equal division, and the early tax records, on microfilm at WRHS, show that this was the case. In 1835, Eliza Garfield paid taxes on fifty acres, Amos Boynton on sixty-nine.

The Garfield farm occupied the southern part of the lot, and was rectangular in outline, its long side running east and west along the present Jackson Road, to the corner of the S.O.M. Center Road.

12. Conwell, pp. 41–45; Johnson, p. 495; Wickham, 2: 601.

13. Johnson, p. 492; Coates, 1: 197. Riddle, *Life*, p. 27, refers to Orange as "hilliest and remotest of townships." The phrase is partly a rhetorical flourish, no doubt, but Riddle grew up only fifteen miles away and was familiar with the area, so it probably is fairly accurate as well.

14. The most detailed account, based apparently on conversations with the Boyntons, is in Conwell, pp. 41–44. A "Memorandum" dated 1 March 1870, in Eliza B. Garfield Diary, JAG Papers, LC, narrates the family's migration to Orange in 1830 as well as its prevous residences. Cf. Boynton, p. 198.

15. L. R. Garfield, "Rough Sketch," p. 3; Bundy, p. 5; Conwell, p. 40; "Memorandum", 1 March 1870, Eliza B. Garfield Diary; Coppess, pp. 91–92; Johnson, p. 495.

16. All the accounts are similar: Bundy, p. 9; Conwell, p. 48; Brisbin, p. 22; Riddle, *Life*, p. 23. The similarity suggests how often the story had been retold. Patterson, "Recollections," supplies the last words. According to a letter from Ellen Larabee Hoppe (Mary's daughter) to [?], 21 January 192[?], in the Henry Boynton Papers, Abram Garfield was buried on the north end of the Boynton farm. His remains were later moved to Roselawn Cenetery in Solon.

17. A couple of parallel instances will illustrate both the commonness of the situation and some of the options available to a widow. Riddle (*Riddle*, pp. 39–42) narrates an instance where the widow remarried within two years; the older children thereupon moved out, though the younger stayed. In Orange, widowed Nancy Odell supported herself and a daughter by weaving, knitting, and spinning for neighbors (Wickham, 2:602). One final piece of data suggests the frequency of remarriage as a solution: in the 1840 manuscript census of Orange, the Garfield household is the only one headed by a woman. Conwell, p. 52, and Patterson, "Recollections," mention neighbors' help with the crop; Bundy, p. 10, the year's support.

18. As stated in the text, evidence for Eliza's remarriage is fragmentary and entirely circumstantial, but I think the possibility is strong enough to warrant mention.

One must begin a discussion of this point by stipulating two facts, both discovered by Allan Peskin some years ago: 1. that Eliza did in fact remarry in 1842, and that the marriage, to a man named Belding, was short-lived and unsuccessful; and 2. That JAG and his family were so sensitive and close-mouthed about this marriage, presumably because they felt it a disgrace, that no biographer before 1960 learned about it. Both facts are discussed further in their proper place, but they need to be kept in mind here.

In a document called "Genealogic Notes," dated 18 July 1858, JAG Papers, LC, Eliza's life is narrated in some detail down to Abram's death in 1833. At that point the narrative breaks off except for the following cryptic note: "1835 m. c. 7m. h. r. a. 7 or 8 y. a. m. b. h. l. in y." In view of the date 1835, this inscription seems to be a continuation of Eliza's story—in cryptic form, evidently, because there was something JAG did not want to record plainly. One thinks immediately of the marriage to Belding; and indeed, the marriage does seem to be referred to. "7 or 8 y." suggests seven or eight years after 1835; that is, 1842. Perhaps, then, "7 or 8 y. a. m. b." is to be read as "seven or eight years after married Belding." In that case, "h. l. in y." probably means "he left in year;" the marriage did in fact last about a year, though according to the record it was Eliza who left.

If this reading is correct, what is one to make of the first six letters: "1835 m. c. 7m. h. r. a."? "7m" seems to suggest another time span. I suggest the following reading: "1835 married C____ seven months he ran away."

Two other pieces of evidence offer some slight support for this conjecture. Mary B. Patterson, in her "Recollections", includes a reminiscence by Eliza's granddaughter Ellen Larabee Hoppe: "Mrs. Garfield married a second time. The man left her, taking with him horse and wagon and any other valuables he saw fit." This recollection does not fit the marriage to Belding in several ways. It implies that the man took goods not rightfully his and would have been open to prosecution. Belding, however, initiated divorce proceedings, was regarded in the courts as the aggrieved party, and two years after the separation was granted custody of three minor children in his family—facts which make it doubtful he acted as Mrs. Hoppe described. Second, this story seems to fit the words "ran away" much better than the breakup of the marriage to Belding. Belding did not run far at all; for at least two years after the separation he was living in Independence, a mere eight or nine miles away, as the tax records show.

The tax records reveal one other suggestive bit of information: in 1835 Eliza paid no tax on personal property, yet she did in 1834 and 1836. The inference is that in 1835 someone else paid her tax.

I conclude, therefore, that Eliza married again in 1835 and that the man ran out on her as described by Mrs. Hoppe. Further investigation may uncover more direct evidence and the name of the man concerned.

It is obvious, at any rate, why JAG and his family wanted to conceal the episode, and why he was so circumspect about it even in his private writings.

I am indebted to Patricia R. Woodward, of Berea, Ohio, for help with this question.

19. Leech and Brown, p. 15.

20. L. R. Garfield, "Rough Sketch," pp. 4–5; Wickham, I, 488. Conwell, p. 52; clipping from Cleveland *Leader*, 25 April 1891, in scrapbook at Lawnfield. JAG to Eliza R. Garfield, 2 October 1856; Mary G. Larabee, in Eliza B. Garfield to JAG, 24 February 1861, JAG Papers, LC. Wickham, 2:601.

21. Gilmore, p. 4, and Wickham, 2:601, mention the crops grown. Patterson, "Recollections," states that JAG remembered using cream rather than butter on his potatoes as a boy, a sign of poverty. On firewood see Conwell, p. 52; on clothing, Bundy, p. 10.

22. Thomas Garfield (clipping from the Cleveland *Leader*, 25 April 1891, in scrapbook at Lawnfield) recalled that the 20 acres were sold before Abram's death. The tax records on microfilm at WRHS, however, show the sale took place in 1836.

23. Wickham, 2:601; Gilmore, p. 4; Conwell, p. 52, Bundy, p. 10.

24. Thomas Garfield to JAG, 15 April 1854, JAG Papers, LC; L. R. Garfield, "Rough Sketch," p. 3; Leech and Brown, pp. 12–15; Bundy, pp. 10–13; Conwell, pp. 54, 63; clipping from Cleveland *Leader*, 15 July 1899, in scrapbook at Lawnfield.

Alonzo Harlow to JAG, 14 June 1880, JAG Papers, LC.

25. Hitty's marriage: Leech and Brown, p. 16, fn. 32, summarizes the marriage well. See also Eliza B. Garfield and Mary G. Larabee to JAG, 12 May 1856, JAG Papers, LC. For Trowbridge's family connections, see Trowbridge, p. 305. The Philomathean Society record book shows that he participated in debate fairly frequently in 1849–50; this fact, together with his activity as a teacher, suggests his verbal skill. JAG, as a young man, called him "a combination of goodness and meanness" (*Diary*, 1:62). The word "meanness," I suggest, denotes not malice, as Leech and Brown, p. 7, seem to think (this usage was rare before the twentieth century), but cheapness, stinginess, and privation. His goodness was evident in the way he befriended young James during his adolescence—for an isolated bit of reminiscence, see Orrin Judd to JAG, 19 March 1872, JAG Papers, LC. His laziness is attested by many sources; Eliza called him "so slack he can hardly draw his breath" (Mary G. Larabee to JAG, 16 August 1854); see also Thomas Garfield to JAG, 1 April 1855, JAG Papers, LC.

First child: Leech and Brown, genealogical chart, facing p. 1.

26. *History of Ottawa County*, p. 96. Note, too, the revealing phrasing of Eliza's letter of 14 February 1862, family history album, JAG Papers, LC, in which Thomas was praised as "thoughtful," "faithful to work," and "dutiful."

27. L. R. Garfield, "Rough Sketch," p. 5; clipping from Cleveland *Leader*, 25 April 1891, in scrapbook at Lawnfield; Leech and Brown, p. 16; Lucretia Rudolph to JAG, 8 June 1855, 5 January 1856, JAG Papers, LC. In the reminiscent letter to his mother, 19 November 1855, in *ibid.*, JAG remembered himself as "the stubborn wilful boy of eight". His dislike for work is mentioned in Eliza's letter of 14 February 1862, family history album, *ibid.*, and Conwell, p. 56.

28. Conwell, p. 59, and L. R. Garfield, "Rough Sketch," p. 4, reflect the role Amos Boynton took, that of surrogate father and disciplinarian. But to judge from

JAG's reminiscent comments in his letter to Thomas and Eliza Garfield, 16 August 1853, JAG Papers, LC, Uncle Amos was neither as strict nor as effective as Conwell suggests. The family's lack of control is evident in Boynton, p. 199, and L. R. Garfield, "Rough Sketch," p. 7.

29. This is documented in *Cuyahoga County Marriage Records*, 1:31. It took place 16 April 1842, in Bedford.

30. The death of Alfred Belding, JAG's onetime stepfather, 14 January 1881, in Byron, Michigan, was reported in several Grand Rapids newspapers. One (the *Grand Rapids Evening Leader*, 15 January 1881) gave his age as seventy and reported that he had died "in reduced circumstances." The U.S. Census taker of the preceding year, however, listed his age as eighty (Manuscript, U.S. Census, Kent County, Michigan, 1880). The census also reported that he had been born in Massachusetts, as had both his parents, and that he was living with a grandson, Nicholas Barnes. The Grand Rapids *Daily Eagle* of 18 January 1881, described him as a man of "good sense, good habits, and good intentions," though disposed to "fussiness and fretfulness." These are all the direct sources on Belding.

Some indirect evidence, however, fills in the picture considerably. A check of Massachusetts vital records for the early 1800s shows that Alfred Baldin, a son of Ezekiel and Phebe Parsons Belden (these spelling variations are from the original), was baptized in Granville, Massachusetts, in 1825, with five other children of the same parents (Granville, Mass., *Vital Records*, p. 12), among them Jabez D., Charlotte, and Sally. Ezekiel and Phebe, according to the same source, were married 17 September 1812, shortly after Alfred's birth if his age in the obituary is correct. The other children were presumably born between 1812 and 1825.

Further, an Ezekiel Belden and a J. D. Belden turn up in the U.S. Census manuscript for the town of Independence, just west of Bedford, in 1840. Ezekiel's household included three men between twenty and twenty-nine, two of whom could have been Alfred and his brother Asahel. This Ezekiel Belden is the same as the one from Granville, as shown by the fact that his daughter Charlotte married an English immigrant, Benjamin Wood, whose manuscript diary is in WRHS. In 1853, Wood referred to his wife's parents' living in Belvedere, Boone County, Illinois, and a check of the 1850 manuscript census there shows Ezekiel and Phebe Belden, ages sixty-five and sixty-one respectively. Charlotte married Wood 20 August 1840, in Cuyahoga County. She named her second son Alfred.

Evidence from the tax records is mostly negative but does not contradict the picture so far presented. In 1840 Ezekiel Belden paid taxes in Independence on four cattle. Alfred did not appear in the tax books. In 1845, after the breakup of his marriage, Alfred turns up in the records paying a property tax in Bedford, while Ezekiel remains in Independence. In 1847 they both disappear from the tax records. At no time did either of them pay tax on land, a fact which strongly suggests they were leasing their farms, like several of the Garfields' neighbors in Orange.

Such legal evidence as exists portrays Alfred Belding as a thoroughly solid citizen. His divorce decree (Court of Common Pleas, Journal S, p. 136, Cuyahoga County Archives) adjudged him "a man of good moral character" who had "always treated the said defendant as an affectionate husband;" though this is largely the language of legal fiction, there was probably more than a shred of reality behind it, for in 1846 the same court had entrusted him with the guardianship of three minor children in his family—Sarah Ann Belden, seventeen; Louisa Belden, fourteen, and William Belden, nine (Court of Common Pleas, Journal Q, p. 15, Cuyahoga County Archives). No evidence shows the degree of kinship between these children and Alfred Belding. The appointment shows, at least, that Belding had a fairly stable home and was not an obviously dissolute person; it suggests that he had some standing in his family and in the community. Joseph Skinner of Bedford, JAG's uncle by marriage, stood surety for Belding as guardian.

Other Beldings appear in sources from Bedford and Independence around this time; some were probably related to Ezekiel and Alfred, some not. "She that was Sarah Belding", whose death was reported by Eliza in 1855 in Bedford (to JAG, 22 February 1855, JAG Papers, LC), could well have been Alfred's sister. The records of the Bedford Disciple Church, with which the Garfields were very familiar, show a Myriam Belding who was immersed in May 1840, but no others of that name (Bedford Disciple Memorandum, WRHS).

In sum, it seems probable that Alfred Belding of Bedford was a son of Ezekiel Belden of Independence; that he was around thirty at the time of his marriage in 1842; that he had lived on his father's farm up to that time; and that he was well thought of in his family and community. If this identification is accepted, though, one puzzling question remains: Why did a man who was, at most, thirty-two, want to marry a forty-one-year-old widow with two teenage children? The records supply no answer, and I confess my inability to suggest a solution.

31. The county tax records supply a little data about the family's moves after Eliza married Belding. In 1843, Eliza continued to pay tax on her land in Orange, under the name "Eliza Garfield"; she did not, however, continue to pay property tax. Instead, Alfred Belding paid taxes on one horse and four cattle in Orange. Eliza, the preceding year, had paid tax on only three cattle; probably the horse was his. This distribution of taxes probably corresponds to the situation soon after the marriage, some time in 1842 when the 1843 tax rolls were made up. Alfred, Eliza, the children, and the livestock were still in Orange.

In 1844, however, neither Alfred nor Eliza appears on the tax list in either Orange or Bedford as paying personal property tax. Eliza continued to pay tax on the Orange farm, a fact which at first blush seems strange, since one would expect the couple to have sold the land if they were leaving Orange. And in fact, a document dated ten years later suggests that this is what they did. The Cuyahoga County Deeds, 67, p. 247, contain a deed, dated 8 October 1853, from Alfred Belding and his wife Eliza, "formerly wife of Abraham Garfield deceased," to Amos Boynton, conveying the thirty-acre farm for $900.00. This deed cannot be taken at face value, for by October 1853 Alfred and Eliza had been divorced for three years, she had received all her property back, and Belding was no longer living in Ohio. The inescapable inference is that the deed had been drawn up earlier, no doubt in 1842 or 1843, but that Amos Boynton had decided for some reason not to have it recorded, perhaps fearing that the marriage of Eliza and Belding would be short-lived, as in fact it was. When Eliza returned to Orange, therefore, she was living on her brother-in-law's land but paying tax on it as though it was hers. When she finally decided to move off it in 1853, Boynton took legal possession by changing the date on the deed and having it recorded. The whole transaction illuminates just how much the flighty Eliza owed to the steadiness and good judgment of her brother-in-law.

In any event, by 1843 Belding and Eliza had definitely left Orange, probably with Amos Boynton's first payment in hand. But they were not on the tax lists of Bedford or any of the neighboring townships. (I have checked all the townships in the eastern half of the county.)

There is reason to believe, though, that the newlyweds lived briefly in Bedford or Independence before moving on. Conwell, pp. 57–58, records a story he probably had from Eliza about James, as a boy, having to traverse a spooky, wooded, three or four-mile stretch of road between his home and that of his Uncle Thomas. Thomas

Garfield's home, however, was a good ten miles from the farm in Orange. On the other hand, if Belding and Eliza were living in northern Independence or Bedford, the distance would have been about right, since Thomas Garfield lived near the south line of Newburgh township.

The absence of Alfred and Eliza Belding from the tax lists of the townships where they had lived gives good reason to suspect that they were not living in Cuyahoga County in 1843–44. Other evidence reinforces this suspicion. Years later, in his diary, JAG recalled (*Diary*, 2: 335), "When I was ten years of age I had never travelled fifteen miles from home." The point of this reminiscence was his limited opportunity as a young man; if this lack of opportunity had persisted up to age twelve or fifteen, he probably would have said so. The inference is that shortly after he was ten he traveled more than fifteen miles from home.

This reasoning is reinforced a little by another entry in the diary. On 19 September 1876, having just visited the brick house where Governor Rutherford B. Hayes was born in Delaware, Ohio, JAG noted (*Diary* 3: 354), "It was a better house than I had ever seen when I was ten years old."

The two entries might seem to suggest that "ten" was a number JAG used casually to represent any age in his early boyhood. Nothing is less likely. JAG was always quite exact numerically in referring to his early life. For instance, on Silas Bigelow (*Diary*, 3: 184): "Twenty-six years ago he was a teacher in Chester and I recited to him." On his teeth (*Ibid.*, 2: 396): "I have lost but one tooth and that a double tooth. I lost it when I was 16 years of age." On carpentry (*Ibid.*, 3: 476): "27 years ago, when I learned to lay flooring."

I suggest, then, that when he was eleven, in the first year of Eliza's marriage to Belding, JAG traveled more than fifteen miles from home for the first time and saw finer houses than he had ever seen, as he accompanied his mother and stepfather en route to their new home.

On the popularity of Michigan with emigrants from Orange, see Thomas Garfield to JAG, 21 May 1854, 23 January 1855, and Eliza B. Garfield to JAG, 19 October 1854, JAG Papers, LC. Two other facts, documented below, seem to me to strengthen Michigan's claims. Mary Garfield Larabee spent the first years of her married life, probably 1845–47, in Michigan, and Thomas, in 1845, somehow obtained a wood-chopping job there.

32. The basic thing to remember about Belding's divorce is the time sequence. The final decree was dated 7 October 1850. The petition for divorce had been filed in 1848. (Neither of these moves is mentioned in the diary which JAG was keeping by then. The fact suggests that Belding obtained the divorce without the involvement of the Garfields.) In the petition, Belding averred that Eliza "had wilfully absented herself from living or cohabiting" with him for over three years, i.e., since 1845 or before, and also that he had been a resident of Cuyahoga County for more than three years. But he also stated that Eliza had left him within a year after their marriage, i.e., before April 1843, and had refused to return despite his appeals.

Why Belding waited until 1848 to file for divorce is not obvious. One possible reason is that he had returned to Cuyahoga County still trying to patch things up with Eliza (his petition mentioned repeated appeals to her to return) and then, having decided in 1845 to sue for divorce on grounds of desertion, had to wait three years to establish residency. In any case, it appears that Eliza and Belding lived together only a year. This time span agrees with my suggested reading (see above) of JAG's cryptic note in the family history.

Why did the marriage break up? There is almost no evidence. The tax records indicate only that before January 1845, both were back in Cuyahoga County, she in

Orange, he in Bedford separate from his father. No stigma seems to have attached to him, for, as mentioned above, in 1846 he was made guardian of three minor children in his family, possibly nieces and a nephew. "It is hard for me to think of the man without indignation," JAG wrote forty years later on learning of Belding's death (*Diary*, 4: 528). And in JAG's version of the affair, if my reading is correct, Belding was the one who left. All the evidence in the surviving legal documents, however, seems to point the other way, to Eliza's leaving. Perhaps this may reflect legal formalities required in filing suit for divorce. In view of the conflicting claims, the surprising lapse of time between the breakup of the marriage and the filing of the divorce petition, and the paucity of other evidence, it is probably unwise to try to speculate further.

33. Coppess, p. 93. Patterson, "Recollections," relates that Mary's first child, Ellen Larabee (later Ellen Larabee Hoppe) was born in the Michigan woods and nursed by an Indian squaw. She had this information from Mrs. Hoppe herself. See also the obituary in the Bedford (Ohio) *News Register*, 25 January 1935, which gives Mrs. Hoppe's birthplace as Germantown, Michigan.

Thomas's woodchopping job is mentioned in Conwell, p. 69; Gilmore, p. 6; and clipping from Cleveland *Leader*, 25 April 1891, in scrapbook at Lawnfield.

34. Cleveland *Plain Dealer*, 26 February, 7 May 1845; Clapp Account Book, WRHS. Fuller, p. 16; Dickinson, p. 84; Howe, p. 189; *Pioneer and General History*, p. 116.

35. Conwell, p. 57.

36. Drinking: There was a flourishing temperance society in Orange in 1844 (Cleveland *Plain Dealer*, 16 October 1844), though by the next year it was reported languishing (*Annals*, 28: 365). At least two taverns operated in the township; during 1845 the Court of Common Pleas granted licenses to Stephen Burnett and Elijah Smith (Court of Common Pleas, Journal P, pp. 69, 200, Cuyahoga County Archives). But the historian of the township, writing in 1879, could summarize its history as that of a very rural community with few taverns.

For glimpses of drinking and drinkers in two other rural townships not far from Orange, see Riddle, *Old Newbury*, pp. 36, 42, 50, and Ryder, pp. 66–68 (Kirtland).

Neighborhood characters are mentioned in L. R. Garfield, "Rough Sketch," p. 5; Riddle, *Life*, p. 396; Bard, p. 26; and Henry, pp. 9, 13. For a list of characters in a comparable township, see Riddle's amusing poems in *Old Newbury*, pp. 33–51.

37. The population of Orange and Solon, even in 1850 after European immigration had begun to have an impact, was much more heavily Yankee than that of neighboring townships. I have tabulated the birthplaces of boys JAG's age (16 through 21) and their fathers, as given in the 1850 census. In Orange, 17 percent of the boys had been born in the New England states; in Solon, 14 percent. In adjacent towns the proportion was much smaller—Warrensville, 8 percent; Independence, 5 percent; Chagrin Falls, 4 percent; Bedford, 3 percent. In all the towns but Independence and Warrensville, over one third of the fathers were New Englanders, but the percentage in Solon was the highest, 46. Other figures were Chagrin Falls, 42; Orange, 39; Bedford, 38; Warrensville, 30; Independence, 29. The difference between Solon and Orange and the neighboring townships, much shaper in the sons' generation than in the fathers', shows that Solon and Orange contained more families who had recently migrated from New England.

In Solon and Orange boys tended to stay in school longer. For the same six towns, I have tabulated the percentage of boys who were listed as being in school for each age from sixteen to twenty-one. In Bedford, Independence, Warrensville, and Chagrin Falls, over half the boys were out of school by the age of eighteen (in Chagrin Falls, indeed, over half had left by age seventeen). But in Solon, about 70 percent of the boys went to school through eighteen years of age, and in Orange more than half were still in school at age twenty. This fact is the basis for my characterizing JAG's neighborhood as "serious-minded."

38. JAG to Lucretia Rudolph, 2 March 1854; to Phebe Boynton, 24 April, 1855, JAG Papers, LC. These letters largely concern migration to the west, but there were other destinations, too. Sheldon Wilkinson, "an old schoolmate" (*Diary*, 2:364), was living in Chagrin Falls by 1850, according to the manuscript census. Another old schoolmate, Philo Stevenson (*Ibid.*, 2:95), had moved to Huron County. Another, Moses Lowe (*Ibid.*, 2:369) had moved out of the neighborhood by 1850 to an unknown destination, though he returned to Chagrin Falls in adult life.

By 1850, according to the manuscript U.S. Census, 21 percent of the boys ages sixteen to twenty-one in Orange were English born. This was the highest proportion of any of the towns studied, and was much higher than adjacent Solon, where the figure was 1 percent. The discrepancy suggests what most other sources (e.g., Erickson, p. 105) confirm—that most English settlement in Orange was in the north, farthest away from the Solon line. Only three English families appear in the Garfields' immediate neighborhood: those of Christopher Whitlock, John Whitlock, and James Parsons. The only other immigrant family in the area were the Rundts, mentioned in the next note.

39. Martin Rundt: The spelling of the family's name gave its American-born neighbors some trouble. The census taker in 1850, and JAG at one point in his diary, spelled it "Runett" (*Diary*, 1: 165); earlier in his diary, JAG had written "Roundt" (*Ibid.*, 1:6, 10, 11, 12). A gravestone in North Solon Cemetery elucidates the confusion (*Cuyahoga County Cemetery Inscriptions*, p. 438). Martin Rundt, who emigrated from the island of Heligoland in 1836, was in his early sixties in 1850—the census and the gravestone differ a few years on the exact age. His wife Christina was a few years younger. Tax records show that the Rundts had first settled near the west line of Orange, two or three miles from the Garfields, but by 1848 were living across from them (Cuyahoga County tax duplicates, microfilm, 1844, 1848, WRHS).

40. Chagrin Falls: Ryder, pp. 74–76; Coates, I, 224–25; Johnson, pp. 427–31; Howe, pp. 125–26.

41. The best way to document this statement is just to set forth, from the county tax records, the personal property on which the Garfields and their nearest neighbors paid tax in 1848 and 1850, and let the reader draw his own conclusions. The list follows:

	1848	1850
T. Garfield	$ 90	$ 48
A. Boynton	314	450
M. Rundt	104	146
R. Judd	362	369
J. Mapes	172	457
M. Frazier	6	24
D. Partridge	56	130
J. Haymaker	37	48
Z. Smith	141	220
C. Warren	177	64

Chapter 4. A Questionable Future

1. Schob, pp. 188–190; F. Lewis, p. 12; Brisbin, pp. 38–39; Welker, p. 13;

Coates, I, 196; Henry, pp. 19, 38, 46, 399; Conwell, pp. 55–56; Starr diary; *passim*; Bard, p. 25; MS autobiography, Hinsdale Papers, p. 12; Riddle, "55 Years," pp. 210–11; *Early Settlers*, 4:157; Weisenburger, p. 57; Howells, p. 86; Clapp Account Book.

2. L. R. Garfield, "Rough Sketch," p. 5. Cleveland *Leader*, 25 April 1891, clipping in scrapbook at Lawnfield. Conwell, p. 63. (On the sharpness of a scythe, cf. Riddle, "55 Years," p. 74.) JAG to Eliza B. Garfield, 19 November 1855, JAG Papers, LC.

3. Leech and Brown, p. 17; Gilmore, *Border*, p. 222; Peskin, p. 9.

4. This was Orrin Judd, who figures often in this story. His age and birthplace are from the manuscript U.S. Census of 1850. The Judd family is not in the 1840 census manuscript; it appears in county tax records, however, as early as 1844.

5. Clipping from *Tribune*, 4–5 July 1880, in JAG Papers, LC; Bundy, p. 15; *Diary*, 3:466.

6. *Diary*, 2:364 (9 September 1874); Conwell, p. 68; clipping from unidentified newspaper, 22–23 September 1881, in JAG Papers, 39, LC. L.R. Garfield, "Rough Sketch," p. 7.

7. JAG to Eliza B. Garfield, 19 November 1855, JAG Papers, LC; Conwell, p. 68; Bundy, p. 15. R. L. Jones, pp. 15–16; Brisbin, pp. 39–40; Tourgee, pp. 7, 9; Henry B. Boynton to JAG, 5 August 1854, JAG Papers, LC.

8. Schob, pp. 67–69, 91, 94–96, 197. The quotation is from pp. 94–95.

9. Corydon Fuller, JAG's college friend and roommate, insisted (Fuller, p. 92) that he had never heard JAG called anything but "James." JAG addressed himself as "James" at some points in his diary (e.g., 1:99, 18 October 1851), never as "Jim." This evidence, however, all pertains to JAG's academy and college days. Given the proclivity of Reserve people for using nicknames, evident in Riddle's novels and in manuscript sources, it would be surprising if JAG had not been called "Jim" in his early years of manual labor, when he had no reason to insist on anything more formal. There is evidence for the use of the nickname in Bundy, p. 21, and the 1877 Notes, p. 11.

10. *Diary*, 1:12 (10 August 1848), 20 (2 August 1849). JAG's dislike for work is obvious from Conwell, p. 56, and L. R. Garfield, "Rough Sketch."

11. Gilmore, *Life*, pp. 5–6; letter of Eliza Garfield, 14 February 1862, in family history scrapbook, JAG Papers, LC. For the way in which JAG absorbed this perception, see the diary entry of 31 October 1852 (Diary, 1:159); and Williams, p. 168.

12. My calculations, from the 1850 manuscript U.S. Census. The exact percentage is 77 if all men over 21 are considered. If only those men with identifiable occupations are considered, the percentage is 87.

13. Riddle, *Bart Ridgeley*, p. 11.

14. Johnson, pp. 427–431; Howe, pp. 125–26.

15. Examples of young men routinely walking seventeen miles and more are in Henry, pp. 39, 66, and Fuller, p. 25.

16. Wickham, 2:602.

17. For the almost impassable condition of roads near Cleveland in the winter see *Plain Dealer*, 13 December 1848, and Ryder, p. 86.

18. Patterson, "Recollections," p. 7, states that JAG occasionally went to Cleveland with his uncle Amos Boynton to sell chestnuts. Cf. L. R. Garfield, "Rough Sketch," p. 4. Landmarks on the way are from Henry, p. 66; *Early Settlers*, 5:493; Coates, 1:281; and *Early Settlers*, 1:4, 31.

19. Weisenburger, pp. 11–12; Orth, 1:24, 59; *Plain Dealer*, 5 March, 20 August 1845, 10 October 1849; Busch, p. 22; Chapman, pp. 50–56, 66–69, 83–93; Ryder,

pp. 114, 142, 146; Rose, pp. 176, 187; Reprint from Springfield *Republican*, in [Ravenna] *Ohio Star*, 30 June 1847; Davis, *Hinsdale*, p. 17; *Annals*, 30:64, 197–210; Handerson, p. 7.

20. *Annals*, 30:64; Baird, p. 220; Hodge, 1:11; Pulszky, p. 92; Howe (1896 ed.), p. 523. Market: Ryder, p. 148. Public Square: Rose, p. 178; Chapman, pp. 47, 55; *Annals*, 35:397; *Plain Dealer*, 10 October 1849.

21. *Plain Dealer*, 10 October 1849; waterfront: *Early Settlers*, 4:256; Rose, p. 116; Orth, 1:24; *Ohio Railroad Guide*, p. 86.

22. Thomas Garfield to JAG, 15 April 1854, shows that the Boynton house was white. Orrin H. Judd to JAG, 19 November 1854, mentions a "chamber" or upper bedroom. Both letters are in JAG Papers, LC. Amos Boynton is described in Burke Hinsdale's sketch in Johnson, p. 496, and in L. R. Garfield, "Rough Sketch," p. 4. William Boynton's diary, 11 September 1855, mentions his helping the hired man pick up stones (Henry B. Boynton Papers, WRHS). On his interest in the minutiae of farming, see Amos Boynton to William Boynton, 14 June 1852; to William, Phebe, and Harriet Boynton, November, 1854, JAG Papers, LC. A set of daguerreotypes of the Boynton family, taken about 1850, is in the WRHS picture collection.

"Go on then my son": to William Boynton, 14 June 1852; cf. Eliza B. Garfield to JAG, 15 June 1855. Both letters are in JAG Papers, LC. JAG's feeling toward him is evident in JAG to Thomas and Eliza Garfield, 16 April 1853, *ibid.*

23. Boynton's holdings in cattle, and those of John Mapes, are from Cuyahoga County tax records, microfilm, WRHS. On dairying in the Reserve in general, see *Ohio Railroad Guide*, p. 80; Schreiber, "Canal," p. 119; Lewis, p. 12; *Plain Dealer*, 13 June 1849; Lloyd, Falconer, and Thorne, p. 97; *Ohio Cultivator*, 4:109 (15 July 1848); and Weisenburger, p. 71. Perry Mapes autobiography, WRHS, has more about Mapes.

The 1850 census shows Nelson Cooper, a laborer, living on the Boynton place with his wife and infant daughter. Elsewhere in letters from the Boyntons there are apparent references to hired workmen; see Amos Boynton to William Boynton, 14 June 1852, JAG Papers, LC, and entry of 11 September 1855, in William Boynton Diary, Henry B. Bonyton Papers, WRHS. On making and marketing cheese, see R. L. Jones, "Dairy," pp. 57–58, and entries of April, 4 September 1855, William Boynton Diary.

24. L. R. Garfield, "Rough Sketch," p. 9, the Boynton family daguerreotypes, WRHS; Phebe Boynton to JAG, 31 [*sic*] April 1854, JAG Papers, LC.

25. U.S. Census manuscript, 1850; *Diary*, 1:64 (11 November 1850) and *passim*; Phebe Boynton to JAG, 31 [*sic*] April 1854, JAG Papers, LC; Perry Mapes autobiography.

26. Schob, pp. 173–75; A. Wilcox, p. 11.

27. JAG's feeling of independence: The following passage from the 1877 Notes, describing JAG at sixteen, is pertinent: "I had been working for myself for a long time and felt that I had a right to go where I pleased provided I did well and made money."

28. Helping Hubbell: Bundy, p. 17; clipping from unidentified newspaper, 22–23 September 1881, in scrapbook; JAG to Eliza B. Garfield, 19 November 1855, JAG Papers, LC.

29. Manuscript, U.S. Census, 1850.

30. Two excellent sources on the details of carpentry, used in this and similar paragraphs, are Frary (see especially pp. 122, 229–32) and Hutslar, especially pp. 174, 237–39. See also Chapman, p. 70, Wheeler, "Building," pp. 35–36, and *Early Settlers*, 5:48.

31. Conwell, p. 70, calls JAG "an indifferent workman." For a later estimate of

his skill that squares well with this one, see chapter 17. Cf. also Riddle, *Life*, p. 38. Operations of carpentry are detailed in Hutslar, pp. 236–37; and Van Wagenen, p. 112. On master carpenter's work, see Wheeler, "Building," p. 36; and any of the several carpenters' manuals for this period, e.g. Asher Benjamin, *The American Builder's Companion*. JAG's attitude is apparent from Fuller, p. 55, and *Diary*, 3:478.

32. Kett, p. 34.

33. Shaw, pp. 86–87.

34. In a letter to Corydon Fuller, 6 January 1858 (Fuller Papers), JAG confessed that his "early prejudices were very strong" against law. He did not say why, but the reasons given in the text seem strong to me. Later his view of the law was that it was too worldly (*Diary*, 1:256—29 June 1854).

35. *Ibid.*, 2:329 (30 May 1874). For one instance of his distorted conceptions see *ibid.*, 1:422.

36. Attending school: Conwell, p 68; Bundy, p. 6. By January 1848, however, when his diary begins, he was attending regularly again.

Attending church: Bundy, pp. 21–22. L. R. Garfield, "Rough Sketch," p. 7, may be a distorted version of this period, or may refer to an earlier episode, but it does at least confirm that JAG was not always willing to attend meeting. The *Diary* entries for early 1848 mention attending meeting only irregularly.

Chapter 5. The Social Season

1. Schob, pp. 101–03; Riddle, *Portrait*, p. 135.

Husking bees were standard in the frontier Midwest and surely occurred in Orange, though I have no direct evidence. The Shakers in adjacent Warrensville had them; see Piercy, p. 205. For barn raisings, see *Diary*, 1:19, 20 (5, 13 July 1849) (Orange); Starr diary, 18 April 1845 (Hudson); Dickinson, p. 69 (Randolph).

2. There is a thorough description of an apple paring in Brisbin, p. 32. Starr diary, 9 November 1847, mentions one in Hudson. Post, pp. 111–12; *Early Settlers*, 6:1, pp. 39–40; Henry, p. 45; *Chagrin Falls Exponent*, 18 August 1933, mention the wild pigeons. As to chestnuts, see Patterson, "Recollections," p. 7, and Post, p. 53.

3. Probably most farmers in Orange still threshed the old way, using the wind. For the slow and irregular advent of machinery in the 1840s, see R. L. Jones, "Machinery," p. 12 and Weisenburger, pp. 63–64. For the process, see Schob, pp. 104–7.

4. Cleveland *Plain Dealer*, 13 December 1848.

5. Henry, p. 37. *Diary*, I, 5.

6. W. A. Knowlton, p. 16; Kenyon, *passim*; Hart, "Westernization," p. 264; Mary G. Larabee to JAG, 16 August 1854; JAG to Phebe Boynton, 24 April 1855; Amos Boynton to William, Phebe, and Harriet Boynton, [November 1854], all in JAG Papers, LC.

7. Joe Cleveland is referred to ironically in Alpha Boynton to JAG, 21 March 1872, JAG Papers, LC. He served a term as secretary of the neighborhood lyceum, and the Philomathean Society Record Book, WRHS, for the winter of 1850–1851 testifies to his shaky grammar and spelling and the ribbing he took from other members about them. See especially the entry of 18 January 1851. On Grant, see Patterson, "Recollections," p. 4. The 1850 manuscript census shows no Grant family living nearby, but Alpha Boynton also referred to a local person of that name in her letter to William Boynton, 23 February [1857], JAG Papers, LC.

8. Idlers at store: These are a regular feature of Albert G. Riddle's stories about

life in the Reserve, *Bart Ridgeley, The Portrait, Ansel's Cave*, and the shorter stories; and the general store itself was an established part of American rural life. But I have found nothing in the Garfield diary or letters, or any other memoir from the neighborhood, to suggest that there was a country store at which most of the residents traded. Such evidence as there is indicates that they went into Chagrin Falls rather than to any rural store.

9. Coates, 1:107–108, gives an example of religious debate from Royalton, Cuyahoga County. See also Schob, p. 242; Henry, p. 45; and Fuller, pp. 12–13. "Every man": *Early Settlers*, 1:1, 51.

10. Debate at Chagrin Falls: Hayden, p. 439.

11. Henry, p. 47.

12. The story is in Brisbin, pp. 59–60. Coates, 1:214, 219, mentions Patrick as an early settler of Hampshire Road. The 1848 tax records show him as a man of substantial property ($261 personal property as compared with, say, Amos Boynton's $314), and the Cleveland *Plain Dealer*, 16 October 1844, mentions him as a pillar of the local temperance society.

13. For examples, see *Diary*, 1:33; *Annals*, 30:103; and Dickinson, p. 85.

14. To give one example, when JAG heard a local Disciple preach 16 January 1850, his only comment was "Fluent" (*Diary*, 1:33).

15. The Western Reserve had its share of standard American political activity, rallies, caucuses, conventions and the like; a glance at the Cleveland *Plain Dealer* or any other party journal is enough to prove the point. Moreover, elections were often close. Though the Reserve as a whole was Whig during the 1840s, quite a few townships—Orange, for instance—usually went narrowly Democratic. But the sources do not reveal the pattern of heavy political activity one might expect in the Orange-Solon–Chagrin Falls areas. On the contrary, JAG's diary mentions political speeches only a few times, and political gatherings not at all. Few rallies are mentioned in the *Plain Dealer*, and none in other sources. This is not to say that political activity was nonexistent in the Chagrin valley and environs in the 1840s; but clearly, it was not very salient.

16. Weisenburger, p. 122; Howells, p. 90. Four townships in the area where the Garfields lived are known to have had lyceums: Orange, Solon, and Warrensville, all mentioned in the *Diary*, and Mayfield, the minutes of whose lyceum are in the Alfred Mewett Papers, WRHS. My description is drawn mainly from the minutes of the Orange and Mayfield lyceums.

The minutes of the Mayfield lyceum show that it met in a schoolhouse. So did the various lyceums that succeeded one another in the Boynton neighborhood—see Riddle, *Life*, p. 25; Conwell, p. 64; Philomathean Society minutes, WRHS; and "Synopsis" for 1855 in the William Boynton Diary, Henry B. Boynton Papers, WRHS.

The Philomathean Society minutes record an expenditure for candles. For fixing them to windows, see *Early Settlers*, 4:373.

Kenyon, p. 402, is the source for "toad-stabbers."

17. The admiring notice of the township of Mesopotamia, in the Reserve, a rural community which counted 341 subscribers to newspapers and periodicals, in *Annals*, 34:58, suggests the region's pride in its literacy.

18. Philomathean Society minutes, 16 March 1850, WRHS: Henry, p. 53; Mayfield Lyceum minutes, Alfred Mewett Papers, WRHS.

19. Not all lyceums had judges. In the Mayfield Lyceum, the president declared the winner of each debate, and in the Philomathean Society of Orange, the vice-president performed the same function, as the constitutions of the respective societies make clear. But the Warrensville Lyceum had a judge, apparently only one (Diary,

1:114), and the Philomathean in the fall of 1851 revised its rules to provide for a panel of three judges at each meeting. From the Philomathean minutes of 1851–52, it becomes evident that half a dozen men were regularly called on to serve as judges, with others occasionally, and that most of these were men who rarely debated. Thomas Garfield, for example, is not recorded as debating, ever, but was named to judge twelve times in that year.

20. In 1849, JAG's school met on Christmas Day, and there is no mention of any special activities (*Diary*, 1:30). In 1850, however, school did not meet on that day, and JAG mentioned the possibility that some celebrating might have taken place, though in a tone that suggested he deplored it ("How many youths have today disgraced themselves"; *Ibid.*, 1:67). For other evidence that Christmas was celebrated rarely, if at all, in the rural Reserve, see Dickinson, p. 69, and George Starr's diary for 25 December 1845 and 1847. In the metropolis of the Reserve, Cleveland, things were different, and the holiday was coming to be the family-oriented, gift-giving, mercantile extravaganza familiar to twentieth-century Americans; see *Annals*, 28:128, and 30:257; Ryder, p. 116. On "Merry Christmas," see *Diary*, 1:110 (25 December 1851); Cowles, p. 37; A. Brocket to O. J. Hodge, 24 December 1849, Hodge Papers, WRHS.

21. JAG to Phebe Boynton, 24 April 1855; Eliza B. Garfield to JAG, 13 August 1854, JAG Papers, LC. Williams, *Wild Life*, p. 93.

22. Dickinson, p. 125; Henry, p. 41. As for masturbation, the roaming around described in these sources, particularly details like running naked on the sand of the riverbank (Henry), and the anxiety of fathers to see that their boys did not waste their time in this way, are strikingly similar to the practices of a rural Missouri community a century later, described in James West, *Plainville, U.S.A.* (New York: Columbia University Press, 1945), pp. 193–94. The parallel is so close that I have felt safe in using the later experience to illuminate the earlier one. Masturbation, as will be shown, later became a source of worry to young Garfield (see notes to chapter 11). MS autobiography, Hinsdale Papers, p. 30, gives a good example of a strict father.

23. On Orrin Judd's physical appearance, see Judd to JAG, 24 August 1854; Judd to JAG, 19 March 1872, JAG Papers, LC. Perry Mapes described, in his manuscript autobiography, WRHS, how a schoolroom incident once set Judd and JAG laughing uncontrollably together. On hunting, see *Diary*, 1:3, 9, 32, 241; Boynton, p. 198; Riddle, *Ansel's Cave*, p. 82; and newspaper clipping of September 22–23, 1881, in scrapbook, 39, JAG Papers, LC. JAG's black dog is mentioned in Conwell, p. 62.

24. Henry, p. 39; Dickinson, pp. 67, 80; Blakeslee, p. 20; Perry Mapes manuscript autobiography, WRHS.

25. Davis, *Hinsdale*, p. 12; Post, p. 53. Howells, pp. 89–90, vividly depicts a fifteen-mile sleigh ride, in unexpectedly cold weather, that turned into a freezing ordeal for two young men in their late teens and early twenties. Dances are mentioned in Riddle, *Bart Ridgeley*, pp. 116–17; Alonzo Brocket to O. J. Hodge, 24 December 1849, and A. B. Gunnison to O. J. Hodge, 17 February 1850, both in Hodge Papers. But as to JAG and dancing, *Diary*, 1:109 (16 December 1851), 115 (28 January 1852), shows his attitude.

26. *Diary*, 1:35, 63, 145; Henry B. Boynton to JAG, 13 December 1853, JAG Papers, LC. Compare the names of the districts thirty years later, as given in Chagrin Falls *Exponent*, 1 December 1881.

27. Rudolph, pp. 1–2; Butler, p. 63; Bard, p. 28; Bundy, p. 11; Conwell, p. 45.

28. The stove with wobbly legs is an authentic memory; see Perry Mapes autobiography, p. 4. The raised platform and other furnishings are typical features mentioned in sources like school directors' records, from Mayfield Districts 2 and 8, both

in WRHS; *Early Settlers*, 2:7, 338–39, and Dickinson, p. 148. For an example of a platform see the restored schoolhouse at the Hale Farm, Bath, Ohio, operated by the Western Reserve Historical Society.

29. JAG to Eliza Garfield, 19 November 1855, JAG Papers, LC; Johnston, p. 191; Weisenburger, p. 167; Snyder, p. 2237; [Ravenna] *Ohio Star*, 12 January 1848.

30. The records of the Boynton district have not been preserved. Nothing, however, suggests that its practices and curriculum were at all different from those in neighboring districts, several of whose records have survived—Districts 2 and 8 in Mayfield, 8 and 10 in Bainbridge, and 1 in Newburgh, all in the manuscript collection at WRHS. I have used the records of these neighboring districts, augmented by recollections and contemporary sources from elsewhere in the Reserve, to reconstruct a picture of school as it probably was in the Boynton district.

The subjects offered in any district school—the "common branches," as they were called—were six: reading, writing, spelling, grammar, arithmetic, and geography. Time and again these were the only subjects in the Newburgh District 1 curriculum. Bainbridge District 10, in 1853–54, offered only these subjects. The Mayfield school board prescribed textbooks for school use in these subjects only. Somewhat farther afield, but still in the Reserve, so did the Erie County Board of Examiners (Sandusky *Clarion*, 30 November 1844).

Other subjects were mentioned infrequently. Burke Hinsdale, writing of his school in Hinckley, Medina County, mentioned chemistry and philosophy as occasional rarities (MS autobiography, Hinsdale Papers, p. 20). David W. Gage, who attended district school in Cuyahoga County until age seventeen, recalled only two terms in which chemistry and philosophy were taught (*Early Setters*, 2:7, 338). In Bainbridge District 8 in 1853–54 philosophy was offered, as was algebra. History was mentioned occasionally (D. C. Knowlton; Hinsdale, *Garfield*, p. 382). So was Latin (Starr diary, 4 September 1847; Lucretia Rudolph roll book, Lucretia R. Garfield Papers, LC).

As to textbooks, three authors had works that were almost universally used in the Reserve: Webster's speller, Ray's arithmetic and algebra texts, and McGuffey's readers. All three are mentioned in Sandusky *Clarion*, 30 November 1844; Mayfield Township School Records, 22 April 1853; Bainbridge District 8 records, 11 March 1854; and MS autobiography, Hinsdale Papers, p. 19, where lists of textbooks in use are given. On grammar texts there was much less agreement. Weisenburger, p. 169, mentions Kirkham's grammar. Others were by Pinner (MS autobiography, Hinsdale Papers, p. 19), Brown (Bainbridge District 8 records), and Bullion (Sandusky *Clarion*, *loc. cit.*). In geography, Morse's text was the most popular, but there were others, e.g. Peter Parley (Starr diary, 10 December 1845).

For mention of high schools in the Reserve, see E. A. Miller, pp. 461–62; Lottich, p. 75; and A. Phelps to A. G. Riddle, 7 March 1849, Riddle Papers. These schools, with trained teachers, scientific apparatus, and regular offerings in history, foreign languages, and music, were far superior to the district schools of the rural Reserve, and underlined the growing difference between town and country. JAG's awareness of them may have added to the frequent bitterness with which, in later life, he spoke of his limited educational opportunities. See, for instance, *Diary*, 2:329 (30 May 1874), and JAG to Harry Rhodes, 19 November 1862, in *Wild Life*, p. 181.

31. For the general contrast between summer and winter schools, see Dickinson, p. 148, *Early Settlers*, 1:4, 63, and MS autobiography, Hinsdale Papers, pp. 18–19.

These sources all state that summer school was normally taught by women; in fact, in all the school district records I have seen I have found no instance of a man teaching summer school. In the Reserve, moreover, where young women were more apt to be teachers than in the rest of Ohio—where, in fact, there were more female than male teachers (Ohio, Secretary of State, *Annual Report. . . on the Condition of Common Schools. . . for the Year 1851*), women also taught winter school, though usually at a lower salary than men (Fuller, p. 40; Dickinson, p. 113; Hinsdale, *Garfield*, p. 382). Harriet Boynton, JAG's cousin, taught the winter term of 1851–52 and dealt with all the problems faced by male teachers, including fights (Fuller, p. 46). Of five winter terms recorded in the Newburgh District 1 records, men taught three and women two; in Mayfield District 2, the proportion was one and three. Despite this general tendency, however, there is no record of any but male teachers in the Boynton winter schools.

That boys over the age of ten or twelve attended only in winter is stated in the Perry Mapes autobiography, p. 3, and Henry, pp. 68–69.

Kett, pp. 20–21 discusses the age range. The figures are from D. C. Knowlton, pp. 73–75. For class size, see Knowlton and Lucretia Rudolph roll book, Lucretia R. Garfield Papers. Hinsdale, *Autobiography*, p. 39, recalls that he had 50 students on his roll in one Summit County district.

32. JAG later put it this way in a letter to his cousin Phebe Boynton (22 January 1853, JAG Papers, LC): ". . . the winter term is generally more unpleasant than the others, on account of having so many poor scholars." See also Starr diary, 23 November 1848; J. Wonsetler to O. J. Hodge, 22 March 1851, Hodge Papers, WRHS; Kett, p. 47; Riddle, *Bart Ridgeley*, pp. 109ff. Dickinson, pp. 148–49; *Early Settlers*, 1:4, 63; and D. C. Knowlton. For examples of both fights and romantic involvements in JAG's own teaching career, see *infra*, chapters 12, 19.

33. The following opening dates, all from district records at WRHS, indicate the lack of system in scheduling school terms: Newburgh, District 1:7 January 1850; 2 December 1850; 8 December 1851; 9 January 1854. Mayfield, District 2: 8 November 1848; 11 November 1850; 25 November 1851. Mayfield, District 8: 12 January 1852. Bainbridge, District 10: 15 November 1853. Bainbridge, District 8: 7 December 1853.

34. *Pioneer and General History*, p. 149; *Diary*, 2:369 (25 September 1874); JAG to Phebe Boynton, 22 January 1853, JAG Papers, LC; Perry Mapes autobiography, WRHS; *Diary*, 1:28, 30, 34 (18 November, 31 December 1849; 26 January 1850); Eliza B. Garfield to JAG, 16 December 1853, 18 April 1854, JAG Papers, LC; Lucretia R. Garfield, "Rough Sketch," p. 4.

35. Starr diary, 19 November 1845; 3 May 1848; *Early Settlers*, 6:3, 37; Bundy, p. 14, Boynton, p. 198.

36. *Annals*, 34:262. Cf. an article on Cuyahoga County schools in Cleveland *Plain Dealer*, 28 March 1849.

37. Hinsdale, *Autobiography*, p. 26. As for the ringleader, Riddle, *Life*, p. 25, says merely "Boynton," but it was most likely William, who was older and a bit more aggressive than Henry.

38. The Morrison affair: The account in JAG's diary, right at the beginning (1:3), is extremely sketchy and opens in the middle of the controversy, with the directors' visit to the school on 3 January. Two later notes (*Ibid.*, 1:62) amplify the picture a little: Morrison is described as "a quick-tempered fellow, unfit to teach a school," and the directors are characterized as "actuated by party feeling and interest." A story, in Riddle, *Life* (p. 25), however, seems to cover the same incident in more detail, except that the teacher's name is not given. The broad outline is certainly the same: student protests against a teacher, a public meeting, and an unpopular decision to retain the teacher. The story seems certain to refer to Morrison; the teachers at the school in the three winters previous, Niece, Rutherford, and the New Englander, were all popular, at least with JAG and his friends. I have therefore consolidated the two accounts, and

all details in the story come from one of the three sources mentioned.

39. In the winter of 1851–52, seventeen of the thirty-nine scholars on the roll in Newburgh District 1 were from outside the district. (District records, WRHS).

40. *Diary*, 1:3–4.

41. *Ibid.*, 1:1; volume 3 of William Boynton's journal is in the Henry B. Boynton Papers, WRHS; it covers roughly the years 1853–56. Extrapolating backward to cover the two missing earlier volumes, it seems likely that William began a journal around this time.

42. *Diary*, 1:4 (17 January 1848), 5 (5, 10 February 1848). "logging it": Kenyon, p. 395. Cf. Starr diary, 1 May 1845: "Thursday I teamed it around hauling cornice stuff. . . ."

43. Boynton, p. 198.

44. Howells, p. 90; Henry, p. 63; and Cherry, pp. 111–13, have good general descriptions. JAG's gentleness is noted in Henry, p. 76.

45. Henry, p. 64; Hinsdale, *Autobiography*, p. 36. Little's singing school: *Diary*, 1:3–6. Usual fee: Porter, p. 12; Chase, pp. 183, 184.

46. Singing schools in general: Chase, pp. 184–85; *Early Settlers*, 2:7, 19; *Pioneer and General History*, p. 236; Abbie [?] to Lucretia Rudolph, 24 January 1848, Lucretia R. Garfield Papers, LC; A. Phelps to A. G. Riddle, 27 December 1848, Riddle Papers, WRHS.

47. Chase, p. 185; Hastings and Warriner, pp. v–viii. Hymns: Porter, p. 23; Welker, p. 51. Many country choirs seem to have contained three or four excellent singers. Most communities had at least one. See Riddle, *Ansel's Cave*, p. 4; Post, pp. 52–53.

48. Green, *Hiram*, p. 396; JAG to Phebe Boynton, 4 April 1855, JAG Papers, LC.

49. *Diary*, 1:5 (8–13 February, 15, 17, 1848). The diary does not mention his attending on any Sunday in January or February; in later months there are specific mentions of attendance (e.g., *Diary*, 1:10).

50. Henry, p. 46; Horton, p. 137; Starr diary, 18, 23 March 1848; Riddle, *Bart Ridgeley*, pp. 133–34; Welker, pp. 33–34.

Chapter 6. Independence

1. Garfields in Independence: Johnson, pp. 460–61, 495; "Memorandum," 1 March 1870, in Eliza B. Garfield Diary, JAG Papers, LC. Thomas Garfield: Coates, I, 282; obituary in Chagrin Falls *Exponent*, 30 June 1881. The Cuyahoga County tax records (microfilm, WRHS) show that he was a successful man; the assessed value of his property in 1848 was $539, more than that of his half-brother Amos Boynton.

Mary Larabee: Wickham, 1:490, mentions her kindness, Henry, p. 297, JAG's closeness to her. (Both sources also mention the "second sight," the mysterious premonitions, that figure in some later accounts of JAG's career. It is not clear, however, how important this trait was at this time in JAG's life.) Eliza B. Garfield, letter of 14 February 1862, family history album, JAG Papers, LC, recalls her dislike for work, which, coupled with the family traditions about second sight, suggests that she had a dreaminess rather like her brother's. Coates, 1:199, records that she was living in Independence at this time, a fact missed by most biographers but easily verified—see following note.

2. Mary's visit and return: *Diary*, 1:6 (19 February 1848) is explicit: "went to Independence to take Mary home." (The diary gives no indication of when she arrived in Orange.) Equally clear are the entries of 23–25 March (*Diary* 1:7). On

23 March JAG "commenced boarding to Larabee's" while still chopping wood in Independence; on 25 March he "went home to Orange."

3. The best sources for this job are, of course, the diary account (1:6, 7) and the 1877 autobiographical sketch in the JAG Papers, LC. Both mention 100 cords of wood; the autobiographical sketch says that it was in Newburgh. Neither states who he was doing it for, but this detail is supplied by his letter to Eliza B. Garfield, 19 November 1855, JAG Papers, LC. The accounts of Brisbin (pp. 46–47) and Coffin (pp. 46–47) state that he was paid twenty-five dollars; no other source gives the wage except Gilmore, who, inaccurate as usual, has it that he chopped twenty-five cords of wood for seven dollars (p. 6). The weather 7 March is from *Diary*, 1:6, and Cleveland *Plain Dealer*, 8 March 1848.

4. Other jobs: *Diary*, 1:7–9. These included chopping wood for Edward Barns and Morehouse Barns, planting for A. H. Brainard, and washing sheep for Ben Fisher. All these men are identifiable in the 1850 U.S. manuscript census for Independence. Boarding: *Ibid.*, 1:6–7; Coates, 1:199. JAG later (*Diary*, 1:62) called Larabee "a very good man, but rather deceitful"; Bard, p. 37, gives a glimpse of him in the 1860s making money by boarding paupers for the town of Solon. Mary's cooking is mentioned in Williams, *Wild Life*, p. 94.

5. Hunting and raisings: Raisings, *Diary*, 1:7 (7, 15 April 1848), 8 (4 May 1848). The hunting is inferred from the fact that he had brought his rifle there from Orange (*Ibid.*, 1:9). On raisings in general, see Frary, p. 231; Coates, 1:97; Starr diary, 19 April 1845; and *Early Settlers*, 2:7, 20.

6. Chopping wood for sale: Schob, pp. 15–19, 150–56. The going rate in the 1840s quoted by Schob, however, fifty to seventy-five cents per cord, is considerably higher than JAG's wage. An advertisement in the Cleveland Weekly *Herald*, 9 June 1847 (*Annals*, 30:100) shows the demand for wood for lake steamboats at this time. See *Diary*, 1:6, 7 (16, 17, 21 March 1848), 9 (26 May 1848).

7. *Ohio Railroad Guide*, p. 89; Lucretia Rudolph, "A Visit to Mount L ______," Lucretia R. Garfield Papers, LC; Holloway, 1:78. Orth, 1:712. 1877 autobiography, JAG Papers, LC.

8. On this long and important canal, whose full name was the Ohio and Erie, there is a sizable body of source material. My treatment of it in this and subsequent chapters depends heavily on a few good secondary sources. Frank Wilcox, *The Ohio Canals*, is an evocative, detailed book. James and Margot Jackson, *The Colorful Era of the Ohio Canal*, though much shorter, is clear, well illustrated, and informative—a model pamphlet. The periodical *Towpaths* contains many useful articles. Other sources which also contributed to the picture presented here are Burton P. Porter, "*Old Canal Days*," a rather overdone treatment which deals mainly with a later period than the 1840s, but nevertheless has some worthwhile information, and Alvin Harlow, *Old Towpaths*, a general treatment of the American canal era. The dimensions of the canal are from F. Wilcox, p. 13; Harlow, p. 251; and B. Porter, p. 244. Its lining is described in Downes, 1:26. April the first seems to have been the standard opening date. The canal opened on that date in 1849 (Cleveland *Plain Dealer*, 21 March 1849), and about 30 March in 1845 (*Annals*, 28:40).

9. *Diary*, 1:8 (16 April, 4 May, 1848); F. Wilcox, pp. 19, 32.

10. The 1850 manuscript U.S. Census shows 26 people in Independence who gave "boatman" as their occupation. A quick summary of their characteristics may be of interest. All were male. The youngest was seventeen, the oldest fifty-three. Their average age was 27.5. Fourteen were married, twelve single. Nine had been born in Ohio, eight in New York, five in Europe.

On Ben Fisher, see Cleveland *Plain Dealer*, 29 November, 1848; manuscript of

U.S. Census, 1850.

11. F. Wilcox, pp. 16, 21; Jackson and Jackson, pp. 15–16; Richardson, p. 39; Coates, 1:95; *Annals*: *Courts*, 1:145. For the use of the term "doggeries," see e.g. Cleveland *Herald*, 23 December 1843, quoted in *Annals*; 26:131. Other newspaper stories deal with the sale of liquor at groceries by the canal; see *ibid.*, 33:18–19; Cleveland *Plain Dealer*, 17 May 1848.

Seventeen-Mile Lock: W. A. Knowlton, p. 26. (Knowlton actually refers to the "Nine-Mile Lock," but there was no such lock in Brecksville; presumably he meant the Seventeen-Mile Lock, the closest to his home.) Swimming: *Ibid.*, p. 18. Criminals: *Annals*, 33:197.

12. On the character of Thomas Garfield see *Diary*, 1:56, 62, and Leech and Brown, p. 14. The Garfields in general were "stout, good-natured and full of fun" (JAG to Eliza Garfield, 30 September 1854), but given to "bullying" (JAG to Thomas and Eliza Garfield, 16 April 1853). Thomas Garfield's sons are mentioned in Eliza Garfield to JAG, 10 December 1854. All three letters are in the JAG Papers, LC.

On the Letcher family, see Coppess, p. 91. Thomas appears in the 1849 Cuyahoga County tax records and in the 1850 manuscript U.S. Census, where he was shown as just having married. For Amos, see the notes to chapter 7; for the Letcher-Fisher connection, *Diary*, 4:459 note.

13. The diary gives no date for Eliza's arrival in Independence, but from the entries of 24, 27, and 28 May (1:9) it is clear that she had been there sick for some time before JAG took her home on 28 May. Her tendency to feel low-spirited in spring is mentioned in JAG to Eliza Garfield, 30 May 1855, JAG Papers, LC. But it is equally possible that she was there to keep a motherly eye on her youngest. Her protectiveness and interest in influencing her son's life are evident at several points—her arranging for him to attend an academy (chapter 9), her taking him off to southern Ohio (chapter 16), and her interference in his first serious romance (chapter 20); her presence at Independence in May 1848 fits easily into the same pattern.

14. *Diary*, 1:9 (25 May 1848).

15. The best source on the operation of the canal is F. Wilcox, pp. 17ff. According to *Towpaths*, 1:1, 3, 5 (1963) mules had begun to replace horses on the Ohio canals by the 1850s; but a later allusion in JAG's diary (1:148) suggests that his experience was with horses.

16. Harlow's account, p. 328, though positive and definite, does not tally entirely with other sources for Ohio Canal boats. According to him, a canal boat's crew might range in number from two to six; a large boat would have a crew of five—two drivers, two steersmen, and a cook. "Often," he adds, "there was a 'bowsman,' though the word didn't mean anything, the bowsman being merely a sort of general deck hand."

A boat on the Ohio Canal in 1845, however, had one steersman, one driver, two bowsmen (who worked in shifts), and a cook in addition to the captain (Cleveland *Plain Dealer*, 6, 13 August 1845). Another in the 1840s had two steersmen, two drivers, a "bowman [*sic*]" and a cook (Richardson, p. 38). Yet another in these years, the exact date not specified, had two drivers, "a bowman to watch the front," and two "pilots" (steersmen). ("On the Old Canal," *Towpaths*, 2:1 (1964), p. 7). Using these data, one might amend Harlow's statement in these respects: 1. there was not always a cook on board; 2. there was generally a bowsman, sometimes two, and they had well defined responsibilities—they handled the front of the boat, while the steersmen took care of the rear.

17. F. Wilcox, pp. 19–22; Downes, 1:128; Jackson and Jackson, p. 19.

18. F. Wilcox, p. 22; Downes, 1:127–28; Scheiber, *Ohio Canal Era*, p. 235; Orth, 1:699–701; Cleveland *Plain Dealer*, 19 April 1848; Aley, p. 59; Koch, pp. 36–37;

Cleveland *Plain Dealer*," July, 1 August 1849.

19. *Diary*, 1:9 (25 May, 30 May, 31 May, 1 June, 1848).

20. *Ibid.*, 1:9–10. This is certainly the same incident narrated at more length in Lucretia R. Garfield, "Rough Sketch," pp. 7–8.

21. *Diary*, 1:10; Walker, p. 38; Dickinson, p. 59. There are two mentions of "tending mason" for Thomas this summer, on 29 and 30 June (*Diary*, 1:10). Thomas was evidently building something, and the only clue to what it was is Brisbin's mention (p. 63) that JAG helped build a barn on the farm in the summer of 1849. Perhaps he did; the diary mentions his working on a barn that summer (1:20) with no indication of who it was for or where it was, but there is a rather clear implication that he was working that summer to earn money and would have sought out a job with someone other than his brother. These entries, in the summer of 1848, are the only times he mentions working with Thomas on a building job, and it is possible that Brisbin had his date wrong and that the barn was really built in 1848.

22. Howe, pp. 125–26; Ryder, p. 76; Blakeslee, pp. 9, 28, 35; Chagrin Falls *Exponent*, 31 December 1896; 18 August 1933.

23. *Diary*, 1:10 (19–25 June), 11 (18–21 July).

24. JAG's opinion of Rundt: *Ibid.*, 1:62. The use of the words "corrupt" and "corrupted" in this passage (7 October 1850) seems to me to refer to some specific vice shared by Davis and Rundt; my conjecture is that it meant excessive drinking, a failing not unknown among rural schoolteachers and German farmers.

25. This was a big event in JAG's early life and consequently turns up in several biographies in slightly different guises, e.g. the newspaper clipping dated 4, 5 July 1880, in scrapbook, 39, JAG Papers; Riddle, p. 37; Bundy, p. 15. The quarrel over the wage, alluded to by Riddle and Bundy, is in *Diary*, 1:11 (27 July 1848).

26. *Diary*, 1:10 (21 June), 11 (30 July).

27. JAG's adult assessments of his early life in Orange were anything but positive. It was a "chaos," an experience of poverty and privation, without inspiration or direction (to Harry Rhodes, 19 November 1862, *Wild Life*, p. 181; Gilmore, *On the Border*, p. 222; Leech and Brown, p. 17). Yet it has been pointed out in a previous chapter that his early memories of home were mainly happy ones. Evidently, then, it was the society around him that he felt responsible for his unhappiness. Among the people he knew, he recalled, his family's poverty elicited him some sympathy, but "the mass of the world"—by which he meant the world of Orange-Solon-Chagrin Falls where almost all his early years were spent—"was cold and chilling" toward him (*Diary* 1:246).

That most people in his area were "cold and chilling" toward him is entirely likely; according to a contemporary, manners in the rural Reserve were typically "cold and blunt" (Howells, p. 76); Reserve farmers, indeed, as a matter of principle cultivated "a brusque, cold manner" deliberately lacking in politeness (Davis, *Hinsdale*, p. 16; for an example, see Henry, p. 72) The Reserve was an unfortunate place to grow up in for a boy who, like Garfield, needed a lot of emotional reassurance. Very probably his neighbors, though not actually hostile, were reserved and distant. Like most neighbors, too, they were probably critical; so the quotation cited in the text suggests.

Garfield, in maturity, tended to sentimentality about his past. He liked to read his old diaries, to get together with old friends, to discuss the various "circles" within which his life had been spent—Orange; Geauga Academy at Chester; Hiram; Williams College, and so on. But revealingly, the circle toward which he showed least enthusiasm was the earliest, Orange. He enjoyed reunions with classmates from Hiram or Williams, and went to some trouble to attend them; but, though his sisters lived in the neighborhood most of their lives, he showed no such interest in reunions with old Orange neighbors. This part of his life was apparently the only one he had no desire to revisit.

28. Clipping from Cleveland *Leader*, 15 July 1899, in scrapbook at Lawnfield.

29. *Diary*, 1:12. Most of the early biographers (e.g., Riddle, *Life*, p. 29; Brisbin, p. 48; Coffin, p. 47; Gilmore, p. 6) state that JAG told Eliza of his intention, that her prayers and entreaties failed to dissuade him, and that he ultimately left either with her permission (Brisbin, Coffin, Gilmore) or despite her objections (Riddle). Conwell, however, who had his version direct from Eliza, maintains (p. 72) that he started "secretly and alone." The detail seems convincing, both because of its source and because it fits with JAG's lifelong tendency to avoid confrontations when possible. Moreover, the 1877 autobiographical notes confirm it: "I had left her without a word of where I was going, or if I had told her it had been only indefinately. . ." (p. 12).

Chapter 7. Making a Break

1. The canal experience in general: This episode, described in this chapter and the next, has received far more attention over the years than anything else in JAG's youth—fascinated and romanticized attention from contemporaries, disparaging and reluctant attention from later biographers who wanted to focus on other aspects of his career but felt that they had to deal with the Canal-boy image. One would expect, then, that the sources on it would be fairly full.

Oddly, this does not seem to be the case. A look at contemporary and later accounts suggests that there are no more than half a dozen sources of information about the canal experience, and that only two or three of these are truly independent. This note attempts to describe each source and assess its reliability:

A. The only contemporary source is JAG's diary. He took it along when he went to Cleveland in August 1848 to seek employment, and kept a consistent record of his first voyage as far as the return from Pittsburgh to Beaver. At that point, however, he stopped making regular entries, and the next entry, which summarizes the whole experience, was written some time after his return home. In terms of accuracy and contemporaneity, the credentials of the diary are first-rate; but the contents are disappointing, brief and dry. They fix the dates of young Garfield's employment and promotion, and make it possible to determine where his boat went while he was working on it; as to incidents, however, they are silent.

B. The next source in order of time is a somewhat vague one. It consists of the conversations JAG had during the Civil War with the Boston-based writer J. R. Gilmore, who found a strange fascination in the General's early life and saw it as a suitable subject for writing up. JAG at one point wrote Gilmore a long account of his early life; this letter was at one time in the Gilmore Papers at the Johns Hopkins University, but has unaccountably disappeared. Until it resurfaces, the best extant account of this source is Gilmore's in his Civil War novel *On the Border*, and to some extent, his biography of JAG, written in 1880 but from the same notes.

JAG liked to talk about his canal days—at least after 1862, when they appeared no longer as a disgrace but as a boyhood adventure with providential overtones—and Gilmore seems to be the first person who recorded his story. His version, thus, is valuable, but not so valuable as it might be. Gilmore plays fast and loose with the truth at times, cannot resist the temptation to embroider, and, in the 1880 biography, uses several sources besides his own notes. It is hard to sort out what is his or to determine how much of it to believe.

C. In the fall of 1876, during a speaking stop on the campaign trail at Athens,

Ohio, JAG again got to recounting his canal days, and again his words were taken down. This time the original is extant, in the form of a twenty-six-page manuscript in the Garfield Papers, with a notation at the top to the effect that it appeared in the 25 August 1877, issue of *The Phrenological Journal*—a statement I have been unable to verify.

Who wrote the article? No name is indicated, but a good guess would be ex-Congressman Albert G. Riddle, a prolific writer who only two years later would write a sketch of JAG for a county history, using essentially the same materials contained in this manuscript. Riddle was an antiquarian and like Gilmore a bit of a romantic (he confessed to Charles Henry, "I idealize . . . everything I touch." [Henry, 385]); some of the account may be overdrawn. But here is the completest version of the story from JAG's viewpoint, with several anecdotes and colorful descriptions. Since this source is headed "Notes made for Benefit of Biographers at Mentor During Summer 1880," I refer to it as the "1877 Notes."

Almost all the 1880 biographers based their accounts on this source. JAG did give a special interview, however, to his official biographer, J. M. Bundy, which may have added a little to his previous stories. Nothing major, however; Bundy's account occupies only a page.

D. The major new source in 1880—and the last one I know of—was a copious account by Amos Letcher. Not all the biographers used it, but Gilmore and General J. W. Brisbin did, in versions that vary significantly; each includes some matter that the other lacks. Though Williams and Brown assert (p. 12) that Letcher gave his interview to Gilmore, I find that hard to believe on the basis of the two versions. It seems more likely that both men got it from a common source, perhaps a newspaper article.

How reliable is Letcher's interview as a source of facts? If corroborative detail is to be trusted, phenomenally good. Letcher recalled the name of the *Evening Star*'s steersman as George Lee—and 1850 manuscript census records confirm that there was a George Lee, a boatman, living in Independence, the *Evening Star*'s home port. Letcher recalled the nicknames of locks on the Ohio Canal accurately, and his assertions about times and distances dovetail precisely with contemporary sources. One reason for this clear recall may be that, for Letcher as for Garfield, canaling was an exciting and unusual phase of early life. Though he stayed at it longer than JAG, he does not seem to have followed the trade more than two years. The 1850 census did not find him in Ohio, and by 1855 he was settled at Bryan, Ohio, well out of canal life. (*Ohio Records and Pioneer Families*, 1: 125.)

It is worth noting, too, that JAG turned to Letcher in 1880 to check his own memories of the canal—evidently recognizing that Letcher's were as good or better (Amos Letcher to JAG, 29 June 1880, JAG Papers).

Several assertions about JAG's canal days are patently false—and though they have not as a rule misled later biographers, it is worth while citing them as examples of the way poor memory or vanity can produce incorrect evidence.

During the Civil War, when Garfield's early career was just beginning to receive publicity, ex-Governor David Tod "recalled" how the *Evening Star* had taken on coal at his mines outside Youngstown and how he had seen young Garfield studiously reading in intervals between work. Now, it is quite likely that the *Evening Star* took on several loads of coal at Tod's mines in August and September 1848, but Tod didn't see JAG then. Tod was in Rio de Janeiro as President Polk's minister to Brazil; evidently he got his dates wrong. (Roy, *Practical*, p. 68)

Burton Porter, in "*Old Canal Days*," (pp. 452–53) records a similar tradition about JAG's studious ways, this time from boatmen at Canal Fulton, some miles south of Akron. But the problem here is that the evidence is almost conclusive about JAG's canal days: he got no farther than Akron on the Ohio Canal. Most of his work was on the Ohio and Pennsylvania, east of Akron.

In 1880 Captain Jonathan Myers, a well-known veteran captain on the Ohio and Pennsylvania Canal—see, for instance, the reference to him in *Annals*: *Courts*, 1:212—gave newspapermen his story of JAG's early service on the canal. Garfield, he said, had come on the canal at age thirteen or younger, and had stayed on his boat for a year or more; he had been taken under the wing of Doctor John P. Robinson (in reality, the name was Robison), who put him through school. (New York *Times*, 14 June 1880). This is all, of course, nonsense, but was so convincingly presented that JAG himself wrote to Letcher to ask who Myers was and whether he had known him. Letcher did not recognize the name, another fact that suggests his career in canaling was short (Letcher to JAG, 29 June 1880, JAG Papers).

The Myers story is both a puzzle and a warning: a puzzle in that it has some subsidiary facts correct, although wrong in essentials, and makes one wonder how the captain could have gotten confused enough to give it as the truth; a warning, in that it serves to remind researchers how very confused or erroneous much of the oral tradition about JAG is.

Much of what purports to tell the story of JAG's canal experience, then, is untrustworthy. The only really credible sources seem to be the diary and the Letcher interview. The two versions by JAG himself, the Gilmore material and the 1877 notes, seem to have been embroidered and somewhat confused in the retelling. There are, to my knowledge, no other sources.

2. Cleveland *Plain Dealer*, 12 December 1849, lists the ships wintering over in Cleveland. Orth, 1:709, has comparable figures for 1844; *Annals*, 33:272–92, comparable figures for arrivals in the summer of 1850. For the weather, *Diary*, 1:12.

3. JAG and captain: "Notes," pp. 6–8.

4. Conversation with Letcher: Brisbin, p. 50. (Compare the account in the "Notes," p. 8, where JAG omitted to mention that Letcher was his cousin.) For the guardlock, see F. Wilcox, p. 11, and Trevorrow, p. 41. On canal boats in river: "A Resourceful 'Canawler'," *Towpaths*, 4:1 (1966), 30; *Annals*: *Courts*, 1:61. Drivers' wages: Harlow, p. 328; interview with Philo Chamberlain, New York *Times*, 27 September 1881.

5. Four hundred boats: Scheiber, p. 235n. Description of *Evening Star*: clipping from the *Tribune*, 4–5 July 1880, in scrapbook in JAG Papers, LC. A serialized account of a canal trip, in Cleveland *Plain Dealer*, 6, 13 August 1845, gives the general layout of a canal boat. Standard dimensions: Scheiber, p. 235; Downes, 1:128. Narrow decks: F. Wilcox, p. 31; Dickens, p. 171.

6. F. Wilcox, pp. 27, 19; Harlow, p. 314; Chamberlain interview, New York *Times*, September 27, 1881.

7. Accident on towpath: I follow the version in Gilmore, p. 7. Depth of canal: The sources differ to some extent. B. P. Porter, p. 244, says that the canal was nowhere over five feet deep; but cf. Harlow, p. 251. All sources agree that four feet was the standard depth. On other details, see F. Wilcox, p. 13, and Harlow, p. 310.

8. Rose, pp. 163–64, gives normal running times on this part of the canal. The conversation with Letcher is from Gilmore, p. 7. Brisbin, pp. 50–51, is a parallel passage, with only a few verbal differences.

9. Bowsman Dave: 1877 Notes, p. 10. George Lee: Gilmore, p. 7; manuscript U.S. Census of 1850 for Independence. Ikey: Brisbin, p. 50. Blacks on canal: Richardson, *passim*; Cleveland *Plain Dealer*, 6, 13 August 1845.

10. Canal settlements: Lane, p. 656; Jackson and Jackson, p. 17; B. P. Porter, p. 250; Blower, *passim*.

11. F. Wilcox, pp. 14, 29, 31; Downes, I, 127; *Towpaths*, 2:1 (1964), 6; Harlow, p. 315; Gilmore, p. 7.

12. Twenty-One Locks: F. Wilcox, p. 41; Grismer, *Akron*, pp. 80, 90; B. P. Porter, pp. 248, 252; Richardson, p. 39.

13. Grismer, *Akron*, pp. 100, 117; Davis, *Canal*, p. 8; Scheiber, pp. 215–17; Davis, *Garfield*, p. 15; Cleveland *Plain Dealer*, 26 August 1848; Lyman, pp. 74, 78; Aley, pp. 57–58; [Ravenna] *Ohio Star*, 16 June 1847, 12 July 1848; *Portage Heritage*, p. 160.

14. Harlow, p. 261.

15. Heydinger, pp. 15–16.

16. Davis, *Canal*, p. 7; Grismer, *Kent*, p. 26; Canfield map.

17. The fourteen falls are from JAG's 1877 Notes, p. 9. The normal average speed on the canals was about three miles an hour; for instance, boats regularly made the 38-mile trip from Cleveland to Akron in thirteen hours (Grismer, *Akron*, p. 90). One could expect the *Evening Star*, therefore, to make at least forty miles a day, since she ran at night at least occasionally. But the *Diary*, 1:12, shows that she left Akron on 17 August and arrived at Beaver, a hundred miles away, eight days later, on 25 August.

18. Landscape: F. Wilcox, p. 91. See also C. D. Wilber to Zeb Rudolph, 7 December 1850, Lucretia R. Garfield Papers, LC, in which a young man from the Reserve expresses his wonder at the steep hills of the Ohio valley. Aley, p. 86; *History of Trumbull*, 1:99; Scheiber, "Canal," p. 119.

19. Corkan, pp. 179–80; Gordon, p. 52; *Annals*: *Courts*, 1:212; Harlow, p. 312.

20. *Annals*: *Courts*, 1:211–12; F. Baxter, p. 41.

21. "A two-story farmhouse": H. D. Gates, p. 84. Being towed upriver: The clipping from the *Tribune*, 4–5 July 1880, in a scrapbook in the JAG Papers, LC, whose account is generally consistent with other evidence and seems to have come from some reliable source, states that the *Evening Star* was towed upriver by the steamboat *Michigan*. I have not yet been able to determine whether there was such a boat on the river at that time, or whether it could have been at Beaver and Pittsburgh on the dates specified.

22. Pittsburgh: Addison, p. 25; *Annals*, 32:42; "Pittsburgh in 1848," pp. 192–93; Dickens, p. 179.

23. Baxter, pp. 38–39; *Diary*, 1:12 (27 August 1848).

24. Roy, *Coal Miner*, p. 291. JAG's diary does not mention the Brier Hill mines by name, but it does mention taking on coal at Youngstown. The Brier Hill mine, opened in 1843, was certainly the biggest operation at Youngstown in 1848 and perhaps still the only one (Eavenson, pp. 269–70). Koch, p. 37, describes a mine on the Ohio Canal which was probably similar in appearance.

The loading is from *Diary*, 1:13 (30 August 1848). Details are from *Annals*: *Courts*, 1:225; Cleveland *Plain Dealer*, 5 April 1848 and Eavenson, p. 268. Sixty tons was probably a full load. According to testimony in *Annals*: *Courts*, 1:225, the coal was not weighed on loading; the weight was simply reckoned by the capacity of the boat. Only when it was sold at Cleveland was it weighed.

25. The best general discussion of mining is Eavenson, pp. 268–71.

26. Cleveland *Plain Dealer*, 13 August 1845; Dickens, p. 177; Scheiber, p. 235; Pearl B. Nye collection, OHS; *Diary*, 1:13. (The entry is under the date of 30 August but was clearly added later.) Prospect of further raises: *Ibid.*, 1:60 (1 October 1850).

27. Iron-tipped pole: Harlow, p. 315.

28. Rascal: The word, JAG recalled, "brought up my blood in a minute." And no wonder; Moreau, p. 347, lists it with "god-damn," "bastard," and "son of a bitch," as one of the improper words used in some Philadelphia stage performances in the 1790s.

29. Fight with Dave: The only source is the 1877 Notes, pp. 9ff., but its account is convincing and internally coherent—for instance, the assertion that the fight took place at Beaver dovetails with the fact that the hold was empty when JAG knocked Dave into the bottom of the boat. Beaver and the return stretch from there to Youngstown would have been the only places where the *Evening Star* carried no cargo. The whole story fits roughly with Letcher's statement that before they got to Beaver on the second trip "the boys all liked him first-rate." (Brisbin, p. 51)

30. 1877 Notes, p. 11.

Chapter 8. The Wild Life

1. From the summary account in *Diary*, 1:13, written by JAG after his whole experience on the canal was over, one can reconstruct the regular route of his boat. To begin with, he states that he made only four round trips from Cleveland. He also states that the *Evening Star* transported 240 tons of coal and ten tons of iron to Cleveland during his service on it. Since, as appears from the same entry, sixty tons of coal was the regular load, that *Evening Star* must have carried a load of coal on each of the four return trips, plus a load of iron on one of them. As for the cargo carried from Cleveland, JAG states that it included fifty-two tons of copper ore. This, we know from the "Notes," was the cargo on his first trip. It follows that the *Evening Star* carried copper ore to Pittsburgh only one time in this period. The other trips must have been along the Crosscut at least as far as Youngstown, in order to pick up coal for the return. Probably they went all the way to Beaver; that, at least, is the implication of Letcher's statement that on the second trip "before we got to Beaver . . . the boys all liked him first rate" (Brisbin, p. 51). Several companies seem to have had fleets of boats that ran regularly between Beaver and Cleveland, see *Annals*: *Courts*, 1:211–12, and *Annals*, 26:34.

2. Aley, p. 58.

3. JAG to Lucretia Rudolph, 25 February 1856, JAG Papers, LC.

4. F. Wilcox, p. 17; Rose, p. 164.

5. To arrive at generalizations about men's dress in the middle nineteenth century, I tried to examine a large number of genre paintings from that period. They are cited below, listed under the name of the book where they are reproduced.

In *Vincent Price Treasury*: Darby, "The Reverend John Atwood and His Family," p. 83; Durand, "Dance of the Haymakers," p. 90; Bingham, "Raftsmen Playing Cards," p. 92, and "Canvassing for a Vote," p. 93; Thompson, "A 'Pic Nick', Camden, Maine," p. 94; Fisher, "Corn Husking," p. 95; Woodville, "Waiting for the Stage," p. 99; Mount, "Eel Spearing at Setauket," p. 106; Mayer, "Independence," p. 109. In Davidson: Bingham, drawing, p. 188; print, "Mike Fink, the Ohio Boatman," p. 189; Bennett, "Burning Fallen Trees in a Girdled Clearing," p. 169. In Buehr: Mount, "The Rustic Dance," p. 113; Wighe, "Rural Court Scene," p. 135; watercolor, 139. From *American Heritage*, February 1971: Oertel, "Country Connoisseurs," p. 17; Inman, "Mumble the Peg," p. 18; Woodville, "The Sailor's Wedding," pp. 24–25.

In addition, on respectable clothing, see R. T. Wilcox, p. 139; Starr diary, 25 June 1847; and Blakeslee, p. 8.

6. "How many": *Annals*, 28: 68. Slighted because of dress: *Diary*, 1:54 (17 August 1850); JAG to Thomas, Eliza, and Mary Jane Garfield, 8 August 1852, JAG Papers, LC. "Looked like a gentleman": Riddle, *Ansel's Cave*, p. 61. For other evidence that people in the rural Reserve paid attention to styles of clothing and used them as social indicators, cf. Carter, pp. 33–34.

7. Working dress: JAG to Lucretia Rudolph, 25 February 1856. JAG Papers, LC, describes his dress as a bowsman. For other data on what working people wore, see the descriptions of two men found drowned in the canal, in Cleveland *Plain Dealer*, 27 June, 19 December 1849. Dickinson, p. 125, mentions the heavy shoes. On underwear, see Welker, p. 38; Dickinson, p. 59; Drake, p. 676; Buley, 1:210. Advertisements are quoted in *Annals*, 26:49–52; 27:430; and 28:59.

8. Sunday clothes: Welker, p. 38; Carter, pp. 33–34. The daguerreotypes of the Boynton family in WRHS show the kind of Sunday clothes worn by Orange farmers: Sunday on the canal is discussed in Harlow, pp. 334–35; and cf. *Annals*, 26:285–86. Roy, *Practical*, p. 68, suggests that coal was not normally loaded on Sunday. Captains' dress: Grimser, *Kent*, p. 33.

9. Cleveland *Plain Dealer*, 1845 August 6; R. T. Wilcox, pp. 140, 147; Dickens, *Martin Chuzzlewit*, p. 321; Welker, p. 22; Drake, p. 679.

10. Knowingly and willingly: JAG later described himself at this time as "an active and will[ing] servant of sin" (*Diary*, 1:194).

11. Profanity: Peskin, 18, mentions JAG's swearing during this period. Later, when his friend A. G. Riddle wrote him during the 1880 presidential campaign that "Grant seems to have knocked S____t out of Hancock" (8 October 1880, JAG Papers, LC), he clearly assumed that JAG could fill in the blank and would not object to the phrase.

On swearwords, see Flexner, p. 173.

12. Harlow, p. 318; *Annals* 34:123–24; Cleveland *Plain Dealer*, 22 August, 31 October 1849; F. Wilcox, p. 90; Aley, p. 59.

13. Gilmore, *Life*, p. 7. Brisbin, p. 51, is a parallel account.

14. Riddle, *Life*, pp. 31–32; 1877 Notes, pp. 12–15. Other fights; Fuller, p. 65; Harlow, p. 320.

15. "To whip": Fuller, p. 65.

16. The only mentions I have found of spirits on board are in Dickens, p. 177, describing the bar on a passenger packet, and Cleveland *Plain Dealer*, 1845 August 13. In two cases where canal boats were robbed, liquor was not among the articles stolen (*Annals*, 28:73; 30:21). The price of three cents a glass, actually, is from a Chagrin Falls tavern (Henry, p. 48). I have found no reference to prices in the taverns by the canal, but they were probably comparable. On alcohol use in general, *Annals*, 36:1, and Cleveland *Plain Dealer*, 1848 September 27, note accidental deaths due to drunkenness among canal men.

17. Harry Brown: Gilmore, *Life*, pp. 17–18. The same man appears in Gilmore, *On the Border*, p. 222, as "Bradley Brown."

18. A high-class Cleveland brothel is cited in *Annals*, 33:461. For Ohio City, see Cleveland *Plain Dealer*, 1849 July 25. A distant vista of Ohio City is in J. Mueller's "Panorama of Cleveland and Ohio City Drawn from Nature," a lithograph printed around 1850, in WRHS. One might add that Scranton's woods, on the Ohio City side of the river, were criticized a few years later as a haunt of "abandoned" men and women who evidently staged wild gatherings there (*Annals*, 34:434). Household number 953 in the 1850 manuscript census of Brooklyn township, which contained Ohio City, may be germane here. Headed by D. W. Poe, age fifty, who gave his occupation as "landlord," it contained four young women in their teens, all unrelated, and a twenty-two-year-old man who gave no occupation.

19. "O! at that time": *Diary*, 1:194 (1853 May 22).

20. *Early Settlers*, 6:3, 68; *ibid.*, 8:4, 43. For muggings and robberies, see, e.g., Cleveland *Plain Dealer*, 1845 October 22; 1848 June 14.

21. Fall overboard: The best source for this story is the 1877 Notes. It also appears

in Gilmore, *On the Border*, pp. 222–224, in substantially the same form. The likeness of the two versions, told ten or twelve years apart, suggests that the narrative had reached a standard form in JAG's mind by the 1860s. A clipping from the *Tribune* (no location), 1880 July 4–5, in a scrapbook in the JAG Papers, LC, gives the location as Breakneck Creek, citing no source. Because of the depth, this seems plausible. Possibly the fall took place in the canal proper, see the note to chapter 7, p. 81, but it seems more likely to have been in a slackwater section of the Crosscut, near either Akron or Youngstown.

22. Many adults could not swim; see, for example, W. A. Knowlton, p. 18. For non-swimmers on the canal, see Cleveland *Plain Dealer*, 1845 June 25; 7 June 1848; *Annals* 31:1, 2; 34:73; 36:2; and 38:2.

23. *Diary*, 1:13.

Chapter 9. Convalescence

1. Malaria in general: The two best accounts I have found, in addition to those in Drake and the *Plain Dealer* cited below, are in Burr, pp. 681–88, and Buley, pp. 244–45. All material on malaria not specifically documented comes from these two sources.

2. Cleveland *Plain Dealer*, 9 February 1848.

3. Drake, p. 734ff.

4. Dickens was one writer who particularly noticed this characteristic. The American section of *Martin Chuzzlewit*, beginning at chapter 16, is full of adjectives like "sallow," "bilious," and "yellow" to describe the characters' complexions.

5. Ackerknecht, p. 15.

6. Henry, p. 34; *Pioneer and General History*, p. 60; Drake, p. 689.

7. *Ibid.*, p. 742.

8. Horton, p. 138; entry of 14 May 1847. George Starr Diary; Eliza B. Garfield to JAG, 15 June 1855, JAG Papers, LC.

9. *Diary*, 1:13; Alexander, p. 114.

10. *Diary*, 1:13. Butler appears in the 1850 U.S. Census manuscript for Chagrin Falls.

11. Quinine: Drake, p. 746; Burr, p. 681. Other treatments: Drake, pp. 749–50. Calomel: *Ibid.*, pp. 743–45, 7766–77; Ackerknecht, p. 116; Buley, 1:274. Ague-cake and spleen: Burr, p. 681.

12. 1877 Notes, p. 20; Riddle, *Life*, pp. 34–35; Burr, p. 686.

13. Polk's message: Cleveland *Plain Dealer*, 6 December 1848. California fever in Bedford: Eliza B. Garfield to JAG, 27 July 1853, JAG Papers, LC. In Newbury, Akron, Farmington, Warren: J. A. Riddle to A. G. Riddle, 12 February 1849, Riddle Papers; Lane, pp. 1107–09; Ferguson, p. 10; Abbie [?] to Lucretia Rudolph, 23 January 1849, Lucretia R. Garfield Papers. In Cleveland: Cleveland *Plain Dealer*, 24 January 1849; and compare the issues for the next few weeks.

14. *Diary*, 1:13. Vincent is described in Blakeslee, p. 13. Canal earnings spent: Bundy, p. 19.

15. Winter diet: Carson, p. 196; *Diary* 1:4 (17 January 1848); Howells, p. 99; Carter, p. 31; letter of Eliza B. Garfield, 7 February 1862, in family history album, JAG Papers, LC.

16. *Pioneer and General History*, p. 119; Henry, p. 35. Family letters emphasize Thomas' kindness and dislike for seeing suffering; e.g., Eliza B. Garfield to JAG, 28 October 1857, JAG Papers, LC.

17. Green, *Hiram*, p. 49; Horton, p. 136; Martha Lane to Lucretia Rudolph, 9 February 1849, Lucretia R. Garfield Papers; Welker, p. 19; letter of Eliza B. Garfield in family history album, 7 February 1862, JAG Papers, LC.

18. Davis, *Hinsdale*, p. 17; Dickinson, pp. 17, 67; Horton, pp. 137–38; Welker, p. 19; *Early Settlers*, 6:2, 26; Martha Lane to Lucretia Rudolph, 9 February 1849, Lucretia R. Garfield Papers. Beverages: Drake, pp. 658ff. Tea or coffee: Dickinson, p. 60.

19. *Annals*, 32:36; Drake, pp. 658–59; Lucretia R. Garfield, "Rough Sketch," p. 8; Horton, p. 137; Carter, p. 31.

20. Dickinson, p. 67; letter of Eliza B. Garfield, 7 February 1862, in family history album, JAG Papers, LC.

21. Drake, p. 656; Orrin H. Judd to JAG, 24 August 1854, JAG Papers, LC; Lucretia Rudolph to Arabella Rudolph, 23 September 1849, Lucretia R. Garfield Papers. These sources suffice to show that Welker's recollection, p. 45, cannot be applied to the Reserve in this period.

22. Leech and Brown, p. 17; Carter, p. 31; Dickinson, p. 65; Davis, *Hinsdale*, p. 18.

23. Cleveland *Plain Dealer*, 6 and 13 August; *Annals*, 29:93; 36:107; Day Book 1, Hodge Papers. The food mentioned in the *Plain Dealer* article is mostly cold leftovers or items like bread and butter bought on shore; nevertheless, the kitchen implements make it clear that cooking was done. For the popularity of pancakes, see Drake, p. 656. Oranges and coconuts are mentioned in a Cleveland advertisement, *Annals*, 29:93. As for drinks on the canal; such sources as *Annals*, 26:107; 30:71; and the *Plain Dealer* article mention only coffee, sarsaparilla, and alcoholic beverages.

24. "Rough Sketch," p. 8; 1877 Notes, p. 21; Coffin, p. 349; Bundy, p. 16.

25. Brisbin, p. 60; Jacoby, pp. 314–15; J. Wonsetler to O. J. Hodge, 22 March 1851, Hodge Papers.

26. Bates' classes: Recollections of Henry B. Boynton, in clipping from unidentified newspaper, 22–23 September 1881, scrapbook in JAG Papers, LC. Bates' own account is in Coffin, pp. 349–50.

27. Conwell, pp. 80–81.

28. Bates, in his own account, quite naturally emphasized his own role in persuading JAG to attend; according to him, Eliza merely "seconded" his efforts (Coffin, p. 350). But JAG, writing a few years later, saw Eliza's influence as paramount. "Those long dreary months of the winter of 1849," he wrote, "she was my good angel when legions of evil ones were besetting my path . . . this was, I fully believe, the only earthly influence that could have melted [me]." (*Diary*, 1:277)

29. On costs at Geauga Seminary, see M. Wood to O. J. Hodge, 5 November 1848, Hodge papers, and 1849 *Catalogue . . . of the Geauga Seminary*. Bundy, p. 18 shows how the money was put together. Lucretia Garfield's "Rough Sketch," p. 9, gives an idea of the difficulties: "On the farm a comfortable living could be gained with very little outlay, especially at that time when much of the cloth was made in the home. But now money must be paid for books, tuition, room rent, etc. From out the two homes enough could be spared to furnish the room with the few things absolutely necessary, and from the home larders provision sent, but some money must be had. By one means and another this was raised. . . ."

On this point, the usually reliable Conwell, pp. 82–83, is in error.

30. Bundy, pp. 18–19; 1877 Notes, pp. 21–22. MS autobiography, Hinsdale Papers, pp. 19–20 is an interesting comparison. On JAG's sense of inadequacy, see Peskin, pp. 16, 20.

31. Coffin, p. 350; Fuller, p. 2, Conwell, pp. 80–83; Davis, *Hinsdale*, p. 47; Rid-

dle, *Bart Ridgeley*, p. 168; Leech and Brown, p. 8; photograph of Alpha Boynton at WRHS.

32. Eliza's argument: 1877 Notes, p. 22. The argument that mathematics would help him to master navigation is mentioned on p. 8 of Corydon Fuller's manuscript lecture, Fuller Papers.

33. Cottom, p. 15.

Chapter 10. A Fresh Start

1. Trip to Chester: The date is from *Diary*, 1: 14. The distance, as given by Henry Boynton, is from an unidentified clipping, dated 22, 23 September 1881, in scrapbook, 39, JAG Papers, LC. Items taken: Brisbin, p. 61. According to Mandanah Wood to O. J. Hodge, 5 November 1848, Hodge Papers, WRHS, students had to provide their own beds. No public affection: Riddle, "55 Years," pp. 141, 145.

2. Corydon Fuller, who first met JAG two years later at Hiram, objected in his book (p. 92) to biographers who referred to his friend as "Jim," and stated that he had never known his to be called by any name but "James." This statement suggests that by 1851 "James" was established as JAG's name; since several people he knew at Hiram had also been classmates at Chester, it also suggests that he had gone by that name for some time. That he switched from "Jim" to "James" when he entered Chester, however, is only my conjecture. The switch happened at some time between 1849 and 1851, and this seems perhaps the most logical time.

3. *Pioneer and General History*, pp. 100–103. There are photos of the seminary building at Lawnfield and in Butler, p. 76. *Chagrin Falls Exponent*, 15 April 1897, mentions the cupola.

4. Bundy, p. 20; *Diary*, 1:4: Brisbin, p. 61.

5. Bundy, p. 20.

6. "There are over one hundred scholars there I believe he said 150," Mrs. D. L. Wood assured her brother John Hodge 5 November 1848 as she told him about Geauga Seminary (letter in O. J. Hodge Papers, WRHS); but in actuality, the number of students at Geauga could be counted in more than one way, and probably there were rarely as many as one hundred students in attendance at one time. The 1849 catalogue lists 211 names, not counting primary students, and gives the impression that the school had an enrollment of that number. But the catalogue covered three terms, fall, winter, and spring, and, as the discussion in the text brings out, attendance at Geauga was rarely continuous; students attended one term and then worked a term or two to earn money for their return. Most of the students named in the catalogue probably attended two terms that year, and many only one.

The typical enrollment for a given term has to be gathered from other sources. The United States census taker, 24 September 1850, managed to find and list eighty-four students, fifty-two male, thirty-two female. Caution in using this source is appropriate, since the person who took the census was not particularly accurate; he listed John Hodge twice and seems to have garbled JAG's name to "John Goffin." But his total figure corresponds to the comment in T. W. Scott to John Hodge, 2 September 1851 (Hodge Papers, WRHS), that "evry [*sic*] thing is going on as usual here there is 85 students now at school," or Matilda [?] to Lucretia Rudolph, 10 January 1850 (Lucretia R. Garfield Papers, LC): "Our school is not as pleasant as last term but pleasanter than I expected, about 80 students. . . ."

7. Students' ages: U.S. Census manuscript, 1850. Interrupted education: Kett, pp, 18–19. Residences of students: 1849 Catalogue.

8. Martha Lane to Lucretia Rudolph, 10 April 1849; cf. same to same, 13 February 1849, both in Lucretia R. Garfield Papers, LC.

9. The point is well made by Peskin, pp. 14–15. See also A. Perry to A. B. Barnes, 15 August 1850, Hodge Papers, WRHS. For comparison, see the account (Carter, p. 60) of the Twinsburg Academy some ten miles south of Orange, which offered, among other things, French, German, geology, chemistry, astronomy, and piano, flute, violin, or cello, at a price comparable to Geauga's.

10. Patterson, p. 151; N. Baxter, pp. 90–91; Gates, p. 66; 1849 and 1850 Catalogues of Geauga Seminary; Brisbin, p. 61.

11. For examples of the use of "Mr." of "Miss," see *Diary*, 1:38, 40, 54; Lucretia Rudolph to Arabella Rudolph, 23 September 1849; and Matilda [?] to Lucretia Rudolph, 10 January 1850, both in Lucretia R. Garfield Papers, LC. Other references are Carter, p. 60; JAG to Eliza B. Garfield, 31 March 1849, JAG Papers, LC; and Day Book no. 1, Hodge Papers, WRHS.

12. JAG to Lucretia Rudolph, 25 February 1856, JAG Papers, LC. On Hall himself, see Hodge, 1:124. A picture is in Tourgee, *The Story of A Thousand*, p. 3. For the use of "b'hoys," see *Annals*, 32:45, 47.

13. *Diary*, 1:14 (12 March 1849); C. Atwater to Lucretia Rudolph, 10 May 1849, in letter of 5 April 1849, Lucretia R. Garfield Papers, LC.

The story about Mrs. Branch's idiosyncratic grammar is in Brisbin, pp. 60–61. JAG's mention in his diary 9 March [Diary, 1:14] that he had purchased Chapin's *Grammar* as a textbook suggests that she may not have been quite so iconoclastic as Brisbin's source painted her. On the other hand, JAG did send home for his Kirkham's grammar as well (JAG to Eliza B. Garfield, 31 March 1849, JAG Papers, LC).

14. JAG's letter to the Board of Trustees, Geauga Seminary, 8 May 1867, reprinted in Fuller, pp. 2–4, *Diary*, 1:14 (12, 14 March 1849), 16 (16, 19 April).

15. *Diary*, 1:14 (12 March 1849), 23 (30 August); Howe, p. 452, Smith, pp. 28–29.

16. Zebulon Sorter: *Diary*, 1:43 (24 May 1850); Lucretia Rudolph to JAG, 18 February 1856, JAG Papers, LC; U.S. Census manuscript, 1850, Mayfield, Ohio. Lucretia Rudolph: Hodge, 1:124. Her small build is apparent from the clothes on exhibit at Lawnfield. John Hodge: *Early Settlers*, 6:3, 79.

17. Lucretia Rudolph to JAG, 18 February 1856, JAG Papers, LC; Hodge, 1:123.

18. *Diary*, 1:17.

19. *Ibid.*, 1:14 (10, 17 March), 15 (24, 31 March), 16 (21 April), 18 (2, 16 June), and *passim*. JAG's friend Corydon Fuller had the impression that JAG had been rejected for membership in a debating society at Geauga because of his background (ms. lecture, p. 9, Fuller Papers). This is not strictly true—JAG was successively a member of the Zetelethian and Sophomethean, and found their proceedings "interesting" (*Diary*, 1:14–15—13, 20, 21 March 1849). But he may well have experienced some social snobbery in the societies.

20. *Diary*, 1:14–18, *passim*. Several letters in the Hodge Papers from another Geauga student are in Pitman shorthand.

21. "A Visit to Mt. L ____," Lucretia R. Garfield Papers, LC; *Diary*, 1, 18 (16 June 1849), 19 (27 June); Lucretia Rudolph to JAG, 18 February 1856, JAG Papers, LC.

22. JAG to Eliza Garfield, 31 March 1849, JAG Papers, LC; *Diary*, 1, 14 (28 March), 18 (13 June), 19 (27, 29 June).

23. A New England commencement is described by Fish, p. 204; this was the model on which Reserve academies drew. But the best depiction of a spring exhibition in the Reserve is fictional, in Albion Tourgée *Figs and Thistles*, pp. 63–64. The academy in the novel is clearly Kingsville Academy in Ashtabula County, which

Tourgée had attended in the 1850s.

24. *Diary*, 1: 19 (30 June 1849); The program is reproduced in the 1849 Catalogue. Cf. *Diary*, 1: 19 (4 July 1849). Hall and Miss Rudolph: Marinda Raymond to Lucretia Rudolph, 28 August 1849, Lucretia R. Garfield Papers, LC; Hodge, 1: 124.

25. JAG to Eliza Garfield, 31 March 1849; to Thomas Garfield, 16 August 1849, JAG Papers, LC.

26. Corydon Fuller's father, a Geauga County carpenter, worked usually for one dollar a day in the 1840s (Fuller, p. 11). Zeb Rudolph, a Portage County carpenter, figured his own labor at $1.25 a day in 1852 but charged from seventy-five cents to a dollar for that of his son John, who was helping him (Account Book, Rudolph Family Miscellany, Lucretia R. Garfield Papers, LC). In view of JAG's limited skills, he probably earned the lower rate.

27. *Diary*, 1: 19–20 (5–27 July 1849). For weather, see *Ibid.*, 1: 19–20 (7, 11, 12, 20, 25 July). Cf. the rainfall figures for Hudson in Alexander, p. 632, and Cleveland *Plain Dealer*, 18 July 1849.

28. *Diary*, 1: 20 (30 July–2 August); Schob, pp. 67–71; W. A. Knowlton, p. 12; Welker, pp. 14–15. Cider or honey-and-water: Schob, pp. 98–101. Many farmers provided whiskey. Ignorance and profanity: *Ibid.*, p. 243; F. Lewis, p. 12.

29. Coates, 1: 202.

30. *Diary*, 1: 20 (4 August 1849). Shopping is not specifically mentioned, but the 1877 Notes, p. 23, make it clear that that was the purpose. For a sample of accidents on Cleveland streets around this time, see *Annals*, 28: 1–2; 32: 2; 34:72–73. The crowded streets are mentioned in *ibid.*, 34: 60, and Cleveland *Plain Dealer*, 11 April, 20 June, and 22 August, 1849.

31. 1877 Notes, p. 23; *Diary*, 1: 21 (8 August 1849).

Chapter 11. The Lure of Respectability

1. In 1880 JAG told his official biographer that not until his conversion, described in chapter 12, did he definitely give up his idea of becoming a sailor: Bundy, p. 22.

2. For instance, people in Newbury, Geauga County, thought ill of A. G. Riddle for studying law rather than working with his hands; they considered it just a glorified way of shirking, and thought he "lazied round living on [his] mother." Riddle, "55 years," p. 142.

3. Woodworth is listed in the 1850 manuscript U.S. Census as a carpenter, age thirty-eight, born in Vermont. *Diary*, 1: 21–22. The amount was later raised to two cents per board; see *ibid.*, 1: 23 (1, 8, 22, 29 September, 6 October), 1877 Notes, p. 23, and Riddle, *Life*, p. 38. "Which will help": JAG to Thomas Garfield, 16 August 1849, JAG Papers, LC.

4. Like other academies, Geauga Seminary issued a catalogue of its offerings every July, at the end of the spring term, with a list of its current faculty. The 1849 catalogue, a copy of which is at Lawnfield, lists Mr. and Mrs. Daniel Branch, George H. Ball, Silas Bigelow, L. S. Coffin (whose wife taught JAG's algebra class), Abigail Curtis, and Joshua Wellman. Of these, only Curtis and Ball reappear in the 1850 catalogue, a copy of which is in the JAG Papers, LC. The Branches, the Coffins, and Wellman appear to have left in summer 1849; they are not mentioned again in JAG's diary. Silas Bigelow is mentioned once in the fall term (*Diary*, 1: 23—30 August), and probably left in the winter. New faculty by 1850 were Spencer and Elizabeth Fowler, John Beach, and Delia Turner. But some other teachers seem to have come and gone between July 1849 and July 1850; JAG's teachers in the fall of 1849 included a Mr. Ward for algebra and C. C. Ames in geography (*ibid.*, 1: 22, 24).

Patterson's statement (p. 151) that the Reverend Ransom Dunn was among JAG's teachers at Chester is incorrect. Dunn apparently left a term or two before JAG's arrival (H. D. Gates, p. 84). But the error is certainly understandable in view of the rapid turnover there.

According to *ibid.*, p. 66, when Daniel Branch left Chester in 1849 George H. Ball succeeded him as principal. The statement seems plausible enough—Branch did leave in 1849 and Ball was there at least through 1850, but the rest of Gates' list of principals is inaccurate enough to make it suspect. It claims that the Reverend George T. Day was principal after Ball "for a short time" and that C. B. Mills and Spencer J. Fowler were the last principals. In fact, Fowler arrived in April 1850 to take over the post (*diary*, 1:39) and left in October of that year (*ibid.*, 1:63), several years before the closing of the school. Neither Day nor Mills is mentioned in JAG's diary or any other source for 1849–50. Thus one is left wondering whether Ball was principal of the school after Branch, or at all.

Actually, there seems to have been no formal head of the school from Branch's departure to Fowler's arrival in the middle of the spring term to take charge of the academy. If anyone was running the school in the interim, it seems quite likely to have been John Beach, whom JAG mentions 6 September (*ibid.*, 1:23) as lecturing him and a number of other students on behavior. Ball is not mentioned in the diary as doing anything that would suggest an administrative capacity.

5. *Ibid.*, 1:24 (13 September 1849).

6. For the five months before August, the entries in the printed *Diary* average 1.2 lines per day, with 1.5 the highest average for any month. For August and the four succeeding months, entries average 2.2 lines per day, with a high of 2.5 in August.

7. *Ibid.*, 1:21 (12 August), 23 (9 September), 24 (23 September), and *passim.*

8. *Ibid.*, 1:22 (19 August). Cf. *ibid.*, 1:42 (19 May 1850), 53 (11 August 1850).

9. *Ibid.*, 1:23 (2 September 1849), 25 (30 September); Tyler, pp. 404ff.

10. *Diary*, 1:24 (21 September 1849), 25 (1 October), 26 (10, 11 October).

11. *Ibid.*, 1:21 (14 August), 22–24 (28, 31 August, 4, 11 September).

12. *Early Settlers*, 5:445. Cleveland *Plain Dealer*, 13 August 1845, and Lorinda C. Davis to Lucretia Rudolph, 14 January 1850, Lucretia R. Garfield Papers, LC, show the common colloquial use of the term "nigger" for blacks. The temperate comment of a close friend of JAG who attended Oberlin in the 1850s is perhaps representative: "There are too many Negroes and Mulattoes here. I should think somewhere between 50 and 75. Were I accustomed to living with them I probably should think nothing of it—but—as it is it is diagreeable." (Symonds Ryder to JAG, 5 September 1854, JAG Papers, LC).

13. *Diary*, 1:23 (6 September 1849).

14. Brisbin, pp. 65–66.

15. Williams, *Wild Life*, p. 181; *Diary*, 1:23 (6 September).

16. *Ibid.*, 1:25 (1 October); Barker-Benfield, p. 135ff; McLoughlin, p. 20ff.

17. Barker-Benfield, pp. 12, 164–67, 178–80; Gilbert, *passim*; Fowler, p. 14.

18. Barker-Benfield, p. 169. (For the inaccurate identification with Onan, see *ibid.*, p. 328.); Fowler, pp. 12–13; Kinsey, p. 499.

19. Fowler, pp. 45ff.

20. *Diary*, 1:216 (10 August 1853): cf. *ibid.*, 1:214 (2 August 1853. Fowler, pp. 49, 50, 53–55; *Diary*, 1:25 (1 October 1849).

21. The best general source is Davies, especially pp. 4 and 178. There is a useful chart on p. 6. For a quick summary of phrenological doctrine by a practitioner of this era, see Sizer, pp. 372–73.

22. Davies, pp. 16–20, 32–34, 156–57.

23. *Ibid.*, pp. 32–34, 54, 61–62. For the appeal of phrenology in northern Ohio, see *American Phrenological Journal*, 9; (1847) 131, (1849) 11:70; *Annals*, 33:208, 24:202; [Ravenna] *Ohio Star*, 1 December 1847. A phrenological lecture is described in Davies, p. 51.

24. The best presentation of the idea is in Horlick, pp. 217–21. The *American Phrenological Journal* for January 1848 (10:15) carried a short article entitled "Young Men—Their Capabilities and Preparation for Active Life." See also Davies, p. 166.

25. *Diary*, 1:5 (15 February 1848): Peskin, p. 16; "Phrenologic Report", 1857, JAG Papers, LC.

26. Rosenberg, pp. 101ff; *Annals*, 32:27, 64–76.

27. *Diary*, 1:24 (13, 15 September 1849); Lucretia Rudolph to Arabella Rudolph, 23 September 1849, Lucretia R. Garfield Papers, LC; *Diary*, 1:54 (22 August 1850), 57 (7 September 1850).

28. Orrin's illness: *Diary*, 1:21 (17 August 1849). James had commented, "I feel very lonesome." New friends: *Ibid.*, 1:24 (17 September) (Page); (18 September) (D. R. Brooks, 27) (27 October) (Bell); Hinsdale, pp. 31–32. Mystic Ten: *Diary*, 1:24, 26 (10, 24 September, 8 October).

29. JAG's letters to Thomas Garfield (16 August 1849) and to Thomas and Eliza (9 September—both in JAG Papers, LC) mention his tentative plans for going south. A diary entry for 4 October (1:25) shows that the talk of doing so was widespread among the students at Geauga. See also Hinsdale, "Popular Education", pp. 48–49. T. W. Scott to O. J. Hodge, 9 September 1851, Hodge Papers, WRHS, illustrates the same point. That a job-hunting expedition to the south could turn out badly is shown by John Wonsetler to O. J. Hodge, 22 March 1851, in *ibid.*

30. *Diary*, 1:25 (5, 15 October 1849). The older student was Alonzo Brocket; there is a letter from him, dated 24 December 1849, in the Hodge Papers, WRHS.

31. JAG's route can be followed in *ibid.*, 1:26 (17–19 October), a brief factual account which does not suggest how much discouragement he felt at his failure. That comes out more clearly in the reminiscent account in Hinsdale, p. 48. The version in Brisbin, p. 64, differs in minor details but may well be a rewrite of the same source.

32. JAG later commented, in a letter to Albert G. Riddle (15 May 1873, Riddle Papers, WRHS), that Riddle's novel *Bart Ridgely*, about a young man growing up in the Reserve, contained "many points . . . that came home to my own struggles & experience." The hero's experience teaching school, he went on, "almost duplicate[d]" his own. It may be worth noting, therefore, that in the novel Bart gets his first teaching job at the instance of only one school director, who hires him despite the other directors' doubts of his fitness (Riddle, *Bart Ridgely*, pp. 108, 113). The diary entry of 20 October (1:26) suggests that something similar happened in this case. Initially JAG talked to only one director; the rest had to be persuaded over the weekend.

33. Johnson, pp. 516–17. Bart Ridgely's first teaching also took place in a newly settled, rather rough neighborhood (Riddle, *Bart Ridgely*, p. 107). For the Herringtons, see *infra*; for the Chamberlains, Bard, pp. 45–46. Bundy, p. 21; Brisbin, p. 64.

34. Bundy, p. 21, says he was known as "Jim" Garfield; Brisbin, p. 64, elaborates with some advice Uncle Amos is supposed to have given: "You will go into that school as the boy 'Jim' Garfield; see that you come out as Mr. Garfield, the schoolmaster." The problem was far from unique; for a parallel case, see Kett, 48–49. For the interview with Harrington, *Diary*, 1:26 (20, 22 October 1849).

35. *Ibid.*, 1:26 (26 October), 27 (3 November). The record of the first meeting is in the Philomathean Society Record Book, WRHS, entry of 3 November 1849, which gives the constitution and the officers elected.

Chapter 12. The Turning Point

1. Johnson, pp. 516–17; JAG to Phebe Clapp, 12 November 1869; clipping from unidentified newspaper, dated 22–23 September 1881, in scrapbook, both in JAG Papers, *LC*.

2. Coffin, p. 61, is in error in supposing that JAG lived at home. For an example of the difference in wages occasioned by boarding, see Dickinson, p. 113. First day: *Diary*, 1:27. Teacher's dress: Perry Mapes autobiography, pp. 3–4.

3. *Diary*, 1:27. I infer that the younger pupils came first from such later entries as 26 November: "Large scholars coming in, feel rather dubious."

4. *Diary*, 1:27–35. His school closed 2 March. He taught on every Saturday except 17 November, 1 December, 26 January, and 9 February. There is a hand-ruled roll book, from a Ravenna school district in the 1850s, in the Lucretia R. Garfield Papers, LC. For weather, see *Annals*, 32:414; A. B. Gunnison to O. J. Hodge, 17 February 1850, Hodge Papers, WRHS; *Diary*, 1:34–35 (14, 16 February 1850); and *Ohio Cultivator*, 61 (15 March 1850) 87 (Portage County).

5. *Diary*, 1:27 (6, 7 November 1849), 28 (16, 23, 24 November), 29 (30 November); A. Perry to O. J. Hodge, 15 January 1850, Hodge Papers, WRHS. Perry's school, in the township of Wayne, was reputed the "next to the worst school in the Co," and, like the one in the Ledge district, had had some teachers locked out by the students.

6. The incidents in this paragraph are from *Diary*, 1:27–28 (7, 8, 12, 23, 24 November).

Samuel Harrington: The diary entry says merely "S. Herrington," but there is a Samuel Harrington, aged eleven, listed in the 1850 U.S. Census in the Alvin Harrington household. *Cuyahoga County Cemetery Inscriptions*, p. 422, shows an S. A. Harrington buried with the Alvin Harrington family in Solon, but gives his date of birth as 1842, which would make him seven the year JAG taught school. If this is the same Samuel Harrington, I cannot explain the discrepancy in year of birth; of the two possible ages, I chose eleven because it seems to fit marginally better with the incident described.

Attendance figures are given in *Ibid.*, 27, 28, 29 (6, 7, 14 November, 4 December). The highest figure was thirty-seven students on 4 December.

7. Kett, pp. 48, 50; J. Wonsetler to O. J. Hodge, 22 March 1851, Hodge Papers, WRHS.

8. *Ibid.*, 1:28 (19 November), 29 (26 November, 4 December), 30 (24 December).

9. *Diary*, 1:33 (4 January 1850); Bundy, p. 21; Brisbin, p. 65.

10. *Diary*, 1:28 (12 November 1849); Brisbin, p. 65; Hinsdale, *Garfield*, pp. 49–50.

11. Gilbert Huddleston: *Diary*, 1:35 (25 February 1850); Wickham, 1:491; 1850 U.S. Census manuscript; *Cuyahoga County Cemetery Inscriptions*, p. 429.

Widow Short: *Diary*, 1:34, 35 (11, 21 February); 1850 U.S. Census manuscript. According to the county tax records, Sarah Short owned no land and paid tax on only eighteen dollars worth of property.

Harrington: *Diary*, 1:30 (10, 18, 19 December 1849); *Cuyahoga County Cemetery Inscriptions*, p. 422. In the county tax records for 1850, Alvin Harrington was listed as owning 120½ acres and paying tax on $226 worth of property.

Sylvester Tinker: In the same source, Tinker owned no land and paid tax on property worth eighty-four dollars. He is listed in the 1850 U.S. Census manuscript. *Diary*, 1:27, 28, 29 (8, 17, 26 November).

Bowl of bread and milk: This traditional feature, so much a part of life in the Reserve that natives could become acutely homesick for it, is mentioned in numerous sources, including Williams, *Wild Life*, p. 105; Cowles, p. 64; Horton, p. 138; and Dickinson, p. 122. Reading aloud: Brisbin, p. 65. Visitors: *Diary*, 1:28 (16 November), 29 (30 November), 30 (11, 12 December).

Reverend Seward: *Ibid.*, 1:33 (10 January 1850). JAG referred to him as "Priest" Seward, a title sometimes given Congregational ministers by members of less formal denominations. For a parallel instance, see Brink, p. 151. He appears in the 1850 U.S. Census manuscript and is mentioned in Coates, 1:219.

On the exhibition, see *Diary*, 1:36 (2 March). Others are mentioned in *ibid.*, 1:35 (22 February 1850), 104 (21 November 1851), and 117 (21 February 1852).

12. *Diary*, 1:28–29, *passim*; Henry, p. 68; *American Phrenological Journal*, 11: (1849) 134; J. M. Riddle to A. G. Riddle, 11 February 1848, A. Phelps to A. G. Riddle, 27 December 1848, Riddle Papers, WRHS; a possible example from an earlier date is in Starr diary, 14 November 1845.)

13. Marenus and Mary Larabee appear in the 1850 U.S. manuscript census of Solon township, taken 10–11 October of that year. They do not appear in the 1850 tax list, which suggests that they moved to Solon in 1850 or late in 1849. Probably 1849 is correct, for the *Diary* for November and December mentions them several times, with no intimation that they were in the area on a visit (1:28, 29—24, 30 November, 1 December).

Drive to Cleveland: *Diary*, 1:29 (1 December); Cleveland *Plain Dealer*, 12 December 1849; Rose, pp. 175, 220. For the inadequate lighting of the streets before this time, see, e.g., *Annals*, 31:259.

14. *Annals*, 32:150. For the European background, see Robert Darnton's *Mesmerism and the End of the Enlightenment in France*. Its progress in America and its combination with phrenology can be traced in Davies, pp. 126–27; Sizer, p. 123; Nelson, p. 53; and *Annals*, 26:208. A detailed account of one mesmerist session is in Blakeslee, pp. 33–34.

15. A good brief defense by a contemporary phrenologist is Sizer, pp. 119–20. At their most expansive, the exponents of animal magnetism attempted to link it with all ongoing scientific progress of the period, as in an article, "Electricity the Great Acting Power of Nature," in the *American Phrenological Journal*, 11:(1849) 151, which began: "Phrenology, Physiology, Animal Magnetism, Clairvoyance, and I am about ready to say, Astronomy, Geology, Mineralogy, and Botany, I regard as servants to the all-powerful and all-pervading influence, agency, and action of Electricity." But their critics could reply, like Alexander Campbell in the *Millennial Harbinger*, 2 (series 4). 10 (October 1852), 556, "That all *bodies*—the human body, as well as any other body, mineral, animal, or vegetable—are the subjects and residences of an electric spirit, there is no one, tolerably initiated into the secrets of nature, who can or will deny. . . . In one class of bodies it is made manifest by friction only; in another class, by sensible communication. Some bodies absolutely refuse to receive electricity by communication. . . . We may talk of the quantities of electricity by denominations of positive and negative; of its residences, transmigrations, transformations, and metamorphoses; but yet its secret chambers, and its domestic laws, no son of earth can penetrate, till he has shuffled off this mortal coil."

Batteries: Blakeslee, p. 33. For another technique, see Cleveland *Plain Dealer*, 12 December 1849; *Annals*, 26:208. A funny illustration of positive and negative charges is in *Diary*, 1:170 (20 January 1853).

16. Charles D. Wilber to JAG, 11 April 1854, JAG Papers, LC; *Diary*, 1:29 (1 December 1849).

17. *Diary*, 1:30 (12, 31 December), 34 (26 January 1850), 35 (22, 23 February).

18. Orrin and the Boyntons: *Ibid.*, 1:28 (11, 16 November 1849), 30 (12, 15 December), 32 (1 January 1850), 35 (17, 22, 23 February). Harvey O. Rutherford: *Ibid.*, 1:28, 30, 34 (18 November, 31 December 1849; 26 January 1850). Henry Deady: *Ibid.*, 1:30 (12 December 1849); Bard, p. 30; *Cuyahoga County Cemetery Inscriptions*, p. 422; 1850 U.S. Census manuscript, Solon.

19. Albert Slade: Slade's first name is not mentioned anywhere in the *Diary* entries for the winter of 1849–50 (unless the reference in the entry of 12 December, which seems to read "T. Slade" is to him); but it seems plausible to identify him with the "old acquaintance, Albert Slade" mentioned in JAG's diary entry of 31 January 1858 (*Diary*, 1:319). The manuscript U.S. Census of 1850 shows an Albert Slade, twenty years of age, living in Bedford; his father was a carpenter, and he gave his own occupation as clerk. This seems just the sort of man who would have been teaching spelling schools and debating at local lyceums in the winter. I have no other information on him.

20. This person is far less easy to identify than Slade, but the brief part he played in JAG's life was so important that the effort is worth making. He does not appear in the *Diary* before December 1849 or after February 1850, except possibly in the entry of 13 February 1852 (1:117). One gathers from the diary entries that he lived within walking distance of northern Solon. The diary also suggests, though it does not state, that Stone was married and lived in a home of his own.

The 1850 U.S. Census manuscript shows no Oliver B. Stone in Solon or any of the adjacent townships, but the tax records for that year show an Oliver Stone paying taxes on fifty acres of land in Bedford, next to the farm of JAG's uncle Joseph Skinner. The 1852 Blackmore map shows an O. Stone settled on a lot in the same part of Bedford, though not the very same lot. There is, then, documentary evidence of an Oliver Stone living in Bedford, in a location that would fit with JAG's acquaintance of 1849–50.

Oddly, however, the family appears in the 1850 census records not in Ohio but in New York. Deeds in the Cuyahoga County records show that the Oliver Stone who purchased Lot 26 in Bedford, and a good deal of land besides, in 1847, was a resident of Cato, Cayuga County, New York, and the 1850 manuscript census of that community turns out to contain his household. This Oliver Stone was a prosperous, fifty-four-year-old farmer, with a wife, Phebe, about the same age—not at all likely to have been JAG's friend. He had a son named Oliver, however, who seems a good deal more likely: twenty years old, with no occupation given. Young Oliver was single and living with his family in July of 1850, when the census was taken.

There are serious difficulties with this identification. To accept it, one must assume that the Stone family was living in Bedford in February 1850; moved back to Cato by July; and was back in Bedford by 1852, when the Blackmore map was made—not an impossible course of events, but not immediately plausible. Moreover, there is the question of the "connubial felicity" JAG observed in his entry of 14 January; if Oliver, Jr., was not married, JAG must have meant Oliver, Sr., and Phebe, and one wonders why he should have been interested in their relationship. On the other hand, if Oliver, Jr., was married in January, it is puzzling that he had no wife by July of the same year.

A not wholly satisfactory alternative to this identification is offered by a passage in Henry, pp. 43–44, where Oliver Stone is depicted as a well-known character, a "gifted 'crazy crank' of a shoemaker and Jack-of-all-trades" who held forth in the Henrys' township of Bainbridge, adjoining Solon on the east, and ten or twelve other towns, during the years of Captain Henry's boyhood, approximately 1845 to 1855.

That he was married appears from *ibid.*, p. 55, where his courtship of a Bainbridge lady, Fidelia Smith, is mentioned. No date is given, but the context seems to place it around 1851. I have found no official record of the marriage.

It is unlikely that Henry's Oliver Stone is to be identified with the man of the same name in the tax and census records. To suppose that the son of a well-to-do farmer like Oliver Stone, Sr., was a shoemaker and local character like the one described by Henry is stretching credibility too far—quite apart from the fact that Henry's Oliver Stone would need to have been several years older than the one in Bedford and Cato to have earned the reputation Henry says he possessed. So there appear to have been two Oliver Stones in the Solon-Bedford-Bainbridge area in the early 1850s. Which one was JAG's Oliver B. Stone remains uncertain at this point.

I am indebted to Patricia R. Woodward of Berea, Ohio, for research on this problem.

21. *Diary*, 1:29 (6 December 1849). For JAG's use of "adventure": cf. *ibid.*, 1:45 (8 June 1850), 99 (18 October 1851), 134 (26 May 1852), 155 (26 September 1852), 156 (2, 3, October 1852).

22. *Ibid.*, 1:26 (19 October 1849). "They were 'Banjoed' terribly," JAG commented. Presumably he was referring to a shivaree of the sort common in some parts of frontier America, a noisy demonstration outside the window of a newly married couple. If so, the fact is somewhat revealing about the Boynton community in 1849, for the custom was felt to be old-fashioned and offensive in other parts of the Reserve. In Geauga County, a "riot, a tin-horning of a newly married pair on their wedding-night," was characteristic only of the most isolated and backward townships (Riddle, *Ross*, p. 381). There was an "up and down serenade" with a fiddle, four cowbells, and many old tin pans in Warren in 1848, but it was attributed to malice rather than local custom, and excited widespread comment (Abbie [?] to Lucretia Rudolph, March 1848, Lucretia R. Garfield Papers, LC). JAG himself, when he ran into a similar sort of serenade in southern Ohio in 1851, called it "a miserable mean piece of business" (*Diary*, 1:75—27 March 1851). Thus its occurrence at Thomas's wedding probably indicated how undeveloped Orange remained in comparison with the other communities around it.

23. *Diary*, 1:30 (16 December 1849). "Mr. Slade": *Ibid.*, 1:33 (7 January 1850). Nights at Stone's house: *Ibid.*, 1:30 (18, 22 December 1849), 33 (14 January 1850), 35 (20 February).

24. *Ibid.*, 1:28 (22 November 1849), 30 (13, 20, 21, 23 December), 31, 32 (31 December 1849), 1 January 1850).

25. *Ibid.*, 1:33 (7, 10, 12 January).

26. *Ibid.*, 1:33 (14 January).

27. This is probably the most appropriate place to review the scanty evidence bearing on JAG's sexual orientation as a young man. Cottom, pp. 80ff., convincingly argues the possibility that he had some homosexual feelings. Moreover, there are a couple of minute pieces of evidence that Cottom overlooked: in JAG's college notebooks for the middle fifties, a brief note reading "'Paederasty' Barnes' Notes on Romans 1:24" suggests an interest in what the Bible said about homosexual behavior (JAG Papers, LC). And in his unhappy letter to Harry Rhodes of 19 November 1862 (Williams, *Wild Life*, p. 181) he lamented, in a revealing phrase, that the absence of a father in his early youth had not permitted him to become "fixed in manly ways."

The reference to pederasty in Barnes' commentary (p. 48) is short and easily quoted: "It has indeed been a matter of controversy whether *paederasty*, or the love of boys, among the ancients was not a pure and harmless love, but the evidence is against it." There follows a list of classical authors who mention the practice, including

Cicero, Virgil, Plutarch, and Seneca. (The passage, incidentally, is part of the commentary on verse 27, not verse 24 as JAG stated in his note.) It is not obvious why JAG considered this reference worth writing down. Possibly the word was new to him; perhaps more likely, he was interested in the list of classical authorities cited by Barnes.

In any event, his interest in the practice does not allow one to infer anything about his behavior. He may have had other reasons for being interested. As mentioned in the preceding chapter, he worried a good deal about excessive masturbation, and some nineteenth-century writers linked masturbation and homosexual behavior together—any masturbator was a presumptive homosexual (Bullough and Voght, pp. 143–55). He may have been trying to explore, through the sources available to him, just what it was he was supposed to be guilty of.

Still, when one considers the totality of the evidence—that cited by Cottom, the bits presented here, and facts like JAG's curious relationship with Oliver Stone, discussed in this chapter and in chapter 19—there seems to be room for conjecture that he was involved in homosexual relationships to some degree. At one or two points in this account, I refer to the possibility, which I think will always remain a possibility; evidence to substantiate or disprove it is not likely to be forthcoming.

28. *Diary*, 1:35 (28 February 1850).

29. *Ibid.*, 1:35 (17 February).

30. *Ibid.*, 1:35 (28 February). The entry suggests that he had already been reading it for some time before that date.

31. Quotations are from Pollok, p. 14; p. 22; p. 373.

32. *Ibid.*, pp. 75–76, 139; *Diary*, 1:35 (28 February 1850).

33. *Ibid.*, 1:36 (1 March); Brisbin, p. 66. Bundy, p. 21, calls Lillie a "good solid old man," but the notice of his career in Hayden, p. 230, shows that he was by no means an old man at the time.

34. *Diary*, 1:36 (2 March 1850). The decorations on such occasions are mentioned in the Perry Mapes Autobiography, WRHS.

35. Bard, p. 30; A. Wilcox, p. 8.

36. *Diary*, 1:36 (3 March 1850). It is not definite that the Clark who was baptized on this occasion is the same as the one mentioned in *Ibid.*, 1:30 (12 December 1849), but it was clearly someone important to JAG, as the entry indicates: "Clark immersed, feel considerably roused on the subject." Talk with Lillie: Bundy, p. 22; Green, *Life*, p. 153.

37. O. H. Judd to JAG, 11 March 1855, JAG Papers, LC. Green, *Life*, p. 153. One other young man baptized at that time was JAG's friend George Warren; see clipping from Cleveland *Leader*, 15 July 1899, in scrapbook at Lawnfield.

38. *Diary*, 1:35 (28 February 1850), 36 (3 March 1850).

Chapter 13. The Young Christian

1. Baird, pp. 479ff; Martha Lane to Lucretia R. Garfield, 10 April 1849, Lucretia R. Garfield Papers.

2. Presbyterians: Baird, pp. 480–81. The same author, p. 473, writing from a Presbyterian viewpoint, criticized the "mere animal excitement" of revivals of the Methodist type. For a Disciple critique of the Methodists, see *Millennial Harbinger*, 2:4th ser. (March 1852), 145. A mild criticism of the Disciples' coldness and formality is in a letter from JAG's Methodist cousin, Ellis Ballou, 14 April, 1854, JAG Paper, LC.

"Cold, speculative": Baird, p. 573. Disciples in the Reserve, moreover, were cold and emotionless even by other Disciples' standards; see Shaw, p. 111.

3. *Diary*, 1:36 (5, 6, 8 March 1850), to Harmon Austin, 1 May 1864; JAG to Lucretia Rudolph, 21 April 1855, JAG Papers, LC; Bundy, p. 22, Riddle, *Life*, p. 38.

4. On the frequency of revivals, see S. Sizer, p. 85. A careful search would no doubt turn up dozens of revivals in Cuyahoga County alone every winter; for mention of three in other denominations, see Coates, 1:108; Henry, p. 43; and Austin White to Isabella Thomas, 20 March 1849, Thomas-Wilson-White Family Papers, WRHS. As for conversion in batches, Baird, p. 472, put it this way: "[T]hat the awakening of one individual is frequently made the occasion of arresting the attention of a number of his associates, and fastening conviction in their minds, is matter of familiar observation in every religious community."

Starbuck, pp. 145–49 uses the term "unselfing"; Kett, p. 80, notes that conversion "involved a selection of some aspects of one's personality at the expense of others. That is, to be converted meant that one had decided to lay aside childhood associations and to embrace the new associations appropriate to adulthood." Word of JAG's conversion: interview with Henry Boynton, *New York Times*, 25 September 1881; clipping from Cleveland *Leader*, 15 July 1899, in scrapbooks at Lawnfield.

5. Starbuck, p. 170; Kett. pp. 82–83; O. J. Hodge to Mandana Wood, 30 December 1848; Z. W. Shadduck to O. J. Hodge, 18 March 1850, Hodge Papers.

6. On the Disciples in general, Harrell, *The Quest for a Christian America*, is a good though rather supercilious source; see also Shaw, *Buckeye Disciples*. E. Gates, p. 106, and Hinsdale, *Garfield*, pp. 17–18, outline Disciple doctrines, both the common ones they held with other Christians and their particular beliefs.

Cottom, p. 24, errs, I think, in maintaining that Disciples' behavior was, "while not peculiar, at least noticeable." On the contrary, in most ways the Disciples were like the other churches around them. Disciples did hold their members to a strict moral standard; see, for instance, Bard, p. 30. But so did Congregationalists (Horton, pp. 121–22), Methodists (Henry, p. 55), and other unspecified denominations (Lyman, p. 105).

The terms "brother" and "sister" were freely used by many Protestant sects, not merely the Disciples, as a glance at almost any novel of nineteenth-century rural American life will show. Cottom, p. 28, is surely right in pointing out that Disciples used them, but wrong in implying that this usage was distinctive. An example of the usage by a young Freewill Baptist is in Alonzo Brocket to O. J. Hodge, 24 December 1849, Hodge Papers, WRHS. Weekly communion: Shaw, p. 69; Jennings, p. 237.

"Nemo est": *Diary*, 1:37 (20 March 1850).

7. For the nickname "Campbellites", see A. Wilcox, p. 8, and Lorinda C. Davis to Lucretia Rudolph, 8 August 1850, Lucretia R. Garfield Papers. Number of members: Shaw, pp. 85–93 and *passim*.

8. T. C. Smith, 1:32; *Diary*, 1:42 (17 May 1850). Hinsdale, *Garfield*, also stresses this point. See also Jennings, p. 226.

9. For examples of JAG's use of "sectarian" in a critical sense, see, e.g., *Diary*, 1:54 (18 August 1850), 62 (11 October 1850).

10. Shaw, pp. 29, 72–75; Fuller, p. 12.

11. *Diary*, 1:25 note, 38 (28 March 1850): Conwell, p. 84; Brisbin, p. 65; ms. lecture, pp. 8¼–8½, Fuller Papers; Interview with Henry B. Boynton, *New York Times*, 25 September 1881; *Diary*, 1:39 (11 April 1850).

12. See the incident recollected by Lucretia R. Garfield, in T. C. Smith, 1:29.

13. *Diary*, 1:43 (27 May 1850), 39 (11 April), 40 (22 April), 41 (1 May), 37–38 (25 March).

14. *Ibid.*, 1:38 (30 March), 39 (15 April), 42 (16 May).

15. *Ibid.*, 1:39 (12 April); 2:180 (16 May 1873). His herbarium and Lucretia Rudolph's are among the items at Lawnfield. For background on the flowers, I used Stupka, *Wildflowers in Color*.

16. *Diary*, 1:42 (9 May 1850), 43 (24 May).

17. *Ibid.*, 1:45 (1 June), Cf. *Ibid.*, 1:43 (22 May).

18. Everest disappears from the *Diary* after October 1849 to reappear four years later (1:199). Lucretia Rudolph and Albert Hall: Hodge, 1:125. Samuel Bates: *Diary*, 1:31; A. Brockett to O. J. Hodge, 24 December 1849, Hodge Papers. Symonds Ryder is first mentioned in *Diary*, 1:37 (22 March 1850). For his appearance and character, see Lucretia Rudolph to JAG, 17 March 1855, and JAG to Lucretia Rudolph, 24 March 1855, JAG Papers, LC.

19. *Diary*, 1:37 (19 March 1850), 39 (9, 13, 16 April), 40 (19, 23, 30 April), 41 (7 May), 43 (28 May), 45 (4 June). Cf. *ibid.*, 1:30 (12 December 1849), and entry of 22 December 1849, in Philomathean Society Record Book, WRHS.

20. This can be followed in any number of standard historical works, e.g. Nevins, *Ordeal of the Union*, 1.

21. N. Baxter, pp. 93–109; *Pioneer and General History*, pp. 102–103; Wickham, 1:57; *Diary*, 1:38 (2 April).

22. *Ibid.*, 1:42n (14 May 1850).

23. A list of doctrines shared by Freewill Baptists and Disciples is in E. Gates, p. 106. The inside cover of Day Book 1 in the O. J. Hodge Papers, WRHS, contains a list of verses in favor of immersion—essential ammunition for either a Baptist or a Disciple.

Freewill Baptist-Disciple differences are covered fairly and in detail by E. Gates, pp. 107–21. See also Conwell, pp. 88–89.

Conwell, who had his information from the Boyntons, mentions (p. 89) "little acts of discourtesy, in refusing to speak when accosted, in shunning companionship . . . in favoritism in school, and on public occasions, and sometimes in angry personal disputes." Specific instances are mentioned in Arabella Rudolph to Lucretia Rudolph, 17 May 1849; Lorinda C. Davis to Lucretia Rudolph, 8 August 1850, both in Lucretia R. Garfield Papers; and interview with Henry Boynton, New York *Times*, 25 September 1881.

Converts from Baptists are mentioned in *Diary*, 1:35 (17 February 1850); *Millennial Harbinger*, ser. 4, 2: (April 1852), 235. In the *Millennial Harbinger*, ser. 4, 2:75–76, 145ff., 276ff., 309ff., there appears a series of letters specifically directed against Baptist criticisms, by an ex-Baptist.

24. Baptist services: *Diary*, 1:37 (17, 24 March 1850), 38 (31 March), 39 (14 April), 40 (28 April), 47 (23 June), 48 (30 June). His frequent criticisms of Elder Ball (e.g., 17, 24, 31 March) may well have been in retaliation for Ball's badgering of Disciple students, noted above. JAG at Presbyterian services: *Ibid.*, 1:40 (5 May 1850), 42 (17 May). Walking to Disciple meetings: *Ibid.*, 1:40 (21 April), 42 (26 May).

25. Shaw, pp. 85, 126; Fuller, p. 13. *Diary*, 1:44 (1 June 1850).

26. *Diary*, 1:44 (1–2 June), 45 (8–10 June).

27. *Ibid*, 1:41 (9 May), 46 (14–15 June), 39 (18 April), 40 (25 April), 42 (17 May), 45 (7 June), 47 (25 June). The Teale family appears in the 1850 manuscript U.S. Census of Orange.

28. Conwell, p. 84.

29. A list of all the commencement speakers, copied from the program, is in *Diary*, 1:49–50, under the date of 2 July. For the quote, see *Ibid.*, 1:47 (25 June).

30. *Ibid.*, 1:47 (25 June), 48 (26, 27 June).

31. On the group, see *ibid.*, 1:38 (1 April), 47 (25 June), 48 (1 July), and *Annals*, 35:195. Chase, pp. 173–76, describes the repertory of the Hutchinson Family, of whom the Spencers were apparently a successful copy; the comment in Fuller, p. 57, about the "trivial character" of the Spencers' pieces suggests that their repertory was the same as that of the Hutchinsons.

A thorough search of the literature of American music has so far failed to unearth the melo-pean, at least not under that name. It is reasonably certain, however, that it was a portable reed organ or melodeon. For one thing, the Hutchinson Family, whom the Spencers imitated, used a reed organ (Brink, p. 41). For another, the instrument had been improved and had gained wide popularity as recently as 1848 (F. O. Jones, pp. 123–124); this popularity is consistent with the frequency with which it appears in JAG's diary for these years. "Melo-pean" may have been the trade name used by some manufacturer whose instruments were sold mainly in the Reserve.

For the quote from JAG, *Diary*, 1:47 (25 June).

32. *Ibid.*, 1:48 (1 July), 48–50 (2 July); Hodge, 1:124. The detail of the silver pitcher is from Tourgée's description (p. 63) of a summer exhibition at Kingsville Academy.

Chapter 14. Disputations

1. *Diary*, 1:50 (2 July 1850); Champion Library: Royal Taylor to Aristarchus Champion, 13 April 1849, Taylor-Champion Letters.

2. *Diary*, 1:50 (3–4 July); *American Phrenological Journal*, 12: (1850), 387. Two months later, JAG was reading a copy of Sizer's *Thoughts on Domestic Life* (*Diary*, 1:58); if it was his own copy, he may have purchased it here. Lecturers generally sold books in connection with their lectures; for an example, see *ibid.*, 1:96 (3 October 1851); probably also 1:86–87 (26 June 1851).

3. On levels of skill in carpentry, the comment of Van Wagenen (p. 112) is relevant: "The man who hewed the posts and beams with ax and broadax, nailed on the siding, shingled the roof, and, in general, did the rougher work on a house and barn, was content to be regarded as a carpenter. The man who built the interior furnishings, the paneled doors, window sashes, stairs, and railing, and who molded the wainscoting and made the fanlights, these men preferred the status of joiner." JAG had already achieved carpenter status, in this terminology; now he was trying to move up to joiner.

4. *Ibid.*, 1:51–53, *passim*. Congdon, p. 27; Wheeler, "Building," p. 37.

5. *Ibid.*, 1:51 (7 July 1850), 52 (21 July).

6. *Diary*, 1:53 (8 August), 58 (21 September), 59 (23 September); JAG to Thomas and Eliza Garfield, 22 August 1850, JAG Papers, LC.

7. *Diary*, 1:54 (16, 17 19–21 August); Wickham, 1:489. JAG to Thomas and Eliza Garfield, 22 August 1850, JAG Papers, LC.

8. *Diary*, 1:52 (28 July), 53 (11 August).

9. Shaw, pp. 66–68; *Diary*, 1:53 (11 August), 54 (18 August), 58 (22 September), 62–63 (13 October).

10. *Diary*, 1:55 (27 August), 60 (2 October).

11. *Ibid.*, 1:55–56 (25 August, 31 August, 1 September).

12. *Ibid.*, 1:59 (3 September).

13. *Ibid.*, 1:51 (6 July).

14. Throughout the period covered by this account—that is, up to 1852—JAG's

attitude toward politics was consistently hostile and distant: cf. the comments in *Diary*, 1:72 (28 February 1851), 149 (17 August 1852), and 159 (2 November 1852). But a later diary entry (1:328—14 April 1858) suggests that as early as 1851 a legal or political career had been a possibility to him. ("The law and the ministry encompass me on either hand. Politics and literature also. I would gladly allow the past seven years to be expunged, could I try life over again.") If this is indeed the case, then it is likely that his contemptuous comments were meant at least partly as admonitions to himself.

15. Nevins, 1:286–343.

16. *Diary*, 1:51 (9, 10, 14 July 1850).

17. *Ibid.*, 1:57 (5, 6 September); Harrell, p. 54.

18. The Miller family appears in the 1850 U.S. Census manuscript of Chester. That young Miller's father was Elder Miller is my deduction, based mainly on the controversy described in *Diary*, 1:63 (14, 18 October), in which Elder Miller served on a committee that awarded John Miller a prize for oratory. Young Miller's personality can be glimpsed in a rather smart-alecky teacher's report he wrote for Bainbridge School District 10 in February 1854; it is in the Bainbridge Town Records, WRHS.

19. *Diary*, 1:57–58 (7–13 September 1850), 61 (2, 6, October).

20. *Ibid.*, 1:60 (29, 30 September 1850); Shaw, p. 141; N. Baxter, pp. 93–109.

21. Alexander, p. 226; *Annals*, 33:463; Henry L. Burnett to O. J. Hodge, 14 September 1850, Hodge Papers.

22. JAG's notes on the 9 October exercises are among the fragments in the JAG Papers, LC. The manuscript is not dated, but the date is easily established by comparison with the *Diary* for the same date (1:62).

In passing, it is worth noting that these declamations were not exactly schoolboy exercises. Of the male participants whose ages can be determined from the U.S. Census manuscript, most were of what we would call college age or older. JAG, at eighteen, was the second youngest of those who spoke on 9 October.

23. *Diary*, 1:54 (16 August 1850), 62 (11, 13 October), 63 (14, 15, 20 October).

24. JAG to Thomas and Eliza Garfield, 22 August 1850, JAG Papers, LC. *Diary*, 1:61 (5 October). One person in particular who may have helped with the Warrensville job was Solyman Hubbell; see the following chapter.

25. *Diary*, 1:63 (18, 21 October). Though JAG won the Latin prize, he showed no desire to monopolize the honor; he arranged for his friend E. S. Gilbert to share it with him.

26. *Ibid.*, 1:63 (20, 23 October), 251–52 (25 June 1854).

Chapter 15. Marking Time

1. *Diary*, 1:64 (28 October–2 November).

2. *Ibid.*, 1:61 (5 October).

3. *Ibid.*, 1:64 (11 November); Wickham, 1:100. I have not found a description of Warrensville Center at this time; my sketch is based on the information in the manuscript U.S. Census of 1850.

4. *Diary*, 1:64–65 (11–16, 18, 21 November 1850), 71 (21 February 1851).

Ibid., 1:20 (11 February 1951), gives a sample of the sort of problems he experienced. A later entry in *Ibid.*, 3:153 (28 September 1875), refers to a "sort of revolt among the large girls that winter," which he had to quell by threatening to flog the girls. This could very well correspond with the entry of 14 January 1851 (1:69), "Sent for 7 whips." As Brown and Williams point out, however, it is not entirely clear whether this incident should be assigned to this winter or the one following.

Ibid., 1:66 (10–11 December 1850).

5. The date for the first settlement in Warrensville is given as 1810; the founding of the first school was in 1815. For Solon the corresponding dates are ten years later—1820 and 1825. (Johnson, pp. 516, 517, 532). The different population densities of the two townships in this period reflect Warrensville's head start—it always contained about 400 more inhabitants than Solon. In 1850 Warrensville had fifty-six inhabitants per square mile; Solon had forty-one.

6. Piercy, p. 100; *Early Settlers*, 1:4, 31–33; *Diary*, 1:65 (26 November 1850). "Kaighan" was JAG's spelling, but the boy was almost certainly the "John Caine" listed in the U.S. Census manuscript, seventeen years old when the census was taken on 14 September 1850, born in Ohio to parents who were both natives of the Isle of Man.

7. *Diary*, 1:66 (11, 12, 13 December 1850).

8. This story does not appear in the *Diary*; it is given by Gilmore, *Life*, p. 8. Gilmore assigns it to JAG's years at Geauga Seminary, but a later biographer, the fictionalized and generally untrustworthy Thayer (pp. 267–68), includes it among the events of JAG's first winter in Warrensville. Oddly, it appears that in this instance Thayer is correct. There was no Stiles family in Chester; on the other hand, JAG boarded repeatedly in the Stiles home in Warrensville (*Diary*, 1:65, 69). In Gilmore, the story is attributed, by inference, to the sheriff of Ashtabula County; this turns out to have been Asa Stiles, presumably the same Asa Stiles who appears in the 1850 manuscript census of Warrensville, with his sisters, Persis and Martha. The fact that it appears in both Gilmore and Thayer suggests that the two got it from some common source, probably a newspaper story; but I have been unable to find this source.

Selling rifle: *Diary*, 1:64 (6 November 1850). Buying clothes: *Ibid.*, 1:67 (17 December).

9. Spelling schools: *Ibid.*, 1:68 (8 January 1851), 69 (22 January), 70 (4 February). Other teachers: *Ibid.*, 1:68 (4 January), 69 (18, 25 January), 70 (8 February).

10. *Ibid.*, 1:66 (14 December 1850), 67 (21 December), 68 (4 January 1851), 69 (18, 24, 25 January 1851), 70–71 (15 February); Philomathean Society Record Book, 25 January 1851. Dr. W. J. B. Darwin is in the U.S. Census manuscript, 1850.

11. *Diary*, 1:69 (12, 26 January); Piercy, pp. 163–64, and *passim*.

12. *Diary*, 1:65 (20 November 1850), 66 (15 December), 67 (21, 29 December), 68 (1, 5, January 1851), 70 (2, 9 February), 86 (14 June). A later comment by JAG, after some years of misunderstanding between himself and the Hubbells, shows that the esteem was mutual, probably from the first: "I should be very much pleased to have a long visit with Brother Solyman. I think he is one of the best of men." (to Phebe Boynton, 1 July 1855, JAG Papers, LC.) The 1850 census taker put Hubbell's name down as "Lyon"; hence my conjecture about the way it was pronounced. On the Hubbell family, see Hubbell, pp. 219, 247; Hayden, p. 472, and U.S. Census manuscript, 1850. Chester Button, tavernkeeper, appears next to the Hubbell family in the 1850 U.S. Census manuscript. JAG to Mary Hubbell, [24 July 1852?], JAG Papers, LC, suggests that Button often sent or received letters for the Hubbells.

13. *Diary*, 1:67 (31 December 1850) records the sending of the poem; a note among the fragments in the JAG Papers identifies it as "The Stilling of the Tempest." The poem itself is in still another part of the JAG Papers, LC.

14. *Diary*, 1:71 (24 February 1851).

15. Green, *Hiram*, pp. 7–18, 24; Lorinda C. Davis to Lucretia Rudolph, 14 January 1850, Lucretia R. Garfield Papers.

16. Green, *Hiram*, p. 74.

17. JAG to Thomas and Eliza Garfield, 22 August 1850, JAG Papers, LC.

18. *Diary*, 1:71 (21 February, 24–26).

Chapter 16. Outlandish Customs

1. Johnson, p. 78; Thom, pp. 109–10 and *passim*.
2. Rose, p. 219.
3. Lucretia Rudolph Diary, 6 September 1851, Lucretia R. Garfield Papers, LC; Busch, p. 24; Alvarez, p. 173. For a sampling of other vivid reactions, see *ibid.*, pp. 30–32.
4. Rose, p. 236; Hornung, pp. 99–107. Each engine on the C., C. & C. had a name—see Thom, p. 112. The Garfields may well have checked most of their luggage to Columbus. The checking system, which worked very well, is described in Alvarez, pp. 121–22.

Impressions of the whistle were evidently subjective: the Pulszkys' train had a shrill whistle (p. 101), but Busch's train, on the same line, did not whistle, but roared (p. 24).

Times of arrival and departure are from *Diary*, 1:71–72 (27 February 1851). The *American Railway Guide*, issued later the same year, does not show this train—only an express leaving Cleveland at 8:30 A.M. and arriving in Columbus at 4:00 P.M. Or perhaps this train was the express, but it left late and had trouble en route.

5. Chambers, p. 161; Pulszky, p. 101; Busch, p. 24; Alvarez, pp. 52–53, 67; *Diary*, 1:71 (27 February 1852).
6. *Diary*, 1:72 (27 February); Alvarez, pp. 60–62; Water for passengers: Thom, p. 113; Chambers, p. 161; *Ohio Railroad Guide*, pp. 64–83.
7. Alvarez, pp. 122–25, suggests that the typical arrangement was for passengers to grab hurried meals at small roadside eating places, and Thom, p. 113, confirms that such places existed later on the C., C. & C. No such place is mentioned in the *Diary*, however, and it seems unlikely that many would have existed only a week after completion of the line; so I conjecture that the passengers had to look after their own meals.
8. Alvarez, pp. 36, 39; Thom, pp. 112–13.
9. Weisenburger, pp. 21–22, 24; Howe, p. 171; Busch, p. 24; Jordan, p. 126; Dickens, p. 221; *Diary*, 1:72 (27 February 1852).
10. According to the Twenty-seventh Report of the Prison Discipline Society of Boston, printed in 1852, the prison earned $2,466 from visitors in fiscal 1851, and had a special guard to show visitors around (pp. 746, 753). One can infer from these facts that JAG probably toured the prison as part of a group, though the *Diary* does not say so.
11. There is a fairly full description of the State Penitentiary in *Diary*, 1:72 (February 28). I also used Howe, pp. 174–75, and O. Lewis, p. 162. I have not actually seen striped clothing referred to, but O. Lewis, pp. 58, 208, shows that the use of striped uniforms in some color combination, not necessarily black and white, had become the practice in many states by 1850. Ohio, I am assuming, had kept up with other states in this regard.

Rothman, p. 100, suggests that the "silent system" was not working by 1851 as well as Howe implies. The *Diary* contains nothing to either confirm or deny this statement.

12. Jordan, pp. 125–26, *Diary*, 1:72 (28 February 1851); *Prison Discipline Society Report*, p. 745. Gamaliel Kent: Riddle, *Life*, p. 39; Brisbin, pp. 68–69. Kent was an early settler of Bainbridge (*Pioneer and General History*, p. 129) and a leading Disciple (Hayden, p. 440).
13. Jordan, pp. 92, 184–85; Hulbert, pp. 461, 463.
14. Hulbert, p. 437; Jordan, pp. 91, 100–102, 124; Shippee, p. 149. JAG (*Diary*, 1:83, 25 May 1851) had praise for the section of road east of Zanesville.

15. Jordan, pp. 125, 188, 195, 198, 201, 257, 266. JAG called his trip "a tiresome and dreary rumble." (*Diary*, 1:72, 28 February 1851)

16. The rail fare is from *American Railway Guide*, p. 50. The stage fare is approximate. Dunbar, p. 595, reproduces a table showing the fare from Columbus to Wheeling in 1848 as eight dollars. From Jordan, p. 185, it appears that the fare between Columbus and Zanesville was about half of that from Columbus to Wheeling, or maybe a trifle less. A fare of $3.50 or $4.00 seems about right.

17. Shippee, p. 149; *Ohio Guide*, pp. 350–51; Jordan, pp. 121–22; *Diary*, 1:72 (28 February 1851).

18. When JAG and Eliza returned through Zanesville at the end of May, they stayed not at the Eagle but at the Buckeye Boarding House, of which JAG commented: "Good cheap fare. It is much better to go to these cheap boarding houses than to go to the City Hotels, where you pay double price for a little more formality." (*Diary*, 1:83 (29 May 1851) I assume that the implied comparison was with the Eagle.

19. *Ibid.*, 1:73 (1 March).

20. *Ibid.*, 1:73 (7, 10 March), 74 (14 March), 75 (25, 27, 29 March), 76 (30 March, 7 April), 78 (20 April), 79 (22, 26, April, 1, 3 May).

21. *Ohio Guide*, pp. 543, 545; *Diary*, 1:75 (29 March 1851), 76 (5 April).

22. *Ohio Guide*, p. 546; *Diary*, 1:78 (17 April), 80 (5 May).

23. *Diary*, 1:73 (5 March).

24. JAG to Harriet, Phebe, and Cordelia Boynton, 30 March 1851, JAG Papers, LC. In general, it seems true to say that JAG was frightened by anything remotely suggestive of sexual contact with women. Some of this inhibition was no doubt due to his concept of how a respectable, Christian young man ought to behave, some to his upbringing in a reserved, unsocial environment, and some to personal experiences and fears. Ever after giving due weight to the first two, a comparison with the letters of O. J. Hodge's friends, for instance, suggests that the third factor was probably the most influential.

25. *Diary*, 1:81 (18 May).

26. *Ibid.*, 1:77 (13 April).

27. The Ballous' religion is not explicitly stated in the Diary or any other source I have seen, but it is clear, to begin with, that they were not Disciples. JAG had been in Muskingum County eight weeks before he found a Disciple, one Brother Morrison, "an advocate of truth, standing alone" as he put it (*ibid.*, 1:79, 25 April), with whom he attended a small, struggling Disciple meeting twelve miles away on Poplar Ridge (*ibid.*, 1:81, 11 May). His interest in Morrison was so intense as to make it clear that this was the first Disciple he had encountered.

The Ballous went to "meeting," in JAG's terminology, at Blue Rock, or occasionally at Virginia Ridge (*ibid.*, 1:73, 74, 2, 23 March). (The Virginia Ridge meeting was clearly not a Disciple meeting; JAG called it a quarterly meeting, which suggests Methodist practice.) Often they did not go to church at all (*ibid.*, 1:74, 79, 80, 16 March, 26 April, 4 May), which bothered JAG slightly.

The clearest expression of his feelings, however, came in his letter to Harriet, Phebe, and Cordelia Boynton, 30 March 1851 (JAG Papers, LC): "I am sure that I never appreciated the privilege which I enjoyed in meeting the brethren and sisters around the Lord's table—and having the drooping and way-worn spirit refreshed by reading from the word of God, and singing praises to his holy name. But though here and surrounded by 'Sectarianism' I can hold sweet communion with my Maker—and learn to do his holy will."

28. *Diary*, 1:74ff. (13 March–20 May 1851); 4:121 (20 September 1878).

29. JAG to Harriet, Phebe, and Cordelia Boynton, 30 March 1851, JAG Papers, LC; Brisbin, p. 69; *Diary*, 1:78 (16 April 1851).

30. To a large extent, JAG's comments cited here tell their own story, but one might add the words that the Western Reserve novelist Albert G. Riddle put into the mouth of his hero in *Bart Ridgely*, p. 32: "The moment you step across the south line of the Reserve you step into a foreign country, and among a foreign people, who speak a foreign language. . . ."

31. *Diary*, 1:74 (20 March 1851), 76 (4 April), 83 (26 May). In the case of the math problem, however, JAG's assumption of superiority was unwarranted. The problem as he stated it in the diary is in fact insoluble; he either copied it down wrong or was not smart enough to realize that nine-eighths and seven-eighths are not reciprocal.

32. The page references for the dates cited in the text are *ibid.*, 1:74, 76, 79. End of school: *ibid.*, 1:82 (19, 20 May).

33. *Ibid.*, 1:83–84 (27 May–3 June).

34. This is a deduction, but it seems to me a legitimate one, from the diary entry of 4 June (1:85). "Bullying" was JAG's own word for the Garfields; see JAG to Thomas and Eliza Garfield, 16 April 1853, JAG Papers, LC. On Solomon Garfield, see Bundy, p. 5, who, however, calls Solomon JAG's grandfather. Brisbin, p. 27, has the relationship right. On Abram Garfield: Brisbin, p. 51. For other instances of Abram Garfield's strength, see Bundy, p. 5, and Conwell, p. 40. On the other hand, a good example of the Ballous is Eliza's description of her father, James the astrologer, summarized in Leech and Brown, p. 8.

35. *Diary*, 1:84 (4 June 1851).

Chapter 17. Reaching Out

1. JAG's own detailed account of this spirit-rapping session is in *Diary*, 1:84–85 (4 June 1851). All details come from this source unless otherwise specified. The procedures followed seem to have been exactly similar to those described in Fornell, pp. 21, 25.

2. Fornell, pp. 11–19, 20–25. On the appeal of the movement, Cross, pp. 348–49, is excellent. For Leah Fish, see Fornell, pp. 18, 29.

3. Dunham House: Chapman, p. 56; Ryder, p. 138. This is not to be confused with another Cleveland landmark, the Dunham Tavern.

4. See, for instance, articles in Cleveland *Plain Dealer*, 11 October 1848, 20 June 1849. Cf. Greene, pp. 124–25.

5. Cross, p. 342; Podmore, pp. 287, 290; Fornell, p. 33; Blakeslee, p. 48.

6. *Diary*, 1:147 (24 July 1852); JAG to Corydon E. Fuller, 16 January 1852, in Fuller, p. 43; Podmore, p. 163.

7. Fornell, p. 20; Hardinge, p. 296.

8. Hardinge, p. 296.

9. Blakeslee, pp. 46, 48; Tyler, p. 83, *Diary*, 1:85 (4 June 1851).

10. *Ibid.*, 1:85 (10 June), 86 (12 June).

11. Woodward's reminiscences, quoted in Fuller, p. 4; *Diary*, 1:86 (16–23 June 1851).

12. *Diary*, 1:86 (22 June 1851), 89 (3 August), 88 (20 July). Bloomer incident: *Ibid.*, 1:88 (27 July).

13. The importance of death was well expressed in a letter from Eliza Garfield to JAG, 26 November 1853 (JAG Papers, LC): ". . . we are passing away may we live in a daily preparation to meet the Monster Death with a smile, let me die the death of the Righteous. . . ." See the excellent discussion of the "death cult" in Wallace, pp. 430–36, and for an example, Abi McIntosh to "Dear Sister," 9 June 1833, Elizabeth Bigelow letters, OHS.

14. Nathan Robinson: *Diary*, 1:89 (31 July 1851); Cotton Harper: *Ibid.*, 1:85 (6 June). For examples of watching with the dead from the Reserve, see Riddle, *Bart Ridgeley*, p. 164; entry of 12 September 1854, William Boynton journal, Henry B. Boynton Papers, WRHS. Edwin Mapes's brother: *Diary*, 1:120–21 (14 March 1852). Mr. Paddock: *Ibid.*, 1:89 (6 August 1851). Farmer Parkman: *Ibid.*, 1:88 (9 July).

15. *Ibid.*, 1:86–88 (24 June to 12 July). Design: Shaw, pp. 25–26.

16. Scoring and hewing: There is no one accepted account of how these were done; compare Needham and Mussey, pp. 96–99; Sloane, *Museum*, pp. 16–17; and Congdon, p. 23. Where these versions differ, I have followed Needham, whose first-hand testimony seems most convincing.

Staple-dogs: Sloane, *Diary*, pp. 62–63.

Uriah Smith: *Diary*, 1:86 (24 June 1851); entry of 19 October 1850, Philomathean Society Record Book, WRHS.

17. Hutslar, p. 236; Sloane, *Museum*, pp. 52, 76; Adkins, pp. 24–25; Frary, p. 231; Needham and Mussey, pp. 101–102; Congdon, p. 23; Sloane, Diary, pp. 18–19.

18. Woodward's reminiscences, in Fuller, p. 5.

19. *Diary*, 1:87 (4 July), 88 (27 July 1851).

20. Western Reserve Eclectic Institute Catalogue, 1851, p. 20; Fuller, p. 27; Hinsdale, *Garfield*, pp. 15–16; Green, Hiram, pp. 21–22. "[L]ike the temple": Western Reserve Eclectic Institute catalogue, 1850, p. 13.

21. Osgood, p. 3; Green, *Hiram*, pp. 47–48, 55–56; Rudolph, pp. 2–3; *Diary*, 1:87 (5–6 July 1851).

22. Sloane, *Museum*, p. 85, *Diary*, 1:87–90 (1 July–20 August 1851).

23. *Diary*, 1:87 (1 July), 89 (7–8 August); Wheeler, "Building," pp. 35–36.

24. Congdon, pp. 45, 55; Benjamin, pp. 19–20, plate 21, pp. 46–47; Frary, pp. 132, 232, 254–58; Sloane, *Museum*, pp. 58–59. "Litigating disputed points": *Diary*, 1:89 (1 August 1851).

25. *Ibid.*, 1:87 (1 July), 88 (11, 16 July). Of course, if one accepts the thesis that JAG as a young man had more or less conscious homosexual inclinations, it is not difficult to divine another reason why he enjoyed these communal showers after work.

26. The attitude, a commonplace at the time, is visible in the *Diary* entry for 1 July 1851 (1:87); Cf. Fowler, pp. 51–52, and *Diary*, 1:91 (30 August 1851).

27. *Diary*, 1:94 (17 September), 86–87 (26 June), 89 (15 August).

28. The brief entry in *ibid.*, 1:89, under 21 June, which suggests that he lost the money on a visit to Cleveland, seems to have been displaced one day if compared with Woodward's reminiscences in Fuller, p. 5. Woodward's story makes much better sense than the *Diary* version. That Dr. Bliss was on the spot and found the money is quite plausible if it was lost on a country road near the Falls; if it was lost in downtown Cleveland, this set of events is almost phenomenal. JAG probably added the brief mention of the incident to his diary some time after it happened and carelessly assigned it to the wrong day.

The words "went on his way" are Woodward's; I have supplied the Scriptural reference.

Chapter 18. The Education of a Disciple

1. Osgood, pp. 2–2; Western Reserve Eclectic Institute Catalogue (1851), p. 20; Ms. Lecture, Fuller Papers, pp. 2–3; Fuller, p. 25; Green, *Hiram*, p. 20.

2. *Diary*, 1:90 (23 August 1851). Women's dresses: Welker, pp. 38–39; *Early Settlers*, 6:1, 53; Marinda Raymond to Corda Starks and Lucretia Rudolph, 14

October 1849; photographs in Henry B. Boynton Papers, WRHS.

3. *Diary*, 1:91 (25 August 1851).

4. Many sources contain descriptions of Hiram, the college and the village. To name only three, there are Green, *Hiram*, pp. 21–22, 393; Davis, *Hinsdale*, p. 25; and manuscript lecture, Fuller Papers, pp. 1–2.

5. On Hayden, see Green, *Hiram*, pp. 31–32; Leech and Brown, p. 31; and Fuller, pp. 194, 217. For JAG's later estimate of him, cf. *Diary*, 3:460 (18 March 1877). On Rudolph: Fuller, p. 55; Green, *Hiram*, p. 56.

6. *Diary*, 1:91 (25 August 1851). Unless otherwise noted, all details in this account of JAG's first day are from this rather long entry.

7. Western Reserve Eclectic Institute catalogue (1850), p. 13. The "red benches" mentioned in Hinsdale, *Life*, p. 391, were probably the same as the three-legged cherrywood desks in Green, *Hiram*, p. 394.

8. Green, *Hiram*, pp. 28–30; *Diary*, 1:91 (27 August 1851).

9. G. L. Applegate to JAG, 10 June 1880, JAG Papers.

10. Bundy, p. 23.

11. Green, *Hiram*, pp. 34, 36, 37; *Diary*, 1:91 (26–27 August 1851).

12. *Diary*, 1:91 (29 August); Fuller, pp. 28–29, 33–34; Green, *Hiram*, p. 394. As Fuller points out, there was one major difference between Hayden's chapel lectures and the ones at Geauga Seminary—Hayden carefully avoided doctrinal points so as not to offend non-Disciple students, of whom there were several.

13. Entry of 1 September 1851, Lucretia Rudolph diary, Lucretia R. Garfield Papers.

14. *Diary*, 1:95–96 (30 September–3 October 1851). Cf. *Annals*, 34:365.

15. *Diary*, 1:97 (9 October), 98 (10, 13, 16 October), 99 (21 October), 101 (5 November). Munnell himself recalled (Green, *Hiram*, p. 35) the impressiveness of JAG's performance.

Progress in Greek: *Diary*, 1:98 (10 October), 99 (21 October). Geometry: *Ibid.*, 1:98 (13 October). Until he came to Hiram, JAG had never seen a geometry text (Bundy, p. 26).

16. *Diary*, 1:94 (18 September); H. D. Gates, p. 84; Grafton, pp. 179, 182, 184, and portrait in frontispiece. Campbell's lecture: *Diary*, 1:92 (2 September); Fuller, p. 35; entry of 2 September 1851, in Lucretia Rudolph diary, Lucretia R. Garfield Papers.

17. *Diary*, 1:97 (6 October), 99 (20 October), 100 (28 October), 101 (6 November).

18. *Ibid.*, 1:93–94 (15 September), 97 (4, 8 October).

19. *Ibid.*, 1:91 (30 August), 95 (27 September), 101 (1 November): Fuller, p. 27, 65; Green, *Hiram*, p. 398.

20. *Diary*, 1:92–93 (6, 7 September), 93 (13 September 1851), 95 (20 September), 96 (4 October), 99 (18 October), 101 (1, 8 November).

21. *Ibid.*, 1:95 (20, 23 September), 99 (18 October), 100 (25 October).

22. *Ibid.*, 1:94 (16 September).

23. *Ibid.*, 1:93 (8 September), 98 (10 October), 100 (27 October).

24. JAG's anguish over the lack of a father can be seen in *ibid.*, 1:246 (23 June 1854); JAG to Mary G. Larabee and Eliza B. Garfield, 2 April 1854, JAG Papers; and JAG to Harry Rhodes, 19 November 1862, quoted in Williams, *Wild Life*, p. 181. In speaking of his loss, he often described himself as an "orphan," e.g. *Diary*, 1:246 (23 June 1854); the usage sounds strange to twentieth-century ears, but is in fact accurate. "Orphan" meant originally deprived of any important person in one's life, mother, father, or even child; as a secondary meaning, this survives in present-day dictionaries.

25. Green, *Hiram*, pp. 60, 395. Fuller, p. 35, refers to two debating societies; he was probably thinking of the separate Ladies' Literary Association (entry of 4 September 1851, Lucretia Rudolph diary, Lucretia R. Garfield Papers). On JAG's participation, *Diary*, 1: 93 (12 September), 94 (18 September 1851), 95 (26 September). Cf. *Ibid.*, p. 99 (17, 24 October).

26. Almeda Booth to Burke Hinsdale, 8 May [?], reproduced in Hinsdale, *Life*, opposite p. 30; *Diary*, 1:94 (18 September 1851), 95 (23 September), 107 (5 December) and note.

27. Manuscript lecture, Fuller Papers, pp. 10–13. This incident is not narrated in the *Diary*, which is not surprising, as JAG was usually modest in assessing his debating prowess. It may correspond, however, to the entry of 19 September (*Diary*, 1:94–95), in which he records that he was on the winning side in a debate before a "house full."

28. Fuller, pp. 11–12, 15, 21–22, 35–36; JAG to Thomas Garfield and Eliza B. Garfield, 16 April 1853, JAG Papers; Fuller to Lucretia Rudolph, 7 April 1853, Corintha Carlton to Lucretia Rudolph, 15 November 1853, Lucretia R. Garfield Papers.

29. *Diary*, 1:99–100 (25 October 1851); Dean, No. 3, p. 9; No. 4, p. 11; Green, *Hiram*, p. 393; Fuller, pp. 26, 80–83. The storekeeper mentioned as "Meeker" in Fuller's book may be the same as Dean's "Bennett." Nathan C. Meeker, who did keep a store in Hiram briefly, is unlikely to have sold liquor under the counter. He was an ardent reformer, whose career, curiously enough, is sketched in the *Dictionary of American Biography*.

30. *Diary*, 1:99 (20 October 1851).

31. *Ibid.*, 1:100 (28 October), 102 (11 November); JAG to Mary Hubbell, 18 June 1852, JAG Papers.

32. *Diary*, 1:101 (8 November 1851). The two girls are not named, but JAG's comment "Tener" (tender) strongly suggests that Mary was one of them.

33. *Ibid.*, 1:102 (10 November). A copy of the speech is in Fuller, pp. 36–38.

34. *Diary*, 1:102 (14, 15 November), 105 (25 November).

35. *Ibid.*, 1:103 (19 November), 104 (21–22 November), 105 (24 November).

36. *Ibid.*, 1:102 (15–17 November), 103–104 (19 November).

Chapter 19. Mary

1. *Annals*, 35:475; *Diary*, 1:100 (26–27 October 1851), 105 (27 November), 114 (12, 19, 20 January 1852), cf. 1:109 (15 December 1851).

2. *Diary*, 1:109 (18 December 1851), 115 (28 January), 118 (21 February).

3. *Ibid.*, 1:114 (14 January 1852); Fowler, p. 11; JAG to Corydon Fuller, 14 February 1852, in Fuller, p. 46.

4. *Diary*, 1:106 (3 December 1851). Teaching geometry: Brisbin, p. 68, as corrected by Fuller, p. 125. Number of subjects: *Diary*, 1:112 (2 Janury 1852), 117–18 (21 February).

5. *Diary*, 1:113 (7, 9 January), 115 (26, 29 January), 116 (4 February); JAG to Corydon Fuller, 14 February 1852, in Fuller, p. 46.

6. Fuller, p. 46, *Diary*, 1:106 (28 November 1851), 110 (30 December), 116 (2 February 1852).

7. *Diary*, 1:113 (8 January 1852); Fuller, p. 43.

8. *Diary*, 1:108 (7 December 1851), 109 (20 December 1851), 110 (21 December), 112 (1 January 1852) 114 (17 January 1852), 117 (14 February).

9. *Ibid.*, 1:107 (6 December 1851), 116 (8 February 1852).

10. "Chosen one" is an expression from Howells, p. 90. Other such indirect expressions are in Albert Perry to O. J. Hodge, 15 August 1850 ("Amour" and "goddess") and Orrin E. Aldrich to Hodge, 4 May 1850 ("center of attraction"), both in Hodge Papers. Fuller, p. 50, uses the phrase "lady friends," but there he is referring to all friends who were girls, not those who were in a special romantic relationship with a young man. See also Flexner, p. 104.

Banter of friends: Fuller, in a letter written before 5 December, referred to Mary as JAG's "attentive student." (Fuller, p. 40).

11. JAG to Mary Hubbell, 25 April 1852, JAG Papers; *Diary*, 1:117 (13 February 1852); A. B. Gunnison to O. J. Hodge, 17 February 1850, Hodge Papers; Abbie [?] to Lucretia Rudolph, 23 January 1849, Lucretia R. Garfield Papers.

12. *Diary*, 1:108 (9 December 1851), 109 (11 December). An album quilt was a quilt made to be presented to a person; generally each piece bore the name or initials of a friend.

13. *Ibid.*, 1:109 (11 December); the transcription in the printed *Diary* has been corrected by reference to the manuscript in the JAG Papers.

14. *Ibid.*, 1:110 (22 to 24 December); Buley, 1:274. On homeopathy in Ohio, see the articles by White and Hertzog.

15. *Diary*, 1:110.

16. *Ibid.*, 1:110 (26–29 December).

17. *Ibid.*, 114 (14 January 1852), 116 (5, 10 February), 117 (17 February).

18. Although there is no definitive history of romantic and sexual mores in the Reserve, enough evidence exists to make it possible to generalize about what young men and young women did when they were alone together.

According to Albert G. Riddle, a qualified witness by virtue of his years of law practice in the Reserve and his obvious interest in sexual behavior, "strict sexual purity" was the rule in the Reserve ("55 Years," pp. 190–94). There were, he admits, exceptions to the rule, and he goes on to discuss some of the more spectacular cases of fornication and bastardy in his experience—always, however, with the implication that they happened among people of little or no social standing. (And cf. Henry, p. 45).

This picture matches the one derivable from the letters of young people of the Reserve in the forties and early fifties. Out-of-wedlock pregnancies were not uncommon and were freely discussed (Abbie [?] to Lucretia Rudolph, 23 January 1849, Lucretia R. Garfield Papers; Z. W. Shadduck to O. J. Hodge, 13 October 1849, Hodge Papers), but generally in a disapproving or ironic, not a sympathetic, tone. The impression one gets is substantially that expressed by a friend of John Hodge: "I don't think your fears about my ruining myself after the girls is [*sic*] well founded the girls around here are perfect virgins." (A. B. Gunnison to Hodge, 15 February 1849, Hodge Papers). Sexual intercourse, then, one can say, was probably very rare between respectable young people.

Other kinds of physical contact my have been more acceptable. In a story of Riddle's, a young man puts his arm around a girl of slightly lower social standing and tries to draw her to him, with the clear implication that he intends to proceed to more advanced lovemaking. She resists. "All girls permit that," the man says. (Riddle, *Ross*, pp. 394–95). Clearly, all girls did not, but one can fairly infer from his saying so that some girls did. With regard to kissing, the situation was similar. Riddle recalls ("55 Years," pp. 180–81) that a highly respectable Painesville woman had claimed before marriage that "she could kiss better and more to the satisfaction of a young man, than any girl present." Thus it appears that some forms of physical contact, holding hands, embracing, and even kissing, were permitted by some girls—as ends in themselves, of course, not as foreplay. Once a couple was understood to be engaged, such intimacies were almost encouraged by the parents, who encouraged the young people to spend time together alone (Riddle, *Ross*, p. 165).

With regard to James and Mary, then, they were operating within a customary framework which, at one extreme, permitted some physical expression of love. Most likely, however, James avoided physical contact; for one thing, he was leery of sexual intimacy with women, for another, he was anxious not to compromise his struggle for respectability by any questionable behavior.

19. *Diary*, 1:118 (23 February 1852), 120 (13 March).

20. *Ibid.*, 1:117 (13 February).

21. Howells, p. 90; Abbie [?] to Lucretia Rudolph, 23 January 1849, Lucretia R. Garfield Papers.

22. On correspondence in courtship, see *Diary*, 1:212 (28 July 1853); for examples of courtships broken off for religious reasons, see Hodge, 1:125, and I. B. Curtis to JAG, 13 June, 1853, JAG Papers, LC. "Rake": *Diary*, 1:171 (22 January 1853), 180 (27 February).

23. *Ibid.*, 1:112 (1 January 1852).

24. It is necessary to document this point with some care, for it became a matter of hot controversy when, in February of 1853, JAG broke off his relationship with Mary. Her position and that of her friends was that they were engaged. JAG's position, though not entirely consistent, was that they were not and never had been.

Two utterances of JAG's seem to say that he and Mary had in fact been engaged: a diary entry of 31 December 1852 (*Diary*, 1:167, "I am inclining to the opinion that young men better not make marriage engagements much before they finish their College course, for it may be a source of much annoyance to them if they do.") and another on 25 June of the following year (*Diary*, 1:200–201, "There is, to my mind a real difficulty in the subject of marriage. It is necessary that two, before they enter into that sacred relation, should know well each other, the inner being, and the whole soul. . . and then should one of the parties retire, having found it best, he is denounced as a rake.") Both quotations imply that JAG formally intended to marry Mary, but neither actually says so.

On the other hand, on three occasions JAG specifically denied that he and Mary had made any formal agreement to marry. On 19 January 1853, he wrote Corydon Fuller, "I have never formally engaged myself to her" (Fuller, p. 73). On 27 February of the same year, when he wrote her to say that he regarded her only as a friend, he noted in his diary, "I never had an intention to deceive her, nor have I ever made a promise to her which this act will break" (*Diary*, 1:180). In this letter he made the same point: "there has been no plighted faith, nor verbal agreement between us" (JAG Papers, LC). A biographer has to respect this repeated clarity; it is evident that JAG was clear in his own mind that there had been no promise. Probably the reason for this clear recall is that he had kept a careful watch on what he said and had especially avoided giving such a promise or setting up a situation where he woud have to do so.

25. Austin, pp. 198–99.

26. *Diary*, 1:117 (21 February 1852).

27. *Ibid.*, 1:118ff. (24 February–20 March). Fuller, p. 47, gives his motive. On Dr. Harlow, see *ibid.*, pp. 47, 67, 124. A certificate from Dr. Harlow is in the Fuller Papers.

28. *Diary*, 1:118 (28 February 1852); I, 1:119 (1 March). Blakeslee's character can be inferred from his history of Chagrin Falls, cited several times in this book. Universalists: *Ibid.*, 1:118 (27 February).

29. Coffin, pp. 350–51; *Diary*, 1:118 (27 February), 119 (5, 6 March), 120 (8, 10 March), 121 (15 March); JAG to Corydon Fuller, 20 January 1852, in Fuller, p. 43.

30. *Diary*, 1:118 (25, 26 February), 119 (1–2 March), 120 (9, 11 March), 121 (15 March), 122 (17 March). One drawing done by JAG, of Younglove's Paper Mill on the Ohio Canal, in the Lucretia R. Garfield Papers, is a copy of a picture which appeared in the Cleveland *Plain Dealer*, 10 October, 1849.

31. *Diary*, 1:115 (31 January 1852); for a view by a member of Kossuth's party, see Pulszky, pp. 90–92. On the Cleveland and Pittsburgh Railway, see Johnson, p. 78; *Annals*, 34:335.

32. *Diary*, 1:120 (13 March 1852), 122 (17, 19 March); Howells, p. 76; Boynton, p. 199; A. B. Shaw, p. 305; Ryder, p. 146.

33. JAG to O. J. Hodge, 1 April 1852, Hodge Papers.

34. *Diary*, 1:113 (10 January 1852), 119–20 (7 March). The music of "The student adieu" is on a loose leaf at the end of vol. 2 of the manuscript diary, JAG Papers, LC.

35. *Diary*, 1:122 (22 March); Hubbell, p. 279.

36. *Diary*, 1:122 (23–24 March), 130 (11 May). These, the only references to bell-ringing in the Diary, are clear and unambiguous. Fuller's assertion (pp. 6, 31) that he rang the bell during his first term at Hiram is, as stated in the text, inaccurate.

A further elaboration of the bell-ringing story, which appears in Henry, p. 80, and in some of the campaign biographies, has JAG appear before the Hiram Board of Trustees and beg for a chance to put himself through school by ringing the bell and working as janitor. It conflicts with almost all other available evidence, in that 1. JAG was not employed as janitor during his first term; 2. he did not have the job alone, but shared it with Ryder; and 3. he does not appear to have been hard up for money at this time. Fuller, p. 126, scoffs at the tale as a "Munchausen story." For the bell hours, see Green, *Hiram*, p. 152.

37. Hinsdale, pp. 26–27; Fuller, p. 31.

38. *Diary*, 1:123–25 (30 March–14 April 1852). Fuller at Rudolph's: Fuller, p. 48; Account Book, Rudolph Family Miscellany, Lucretia R. Garfield Papers.

39. *Diary*, 1:122 (23 March); Brisbin, pp. 69–70; *Diary*, 1:125 (17, 19–20 April).

40. Penmanship lessons: *Ibid.*, 1:125 (13, 15 April etc.); Gilmore, p. 9. Debating: *Diary*, 1:125 (16, 23 April etc.). "I can feel": *Ibid.*, 1:126 (29 April).

41. *Ibid.*, 1:124 (10 April); JAG to Mary Hubbell, 9 April 1852, JAG Papers, LC.

42. For the five months from December 1851, to April 1852, the average length of a daily entry in the printed *Diary* is 3.8 lines. In May this figure jumps to 8.2; in June it is 7.2. For the quotes, see *Diary*, 1:128 (4 May 1852), and 127–28 (3 May).

Chapter 20. Pressure

1. By far the fullest account of JAG's debate with Treat is in Fuller, pp. 52–54, and it is on this that later biographers have relied. According to Fuller, Treat was essentially an early Robert Ingersoll, preaching skeptical agnosticism or perhaps out-and-out atheism. Fuller's recollection, however, was a thirty-odd years' distance; sources closer in time describe Treat as a lecturer on the spirit-rapping (*Diary*, 1:128 [5 May 1852], 133 [24 May]; to Mary Hubbell, 18 June 1852, JAG Papers, LC). Years later, JAG remembered Treat as "a public lecturer of Spiritualism" (*Diary*, 3:139 (2 September 1875).

What, then, exactly, was Treat speaking on? The evidence of his own later writings, together with the statements cited below that many spiritualists were ex-Christians or critics of Christianity, makes it plausible that the basic thrust of his lectures was agnostic; apparently, however, he was capitalizing on popular interest in the spirit-rappings by making them the ostensible subject of his talks.

Sizer, pp. 252–54, contains an interesting anecdote about a Joseph Treat, a writer and speaker "of a fiery, struggling talent, misdirected, and therefore antagonistic to all settled lines of thought," who was probably the same man who debated JAG. He was, according to Sizer, a young man at this time. One of his works, "A Card to the World: Rationale of Spiritual Manifestations," was distributed from Garrettsville, Ohio, only a few miles from Hiram—where, according to Kennedy, p. 90, a Joseph Treat had been pastor of the Congregational church since 1836. I assume that this was his father.

"A Card to the World," a prolix, complicated, highly rhetorical manifesto, gives an idea of the ideas Treat espoused in 1855. It is roundly atheistic, but looks for some alternative explanation of the universe. By 1855, however, Treat's ideas were changing. His tract begins: "Progression bears us all along. The writer has for years been a staunch Spiritualist, and a Spiritual medium; but he is so no longer. He now rejects the whole Spiritual theory. . . ."

It would seem, therefore, that Fuller's picture of a cocky, smooth agnostic lecturer needs to be replaced by that of a young, articulate, highly verbal and terribly confused man who was trying to sort out his own ideas even as he and JAG debated.

2. Hardinge, pp. 297–301; Fornell, p. 89; Howells, p. 79; Henry, pp. 16–17; Cherry, pp. 150–52; Welker, pp. 84–85; Wickham, 2:683. Cross's discussion of superstition and spiritualism, pp. 348–49, is again excellent.

3. Howells, p. 367; Fornell, p. 89; G. Wonsetler to O. J. Hodge, 13 August 1852, Hodge Papers.

4. Blakeslee, pp. 46–47; cf. Howells, p. 92.

5. Fornell, p. 89; Podmore, pp. 287, 290; Blakeslee, pp. 46, 48; *Millennial Harbinger*, 4th ser., 2:10, 560.

Of the dozens of possible sources, Orestes Brownson's *The Spirit Rapper* probably illustrates best the linkage between spiritualism and reform. For a vivid example of how spiritualism affected one individual life, see the story of Judson Hutchinson in Brink, p. 147ff.

6. e.g., *Diary*, 1:112 (1 January 1852).

7. Podmore, pp. 164, 217; Blakeslee, p. 47; *Diary*, 1:130 (16 May 1852), 143 (27 June); JAG to Mary Hubbell, 18 June 1852, JAG Papers, LC.

8. Quoted in Hardinge, p. 306; Howells, p. 76.

9. An account of this debate is in *Diary*, 1:128–29 (5 May 1852); and cf. Fuller, pp. 52–53.

10. Fuller, pp. 52–53, maintains that the suggestions came from other Hiram students; JAG, in his letter of 18 June to Mary Hubbell, said they came from teachers. Probably both played a part. *Diary*, 1:131 (18 May 1852).

11. There are two sources for this debate, neither as informative as one would like. Fuller's rather overdramatized account (pp. 53–55) concentrates on the very beginning. JAG's diary entry (1:131) is cursory: "Had a warm time. Staid till half-past 10 o'clock." Thus it is not entirely clear what was discussed, or how the discussion went. From both Fuller's and JAG's versions one can infer that the reliability of the Bible was a principal topic. Perhaps it was the only one; I discuss this subject further in a subsequent note. In any event, it is clear from the diary entry that Treat was not completely crushed, as Fuller suggests.

12. *Diary*, 1:132 (21 May 1852), 133 (23 May), 131 (20 May).

13. As noted above, Fuller's account makes it appear that Garfield and Treat held only one debate, whose results were so conclusive that Treat did not attempt to debate

again. JAG's diary, however, makes it clear that there were two; at the second, on 24 May, there was "considerable excitement" and a "warm discussion." Fuller does not describe this second debate at all; his account, which deals with JAG's first response to Treat's challenge, must refer to 20 May. Thus there is only the diary entry to go by. According to it, JAG and Treat gave alternate half hour speeches "upon the spirit rappings," but again it is unclear just what topics were debated.

A fragment in the JAG Papers, LC, offers a glimpse of what they probably talked about. It is a list, undated and untitled, of seventeen arguments against the Bible, noted in abbreviated form, beginning "1. The Bible does not claim Inspi." and ending "16. Sanctions of Slavery; 17. Retards science." It appears hastily written and may have been written for use in a debate. In any case, it summarizes most of the arguments used by anti-Christian lecturers and can stand as a good example of that school of thought, whether or not it was actually used in these debates.

Assuming for the moment that the document does come from JAG's debate against Treat, it is impossible to asign a definite date to it. It may consist of Treat's arguments on 20 May, taken down by JAG in preparation for a later debate. It could even be notes taken during the lecture of 18 May which JAG attended. I have used it at this point because it reflects Treat's views accurately and offers the only possible source about what the debaters discussed at their second encounter.

In sum, then, it is possible to say with confidence what Treat and JAG debated about, but not what they debated on which night. Their clash about the Bible may have taken place the second night, and a mixture of several topics, including the spirit-rappings, could have been discussed the first. The reverse is equally possible. My reconstruction here is wholly conjectural.

14. His letter of 29 May 1852, does not mention the debate at all; the letter of 18 June mentions it briefly. Both are in JAG Papers, LC. On the "Literary offering," see *Diary*, 1: 132–34 (22–29 May).

15. Fuller, pp. 49–50, 57.

16. *Diary*, 1: 130 (10, 16 May 1852), 131 (18 May), 134 (30 May), 135 (1, 2 June), 138 (10 June), 139 (14 June); Fuller, p. 50.

17. JAG to Mary Hubbell, 25 April 1852, JAG Papers, mention his dejection after Harriet Boynton turned him down.

18. Fuller, p. 50; Mary B. Patterson recollections, Hinsdale Papers, WRHS.

19. When Ceylon Fuller, Corydon's brother, got into trouble with Squire Udall, in whose house he was boarding, about seeing girls too frequently, he solved his problem by moving to the Raymonds'. Later, however, he was reprimanded by Hayden for being seen on campus after nine o'clock walking with a girl. JAG to C. E. Fuller, 16 May 1853, Fuller Papers.

20. See the reference to "two hot irons in the fire at the same time," in *Diary*, 1: 131 (18 May 1852). On JAG's engagement, see Fuller, p. 72; JAG to C. E. Fuller, 19 January 1853, Fuller Papers.

21. JAG to Mary Hubbell, 9 April 1852, JAG Papers, LC.

22. Gilmore, p. 9. The student was probably Ada Becket, who studied painting with JAG this term (*Diary*, 1: 135 [1 June 1852]). "Disposition to cling to": Philip Burns to JAG, 28 June 1854, JAG Papers, LC. This point is well discussed in Leech and Brown, p. 15, from which I borrow it.

23. *Diary*, 1: 136 (4 June 1852); Gilmore, p. 9, probably quoting Ada Becket, who was on the excursion; Fuller, p. 47.

24. JAG to Mary Hubbell, 18 June 1852, JAG Papers, LC. How the phrenologist associated JAG with Leo is not at all clear. JAG's birthdate, 19 November, made him a Scorpio.

25. *Diary*, 1:135 (1, 2 June 1852), 138 (11 June), 139 (15, 17 June), 140 (22, 23 June), 142 (25 June). According to the diary, the oration was originally supposed to be in Latin; on the commencement program, however, JAG is shown as delivering an English oration, another student, John Harnit, is assigned the Latin one (*ibid.*, 1:141–42). I cannot explain the discrepancy.

26. *Ibid.*, 1:139 (16, 19 June), 140 (21, 23 June).

27. Osgood, p. 3; *Diary*, 1:140–42 (24, 25 June 1852); Fuller, pp. 88, 194; Green, *Hiram*, pp. 79–80. Incident with Lucretia Rudolph: Lucretia Rudolph to JAG, 31 December 1855, JAG Papers, LC. An interview with O. J. Hodge in the Cleveland *Plain Dealer*, 12 August 1907, in which Hodge maintains that JAG was in love with Lucretia Rudolph and/or her friend Hannah Morton at this time is, so far as I can determine, completely erroneous.

28. Fuller, pp. 55, 57; entries of 1 January, 19 May 1854, Lucretia Rudolph Diary, Lucretia R. Garfield Papers; Lucretia Rudolph to JAG, 3 March 1854, JAG Papers, LC. The story from Hall's side is in Hodge, 1:125.

29. *Diary*, 1:142 (25 June 1852). Charley Foote was a fine speaker; see *ibid.*, 1:184 (3 March 1853), 190 (1 May), 195 (29 May). See also Fuller, p. 195. On Calista Carlton, see Fuller, p. 56 and Corintha Carlton to Lucretia Rudolph, 9 October 1852, Lucretia R. Garfield Papers. On the performance of the colloquy: Fuller, p. 56. JAG was more modest in his assessment: It "went much better than I expected considering the circumstances." (*Diary*, 1:142)

30. *Diary*, 1:142; Fuller, p. 57.

31. JAG to Mary Hubbell, 25 April 1852; Same to same, 29 May, 1852; Same to same, 2 July 1852, JAG Papers, LC.

32. Davis, *Hinsdale*, p. 47; Riddle, *Bart Ridgeley*, p. 168.

33. The story that JAG, doubting his fitness for college, went to his parents' old friend Dr. John Robison to get an expert opinion first appeared in 1880. In Gilmore's biography, p. 8, it is credited to Robison himself, Riddle's *Life*, p. 388, in a final chapter added during the campaign, contains the same story with a number of variations in detail. Evidently both biographers had picked it up from an interview given by Robison soon after the nomination.

But is it true? Robison, though a longtime friend of JAG, was something of a blusterer, given to self-aggrandizement. Besides, Fuller, pp. 65–66, records that during the campaign of 1880 JAG told him explicitly that the story was false. Leech, in Leech and Brown, pp. 33–34, argues that the story nevertheless is believable; her reasoning does not seem altogether credible to me, but there can be no question that JAG was concerned about the effects of hard study on himself (*Diary*, 1:129 [7 May 1852]); so was his mother (Eliza Garfield to JAG, 27 July 1853, JAG Papers, LC). Probably Robison's story was highly exaggerated; but probably it started from a germ of truth.

34. For two examples of JAG's wrestling with this problem at some length, see *Diary*, 1:132 (21 May 1852), 154 (21 September).

35. If one asks, as the Hubbells were no doubt asking in the summer of 1852, what JAG's long-term intentions were with regard to Mary, the answer is quite clear on the basis of all available evidence: though his plans were vague, his feelings were deeply serious. Fuller, p. 78, says: "I do not doubt that for nearly or quite two years he regarded her as his future wife." JAG, looking back from the distance of a year, confessed to his diary on 31 December 1853 (*Diary*, 1:233) that "foolish visions of the future" had misled him in his relationship with her. And in January of 1853, just after he had decided to break up with Mary, he lamented in a despairing letter to his cousin Phebe Boynton, "Every plan of my own, that I have ever made, for happiness, has

signally failed. . . ." He had great emotional capital invested in his relationship with Mary; his problem was that he refused to see the incompatibility between his goals and hers.

Working for Kilby: Fuller, p. 58; JAG to Mary Hubbell, 18 June 1852, JAG Papers, LC; *Diary*, 1:143 (28 June 1852).

36. *Diary*, 1:143 (27 June). Eliza's later attitude, evident in her letter to JAG, 16 December 1853 (JAG Papers, LC), was that JAG had been entrapped by the whole Hubbell family. That, however, was over a year later; there is no real way of telling why she objected to Mary in June 1852.

37. *Diary*, 1:145–46 (17, 18 July 1852). JAG to Mary Hubbell, [28 July 1852], JAG Papers, LC. Eliza's father: Leech and Brown, p. 8. Mary Larabee: Wickham, 1:490.

Chapter 21. Up from the Herd

1. The reference is to Horace's *Satires*, 1:3, 99–100. The phrase evidently held much meaning for JAG; he used it repeatedly (e.g., *Diary*, 1:294 [13 October 1857]; JAG to Harry Rhodes, 19 November 1862, in Williams, *Wild Life*, p. 181) to designate common, average, run-of-the-mill people with whom he emphatically did not want to be identified. The usage is the more striking in that it was not Horace's. Horace was describing a stage in the development of human society based on Lucretius' *De rerum natura*; JAG, appropriated the words and it would seem, applied them to his own social development.

2. *Diary*, 1:143 (28 June 1852). By the middle fifties the Eclectic campus was surrounded with a picket fence, outside which there ran a street. Just when the street acquired the names South Campus, West Campus, etc., is uncertain, but within a year or two of the institute's founding houses were being built on these streets (Dean, No. 4, p. 11). Several of these houses appear in a photograph album in the Hiram College Library, among them the Dean House, which, according to tradition, was the house Kilby built in the summer of 1852. Fuller located it "a few rods southwest" of the main building (pp. 219–20). There seems to be no reason to question the tradition, which agrees with all other available evidence.

Only photographs of the Dean House are available; the house itself was demolished about 1950.

On the boardinghouses, see Dean, No. 4, p. 12; Green, *Hiram*, p. 49. One of the houses, known as Tiffany Hall, still stands. It is probably not the one JAC roomed in fall 1852, but was no doubt almost identical in original design. A photograph is in the album mentioned in the preceding note. Other construction is from Osgood, p. 3; Fuller, p. 58; Davis, Hinsdale, p. 25; photograph album, Hiram College Library.

3. *Diary*, 1:143 (30 June 1852); JAG to Mary Hubbell, 2 July 1852, JAG Papers, LC. *Diary*, 1:144 (5 July 1852).

4. Fuller, pp. 55, 58, 59; *Diary*, 1:143 (1 July), 144 (8 July), 148 (5 August), 149 (17 August). Although Fuller says that his diary recorded eight times when he spent the night with JAG and almost as many when JAG spent the night with him, it is worth noting that JAG recorded only four of the former instances and none of the latter—a sobering reminder of how very sketchy the Garfield diary can be.

5. For the phrase, and the longing associated with it, see JAG to Fuller, 30 July 1854, in Fuller, p. 132; JAG to Fuller, 6 May 1859, Fuller Papers. An entry in the *Diary* for 2 July 1853 (1:205), though it does not use this particular phrase, conveys the urgency of JAG's hunger for recognition: ". . . I can not relate the world of

thoughts that filled my soul while pondering upon myself and my relations to the world, Science, myself and my God. So few ever accomplish anything in the world, I almost despair."

6. Fuller, pp. 12, 51.

7. *Ibid.*, p. 72.

8. His plans for the new year, in the diary entry of 1 January 1853 (1:168), suggest that he had been thinking about college fairly specifically for some time, probably since July and the offer from his unnamed friend, mentioned in *Diary*, 1:145 (15 July 1852). The conjecture that it was Dr. Robison is in Leech and Brown, p. 34.

9. *Diary*, 1:144 (10 July 1852), 148 (8 August), 151–52 (26 August).

10. *Ibid.*, 1:145 (17 July); JAG to Mary Hubbell, 12 August 1852, JAG Papers, LC.

11. *Diary*, 1:146 (19, 23 July), 147 (28 July), 149 (14 August), 1:150 (18 August); JAG to Mary Hubbell, 2 July 1852, JAG Papers, LC. A photograph of the Dean House is in the photograph album, Hiram College Library, with a note that a carpenter, Erastus Bates, said that he saw JAG put the kite-shaped piece in.

12. *Diary*, 1:149 (10, 13, 17 August), 150–51 (21–24 August).

13. *Ibid.*, 1:152 (29 August), 156 (3 October).

14. *Ibid.*, 1:151 (25, 26 August), 153 (2 September). Founding of Philomathean: *Ibid.*, 1:152–53 (1 September), 153 (3 September); Green, *Hiram*, p. 60. O. C. Atwater's impression, quoted in *ibid.*, p. 395, that Fuller was the leading spirit in founding the society, is probably inaccurate. Atwater was not close to the people involved, but it is interesting in suggesting that, to some students, Fuller appeared older and more knowledgeable than JAG.

15. *Diary*, 1:152 (29 August 1852), 154 (20 September), 155 (26 September); JAG to Thomas, Jane, and Eliza Garfield, 8 August 1852, JAG Papers, LC.

16. *Diary*, 1:154 (13, 14, 15, 17, 18, 19 September), 155 (29, 30 September), 156 (4 October).

17. *Ibid.*, 1:141 (25 June); Philip Burns to JAG, 28 June 1854, JAG Papers, LC. A photograph, with JAG and Lucretia Rudolph, is in Butler, p. 77. On John Harnit, see Fuller, pp. 61, 63, 68.

18. Hinsdale, *Life*, p. 390; Henry, p. 91; Bundy, p. 37; *Diary*, 1:133 (23 May 1852), 138 (11 June), 146 (22 July): Wilber to Zeb Rudolph, 7 December 1850, Lucretia R. Garfield Papers.

19. Wilber to Zeb Rudolph, 7 December 1850; Wilber to JAG, 11 April 1854. The change of tone between these two letters, from naive and earnest to sardonic and elliptical, is worth noting. Except for a characteristic carefree verbal extravagance, it is hard to believe that the same person wrote both letters. Of course, the two letters' being written to different recipients undoubtedly accounts for some of the differences in tone; but one wonders whether the breakup of Wilber's engagement or his subsequent illness did not change his outlook on life substantially.

Engagement to Laura Clark: Fuller, p. 56; JAG to Lucretia Rudolph, 18 June 1855; JAG to Henry Boynton, 21 March 1856, JAG Papers, LC; Corintha Carlton to Lucretia Rudolph, 7 February 1853, Lucretia R. Garfield Papers. "Almost criminal": JAG to Corydon Fuller, 19 January 1853, Fuller Papers. In the printed version of this letter, Fuller omitted the identifying initials "C. D. W."

20. Hinsdale, *Garfield*, pp. 396, 416, 420; Fuller, p. 56; entry of 27 September 1854, Lucretia Rudolph Diary; Corintha Carlton to Lucretia Rudolph, 4 December 1852, both in Lucretia R. Garfield Papers; Green, Hiram, p. 71. See the perceptive portrait in Leech and Brown, p. 37.

21. Hinsdale, *Garfield*, p. 391; Diary, 1:250 (24 June 1854).

22. Entry of 2 December 1852, Benjamin Wood Diary; *Diary*, 1:157 (19, 20 October 1852).

23. *Diary*, 1:158 (24 October 1852—Campbell's article is in the October number of the *Millennial Harbinger*, pp. 541–67), 157 (20, 21, 22, 23 October), 158 (24, 26 October), 159 (30 October, 1 November).

24. Mary's possessiveness: Cf. a letter from JAG to her, without date but probably December 1852, in JAG Papers, LC. "This is a sign": *Diary*, 1:158 (24 October).

25. On 28 October JAG recorded in his diary (1:158) that he had received a letter from the Reverend James Ballard of Grand Rapids, Michigan. Grand Rapids was where Corydon Fuller's family lived, and Ballard, a Congregational minister, was in 1852 the principal of Grand Rapids High School (Grand Rapids Public Library, vertical file). There is no other discoverable connection between him and JAG, so I conjecture that his letter concerned a teaching job. The reasons why JAG might have wanted to teach somewhere besides Warrensville are obvious. Furthermore, when Sutton Hayden offered JAG a position at the Eclectic that winter, JAG's immediate reaction was consternation: "I know not what to do" (*Diary*, 1:158). This reaction is difficult to explain unless JAG was already partly committed to work elsewhere that winter; otherwise he would have accepted with enthusiasm.

26. Fuller, pp. 61–62, *Diary*, 1:158 (26 October 1852), 161 (12 November). JAG to Thomas and Eliza Garfield, 27 October 1852, JAG Papers, LC, shows that by the day after Hayden offered him the job he was leaning toward accepting it; but there is no record of his formal acceptance.

27. *Diary*, 1:160–161 (12 November). Fuller was going to Chagrin Falls to study with Dr. Harlow (Fuller, p. 67); Ryder was teaching in Randolph (*Diary*, 1:170 [19 January 1853]); and Henry Boynton was teaching somewhere (A. W. Maxwell to JAG, 6 December 1852, JAG Papers, LC).

Friends at Hiram: Fuller, pp. 68–72 (Harnit); *Diary*, 1:169 (4, 6 January 1853), 178 (18 February).

Mary Hubbell at Hiram: *Diary*, 1:182 (12 March) strongly suggests that she had been a student that term; so does the undated letter to her, if the attribution to December 1852, is correct.

28. *Ibid.*, 1:150 (17 August 1852), 159 (2 November); Harrell, p. 54.

29. *Diary*, 1:161 (12, 13 November 1852), 150 (22 August).

30. *Ibid.*, 1:161 (16–17 November). The diary entries for 9 December (1:163) and 18 (1:164) show that JAG's dilemma was as puzzling as ever at that time.

31. *Ibid.*, 1:161–62 (19 November 1852).

Bibliography

1. Manuscripts

Batsdorff, Hattie Harper. "The Making of a President." Western Reserve Historical Society. (Hereafter cited as WRHS.)

Bedford, Ohio, Disciple Church of Christ. Memorandum. WRHS.

Bigelow, Elizabeth. Papers. Ohio Historical Society.

Boynton, Henry B. Papers. WRHS.

Clapp, Thomas J. Account Book. WRHS.

Fuller, Corydon E. Papers. Iowa State Department of History and Archives.

Garfield, James A. Papers. Library of Congress.

———. Papers. WRHS.

———. Scrapbooks. James A. Garfield National Historic Site.

Garfield, Lucretia R. Papers (including "Rough Sketch of an Introduction to a Life of General Garfield"). Library of Congress.

Gilmore, James R. Papers. Johns Hopkins University.

Hinsdale, Burke A. Papers. WRHS.

Hodge, Orlando J. Papers. WRHS.

Mapes, Perry. Autobiography. WRHS.

Mewett, Alfred. Papers. WRHS.

Nye, Pearl B. Papers. Ohio Historical Society.

Patterson, Mary Buckingham. "Recollections of James A. Garfield." James A. Garfield Papers. WRHS.

Perkins Papers. "Notes and Descriptions of Lands in Orange" fragment. WRHS.

Philomathean Society Record Book. Henry B. Boynton Papers. WRHS.

Prentiss, Luther. Docket Book. WRHS.

Riddle, Albert G. Papers (including "Fifty-five Years of Lawyer Life"). WRHS.

Starr, George. Diary. Hudson Historical Society.

Taylor-Champion Letters. Ohio Historical Society.

Thomas-Wilson-White Family. Papers. WRHS.

Wood, Benjamin. Diary. WRHS.

2. Government Documents

Bainbridge, Ohio. Town Records. WRHS.

Cuyahoga County, Ohio. Court of Common Pleas Records. Cuyahoga County Archives.

Cuyahoga County, Ohio. Deeds. Cuyahoga County Archives.

Cuyahoga County, Ohio. Tax duplicates, microfilm. WRHS.

Mayfield Township Schools. Records. 1842–64. WRHS.

Newburgh, Ohio. School District No. 1, Records. WRHS.

U.S. Bureau of the Census. Manuscript census returns for Cuyahoga County, Ohio, 1840 and 1850; Boone County, Illinois, 1850; Kent County, Michigan, 1880. National Archives.

3. Primary Sources

Addison, Daniel D. *Lucy Larcom: Life, Letters, and Diary*. Boston: Houghton Mifflin, 1895.

American Railway Guide and Pocket Companion. New York: Curran Dinsmore and Co., 1851.

Annals of the Early Settlers Association of Cuyahoga County. 8 vols. Cleveland: N.p. 1880–1919.

Austin, John Mather. *Golden Steps to Respectability, Usefulness, and Happiness*. Auburn, N.Y.: Derby and Miller, 1850.

Baird, Robert. *Religion in the United States of America*. Glasgow: Blackie and Son, 1844.

Barnes, Albert. *Notes on the New Testament: Romans*. 1832. Reprint. Grand Rapids, Mich.: Baker Book House, 1953.

Baxter, Frances. "Rafting on the Alleghany and Ohio, 1844." *Pennsylvania Magazine of History and Biography* 51 (1927): 27–78, 143–71, 207–43.

Beecher, Henry Ward. *Lectures to Young Men*. 1844. Reprint. New York: M. H. Newman and Co., 1853.

Benjamin, Asher. *The American Builder's Companion*. Boston: R. P. and C. Williams, 1827.

Blackmore, Harris H. *Map of Cuyahoga County, Ohio*. Cleveland: N.p. 1852.

Blakeslee, Chiles T. *History of Chagrin Falls and Vicinity*. 1903. Reprint. Chagrin Falls, Ohio: Friends of Chagrin Falls Library, 1969.

Boynton, Henry B. "Early Life of Garfield." *Hiram College Advance* 6 (June 1896): 198–99.

Brownson, Orestes. *The Spirit Rapper: An Autobiography*. Boston: Little, Brown, 1854.

Buehr, Wendy, ed. *American Manners & Morals*. New York: American Heritage, 1969.

Busch, Moritz. *Travels Between the Hudson and the Mississippi, 1851–1852*. Ed. and trans. by Norman H. Binger. Lexington: The University Press of Kentucky, 1953.

Canfield, J. *Map of Mahoning County*. Youngstown, Ohio: N.p. 1860.

Catalogue of the Officers and Students of the Geauga Seminary. . . for the Year Ending July 4, 1849. Cleveland: M. C. Younglove, 1849.

Chambers, William. *Things as They Are In America*. 1854. Reprint. New York: Negro Universities Press, 1968.

Grace Victorious; or, The Memoir of Helen M. Cowles. Oberlin, Ohio: J. M. Fitch, 1856.

Cutter, William. *The Life of Israel Putnam*. New York: George F. Cooledge and Brother, 1847.

Cuyahoga County Cemetery Inscriptions. Vol. 1. WRHS, [1934] Mimeographed copy.

Cuyahoga County Marriage Records, vol. 1. Cleveland: WRHS, 1934.

Davidson, Marshall B. *Life in America*. 2 vols. Boston: Houghton Mifflin, 1951.

Dickens, Charles. *American Notes*. 1842. Reprint. Greenwich, Conn.: Fawcett Publications, 1961.

Drake, Daniel. *A Systematic Treatise, Historical, Etiological, and Practical, on the Principal Diseases of the Interior Valley of North America*. Cincinnati; Ohio: Winthrop B. Smith, 1850.

[Ellms, Charles, comp.] *The Pirate's Own Book*. 1837. Reprint. Salem, Mass.: Marine Research Society, 1924.

Ferguson, Charles D. *The Experiences of a Forty-Niner*. . . Cleveland: Williams Publishing Co., 1888.

First Annual Catalogue of the Western Reserve Eclectic Institute. . . Cleveland: Steam Press of Harris, Fairbanks, 1851.

Fowler, Orson S. *Amativeness; Embracing the Evils and Remedies of Excessive and Perverted Sexuality*. . . 1844. New York: Fowler and Wells, 1889.

Fuller, Corydon E. *Reminiscences of James A. Garfield, with Notes Preliminary and Collateral*. Cincinnati; Ohio: Standard Publishing Co., 1887.

Garfield, James A. *Diary*. Ed. by Harry James Brown and Frederick D. Williams. 4 vols. East Lansing, Mich.: Michigan State University Press, 1967–78.

Gilmore, James R. [Edmund Kirke]. *On the Border*. Boston: Lee and Shepard, 1867.

Goodrich, Rev. Charles A. *A History of the United States of America*. 3d ed. Hartford: Barber and Robinson, 1823.

Granville, Mass. *Vital Records of Granville, Massachusetts, to 1850*. Boston: New England Historic Genealogical Society, 1914.

Handerson, Henry E. *Yankee in Gray: The Civil War Memoirs of Henry E. Handerson*. Cleveland: The Press of Western Reserve University, 1962.

Hastings, Thomas, and Solomon Warriner. *Musica Sacra*. 3d ed. Utica, N.Y.: William Williams, 1822.

Hodge, Orlando J. *Reminiscences*. Vol. 1, Cleveland: The Imperial Press, 1902; Vol. 2, Cleveland: The Brooks Co., 1910.

Holloway, Emory, ed. *The Uncollected Poetry and Prose of Walt Whitman*. 2 vols. Garden City, N.Y.: Doubleday Page, 1921.

Howe, Henry. *Historical Collections of Ohio*. Cincinnati: Derby, Bradley and Co., 1847.

———. *Historical Collections of Ohio*. 2 vols. Norwalk, Ohio: Laning Printing Co., 1896.

Howells, William Dean. *Years of My Youth and Three Essays*. Ed. by David J. Nordloh. Bloomington: Indiana University Press, 1975.

Jackson, Daniel, Jr. *Alonzo and Melissa; or, The Unfeeling Father*. 1811. Reprint. Philadelphia: Claxton, Remsen and Heffelfinger, 1879.

Johnston, William Graham. *Life and Reminiscences from Birth to Manhood*. Pittsburgh: N.p. 1901.

Koch, Dr. Albert C. *Journey Through a Part of the United States of North America in the*

Years 1844 to 1846. Trans. by Ernest E. Stadler. Carbondale: Southern Illinois University Press, 1972.

Lake, J. *Atlas of Cuyahoga County, Ohio*. Philadelphia: Titus, Simmons and Titus, 1874.

Lane, Samuel A. *Fifty Years and Over of Akron and Summit County*. Akron, Ohio: Beacon Job Department, 1892.

Lewis, Frederick Wheeler, ed. *Hiram Wheeler Lewis: A Partial Auto-biography* . . . . Albion, N.Y.: Eddy Printing Co., 1941.

Moreau de St. Mery's American Journey. Ed. by Kenneth Roberts and Anna M. Roberts. Garden City, N.Y.: Doubleday, 1947.

Ohio. Secretary of State. *Annual Report . . . on the Condition of Common Schools- . . . for the year 1852*. Columbus, Ohio, 1852.

The Ohio Railroad Guide, Illustrated: Cincinnati to Erie, via Columbus and Cleveland. Columbus: Ohio State Journal Co., 1854.

"The Personal Reminiscences of General Chauncey Eggleston," *Ohio Archeological and Historical Quarterly* 41 (April 1932): 284–320.

Pickups from the "American Way": Early Life and Civil War Reminiscences of Captain Joseph Rudolph. Hiram Historical Society Publications, ser. 2, no. 1. Ann Arbor, Mich.: Edwards Brothers, 1941.

"Pittsburgh in 1848." *Western Pennsylvania Historical Magazine* 17 (September 1934): 190–97.

Pollok, Robert. *The Course of Time*. Edinburgh: William Blackwood, 1828.

Post, Charles A. *Doans Corners and the City Four Miles West*. Cleveland: Caxton Co., 1930.

Pulszky, Francis and Theresa. *White Red Black: Sketches of Society in the United States*. 3 vols. 1853. Reprint. New York: Negro Universities Press, 1968.

Reports of the Prison Discipline Society of Boston. 6 vols. Patterson Smith Reprint Series in Criminology, Law Enforcement, and Social Problems, no. 155. Montclair, N.J.: Patterson Smith, 1972.

Riddle, Albert G. *Ansel's Cave*. Cleveland: Burrows Brothers, 1893.

———. *Bart Ridgeley: A Story of Northern Ohio*, Boston: Nichols and Hall, 1873.

———. *Elmer Riddle: A Sketch of His Life*. Cleveland: W. W. Williams, 1884.

———. *The House of Ross and Other Tales*. Boston: Hall and Whiting, 1881.

———. *Old Newbury and The Pioneers*. Cleveland: W. W. Williams, 1885.

———. *The Portrait*. Cleveland: Cobb, Andrews, 1874.

Roy, Andrew. *The Coal Miner*. Cleveland: Robinson, Savage, 1876.

———. *The Practical Miner's Companion*. Columbus: Westbote Printing Co., 1885.

Ryder, James F. *Voigtländer and I in Pursuit of Shadow Catching*. 1902. Reprint. In The Literature of Photography Series. New York: Arno Press, 1973.

Sacred Songs for Family and Social Worship. New York: American Tract Society, 1855.

Second Annual Catalogue . . . Cleveland: Steam Press of Harris, Fairbanks, 1852.

Shippee, Lester B., ed. *Bishop Whipple's Southern Diary*. Minneapolis: University of Minnesota Press, 1937.

Sizer, Nelson. *Forty Years in Phrenology*. New York: Fowler and Wells, 1882.

Sleeper, John Sherburne [Hawser Martingale]. *Tales of the Ocean*. Boston: S. N.

Dickinson, 1843.

Tourgee, Albion W. *Figs and Thistles*. New York: Fords, Howard and Hulbert, 1879.

———. *The Story of A Thousand*. Buffalo N.Y.: S. McGerald & Son, 1896.

Treat, Joseph. *A Card to the World*. Garrettsville, Ohio: The Author, 1855.

The Vincent Price Treasury of American Art. Waukesha, Wis.: Country Beautiful, 1972.

Welker, Martin. *Farm Life in Central Ohio Sixty Years Ago*. Wooster, Ohio: Clapper's Print, 1892.

Wickham, Gertrude Van Rensselaer, ed. *Memorial to the Pioneer Women of the Western Reserve*. 2 vols. Cleveland: J. B. Savage, 1897.

Wilcox, Alanson. *An Autobiography*. Cleveland: Press of the Judson Printing Co., 1912.

Williams, Frederick D., ed. *The Wild Life of the Army: Civil War Letters of James A. Garfield*. East Lansing: Michigan State University Press, 1964.

Works Progress Administration. *Annals of Cleveland, 1818–1935: A Digest and Index of the Newspaper Record of Events and Opinions*. 59 vols. Cleveland: 1938.

———. *Annals of Cleveland: Court Record Series*. 9 vols. Cleveland: Cuyahoga County Archives Survey, 1939.

4. Secondary Sources

Ackerknecht, Erwin H. *Malaria in the Upper Mississippi Valley, 1760–1900*. Supplement to the Bulletin of the History of Medicine, no. 4. Baltimore: Johns Hopkins Press, 1945.

Adkins, Jan. *Toolchest*. New York: Walker, 1973.

Alexander, William Henry. *A Climatological History of Ohio*. Ohio State University Bulletin, vol. 28, no. 3. Columbus: Engineering Experiment Station of the Ohio State University, 1923.

Aley, Howard C. *A Heritage to Share: The Bicentennial History of Youngstown and Mahoning Country, Ohio*. Youngstown, Ohio: Bicentennial Commission of Youngstown and Mahoning County, Ohio, 1975.

Alvarez, Eugene. *Travel on Southern Antebellum Railroads, 1828–1860*. University: University of Alabama Press, 1974.

Bard, Nelson P. *Pioneers with Web Feet*. Solon, Ohio: Solon Sesquicentennial Committee, 1970.

Barker-Benfield, G. J. *The Horrors of the Half-Known Life*. New York: Harper and Row, 1976.

Baxter, Norman Allen. *History of the Freewill Baptists: A Study in New England Separatism*. Rochester, N.Y.: American Baptist Historical Society, 1957.

Blower, Arthur H. "Johnny Cake Lock," *Towpaths* 7 no. 1 (1969): 1–2.

Brink, Carol. *Harps in the Wind: The Story of the Singing Hutchinsons*. New York: Macmillan Co., 1947.

Brisbin, James S. *From the Tow-Path to the White House: The Early Life and Public Career of James A. Garfield*. Philadelphia: Hubbard Brothers, 1880.

Buley, R. Carlyle. *The Old Northwest: Pioneer Period 1815–1840*. 2 vols. Bloomington: Indiana University Press, 1950.

Bullough, Vern L., and Martha Voght. "Homosexuality and Its Confusion with the 'Secret Sin' in Pre-Freudian America." *Journal of the History of Medicine* 28 (April 1973): 143–55.

Bundy, J. M. *The Life of General James A. Garfield.* New York: A. S. Barnes, 1880.

Burr, C. B., ed. *Medical History of Michigan.* 2 vols. Minneapolis, Minn. Bruce Publishing Co., 1930.

Bulter, Margaret Manor. *A Pictorial History of the Western Reserve.* Cleveland: Early Settlers Association of the Western Reserve, 1963.

Carson, Gerald. *The Old Country Store.* New York: Oxford University Press, 1954.

Carter, Lena M. "Centennial History of Twinsburg, Ohio," Part 1 of *Twinsburg, Ohio: 1817–1917.* Twinsburg, Ohio: Samuel Bissell Memorial Library Association, 1917.

Chapman, Edmund H. *Cleveland: Village to Metropolis.* Cleveland: The Press of Western Reserve University, 1964.

Chase, Gilbert. *America's Music.* New York: McGraw-Hill, 1955.

Cherry, P. P. *The Western Reserve and Early Ohio.* Akron, Ohio: R. L. Fouse, 1921.

Coates, William R. *A History of Cuyahoga County and the City of Cleveland.* 3 vols. Chicago: American Historical Society, 1924.

Coffin, Charles Carleton. *The Life of James A. Garfield.* Boston: James H. Earle, 1880.

Congdon, Herbert Wheaton. *Early American Homes for Today: A Treasury of Decorative Details and Restoration Procedures.* Rutland, Vt.: Charles E. Tuttle, 1963.

Conwell, Russell H. *The Life, Speeches and Public Service of General James A. Garfield of Ohio.* Boston: B. B. Russell, 1880.

Coppess, Margaret. "Garfield-Boynton Family Records." *Michigan Heritage* 8 (Winter 1966): 91–98.

Corkan, Lloyd A. M. "The Beaver and Lake Erie Canal." *Western Pennsylvania Historical Magazine* 17 (September 1934): 175–88.

Cross, Whitney R. *The Burned-Over District: The Social and Intellectual History of Enthusiastic Religion in Western New York.* 1950. Reprint. New York: Harper and Row, 1965.

Damon, Bertha. *Grandma Called It Carnal.* New York: Simon and Schuster, 1938.

Darnton, Robert. *Mesmerism and the End of the Enlightenment in France.* New York: Schocken Books, 1970.

Davies, John D. *Phrenology: Fad and Science.* Yale Historical Publications: Miscellany, no. 62. New Haven: Yale University Press, 1955.

Davis, Harold E. *Garfield of Hiram.* Hiram Historical Society Publication no. 4. Hiram, Ohio: N.p. 1931.

———. *Hinsdale of Hiram: The Life of Burke Aaron Hinsdale.* Washington D.C.: The University Press, 1971.

———. *The Pennsylvania and Ohio Canal 1823–1877.* Hiram Historical Society Publications, no. 1. Hiram, Ohio: N.p. 1929.

Dean, B. S. "The Story of Hiram Village." *Hiram College Advance* 22, no. 3 (December 1911): 7–9; no. 4 (January 1912): 10–12.

Dickinson, Walter Johnson. *Pioneer History, 1802–1865.* 1896–97. Reprint. Ravenna, Ohio: Record Publishing Co., 1953.

Downes, Randolph C. *History of Lake Shore Ohio.* 3 vols. New York: Lewis Historical Publishing Co., 1952.

Dunbar, Seymour. *A History of Travel in America*, I. Indianapolis, Ind.: Bobbs-Merrill, 1915.

Eavenson, Howard N. *The First Century and a Quarter of American Coal Industry*. Pittsburgh, Pa.: Privately printed, 1942.

Erickson, Charlotte. *Invisible Immigrants: The Adaptation of English and Scottish Immigrants in Nineteenth-Century America*. Coral Gables, Fla.: University of Miami Press, 1972.

Fish, Carl Russell. *The Rise of the Common Man, 1830–1850*. In *A History of American Life*. Ed. by Arthur M. Schlesinger and Dixon Ryan Fox, vol. 6. New York: Macmillan Co., 1927.

Flexner, Stuart Berg. *I Hear America Talking*. New York: Van Nostrand Reinhold, 1976.

Fornell, Earl Wesley. *The Unhappy Medium: Spiritualism and the Life of Margaret Fox*. Austin: University of Texas Press, 1964.

Frary, I. T. *Early Homes of Ohio*. Richmond, Va.: Garrett and Massie, 1936.

Gates, Errett. *The Early Relation and Separation of Baptists and Disciples*. Chicago: R. R. Donnelley, 1904.

Gates, Helen Dunn. *A Consecrated Life: A Sketch of the Life and Labors of Rev. Ransom Dunn, D. D.* Boston: Morning Star Publishing House, 1901.

Gilbert, Arthur N. "Doctor, Patient, and Onanist Diseases in the Nineteenth Century." *Journal of the History of Medicine* 30 (July 1975): 217–34.

Gilmore, James R. [Edmund Kirke]. *The Life of James A. Garfield*. New York: Harper and Brothers, 1880.

Gordon, Thomas F. *A Gazetteer of the State of Pennsylvania*. Philadelphia: T. Belknap, 1832.

Grafton, Thomas W. *Alexander Campbell, Leader of the Great Reformation of the Nineteenth Century*. St. Louis, Mo.: Christian Publishing Co., 1897.

Green, Francis M. *Hiram College and Western Reserve Eclectic Institute: Fifty Years of History, 1850–1900*. Cleveland: O. S. Hubbell Printing Co., 1901.

———. *A Royal Life, or The Eventful History of James A. Garfield*. Chicago: Central Book Concern, 1882.

Greene, John C. *The Death of Adam: Evolution and Its Impact on Western Thought*. Ames: Iowa State University Press, 1959.

Grismer, Karl H. *Akron and Summit County*. Akron, Ohio: Summit County Historical Society, 1952.

———. *The History of Kent*. Kent, Ohio: Courier-Tribune, 1932.

Ham, Frank Mapes. *The Mapes Family in America*. Bridgeport, Conn.: N.P., 1962.

Hardinge, Emma. *Modern American Spiritualism*. New York: The Author, 1870.

Harlow, Alvin F. *Old Towpaths: The Story of the American Canal Era*. 1926. Reprint. Port Washington, N.Y.: Kennikat Press, 1964.

Harrell, David Edwin, Jr. *Quest for a Christian America*. In *A Social History of the Disciples of Christ*, vol. 1. Nashville, Tenn.: Disciples of Christ Historical Society, 1966.

Hart, Albert B. "The Westernization of New England." *Ohio Archaeological and Historical Quarterly* 17 (April 1908): 259–74.

Hayden, A. S. *Early History of the Disciples in the Western Reserve, Ohio*. Cincinnati, Ohio: Chase and Hall, 1875.

Henry, Frederick A. *Captain Henry of Geauga*. Cleveland: Gates Press, 1942.

Hertzog, Lucy Stone. "The Rise of Homeopathy." *Ohio Archaeological and Historical Quarterly* 49 (October–December 1940): 332–46.

Heydinger, Earl J. "The Pennsylvania and Ohio Canal." *Towpaths*, no. 2, 5 (1956): 15–16.

Hinsdale, Burke A. "The History of Popular Education on the Western Reserve." *Ohio Archaeological and Historical Society Publications* 6 (January 1898): 45–58.

———. *President Garfield and Education: Hiram College Memorial*. Boston: James R. Osgood, 1882.

History of Ottawa County, Michigan. Chicago. H. R. Page & Co., 1892.

History of Trumbull and Mahoning Counties. . . . Vol. 1. Cleveland: H. Z. Williams and Bro., 1882.

Holm, James B., ed. *Portage Heritage*. Ravenna, Ohio: Portage County Historical Society, 1957.

Horlick, Allen Stanley. *Country Boys and Merchant Princes*. Lewisburg, Pa.: Bucknell University Press, 1975.

Hornung, Clarence P. *Wheels Across America*. New York: A. S. Barnes, 1959.

Horton, John J. *The Jonathan Hale Farm: A Chronicle of the Cuyahoga Valley*. Publication no. 116. Cleveland: Western Reserve Historical Society, 1961.

Howe, Gilman B. *Genealogy of the Bigelow Family*. Worcester, Mass.: Charles Hamilton, 1890.

Hubbell, Walter. *History of the Hubbell Family*. . . .New York: Privately printed, 1915.

Hulbert, Archer Butler. "The Old National Road—The Historic Highway of America." *Ohio Archaeological and Historical Society Publications* 9 (January 1901): 405–519.

Hutslar, Donald A. "The Log Architecture of Ohio." *Ohio History* 80 (Summer–Autumn 1971): 172–271.

Jackson, James S., and Margot Jackson. *The Colorful Era of the Ohio Canal*. Cleveland: Ohio Canal Sesquicentennial Commission, 1977.

Jacoby, J. Wilbur. *History of Marion County, Ohio*. . . . Chicago: Biographical Publishing Co., 1907.

Jennings, Walter Wilson. *Origin and Early History of the Disciples of Christ*. N.p.: Standard Publishing Co., 1919.

Johnson, Crisfield, comp. *History of Cuyahoga County, Ohio*. Cleveland: D. W. Ensign, 1879.

Jones, F. O., ed. *A Handbook of American Music and Musicians*. 1886. Reprint. New York: Da Capo Press, 1971.

Jones, Robert L. "The Dairy Industry in Ohio Prior to the Civil War." *Ohio Archaeological and Historical Quarterly* 56 (January 1947): 46–69.

———. "The Introduction of Farm Machinery into Ohio Prior to 1865." *Ohio Archaeological and Historical Quarterly* 58 (January 1949): 1–20.

Jordan, Philip D. *The National Road*. 1948. Reprint. Gloucester, Mass.: Peter Smith, 1966.

Kennedy, William S. *The Plan of Union: or A History of the Presbyterian and Congregational Churches of the Western Reserve*. Hudson, Ohio: Pentagon Steam Press, 1856.

Kenyon, John S. "Western Reserve." Part 6. *Dialect Notes* 4 (1917): 386–404.

Kett, Joseph F. *Rites of Passage*. New York: Basic Books, 1977.

Kinsey, Alfred C., Wardell B. Pomeroy, and Clyde E. Martin. *Sexual Behavior in the Human Male*. Philadelphia: W. B. Saunders, 1948.

Knowlton, Daniel C. "A District School Teacher of a Hundred Years Ago." *School and Society* 80 (4 Sept 1954): 73–75.

Lake County Historical Society. *Here is Lake County, Ohio*. Cleveland: Howard Allen, 1964.

Leech, Margaret, and Harry J. Brown. *The Garfield Orbit*. New York: Harper and Row, 1978.

Lewis, Orlando F. *The Development of American Prisons and Prison Customs, 1776–1845*. "Patterson Smith Reprint Series in Criminology, Law Enforcement, and Social Problems." No. 1. Montclair, N.J.: Patterson Smith, 1967.

Lloyd, W. L., J. I. Falconer, and C. E. Thorne. *The Agriculture of Ohio*. Bulletin 326 of the Ohio Agricultural Experiment Station. Wooster, Ohio: Ohio Agricultural Experiment Station, 1918.

Lottich, Kenneth V. *New England Transplanted*. Dallas, Tex.: Royal Publishing Co., 1964.

Lyman, Lima. *Lyman's Histories and Stories of Newton Falls*. Chicago: Adams Press, 1970.

McLoughlin, William G. *The Meaning of Henry Ward Beecher*. New York: Alfred A. Knopf, 1970.

Miller, E. A. "High Schools in Ohio Prior to 1850." *School Review* 28 (June 1920): 461–62.

Needham, Walter, and Barrows Mussey. *A Book of Country Things*. Brattleboro, Vt.: Stephen Greene Press, 1965.

Nelson, Geoffrey K. *Spiritualism and Society*. New York: Schocken Books, 1969.

Nevins, Allan. *Ordeal of the Union*. Vol. 1. New York: Charles Scribner's Sons, 1947.

Null, Anne. "The Garfield Log Cabin." *Western Reserve Historical Society News* 29 (May–June 1975): 2–6.

Orth, Samuel P. *A History of Cleveland, Ohio*. 3 vols. Cleveland: S. J. Clarke Publishing Co., 1910.

Osborne, William S. *Caroline M. Kirkland*. New York: Twayne, 1972.

Osgood, Elliott I. *In the Days of Old Hiram*. Publications of the Hiram Historical Society, no. 3. Hiram, Ohio: N.p. 1931.

Patterson, John C. "History of Hillsdale College." *Michigan Historical Collections* 6 (1884): 137–65.

Peskin, Allan. *Garfield*. Kent, Ohio: Kent State University Press, 1978.

Piercy, Caroline B. *The Valley of God's Pleasure*. New York: Stratford House, 1951.

Pioneer and General History of Geauga County. N.p.: Historical Society of Geauga County, 1880.

Podmore, Frank. *Modern Spiritualism*. Vol. 1. London: Methuen, 1902.

Porter, Burton P. "*Old Canal Days*." Columbus, Ohio: Hess Printing Co., 1942.

Richardson, L. W. "John Malvin: Canal Boat Captain." *Towpaths* 4, no. 1 (1966): 38.

Riddle, Albert G. *The Life, Character, and Public Services of Jas. (James) A. Garfield*. Philadelphia: William Flint, 1880.

Rose, William Ganson. *Cleveland: The Making of a City*. Cleveland: World Publishing Co., 1950.

Rosenberg, Charles E. *The Cholera Years*. Chicago: University of Chicago Press, 1962.

Rothman, David J. *The Discovery of the Asylum*. Boston: Little, Brown, 1971.

Scheiber, Harry N. *Ohio Canal Era: A Case Study of Government and the Economy, 1820–1861*. Athens: Ohio University Press, 1969.

———. "The Pennsylvania and Ohio Canal: Transportation Innovaion, Mixed Enterprise, and Urban Commercial Rivalry, 1825–1861," *Old Northwest* 6 (Summer 1980): 105–36.

Schob, David E. *Hired Hands and Plowboys: Farm Labor in the Midwest, 1815–1860*. Urbana: University of Illinois Press, 1975.

Shaw, Archer H. *The Plain Dealer: One Hundred Years in Cleveland*. New York: Alfred A. Knopf, 1942.

Shaw, Henry K. *Buckeye Disciples: A History of the Disciples of Christ in Ohio*. St. Louis, Mo.: Christian Board of Publication, 1952.

Sizer, Sandra S. *Gospel Hymns and Social Religion*. Philadelphia: Temple University Press, 1978.

Sloane, Eric. *Diary of an Early American Boy*. 1962. Reprint. New York: Ballantine, 1974.

———. *A Museum of Early American Tools*. New York: Funk and Wagnalls, 1964.

Slotkin, Richard. *Regeneration Through Violence*. Middletown, Conn.: Wesleyan University Press, 1973.

Smith, Theodore Clarke. *The Life and Letters of James Abram Garfield*. 2 vols. New Haven: Yale University Press, 1925.

Snyder, E. P. "Incidents of the Early Settlement of Norwich Township," *Firelands Pioneer* n.s. 21 (January 1920): 2237–38.

Starbuck, Edwin D. *The Psychology of Religion*. New York: Charles Scribner's Sons, 1903.

Stupka, Arthur. *Wildflowers in Color*. New York: Harper and Row, 1965.

Thayer, William M. *From Log-Cabin to the White House*. Boston: James H. Earle, 1881.

Thom, William B. "Early History of the Old Bee Line R. R. and Its Completion by Hon. Alfred Kelley in 1851," *Firelands Pioneer*, n.s. 22 (January 1921): 104–22.

Trevorrow, Frank W. *Ohio's Canals*. WHRS, 1973. Mimeographed booklet.

Trowbridge, Francis Bacon. *The Trowbridge Genealogy*. New Haven, Conn.: Privately printed, 1908.

Tyler, Alice Felt. *Freedom's Ferment*. Minneapolis: University of Minnesota Press, 1944.

Van Wagenen, Jared, Jr. *The Golden Age of Homespun*. Ithaca: Cornell University Press, 1953.

Wallace, Anthony F. C. *Rockdale: The Growth of an American Village in the Early Industrial Revolution*. New York: Alfred A. Knopf, 1978.

Weisenburger, Francis P. *The Passing of the Frontier, 1825–1850*. Vol. 3, *The History of the State of Ohio*. Ed. by Carl Wittke. 6 vols. Columbus: Ohio State Archaeological and Historical Society, 1941.

Wheeler, Robert A. "Building in the Western Reserve, 1800–1870," *The Western Reserve Magazine* 6 (November–December 1978): 33–40.

White, Frederick C. "Thomsonianism in Ohio," *Ohio Archaeological and Historical Quarterly* 49 (October–December 1940): 322–31.

Wilcox, Frank. *The Ohio Canals*. Kent, Ohio: Kent State University Press, 1969.

Wilcox, R. Traver. *Five Centuries of American Costume*. New York: Charles Scribner's Sons, 1963.

Withers, Carl [James West]. *Plainville, U.S.A.* New York: Columbia University Press, 1945.

Works Progress Administration. Writers' Program. *The Ohio Guide*. 1940. Reprint. New York: Oxford University Press, 1976.

"Young America: 'Life Style' in the Nineteenth Century," *American Heritage*, 22 (February, 1971), 16–32.

5. Periodicals

American Phrenological Journal, 1845–52.

Bedford News Register [Bedford, Ohio], 1935.

Chagrin Falls Exponent, 1880.

Cleveland Plain Dealer (weekly), 1844–45, 1848–49.

Grand Rapids Daily Eagle, 1881.

Grand Rapids Evening Journal, 1881.

Millennial Harbinger, 1852.

New York Times, 1880–81.

Ohio Cultivator, 1848–49.

Ohio Records and Pioneer Families, 1960.

Ohio Star [Ravenna], 1847–48.

Sandusky Clarion, 1844.

6. Dissertations and theses

Cottom, Robert I. "To Be Among the First: The Early Career of James A. Garfield, 1831–1868," Ph.D. diss., Johns Hopkins University, 1975.

George, Milton C. "The Settlement of the Connecticut Western Reserve of Ohio, 1796–1850," Ph.D. diss., University of Michigan, 1950.

Holm, James N. "A Rhetorical Study of the Public Speaking of James A. Garfield, 1851–1859," Ph.D. diss., Western Reserve University, 1957.

Porter, William Harvey. "Musical Development of the Western Reserve," Master's thesis, Western Reserve University, 1946.

7. Miscellaneous

Mueller, J. "Panorama of Cleveland and Ohio City Drawn from Nature." Cincinnati: Onken's Lithography, c. 1850. Lithograph.

R. M. Baxter Photograph Album No. 2, Photograph Collection, Hiram College Archives.

Index